Vincent O'Brien
The Man and
The Legend

Cover Pictures

FRONT COVER: Vincent O'Brien in relaxed mood on the golf course at Lyford Cay, Nassau, in the Bahamas, in the week in April '97 when he celebrated his 80th birthday. This picture was taken by his wife Jacqueline.

BACK COVER: Vincent O'Brien's Last Hurrah at Royal Ascot as he leads in College Chapel, with Lester Piggott in the saddle, after victory in the 1993 Cork and Orrery Stakes. Charles O'Brien (centre) who chose to train on his own in Co. Kildare rather than take over at Ballydoyle on his father's retirement at the end of the 1994 Flat season and (bottom) Aidan O'Brien (right), with owner Michael Tabor and Christy Roche, holding trophy aloft, after Desert King had won the 1997 Lexus Irish 2,000 Guineas.
(Pictures: Bernard Parkin and Caroline Norris)

i

Other books by Raymond Smith include:

Under the Blue Flag (1980)
The Poker Kings of Las Vegas (1982)
Charles J. Haughey: The Survivor (1983)
Garret: The Enigma (1985)
Haughey and O'Malley: The Quest for Power (1986)
Vincent O'Brien: The Master of Ballydoyle (1990)
The High Rollers of the Turf (1992)
Tigers of the Turf (1994)
Urbi Et Orbi And All That (1995)
Better One Day As A Lion (1996)

Vincent O'Brien
The Man and
The Legend

By
RAYMOND SMITH

Sporting Books Publishers
Dublin
1997

Vincent O'Brien
The Man and
The Legend

First Published 1997
Copyright © Raymond Smith 1997

Published by Sporting Books Publishers, Dublin
Cover design by Maurice Moore, *Irish Independent*
Origination and Picture Sections by ICR Group Ltd.,
Unit 15, IDA Centre, Pearse Street, Dublin 2.
Printed by Colour Books

Contents

Author's Note

When Vincent O'Brien passed the milestone of his 80th birthday in April, 1997, I concluded that the time was rife to write a new assessment of the man and the legend.

It seemed fitting also, as we approached the new Millennium, that there should be available a definitive biography covering all the essential aspects of his life and times, giving also revealing insights by those who worked closely with him when he was Master of Ballydoyle and incorporating some of the tributes paid to him by his peers when he finally stepped down at the end of the 1994 Flat season.

My original biography, first published in a hardback edition in 1990 and re-issued in paperback in 1992, has been sold out for some time, which means that there is a need to fill a void on the man, described simply by Lester Piggott as "the world's greatest trainer".

There is the vital need also to bring the story right up to date. On Vincent's retirement, his younger son, Charles, who had been his assistant, decided against following in his footsteps by taking over at the helm at Ballydoyle but went out on his own in County Kildare. David had called it a day after training Assert to win the French Derby and Irish Derby and Secreto to shock 'wonder colt' El Gran Senor in the Epsom Derby. He lives today with his wife Catherine and family at Chateau Vignelaure in Aix-en-Provence in the south of France and has found contentment in the wine-making business.

We look at the dream behind the establishment of Classic Thoroughbreds and explore also the reasons why the curtain came down eventually on what Dr Michael Smurfit described as "this noble and unique experiment".

The book is in six sections. Part One deals with the methods that were at the heart of the tremendous strike rate that Vincent O'Brien enjoyed in the Golden Era of Ballydoyle. We look at his attention to detail, his perfectionist approach and the emphasis he placed on the speed factor. We look also at the jockeys, Lester Piggott in particular, who were an integral part of the success story.

Most important, we give vital insights from those who passed through the portals of Ballydoyle as assistant trainers and of particular relevance are the views of Michael Kauntze and Brian Molony who were associated closely with The Master when he had in his charge horses immortalised in the history of the Turf.

Part Two puts the spotlight on the Shaping of The Man – on Vincent's early days in Churchtown, Co. Cork and we see how the Hinge of Destiny brought all the pieces together on the board so that he was able to follow in the footsteps of his father, Dan and set up on his own as a trainer.

We follow his progress up the ladder in Parts Three and Four – as he made his initial assault on Cheltenham and became Master of the Jumping Scene, then King of The Flat. We assess the Great Horses he handled and name the Top Ten in order and this is certain to be the source of keen debate, as every racing enthusiast will have an individual opinion.

Part Five throws new light on the Battles with the Turf Club and especially on "The King's Lake Affair", which was not dealt with in my original biography.

Finally, in Part Six we see what a lasting imprint David O'Brien left on the Classic scene before he was 30 and why he decided to opt out and we reveal why Charles did not take over his father's mantle at Ballydoyle but decided instead to establish his own training quarters in County Kildare. Charles, incidentally, came within a length through Dr Johnson – carrying his father's colours – of winning the 1997 Budweiser Irish Derby.

Vincent and Jacqueline O'Brien were enjoying a winter holiday at Lyford Cay, Nassau in the Bahamas when Vincent's 80th birthday was celebrated.

I wrote a feature for the *Sunday Independent* to mark the occasion, pointing out how he kept himself fully informed and right up to date with all developments worldwide in the racing and breeding spheres. Each morning he received from Coolmore a long fax with racing news from all countries. He also attended to questions that arose from day to day.

He walked a mile every morning and managed also in the day to get in nine holes of golf. He was never one to dwell on age or the passage of time and he didn't wish to have the fanfares sounding on his 80th birthday. In keeping with his wishes, Jacqueline ensured that it was a quiet family affair, David and Catherine and family flying in from France to share the occasion. Other members of the O'Brien family had visited Vincent and Jacqueline at Christmas.

This book, we trust, will show for posterity the immense breadth of his achievement and the establishment of a record in the National Hunt and Flat sphere that can never be surpassed. It offers too new perspectives from insiders into what set him on a plane apart.

The teacher in Churchtown National School had predicted it correctly when he said: "This lad is something different".

Yes, something different entirely...

Raymond Smith

Acknowledgements

This new biography of Vincent O'Brien would not have been possible but for the tremendous co-operation and assistance which I received from a great many people and different concerns.

I would like to record grateful thanks for the authoritative input of Tony Sweeney, an acknowledged expert on racing facts and statistics and on essential background data required by any writer in the field of racing and bloodstock matters, for so quickly answering the queries I put to him, extending back to earlier decades in Vincent O'Brien's career and also to the days when his father, Dan was training in Churchtown.

The Appendices, setting out The Fabulous Vincent O'Brien Record, at the end of this book, represents the painstaking work of Tony Sweeney and his wife, Annie. I feel it will prove an invaluable record for all those who want to see for the first time in tabulated and easily readable form all the big-race successes and title wins of the Master of Ballydoyle.

I deeply appreciate also the depth of knowledge and experience that my colleague, Tom MacGinty, Racing Editor of the *Irish Racing Annual* brought to the task of reading and checking the manuscript.

My thanks to the editors of newspapers and racing papers and magazines and other publications for permission to quote from various interviews, reports and features and also for photos made available to me.

I thank, in particular, Alan Byrne, Editor of the *Racing Post,* Tom Clarke, Editor of the *Sporting Life,* the Editors of Timeform who produce the annual 'Bible', *Racehorses,* which we have quoted in relation to Vincent's great horses, Conor Brady, Editor of the *Irish Times* for permission to quote from an interview by Eileen Battersby with Jacqueline O'Brien, Aengus Fanning, Editor of the *Sunday Independent* for allowing me to reproduce quotes from different features and for his personal support and encouragement with this as with earlier projects of mine. I value it as I value our friendship going back to our days together covering the EU scene from Brussels to Luxembourg and other Continental centres.

I express my appreciation to Michael Daly and the staff of the Independent Library who have proved unfailing in their co-operation at all times.

I thank also the various photographers who provided valuable prints including Caroline Norris, Peter Mooney, Liam Healy, Bernard Parkin, Colin Turner, Ed Byrne. In the field of assisting with the photographic sections, Jacqueline O'Brien, an outstanding professional photographer in her own right, was most co-operative and she provided the front-cover picture of Vincent relaxing on the golf course at Lyford Cay in the Bahamas in the week in April '97 when he celebrated his 80th birthday.

While this book has much new material that was not included in my first biography, *Vincent O'Brien – The Master of Ballydoyle,* which is now out of print, I decided that it was essential that aspects of Vincent's childhood, youth and days as assistant to his father in Churchtown and then the move to Ballydoyle, should be incorporated again in edited form to give the fullest possible picture of the life and times of 'The Master'.

I could not have gathered so much invaluable data during the research I pursued in the Churchtown and Buttevant areas into Vincent's family background but for the help I received from D.A. (Tony) O'Neill of Buttevant, a veritable mine of information, and Noel and Margaret O'Brien of Churchtown House. I shall always cherish the memory of the times I have spent in this area of County Cork which became the base of Vincent O'Brien's initial successful onslaughts on the Cheltenham Festival meeting.

It was as if the wheel had turned full circle when I returned in July, 1997 for the unveiling of a plaque to Vincent and I had the pleasure of renewing acquaintanceship with Noel and Margaret and with outstanding characters like Jack Murphy and Jimmy Gordon. Yes, it was a night to remember!

Grateful thanks to the Keeneland Association, Inc., for all the facilities provided to me during my research in Kentucky and also to John Magnier who also ensured that my way was smoothed in the Bluegrass country as I visited Ashford Farm, a wing of the Coolmore complex. And I must not overlook either the co-operation so readily forthcoming from John and from Bob Lanigan and Richard Henry when I was researching the background to the establishment of Coolmore.

I express my warmest appreciation to the members of the O'Brien family who so willingly gave of their time to help me in my research – firstly, Dermot and Phonsie, Vincent's brothers, who were such an integral part of his success story; Vincent's sister, the late Pauline Fogarty and the five children, Susan, Jane, Liz, David and Charles.

And, of course, Vincent and Jacqueline merit my deepest thanks and appreciation. Before Vincent retired at the end of the 1994 Flat season, I had visited Ballydoyle more than once. I stood on the gallops with him as he over-saw the string at work and later sat chatting with him over coffee in the sun lounge. Always those moments were precious in the company of the Master. A man of few words but everything he said had a lasting significance, especially when he talked about the great horses he had handled and he looked down the span of years from those early days in Churchtown to the peaks attained when he had become a global figure at Ballydoyle.

I was covering the World Cup '97 in Dubai in the countdown to the celebration in April '97 of Vincent's 80th birthday. I was in touch with Vincent and Jacqueline in their holiday home in Lyford Cay, Nassau in the Bahamas and they readily responded to my queries for the special birthday feature I wrote for the *Sunday Independent*. Jacqueline too provided me with the prints to mark Vincent attaining that milestone.

I thank them both for checking factual data in the Mss of this book and ensuring that it will be a definitive record of the epoch-making moments in the career of the man recognised as the greatest trainer this country has produced and unquestionably the world's greatest by the sheer level of his achievements in the National Hunt and Flat spheres.

Let me stress, however, that it is not presented as the official biography of Vincent O'Brien. In its range and scope it seeks to cover his rise from small beginnings in Churchtown to the stature he attained over half-a-century, culminating in a moment at Belmont Park, New York in 1990 when, after renewing his partnership with Lester Piggott they pulled off together the Breeders Cup Mile (Turf) with Royal Academy, which Vincent had bought at the Keeneland Select Sales in July, 1988 as a yearling for $3.5 million – his last throw of the dice in the Bluegrass country of Kentucky and a throw-back to 1975 when 'The Syndicate' (comprising John Magnier, Robert Sangster and himself) had made their first grand assault on Keeneland.

Incidentally, I proffer my deepest thanks to Robert Sangster and Lester Piggott who proved so co-operative in every way.

I could not have finished this book to the publication deadline set without the facilities provided for me in ideal settings by my very good friends Terence and Annette Sweeney and Aidan and Mary Moriarty.

My thanks also to Peter and Noreen Fox of Rosslare Strand, who in July '97 celebrated the 25th anniversary of the French Connection Boutique and Rosslare Beach Villas. They brought together for the occasion at a celebratory lunch over 100 guests, among them Mary Griffin, wife of local hotelier Liam Griffin, who forged a special niche for himself in hurling history in '96 by guiding Wexford, as team manager, to their first All-Ireland title since 1968. Also present was Isabelle Kelly, wife of Bill Kelly, proprietor of Kelly's Rosslare Strand Hotel.

Incidentally, I must again put on record my deepest thanks and appreciation to Bill Kelly and all the staff of Kelly's Hotel, who were so courteous and co-operative in every way, also to my friends Austin Skerrit and Padraig Conway in Rosslare Golf Club (I derived much pleasure in playing this fine Links course on days when the lap-top computer was set aside) and to Phil Meagher of O'Ryans of Rosslare, who engaged me in memorable conversations on hurling, gaelic football and racing. Rosslare Strand holds a special place for me now as my four most recent books were finished there and I value the friendships I have made among its people.

And the understanding of my wife, Sheila and her input and advice lightened the burden of pressurised days. Thanks also to my daughter Bairbre, for her contribution and to my son Stephen.

It has been a labour of love writing this book about a man whose greatness has transcended greatness in the normal sense. I trust that in time it will be read by new generations in the new Millennium and that thus what he achieved will continue to be acclaimed down the decades.

I dedicate this book to the incomparable Lester Piggott who played such a key role in some of Vincent O'Brien's greatest victories on the Flat, especially in the Epsom Derby. I was proud to have savoured the hospitality of his Newmarket home and to have garnered insights from him about Nijinsky, Sir Ivor, The Minstrel and Alleged that cannot but add a vital additional dimension to this biography.

RAYMOND SMITH
Dublin,
October, 1997

Vincent O'Brien (left) in relaxed mood on the golf course at Lyford Cay in Nassau in the Bahamas and (below) with Jacqueline at their Nassau holiday home as he reached the milestone of his 80th birthday in April, 1997.

PART ONE

MAKING THE LEGEND

1

'Let's Keep Things In Perspective'

Out in a desert location beyond Dubai on the occasion of the Arabian Night extravaganza, coinciding with the 1997 World Cup Race, I put it to John Gosden, trainer of the 1997 Epsom Derby winner, Benny The Dip, that someone had written recently that Martin Pipe had to be rated the greatest. The Newmarket trainer just smiled and said: "Let's keep things in perspective."

"There was only one Vincent O'Brien", he continued. "No one will emulate or surpass his achievements."

It could be argued, of course, that Gosden was biased as he had been assistant trainer to Vincent O'Brien but his period at Ballydoyle enabled him to assess the Master's qualities in a rather privileged manner and he summed up: "In the end, I suppose he had that indescribable sixth sense. If you sat down and asked Mozart how he wrote the overture to *Don Giovanni,* he couldn't have explained how. The same is true of Vincent. He would have excelled at anything he chose".

Lester Piggott, not given to over-lauding either horse or man, put it succinctly in eight words: "Vincent was the best trainer of all time".

It was in the aftermath of Martin Pipe turning out four winners at Cheltenham '97 that some went over the top in applauding his achievement. True, in these days when the competition at the Festival meeting is awesome, Pipe deserves every credit for supplementing Make A Stand's scintillating triumph in the Smurfit Champion Hurdle on the Tuesday by winning the Guinness Arkle Chase with Or Royal and then on the Wednesday he took the Coral Cup Handicap Hurdle with Big Strand and the Mildmay Of Flete Chase with Terrao. In the process he equalled the record set by Tom Coulthwaite in 1923 but, remember, the meeting was a much more low-key affair then than it is now and none of the races was a true championship test.

We can appreciate why John Gosden said that things must be kept in perspective when we set Pipe's quartet of 1997 winners against Vincent O'Brien's overall record at Cheltenham. He won 23 races (including victory in the 1949 Gold Cup, run a month after the Festival meeting itself)– only three behind Tom Dreaper, the leading Irish trainer at the Festival meeting, but Vincent's total was compressed into roughly a decade(1948-'59) as against a span of 25 years in Tom's period of turning out winners. Dreaper's first winner was in 1946 (Prince Regent in the Gold Cup) and his last in 1971 (Alpheus in the Arkle Chase).

Vincent's initial runner was Cottage Rake in 1948 – winner of the Gold Cup. In fact, his first five runners (1948-'51) all won and Hatton's Grace was the only challenger in '5I. Nine out of twelve runners sent over in the years 1948-'52 were successful. The last Vincent O'Brien-trained challengers at the Festival meeting were York Fair and Courts Appeal in the two Divisions of the Gloucestershire Hurdle in 1959. T. P. Burns rode York Fair to victory in the first Division.

One can only surmise how many more Cheltenham winners he would have produced – and Aintree winners also – if he had not decided to turn his attention completely to the Flat in 1959.

Leaving aside his four Gold Cup triumphs (three-in-a-row for Cottage Rake, 1948-1950 and Knock Hard in '53) and three Champion Hurdle victories (Hatton's Grace 1949-'51), I am convinced that it was Vincent's record in the Gloucestershire Hurdle that really set him on a pedestal apart as a Cheltenham trainer.

Now the Supreme Novices' Hurdle, it was run then in two Divisions. And Vincent made a point of laying out horses specially with this race in mind. Paddy Norris who was Vincent's Travelling Head Man for years, happened to mention to him one day that he felt that a particular three-year-old that had shown promise in his first outing of the season should pick up a race before long and Vincent quietly responded that he had already earmarked him in his mind for one of the Divisions of the Gloucestershire Hurdle – and, of course, that was thinking a long way ahead.

In fact, Dermot O'Brien, who was Vincent's right-hand man for a lengthy period and a key figure in his success, thinks that unquestionably the outstanding achievement of his brother's career was the unparalleled strike rate in the Gloucestershire Hurdle and Phonsie O'Brien agreed that it was "out of this world".

The record reads: ten winners out of twelve runners in the period 1952-'59. The other two, Knockabout and Courts Appeal, finished second. In an era when the French were playing a strong role over hurdles as well as on the Flat, Tasmin, ridden by Rene Amery and trained in France, started the 5-1 second favourite and got up on the line to beat Knockabout (T. P. Burns), the 7-4 favourite by a head. Albergo (Doug Page) was backed from 100-8 to 9-1 and beat the even-money favourite, Courts Appeal (T. P. Burns) by six lengths. The following year Albergo was runner-up to the Paddy Sleator-trained Another Flash in the Champion Hurdle and was definitely one of the outstanding horses trained by Clem Magnier.

Vincent's tremendous strike rate in the Gloucestershire Hurdle, according to Phonsie, could be attributed to the schooling over obstacles the horses

2

were given. "You might say that they were taught to jump before they could gallop. The ones aimed at this particular event had the jumping ability of handicap hurdlers before they were entered for this very competitive race.

"Once the going became good to soft in September, Vincent would have four hurdles and four fences put out. Every horse that was going to have a dual purpose in life jumped eight hurdles or eight fences every Tuesday and Friday. It was a case of jumping the four and then coming back and jumping them again. No other trainer schooled his horses to jump as Vincent did."

He maintained that it was very difficult to teach horses to jump after they began to run races on the Flat. You might then find yourself trying to eradicate faults which might not have developed if you had made your horses proficient jumpers from the outset.

"Once a horse of Vincent's reached handicap class as a chaser, he was never schooled over fences again. A chaser might be popped over the four fences before his first race of the season simply to sharpen him and then just given a 'pop' occasionally to keep his eye in.

"In the case of the Aintree Grand National challengers, he didn't school them over jumps similar to Becher's or Valentine's or The Chair. They would never have seen anything like these jumps before they got to Aintree; yet they were so schooled early on in their jumping careers that they had the ability ingrained in them to jump any jump, no matter how formidable.

"The National fences were much tougher in those days than they are now. Vincent knew exactly the type of horse required for the race. He knew they had to be able to jump. If they did not meet this requirement, then other attributes would not suffice at Aintree."

Phonsie summed up by saying that "everything" would have to be right before Vincent would allow one to take its chance in a bid for an important prize like those rich Cheltenham races or the Grand National. There were no "ifs" and "buts" in his vocabulary. He was a perfectionist through and through.

Prize-money in Ireland then was minimal, especially in the National Hunt sphere. It couldn't be compared with what was there to be won at Cheltenham. To lift a race at the Festival meeting valued £8,000 meant winning a prize worth many times that amount by the money values of today.

But at the same time it has got to be recognised that Cheltenham was not casting its net wide then to catch the "big fish" in the sponsorship arena as is the norm today. There are plenty of concerns that are only too happy to be identified with Cheltenham. Dr Michael Smurfit, a great lover of National Hunt racing and, as an owner, an outstanding supporter of the Sport of Kings, put the Smurfit name to the Champion Hurdle and Guinness put their name to the Arkle Chase.

✳   ✳   ✳

Vincent O'Brien arrived in the era as a trainer – that is in the early Forties

– when he was an "unknown" aiming to win big prizes from his County Cork base in Churchtown, where his father, Dan had trained before him. There were high-profile trainers in the Curragh who thought he would be just another morning glory who would vanish from the scene as quickly as he had sprouted. Quietly they scoffed at his ambitious approach and they were jealous too of him as he began to hit the headlines.

From the very outset, however, Vincent O'Brien's star was set for greatness. Tom Tierney, one of Vincent's teachers and Principal of Churchtown National School had predicted it correctly when he said prophetically: "This lad is something different".

Yes, something different entirely…

And the big rails bookies in England and their counterparts in Ireland would come to bemoan the day he ever took out a trainer's licence. In fact, some of the English layers had been taken to the cleaners again and again before they woke up and realised just how good Vincent was at planning a gamble.

There came a moment at York in 1958 – the season that Vincent through the successes of Gladness and Ballymoss could do no wrong – when William Hill, the most fearless bookmaker of his time, walked over to the Master of Ballydoyle who was chatting with Noel Murless and Sir Cecil Boyd Rochfort.

Hill remarked to him in the hearing of the other two: "I would have saved myself literally thousands of pounds if I had had you done away with ten years ago".

"We had to gamble to survive", said Vincent to me quite frankly.

He had owners who had the 'readies' and who loved to have a bet when Vincent told them one was 'expected. 'They could afford to put on £500 or £1,000 and more and not find themselves in deep water if a gamble became unstuck.

"I had to come up with the goods to stay in business. It was me against the bookies and though the pressure was enormous, we did all right", he said.

"We did all right". Never was there such an understatement.

Dermot assisted Vincent in keeping a complete ledger of all bets made at the time. Invariably they came out right at the end of each season, legendary bloodstock agent, Jack Doyle making the very significant point to me that "Vincent seldom if ever left it behind with the bookmakers. And if a gamble became unstuck, you could say the money was only on loan. Invariably Vincent would get it back – with interest".

One of the biggest gambles of all at Cheltenham – as the famous ledger revealed to me – was that on Ahaburn to win the County Handicap Hurdle in 1952. The amount invested was £1,452, equivalent to well over £20,000 by today's values. Aubrey Brabazon was in the saddle. In the parade ring beforehand, Vincent said quietly to 'The Brab': "I think this one should win". When Vincent ventured something like that Aubrey knew that the horse was fancied no end.

"We were only cantering at the second last and I said to myself – 'This is going to be easier than Vincent himself imagined'. Then Ahaburn suddenly stopped as if he had been shot and finished in the ruck in ninth place," recalled Aubrey.

"I could see that Vincent was mystified and very dejected at what had happened. He would never say a word to me in a situation like that. He kept his feelings bottled up and I never knew him in all the years we were associated with each other to vent anger or disappointment. That day he was just strangely quiet and I realised it was bothering him deeply that Ahaburn could have stopped to nothing.

"It wasn't until two days later that we discovered what had happened – that is when Ahaburn was on his way back to Ireland. The man travelling with him noticed the stone-black droppings. The horse had burst a blood vessel internally. In such situations instead of bleeding from the nose, the blood will be retained in the system and it's the droppings that reveal to you what has happened".

Aubrey added that Ahaburn was injected for the problem and made amends by winning the Irish Cesarewitch later that year. Yes, the money lost at Cheltenham wasn't left behind!

And three years later at the Festival meeting, the bookies had cause to remember the name 'Ahaburn' when, with T. P. Burns up, he landed a massive gamble in taking the Birdlip Hurdle – the selling hurdle later withdrawn from the Cheltenham programme.

As the bookies squirmed under the O'Brien onslaughts on them, it was not surprising that efforts were made to nobble horses Vincent sent over to Cheltenham and judged to be 'good things' for their particular races.

Alberoni, backed as if defeat was out of the question in the County Handicap Hurdle in 1950, was 'got at'.

"When we searched for a reason why he finished out of the money, we discovered that someone had placed acid under his shoes", Dermot O'Brien revealed to me. "There was a hole showing in each foot where the acid had burned into the foot. That cost us a good bit of money".

But Vincent took his own measures – and very wise ones they were – to thwart the nobblers. He instructed his staff that when anyone enquired the name of a horse running at Cheltenham, they were to mix a cocktail, so to speak, in responding to the inquisitive. Thus, Alberoni became Hatton's Grace and Hatton's Grace became Alberoni. The "Tipperary cocktail" worked in the sense that it saved Hatton's Grace, 5-2 favourite to win his second successive Champion Hurdle in 1950, from being "done". My research into this episode has convinced me that the nobblers believed they were ending the victory hopes of Hatton's Grace when they put the acid under Alberoni's shoes.

It certainly was not wine and roses all the way. Never is when a stable is "going to the well" seeking to land big gambles.

"I remember one season when the going was very hard and we backed a string of losers", Vincent recalled. "When the big gambles came off people tended to forget the setbacks".

"Ginger" Dyson was brought over from England to ride Ahaburn in the 1951 Irish Cesarewitch. He started evens favourite after a whirlwind gamble but could only finish third in a seventeen-horse field, beaten two lengths and five lengths by Le Roi Soleil and Sontongo. "He ran into all sorts of trouble", said Dermot O'Brien. "I could have bought myself a nice small farm with what I lost on him that day".

*　*　*

The English bookmakers first reeled under a Vincent O'Brien onslaught on the Gloucestershire Hurdle when Cockatoo, with Phonsie up, won Division One of the event in 1952 starting at 4/1. "Unfortunately, we never got the same odds in the race again", said Dermot.

Vincent had a couple of people he had complete faith in to put the money down whether for himself and a couple of close friends or any owner who wanted a "monkey" (£500) or more on. The late Nat McNabb of Dublin and Bob Mulrooney of Limerick were the trusted lieutenants who entered the firing line against the bookmakers. Nat McNabb told me that when he crossed over to England he had accounts with all the leading rails bookies and had no trouble in executing his bets "on the nod". Dermot would sometimes step in, also, to fire a salvo or two on days of fearless gambles in England.

But there were outstanding layers also in the Irish ring – Dick Power, Jim Rice and Patsy McAlinden being possibly "The Big Three" of their time.

Nat McNabb recalled that the biggest individual bet he had on a horse in Ireland for Vincent O'Brien was the £3,000 he placed on Good Days in a race at Naas in the Forties. Multiply that by twenty and you get a clearer picture of the "investment" by today's money values.

"I knew that with that kind of bet I had to get the best price that would obtain that day", Nat recalled. "I knew, too, that if I began to put it on piecemeal, the market could quickly vanish on me and I might even end up having to take-odds on to some of the money. So I had a chat with Patsy McAlinden and I said to him, 'I'm going to back this horse today and I will be backing it big. What price will you lay me?

"Patsy did not flinch. His immediate response was, 'I'll take the bet and lay you the best available odds provided you don't have another bet'. I agreed. Patsy recovered the £3,000 and more by backing Good Days around the ring, so we were both happy when he came home a very easy winner."

The period immediately after the Second World War was the boom period for betting, he said, and it was one marked by fearless gamblers and by bookmakers prepared to take them on.

It was the period also when there was a phenomenal amount of black market money around in England and the only way to get it laundered was to get a cheque from a bookmaker. Of course, there was a lot of black market money too in Ireland and there was a stigma on the blackmarketeers for the manner in which they charged for tea, especially, at a time when people had tea in the evening instead of dinner. If you walked into a bank on Monday with cash from blackmarket transactions, you would be let know indirectly what was thought of this "blood money". So naturally the blackmarketeers preferred to lodge a cheque from a bookmaker – just as the drug barons of the current era have been known to launder their money in a similar fashion.

Nat McNabb remembered going over to the Liverpool Grand National meeting just after the War. "I had my eyes opened to the scale of the betting and how much you could take out of the ring if you brought off a successful coup."

He recalled standing beside William Hill's perch before one particular race. "This little Jew boy came in and said "£9,000 to £3,000" as Hill was shouting "3-1 the field". William Hill never batted an eyelid but continued to shout "3-1 the field". Another chap came in and took "£9,000 to £3,000". And a third. It was only then that Hill dropped the price to 11-4.

"I had seen nothing like it and I knew in my heart that we had a market once Vincent decided to tilt at the big prizes in England. We stung them very badly with Hatton's Grace the first year he won the Champion Hurdle in 1949. I know the starting price was 100-7 but we backed him ante-post at 33-1, 25-1 and 20-1 and continued to back him right down the line."

Reflecting on the day – 19th November, 1952 – that Knock Hard, with Tim Molony up, ran in the Nuneaton Hurdle at Birmingham, Nat said: "He must have been the greatest certainty of all time when you consider that he had won the Irish Lincolnshire with 8st 12lbs".

Nat had £10,000 to put on him that day and Knock Hard won even more easily than Gay Future did on an unforgettable occasion at Cartmel.

The headlines are made today by J. P. McManus when he "goes to war" in the ring at Cheltenham and he may lose £250,000 the first day and put the wheel back on the bike by backing a horse like Istabraq, which carried his colours on the second day of the 1997 Festival meeting and obliged like the Irish-trained banker bet of the meeting he had been hailed in advance.

But I contend that it was when he was dubbed "The Sundance Kid" in the Seventies by Hugh McIlvanney that McManus showed courage comparable with that shown by Vincent O'Brien. Skint more than once as a bookmaker and skint too as a gambler in the impetuous days of his twenties, McManus survived and is a different animal entirely now in the maturity of his forties.

Now when he loses gambling on the horses it's relative to his resources. For he's a millionaire concerned primarily with playing the financial markets from his base in Geneva. The computer in his spacious suite of offices in the Rue du Rhone indicates in red immediately any currency fluctuations. He watches it constantly.

At dinner in the Restaurant Roberto or the famous Lion D'Or he may take a call on his mobile phone which may mean that he has made a "killing" that day in the financial markets.

The vultures can hover in vain waiting to pick his body clean after the bookies have done with him. He won't suffer, I am sure, the same fate as Terry Ramsden who came a cropper through a combination of Glen International crashing on "Black Monday" in October, '87 and losing an estimated £57 million to £80 million to the bookies in crazy gambling.

When Vincent O'Brien got Nat McNabb to put £3,000 on Good Days at Naas and £10,000 on Knock Hard at Birmingham, you might say that he was going for broke on his judgement and his uncanny ability to bring a horse to its peak on the day that really mattered. He had no resources behind him to fall back on if he failed.

I reckon that was the period when he showed nerves of steel and courage beyond the normal meaning of courage. The money garnered from successful gambles, in particular the ante-post coups on Cottage Rake and Hatton's Grace and Alberoni with Aubrey Brabazon winning the Leopardstown Handicap Hurdle under 10st 2lbs in July 1950 plus a substantial bank loan, enabled Vincent to buy the house and land in the shadow of Slievenamon in County Tipperary in the Spring of 1951 that would become his new Ballydoyle training establishment. And it would be developed in time into a model of its kind as one of the finest training centres in the world. And it enabled him, as we shall see in Chapter Three, to enter a new phase as a trainer when the gambling on his eye and his judgement was of an entirely different nature.

*　　*　　*

In the count-down to the Dubai World Cup Race '97, trainers, owners, jockeys, racing writers and others gather in the Clubhouse of the Nad Al Sheba track for breakfast after the horses have completed morning work on the track. A cosmopolitan set, English trainers Michael Stoute, John Gosden and Clive Brittain rubbing shoulders with Ellie Lellouche from France, trainer of 1996 Prix de l'Arc de Triomphe winner, Helissio (who as events turned out did not run after all in the rescheduled race); Gai Waterhouse from Australia; Takao Nakano from Japan; and the Americans William Perry and Richard Mandella.

The Californian Mandella, one of the most successful trainers on America's west coast, handles the favourite, Siphon, beaten in a battle royal over the last few furlongs by the Michael Stoute-trained Singspiel (winner in '96 of the Canadian International and the Japan Cup and second in the Breeders' Cup Turf), who certainly did Europe proud and also Sandpit who would take third place.

Richard Mandella told me how proud he was to have met Vincent O'Brien – "the idol of my young days" – on a recent visit to Lyford Cay, Nassau in the Bahamas, where Vincent reached the the milestone of his 80th birthday on Wednesday, April 9th, '97, celebrating the occasion with a quiet dinner in the holiday home with Jacqueline and his eldest son, David and his wife Catherine and four children, Andrew, Robert, Charles and Alexandra.

Talking to Richard Mandella, I could not but recall what D. Wayne Lukas said to me at the Keeneland July Sales in 1988 in reply to my question : "What in your estimation made Vincent O'Brien such a great trainer?"

"Longevity", came the cryptic response. "Many in this game can have a good year, maybe even a few good years. But what made Vincent O'Brien one of the greatest trainers in the history of racing globally was the manner in which he stood the test of time. The records show that he was turning out champions over the jumps as far back as 1948 and forty years later he still commanded the deepest respect among racing folk, though then training exclusively on the Flat.

"A good horse can make anybody look good. In Vincent O'Brien's case, however, he did not just depend on one great animal to catapult him on to a level where his name became known in every corner of the world. There was this constant search for excellence. He displayed qualities that can only be recognised as true genius.

"When I first came into this game, Vincent O'Brien was setting the standards for most of us to follow. I know there are American trainers who would say they had been outstandingly successful if they achieved even half of the goals that Vincent O'Brien achieved.

"The cruel reality that emerges from a close study of the history of racing is that nobody can buy success. In a word, money alone doesn't guarantee Classic or big-race victories. Vincent O'Brien picked them out when he had nothing like the money at his back that would come later in his career. Let me repeat – it takes genius to accomplish all that he accomplished in a lifetime at the game".

That analytical tribute from D. Wayne Lukas must be set against this brilliant American trainer's own record of achievement which saw him turn out three winners on Breeders' Cup Day 1988 at Churchill Downs but, more so, his successes in America's Triple Crown Classic events, including his Kentucky Derby victories.

The more you reflect on it, the more you agree with Lester Piggott's considered opinion that Vincent "was the best trainer of all time".

He was the mainspring of the breaking of moulds and setting new ones. He was the creative force in bringing about the dawn of modern training methods. The innovations he introduced at Ballydoyle are taken for granted by other trainers today.

September 16th, 1997 marked the 20th anniversary of Maria Callas's death in Paris. She was to the world of grand opera what Vincent O'Brien was to racing. You have only to reflect on how Visconti summed up her Violetta in *La Traviata*. "All the *Traviatas* of the future will contain a little of Maria's *Traviata,* then much, then all of it."

And, thinking of her other great and riveting performances in *Norma, Lucia de Lammermoor, Tosca, Il Pirata, La Gioconda* and *La Sonnambula,* he added: "These are precious, indelible memories."

Vincent O'Brien's summit stands unconquered, as Maria Callas's summit remained unconquered.

2

The Record

In the year – 1990 – when St. Jovite scored his awesome record-breaking twelve-lengths victory in the Budweiser Irish Derby, Jim Bolger sat back at lunch one day in Dublin's Berkeley Court Hotel and remarked to me that even if he were to go on and scale every peak attainable in the Flat arena, he still could not emulate or surpass Vincent O'Brien's record.

"You see, even if I were to win all the Classic and Group races that Vincent won, there would still be his unparalleled record of achievement over the jumps and that of itself puts him on a pedestal apart".

Describing Vincent O'Brien as "the world's greatest – there was no second to him", Jim Bolger dubbed him aptly also "the Christopher Columbus of Irish racing".

Long before Godolphin loomed on the horizon, in fact, thirty years before great play was made of the benefit of wintering potential Classic colts and fillies in the sunshine and warmth of Dubai, Vincent O'Brien wintered Sir Ivor and seven other horses in Italy. The mild weather around Pisa seems to have been of marked benefit to Sir Ivor, for in his very first outing as a three-year-old in 1968 he won the Ascot 2,000 Guineas Trial despite the heavy going and then went on to master Petingo, the Gimcrack and Middle Park Stakes winner in the 2,000 Guineas itself on his way to a brilliant success in the Epsom Derby.

In true Christopher Columbus fashion, Vincent O'Brien then was a pioneer and Jim Bolger made one other very relevant point to me. It had often been claimed, he said, that Vincent would not have achieved all he did in the Flat sphere, in particular, without the backing of millionaires. "But I maintain that if he had been placed at the top of a mountain and asked to start from there, he would still have been an achiever supreme. It was when he was an unknown trainer in Churchtown with no big money behind him and depending on gambling to survive that he recorded some of his most notable successes like Cottage Rake's three successive Gold Cup victories and the three successive triumphs of Hatton's Grace in the Champion Hurdle".

John Randall, the expert on statistical matters for the *Racing Post,* went on record to describe Vincent on his retirement in 1994 as "the greatest racehorse trainer of modern times".

"Starting out from the humblest beginnings, he has been at the top of his profession for half a century, producing a long line of champions first over jumps and then on the Flat", wrote Randall.

"Even if Vincent had never trained a Flat winner, he would still rank among the greatest of his profession, for in the late Forties and throughout the Fifties, for sheer quality in depth his stable dominated the jumping scene like no other before or since", added Randall.

He noted also that, after Vincent turned his attentions solely to the Flat, "he built up at Ballydoyle one of the finest training establishments in the world, a stable which became synonymous with excellence in the thoroughbred".

✳   ✳   ✳

A cold analysis of Vincent O'Brien's record confirms immediately why Robert Sangster should say simply when he learned of Vincent's retirement: "I could talk all night about Vincent and what he achieved, but I am only going to give you two words: 'The Greatest'."

Consider first the Gold Cup. After Cottage Rake's three successive triumphs in 1948-'50 only one horse, the peerless Arkle, succeeded in recording the three-timer (1964-'66). Of course, Golden Miller won five in the period 1932-'36 (between the ages of five and nine); there was no race in 1937 and he was back in 1938, finishing second that year at the age of eleven to The Pilot, beaten two lengths.

I have no doubt that Arkle could have won five-in-a-row had not injury summarily cut short his career. After he had broken the heart of Mill House in that epic duel in 1964, he started at 3/10 in 1965 and at 1/10 in 1966. Could you imagine Woodland Venture, the 1967 winner at 100/8 or Fort Leney, the 1968 winner at 11/2 lowering the colours of Arkle if he had gone to the start in each of those years fighting fit?

Glance down the records since 1966 and you will find that ill-luck or a combination of circumstances all contrived to prevent seemingly good Gold Cup winners going on and making it two back-to-back, not to mind any possibility of the treble being recorded.

Tied Cottage lost it at the last against Alverton in the snow in 1979 and while he made ample amends the following year, he was disqualified subsequently on technical grounds. Forgive 'N' Forget, the 1985 winner, might well have won a second but Lady Luck certainly did not smile on him in 1987.

Desert Orchid, successful in 1989, surrendered his crown to the 100/1 outsider, Norton's Coin the following year. The Fellow might have won three-in-a-row for France but had to be content with one (1994).

Imperial Call was only seven when he triumphed for Fergie Sutherland

and Ireland in 1996 and, as the Cork hordes acclaimed his success in the winner's enclosure and sang "The Banks Of My Own Lovely Lee" as they unfurled the banner with the words "Imperial Call" on it, there seemed no reason why the gelding should not go on and complete the three-in-a-row.

But Fate stepped in and a last-fence fall at Punchestown on his seasonal debut in 1996-'97 when he had the race at his mercy was the prelude to other misfortunate mishaps that saw him go to Cheltenham without being the horse he was the previous year. He was never sparking and Conor O'Dwyer actually pulled him up when he saw his chance was gone.

In this highly-competitive era, if any chaser were to complete the three-timer in the Gold Cup he would be talked about in the same breath as Golden Miller and Arkle – even though he might not live with either of them. Likewise if a hurdler were to record three-in-a-row he would be put up there with Hatton's Grace (1949-'51), Persian War (1968-'70) and See You Then (1985-'87). But since See You Then completed his three-timer, no horse (up to and including the 1997 Festival meeting) has even won two back-to-back in the Champion Hurdle.

✳   ✳   ✳

Such was the level of Vincent O'Brien's achievements subsequent to 1959 when he was training solely on the Flat that people tend today to overlook the full significance of Vincent not alone winning four Gold Cups and three Champion Hurdles but his amazing strike rate in other events at the Festival meeting that saw him end up with a total of 23 winners in a decade (the trainer with the most Cheltenham Festival winners was Fulke Walwyn, who amassed 40 but it was over a period of forty years from 1946 to 1986 while Fred Winter stands second with 27, achieved in eighteen years from 1970 to 1986).

Since 1946 and the passage of over half-a-century, no other trainer has succeeded in winning three successive Aintree Grand Nationals, as Vincent did with Early Mist (1953), Royal Tan (1954) and Quare Times (1955), though 'Ginger' McCain won two-in-a-row with Red Rum (1973-'74) and won again with the same horse in 1977.

What made Vincent's feat unique was that he won with a different horse each year over three years – Early Mist (1953), Royal Tan (1954) and Quare Times (1955). If Martin Pipe or Jenny Pitman were to accomplish that feat today, it would be viewed as breaking through the realms of normal possibility.

✳   ✳   ✳

Consider now Vincent's record on the Flat. It dwarfs again, at the level of major prizes alone, his unique collection of "scalps" garnered in the National Hunt arena, though it has to be repeated that he now had millionaires' money at his back whereas in Churchtown, he depended on the

12

money he took from the bookies' satchels or what was lent by a kindly and understanding bank manager in Cork to see him through.

Six Epsom Derbys… six Irish Derbys… one French Derby.

Would not thirteen Derbys suffice to put any trainer you like to name up there with the Gods of racing?.

In addition, however, he won the English Oaks twice and the Irish Oaks four times. He took the English 2,000 Guineas four times and the Irish equivalent five times. Likewise with the 1,000 Guineas – he has four to his name (one English and three Irish) and in the case of the St. Leger a tally of twelve (nine Irish and three English).

He won the King George VI and Queen Elizabeth Stakes three times, the Eclipse Stakes four times, the Champion Stakes twice, the Benson and Hedges Gold Cup twice. And he took one of the most prestigious and most difficult races of all to win on the European stage – the Prix de l'Arc de Triomphe – three times. On the global plane, outside of Ireland, Britain and France, he won the Washington DC International Stakes and the Breeders Cup Mile (Turf).

You simply cannot overlook either his tremendous strike rate in other important races like those on the domestic front in Ireland – the Tetrarch (twelve successes), the Gallinule (fifteen victories), Pretty Polly (seven), Desmond (thirteen). Blandford (fourteen), Ballymoss (four) and Joe McGrath Memorial Stakes (four), Cambridgeshire (five) and Cesarewitch (five).

He exerted a marked dominance, especially in the Sixties, Seventies and early Eighties, on major two-year-old events at home like the Railway Stakes (fourteen victories), Anglesey Stakes (fourteen), National (fourteen) and Beresford (fifteen).

In Britain he left an indelible mark on the Dewhurst Stakes winning it seven times and between 1958 and 1990 his impact on the Royal Ascot meeting was profound. There was nothing finer than his achievement in saddling six winners from seven runners in 1975 (making it a "bag" of seven for the week by turning out another winner at the Ascot Heath meeting on the Saturday).

He trained several notable sprinters and took the King's Stand Stakes five times, the Cork and Orrery Stakes four times and the Diadem Stakes four times. At Newmarket he landed the July Cup five times and at Goodwood the Sussex Stakes four times. On the domestic front he won the Phoenix Stakes ('1,500') twice with Cloonlara ('76) and Achieved ('81).

From Epsom to Ascot… Newmarket to Goodwood, and York to Doncaster, Vincent O'Brien commanded total respect. Ironically in a way, the dazzling Derby triumphs and in particular the headlines made by Sir Ivor, Nijinsky, Roberto, The Minstrel and Golden Fleece tended to overshadow the level of his overall achievements and the manner in which he rode the High Sierras for decade after decade over a span of half-a-century. In a word, triumphs that would cement the reputation of another trainer were taken almost for granted in Vincent's case.

Tony and Annie Sweeney compiled the full record of big-race successes achieved by Vincent O'Brien at home and abroad that we carry at the end of this book and it represents the finest tribute of all to Vincent's place in the annals of racing globally.

Little wonder then that when Vincent announced his retirement in '94, Peter O'Sullevan, the doyen of racing commentators (who retired himself as 'The Voice of the BBC' at the end of the 1997 Flat season) should say of the Master of Ballydoyle: "He was the greatest all-round trainer of all time. I cannot think that his achievements in the dual disciplines of the sport, both National Hunt and on the level, will ever be matched by anyone.

"He set standards which others followed and I think that it is important to say that both Vincent and long-time colleague P. J. 'Darkie' Prendergast were the men who put Irish racing and bloodstock on the international map".

Vincent O'Brien won an amazing total of 44 Classics and his harvest of Group successes went well beyond the century mark.

He was leading trainer in Britain four times – twice in the National Hunt sphere (1952-'53 and 1953-'54) and twice on the Flat – 1966 and 1977 (with a then record £439,124 in prize-money). We must not overlook here that P.J. ('Darkie') Prendergast, a trail-blazer with Vincent, was leading trainer on the Flat in Britain three years in succession (1963-'65).

It is generally accepted that his record with colts outstripped that with fillies. But that is quite understandable when you reflect on the policy of "making stallions" which was pursued so successfully from 1975 when Vincent O'Brien along with Robert Sangster and John Magnier made the first big assault on the Keeneland Sales and by going for Northern Dancer blood changed the whole face of breeding.

Northern Dancer's son, Sadler's Wells, the pride of Coolmore, would become the world's leading sire of Stakes winners with 19 in 1996 alone when he was champion sire in Great Britain and Ireland for the fifth successive year (a 20th century record). Another son, Nijinsky became a great sire and sire of sires. One has only to instance Caerleon, King's Lake, Solford, Royal Academy and the ill-fated Golden Fleece.

One must not overlook either other sons of Northern Dancer like Be My Guest, Fairy King, El Gran Senor and Storm Bird, who in turn sired Storm Cat, now established as a top-class sire.

The tentacles of the Coolmore complex stretched to Ashford in Kentucky and to Coolmore Australia in Jerry's Plains in New South Wales.

Vincent's decision in 1975 to gamble on Northern Dancer blood, before anyone had awakened to the possibilities, became gambling of a far, far different kind than that on the horses sent out from Churchtown initially and aimed at big Cheltenham prizes.

In the next chapter we shall see how he was again a step ahead of everyone else... yes, truly the Christopher Columbus of racing and breeding.

3

Gambling With A Difference

Christy Roche, who rode for P. J. 'Darkie' Prendergast, David O'Brien, Jim Bolger and Aidan O'Brien, was associated with Ballydoyle in the days when it was no longer necessary for Vincent to gamble to survive.

But, as Christy put it to me: "It was now gambling on a different plane entirely. In one way you could say perhaps that the pressure was even greater than in the days when the money was being put down fearlessly on horses that were considered near-certainties."

"Vincent was putting his judgement on the line at the yearling sales, at Keeneland in particular on the basis that the colts he bought for his patrons would not alone win Classics but be syndicated for millions as sires.

"I was there in the era of the making of stallions. With rich patrons behind him, Vincent's concentration was totally on ensuring that the quality two-year-olds in the yard would first make their mark in the events marked out for them while at the same time leaving no stone unturned in endeavouring to ensure that they would train on and develop into potential Classic winners as three-year-olds."

It was a fascinating time. Epoch-making too in the sense that it saw Vincent O'Brien transform the game and change all preconceived assumptions about breeding on this side of the Atlantic.

Everything in a way was in his eye for a yearling combined with the other essential prerequisite – knowledge of pedigrees. One cannot be divorced from the other.

It was said of Vincent that when he was four he used to sit on his father's knee and reel off the breeding of the horses in Dan's yard, as another child would recite his sums. He became a walking encyclopaedia where pedigrees were concerned.

As a youth Vincent went everywhere with his father who in today's terminology would be seen as a permit-holder, that is, he only trained horses owned by himself.

"We went to races, to sales and around the country to various farms looking for young stock to make hunters, point-to-pointers and chasers", said Vincent.

And he smiled when he recalled that once he had the audacity in the hearing of grown-ups to advise his father quite seriously against buying a particular animal in a field because of something he had spotted about his forelegs. He was already on the road, without realising it, to Lexington and the Keeneland Sales – half a century before he made the initial onslaught with "The Syndicate" in 1975.

He would never forget the debt he owed his father for introducing him so young to the world of the judgement of horseflesh – for helping him acquire "the eye" that can be acquired in no university or any seat of learning but only in the hard school of experience.

"Whatever knowledge I may have of horses, I owe a great deal to my father", said Vincent to me one day out in the gallops in Ballydoyle when he was still training. "I learnt so much in those years going around with him and I have no doubt my father realised my great interest in and love for horses and he did everything possible to foster it".

John Magnier, the Boss of Coolmore, which his father-in-law helped to found, said, choosing every word deliberately: "Nobody before Vincent, or likely to come after him, could ever match his knowledge of pedigrees or bloodlines. It's uncanny really. People can today, with the benefit of the computer, call up statistics and other vital data that will prove very beneficial to those making vital decisions at yearling sales.

"In Vincent's case, however, it was almost as if all this knowledge was inbuilt. He would take it, as it were, subconsciously into account as he reached his decisions. He would look at a colt and say, 'That is a Buckpasser head' and although he never trained Buckpasser he would know everything that you needed to know about the Buckpasser line. He left you gasping in wonder at his knowledge".

John Magnier then went on to relate how Vincent in an inspired moment – which in itself showed the intuitive brilliance that stemmed from a masterful eye for selecting potential champions – came to pick Nijinsky, winner of the Triple Crown in 1970, when there was absolutely no prior thought of going for the bloodline this champion of champions represented.

"Vincent, at the behest of Charles Engelhard, went to look at a Ribot colt at Edward P. Taylor's Windfields Farm in Canada but ended up advising Engelhard that he buy a colt by Northern Dancer out of Flaming Page. The colt was purchased by Engelhard's representative for 84,000 guineas, a Canadian record at the time.

"Vincent often told me that from the moment he first saw Nijinsky the colt 'filled his eye', that he had 'the look of eagles' and struck him as a real champion in the making. This was a perfect example of Vincent bringing all his accumulated knowledge into play, his penchant for spotting that vital 'something' that would later emerge in Classic success.

"At the time Northern Dancer had not, as yet, arrived as a name sire. Nijinsky was one of his second crop. The era when he would become the single most dominant force in the world of breeding was still some years away. And Vincent, by picking colts like Nijinsky and The Minstrel, helped establish the reputation of Northern Dancer on this side of the Atlantic.

"Vincent, as I have already indicated, had no doubts in the case of Nijinsky. But before purchasing The Minstrel he was riven with doubt. I remember as vividly as if was only yesterday the team arriving in Kentucky for the 1975 Keeneland Sales. Naturally, The Minstrel was a prime target, being by Northern Dancer, Nijinsky's sire and out of Fleur, daughter of Nijinsky's dam, Flaming Page. But there were immediate and obvious worries about how small he was and, even worse, that this flashy chestnut had four white legs and feet."

John Magnier did not have to spell out the significance of those four white feet, or quote the old breeding maxim: 'One white foot, buy a horse; two white feet, try a horse; three white feet, look well about him; four white feet, do without him'.

It would have been so easy for Vincent O'Brien to "do without him" but, having accepted all the advice against the purchase and having had all the negative points impressed upon him, he still decided to go ahead and purchase. He deserved a special accolade for his courage in doing that.

Vincent went to $200,000 for The Minstrel. "He allowed Lyphard to be led out of the ring unsold at Newmarket because of his size and didn't lose any sleep over that decision", said John Magnier. "Subsequently, Lyphard, after a successful racing career in France, went on to become a very big success as a sire in America. Vincent picked The Minstrel despite his size and had the satisfaction of seeing him syndicated for $9 million. Yes, the $200,000 buy had turned out to be some investment".

✳   ✳   ✳

Colourful County Down-born bloodstock agent, Billy McDonald, a born character who has lived more than nine lives and got a bit part in the classic hilarious film "Let It Ride" earned the tag of "The Man Who Bought Alleged" – the colt that Vincent O'Brien trained to win two successive Prix de l'Arc de Triomphes in the colours of Robert Sangster in 1977 and '78 with Lester Piggott in the saddle. He also earned the tag of "The Man Who Discovered Fairy Bridge".

Billy acknowledged to me at breakfast in the Hyatt Regency Hotel in Lexington one day that his star was set right in the constellation the morning in Kentucky that he spotted Fairy Bridge. He was in the Bluegrass country looking at yearlings on the stud farms in advance of the Keeneland July Sales.

"It is generally the custom to put them out at night in the paddocks because of the heat", he told me.

"It was early morning and I saw this filly in a paddock with other yearlings. She was very small but what really caught my eye was that when the man came with the bucket of feed, she beat all the others nearly 100 yards in racing towards him. I took a mental note there and then, enquired about her breeding and said to myself that when she came into the ring eventually we would not let her go.

"I rang Vincent at Ballydoyle and I told him – 'I have seen this filly in a paddock and she's an absolute flyer'.

"He came to the Keeneland Sales in due course and went to look at her. He loved the pedigree. She was by Bold Reason out of the Forli mare, Special, who in turn was a sister of Thatch and a half-sister to the top-class King Pellinore. She was small but Vincent repeated more than once that she was 'a very nice filly'."

Vincent was standing with John Magnier and Billy McDonald when the filly came into the ring.

Billy McDonald did the bidding, securing her for $40,000. "Vincent, Robert Sangster and John Magnier took a quarter share each and I retained a quarter share myself", recalled Billy McDonald.

"The filly went into training with Vincent and won twice in succession as a two-year-old at the Phoenix Park in July of 1977, winning her second race by five lengths.

"She was the dam of Sadler's Wells."

Alleged turned out to be one of the best and most profitable buys in the whole history of bloodstock transactions.

"When he was offered for sale as a yearling at the 1975 Keeneland July Sales, he was led out unsold at $34,000," Robert Sangster recalled one morning over coffee in the Dublin's Berkeley Court Hotel. He was very immature and scrawny looking and, indeed, one onlooker went so far as to comment that he was like a drowned rat in appearance."

Billy McDonald (acting on Sangster's behalf) spotted something in the colt that he liked, so he helped trainer Monty Roberts to buy him privately for $34,000. Monty had the idea that he would re-submit him as a two-year-old at a sale in California.

"I didn't make it to the sale in California", said Robert Sangster, "but Billy McDonald was there acting for me and knew where to contact me. He bought Alleged for $120,000 before he went into the ring. On my instructions the colt was then allowed to be put up for auction and I was actually prepared to let him go if he reached $200,000. Billy bought him back for $175,000.

"Hoss Inman was the underbidder. After Billy had signed the docket, Hoss, wearing a white Texan hat, came up to him and asked 'Will you take a profit?'

"Billy asked $225,000. Hoss's reaction was – '$200,000 dollars is my limit. No deal, son.' "I was so lucky that Billy decided to add on that additional $25,000 and that Hoss dug in his heels at $200,000".

Robert Sangster was bid $1 million for Alleged after he won the Great Voltigeur at York in 1977 by eight lengths and trailing behind him were Hot Grove, second to The Minstrel at Epsom and Lucky Sovereign and Classic Example, second and third respectively to the same colt in the Irish Derby.

Some commentators raved about that performance and Vincent O'Brien remarked to Sangster that he could hardly believe the ease of it.

Having turned down the $1 million offer Sangster actually bought out Shirley Taylor's share in Alleged and now he was sitting on a gold mine – even though the colt was to be beaten in the St. Leger on his way to Longchamp.

After winning the Prix de l'Arc de Triomphe for the second year running in 1978 Alleged was syndicated for $13 million in Kentucky. Set that against the $120,000 that Sangster originally paid for him and you can really appreciate what a steal he was when Billy McDonald picked him out.

From the time he was knee-high to a grasshopper Billy McDonald had an absorbing interest in racing and bloodstock, not surprising in a way when you reflect on the fact that his family were very prominent in the show jumping world, his father being President of the Northern Ireland Show Jumping Association. Billy acknowledged to me that he "travelled on Vincent O'Brien's shirt tails when I started going to the sales".

He goes further and readily admits that anything he learned about the judgement of a yearling he learned from Vincent. He contended that Vincent had the greatest eye in the world when it came to judging a yearling.

"Nobody advised Vincent. He was on a plane apart. I would not speak about anyone else in the same breath as him".

He went on: "Carping critics of Vincent liked to advance the argument that he had vast resources at his back when he picked out champions like Golden Fleece and El Gran Senor. But what these people invariably forgot was that all through his life Vincent was able, with that uncanny eye of his, to buy real horses inexpensively.

"I do not know of any other man who would have bought Apalachee and it was the same with Lomond. He was able to see things about a horse that I venture to say that no one else could have seen. Many people can see the faults that it's easy to see – the things that people in the bloodstock business can crab a yearling for; there are no kudos in that.

"But Vincent could look beyond this aspect, could even forgive where his inner eye had caught something special in a colt or filly, as in the case of The Minstrel. Now there was a classic instance where he went dead against the experts crabbing the Northern Dancer colt because he was so small and had those four white stockings. While many told him he was crazy when he went to $200,000 for him, he proved in the long run that he had acquired a real bargain at that price.

"You see, money wasn't the criterion that mattered – it was judgement, and many of those who passed up The Minstrel had reason to respect even more Vincent's uncanny eye, especially when the colt was syndicated for $9 million."

Turning to the criteria that swayed Vincent O'Brien, Billy McDonald said that he placed tremendous importance on the fact that a colt had to have a man's head and a good eye.

"He spent more time endeavouring to assess the character of a horse by looking at the eye and the head than at anything else. He also placed a lot of emphasis on the fact that the legs must be right.

"He would, of course, have spent hours on end studying the pedigrees before he ever looked at a colt or filly. Having assessed the pedigree of a yearling exhaustively, he would then seek to look into its soul – through the eye. 'The eyes, Billy, are the mirror of the soul and the eye can reveal bravery and courage', he advised me once.

"And if he didn't see a certain look of kindness in the eye, a certain expression that ruled out the tell-tale trait of a rogue, then he could pass one by – despite its pedigree. Sometimes he discovered the look of eagles as he discovered it in Nijinsky and then he knew with an exactness beyond words that he had found a champion.

"You can't learn that from books – Vincent started to acquire it from the moment that he began to go around with his father and that was the university he attended and he graduated, you might say, with an honours degree in the judgement of horseflesh that no one in the world has ever been able to match".

✳   ✳   ✳

The policy of making stallions that in time became sires of sires of notable distinction paid rich dividends for Vincent O'Brien, Robert Sangster and John Magnier from the moment they made their first big raid on the Keeneland July Sales in 1975 and brought back a batch of horses that included The Minstrel, Artaius and Be My Guest.

One of Vincent O'Brien's great strokes at Keeneland, after The Minstrel, was to pick out Storm Bird – the colt by Northern Dancer (out of South Ocean) that was closely related to Nijinsky and The Minstrel. BBA (Ireland) paid $1 million on behalf of the Sangster-O'Brien Syndicate and it ran in the colours of Robert Sangster.

Rated top juvenile in Europe in 1980 after five successive wins as a two-year-old, Storm Bird was installed winter favourite for the English 2,000 Guineas and at the same time was viewed as a potential Epsom Derby winner. But he failed to win anything as a three-year-old and yet, as we shall see, Sangster made a real "killing"on him.

He was valued at the end of his two-year-old season at $20 million, according to Sangster, who insured him for $15 million with Hughes, Gibbs and Co. in the City for a premium of £208,000.

That was before his mane and tail were cut off before the 1981 season opened in a sad, bizarre incident (Vincent O'Brien was on a winter holiday with Jacqueline; David, then his assistant, was holding the fort at Ballydoyle and had to handle the clamourings of the media).

Vincent O'Brien maintained at the time that Storm Bird was unaffected by the experience and all seemingly went well with him. However, when he was taken to Naas racecourse for a public gallop he showed little of the sparkle of his two-year-old season. The bad ground could hardly be advanced as the sole reason. Then he suffered a minor setback.

That was enough to cause him to miss the English 2000 Guineas. Vincent was confident, however, that he would have him ready for the Derby. Indeed, he came strongly into the ante-post market but then disappointed in his final work-out and was withdrawn.

Now Robert Sangster takes up the story of how Storm Bird came to be sold for twenty-four times his original purchase price – even though he failed to win a Classic.

"I remember we were in the Hyatt Regency Hotel in Lexington during the 1981 Keeneland July Sales – Vincent, John Magnier and myself. I was just leaving the breakfast table when bloodstock agent George Harris came over and asked me what value I would put on Storm Bird. I said '$15 million'. I didn't think any more of it until that evening George came to me again after the sales session and told me he had a client who was willing to pay $15 million.

"I pointed out that when I had put a valuation of $15 million on Storm Bird, I did not mean that I would sell at that price. It was simply a minimum valuation on the colt – a figure below which there could be no negotiations. George Harris was not in the least taken aback by that. He replied – 'my client is quite willing that negotiations start from a base of $15 million'.

"Immediately I went into private discussion with Vincent and John, knowing now that George Harris and his client really meant business. We decided that we would not sell for less than $25 million.

"So Vincent and John accompanied me to George Harris's suite and after an hour's negotiations, it was clear that they were prepared to go to $24 million at least to acquire the colt. We gave the impression that we were playing tough by asking for time to consider, and then later went back to George Harris's suite and shook hands on $24 million.

"Every time I reflect on that amazing day, I just cannot believe how smoothly the whole business went. At the time $24 million became like so many chips in a big poker game in Las Vegas in the cut and thrust of negotiation. You know what I mean, you forget momentarily the astronomical sums you are dealing with, as you battle to clinch the deal".

George Harris was acting for Robert Heffner, an oil and gas magnate from Oklahoma (and no relation to Hugh Hefner).

Storm Bird remained in training with Vincent O'Brien. The target now set for the colt was the Prix de l'Arc de Triomphe and if he were to win it, there was no doubt that it would compensate in one magnificent stroke for missing out on the English 2000 Guineas and the Epsom Derby.

Vincent decided that Storm Bird should have a preliminary run in the Prix du Prince d'Orange at Longchamp on Sunday, 20 September, 1981. The going was soft.

Robert Sangster lunched at the Pre Catilan restaurant near the course with Robert Heffner's lawyer and accountant. "The thought of Storm Bird losing did not enter our minds that day", recalled Sangster. "It was simply a question of how much he would win by. He started favourite at 7-4. "

Ridden by Pat Eddery, the colt was in the lead after half-a-mile but was soon beaten and finished seventh behind the Aga Khan's Vayrann (Yves Saint-Martin) and Bikala.

"I never saw Vincent so shattered after any failure as he was that afternoon in Paris", said Robert Sangster. "I recall about twenty pressmen crowding round me, asking me what had gone wrong. All I could say was: 'I do not know. I don't own the horse any more. I cannot explain it.'

"Storm Bird had not had a race since the Dewhurst Stakes the previous season. It was now mid-September. I think he lost interest in racing in the meantime as he had not been asked a serious question for a year. All right, I know he had been worked at home and that he had looked exceptional at times, and that his work had led Vincent to believe that he would come good at Longchamp. Yes, it was a great shock. Perhaps if he hadn't suffered that setback when his tail and mane were cut, things might have been different. We shall never know".

Storm Bird did not contest the Prix de l'Arc de Triomphe. He was syndicated for $30 million to stand at the Ashford Stud in Kentucky, an arm of Coolmore. As a sire carrying on the valued Northern Dancer line, he did not lack patronage and soon the winners began to flow.

In 1989 he finished fourth in the British and Irish sires list thanks to the exploits of the top-class four-year-old filly Indian Skimmer and the Irish 2000 Guineas winner, Prince of Birds (who was sold to Japan). The Ashford Stud sire was also represented by the Italian 1000 Guineas winner, Lonely Bird and the US graded stakes winner, Conquering Hero.

There were even better days ahead for him.

By the end of 1996 he had established himself as a world-class sire with nearly 50 Stakes winners and 31 individual Group winners to his name, including 10 individual Group One winners and five Classic winners.

Fittingly too, as a son of Northern Dancer he had become a very successful sire of sires with Storm Cat, Bluebird and Summer Squall all proving to be very successful stallions. Indeed, Storm Cat had sired 40 Stakes winners by the end of '96, including November Snow, Hennessy, Missed The Storm, Tabasco Cat, Sardule and Harlan. And Hennessy was going to stud at Ashford.

It was not surprising that Robert Sangster should have raced three of Storm Bird's best sons, Bluebird, Prince of Birds and Stonehatch. He had the immense satisfaction also of seeing a daughter of Storm Bird, namely Balanchine, which he bred, emerge as the best three-year-old in Europe in 1994, winning the Budweiser Irish Derby in the colours of Godolphin by four lengths from King's Theatre with Colonel Collins third. She became only the second filly this century to achieve this feat.

Yes, Storm Bird had more than justified the $24 million paid for him.

4

The Perfectionist

Vincent O'Brien was a perfectionist from the very outset of his career as a trainer. Indeed, his attention to detail contributed to some of his greatest triumphs in the National Hunt sphere and later when he turned his attention solely to the Flat.

Instance the 1955 Aintree Grand National. Vincent actually ran four that year and, as Pat Taaffe recalled, once he knew what horses he would be entering, he had already lined up the jockeys he judged were among the best over the Aintree course. Bryan Marshall was automatically earmarked for Early Mist which he had ridden to victory in the 1953 National and which had missed the 1954 race because of injury. Dave Dick was engaged for the 1954 winner, Royal Tan; Fred Winter was chosen for Oriental Way and Pat Taaffe had the mount on Quare Times, which he had been riding since the outset of the 1954-'55 season and knew the horse perfectly.

On the eve of the race – Friday 25th March to be exact – Vincent gathered his four National jockeys in his suite in Liverpool's Adelphi Hotel, scene of mind-boggling victory parties thrown by 'Mincemeat' Joe Griffin after Early Mist and Royal Tan had carried his colours to victory in 1953 and 1954.

"Yes, Vincent was exceptional in the way he planned things", said Pat Taaffe. "He left absolutely nothing to chance. Not alone did he go after three of the top jump jockeys in Britain for Royal Tan, Early Mist and Oriental Way but he insisted on having a spare rider standing by for each of his chosen jockeys in case any of them got injured or had to cry off at the last moment for some other reason".

Vincent played the films of the two previous Nationals. As Bryan Marshall had won on Early Mist and Royal Tan, it was only natural that Vincent should ask Fred Winter, Dave Dick and myself to study closely the tactics employed by Bryan in victory and use these tactics as our guidelines", Pat Taaffe continued. "He ran through those films again and again, pointing out what he felt we should avoid and indicating the best route to take, especially in the very tricky run to Becher's Brook. At that stage it looked as if the going was going to be goodish. But it rained all night, a torrential downpour. Next morning at 10. 30, Vincent got on to me and asked me up to his suite to discuss new tactics in the light of the changed going.

"I suggested to Vincent that he should get Bryan Marshall to ride Quare Times and I would take the mount on Early Mist, but he wouldn't hear of that. His approach to the riding of Quare Times was that I should go on a mile from home to utilise the stamina which he had shown in winning the National Hunt Chase over 4 miles at Cheltenham the previous year. But I had already made up my mind that I would wait as long as possible. T. P. Burns had told me that Quare Times was leading the two-year-olds at home on the gallops and that proved to me that he wouldn't be beaten for a turn of foot in the long run-in, if it came to a battle from the last.

"I left Vincent's suite without telling him how I planned to ride Quare Times. I believed that Quare Times had the ability to win the race bar the accidents that can happen to any runner in the National. I was quite confident".

In that 1955 Grand National, Pat Taaffe's brother, 'Toss' was on Carey's Cottage, trained by his father, Tom J. Taaffe at Rathcoole, County Dublin. When they both jumped Becher's Brook safely the second time round and were right there with the leaders, with the odds favouring one of them to win, Pat, glancing across at 'Toss', said to himself: "What will the public say if both of us fall now!"

They didn't fall. And what a thrill they gave their parents and other members of the family who had travelled over, by finishing first and third. And Pat's fiancee (Molly Lyons) was in the stand to cheer him to victory.

For the record, Quare Times won by twelve lengths and Vincent O'Brien had the satisfaction of seeing his two previous Grand National winners get round unscathed. Early Mist, shouldering 12st 3lbs in the mud finished ninth and Royal Tan (owned then by Prince Aly Khan), an eleven-year-old that season and set to carry 12st 4lbs, came home twelfth. Vincent's fourth challenger, Oriental Way was brought down at the eleventh fence, falling over the prostrate No Response.

Incidentally, Vincent O'Brien had sent a record five challengers for the 1954 National and had the pleasure not alone of seeing Early Mist take the honours of the day but Churchtown (Toss Taaffe), whom he had given as a gift to Jacqueline, finished fourth despite bursting a blood vessel between the last two fences. Jacqueline had put on £5 each-way at 40-1.

✳   ✳   ✳

Vincent O'Brien was ahead of his time in almost every aspect of the training profession. What is more he was thinking big even when he was an "unknown" in Churchtown. At a time in the late Forties when it was the custom for Irish trainers, sending horses to challenge for prizes in England, to transport them by ferry, normally from Rosslare to Fishguard, Vincent saw the advantage of sending his challengers by plane. March 1949 marked the first time that he sent challengers for the Cheltenham Festival meeting by air. His three runners that year, Cottage Rake (his challenger for the

Gold Cup, postponed a month because of frost), Hatton's Grace (who won his first Champion Hurdle) and Castledermot (winner of the National Hunt Chase) were flown over in a flight arranged by the Curragh Bloodstock Agency – actually a reconstructed bomber flying out of Shannon to Bristol.

Vincent's brother, Dermot, Danny O'Sullivan and Jimmy accompanied the horses. Dermot knew that Cottage Rake was a nervous traveller even when taken by road and sea. Now he wondered what would 'The Rake's' reaction be to his first experience of coasting down a runway before take-off.

He had warned the pilot to be extra careful, especially when turning round to straighten out to face the plane down the runway. But, unfortunately, the plane gave a lurch and Cottage Rake, taking fright, began to go down. "I knew if he went off his feet we were sunk", said Dermot. "There I was holding on to Cottage Rake for dear life, hoping and praying that I could prevent disaster. Danny and I took turns during take-off and during the flight itself swinging, you might say, off his tail and there were some terrible moments when we felt we had an impossible task on our hands. Thank God, we reached Bristol without mishap. But it was a near thing, a very near thing. "

In those days planes were non-pressurised and, therefore, could not get over the weather. The result was a very rough trip when a plane ran into bad weather.

There came a day when Vincent O'Brien had his own landing-strip at Ballydoyle for the flying of horses to Britain and Continental destinations.

A far cry this from the time when, as Assistant trainer to his father, Dan, he was the inspiration behind the landing of the Irish Cambridgeshire in 1938 through Solford and the Irish Cesarewitch in 1941 with Astrometer. "Trained D. P. O'Brien" was entered after each horse in the record books but Vincent, though he was the guiding genius behind those coups, was happy to let his father bask in the glory, for he was already thinking ahead. He was only 21 at the time of Solford's success.

Solford and Astrometer would both have been walked from Churchtown to the local railway station in Buttevant, Vincent with the bike in the other hand, led the horses earmarked to win the principal handicaps in the Irish racing calendar. "I would throw the bicycle in the Guard's van and then the horses would be loaded on to the train and I would stay with them for the journey until we reached our destination", he told me.

When the train got into the Curragh, Vincent would retrieve his bicycle, supervise the unloading of the horses and then walk them to the course where they would be stabled. Normally this would be on the eve of racing. Having booked into some guest-house in Kildare, he would cycle up to the racecourse later in the evening to feed the horses and ensure that they were bedded down comfortably for the night.

Contrast that with the helicopter whisking Vincent from Ballydoyle to the Curragh in later decades and back home again after racing. A far cry too from Concorde.

An even farther cry from the moment after the sensational defeat in a photo finish of 'wonder colt' El Gran Senor in the 1984 Epsom Derby when the Queen insisted that he join his son David, trainer of Secreto, for a drink in the Royal Box. Normally the trainer of the runner-up would not normally be invited but the Queen recognised that the race this time was "a family affair".

✳ ✳ ✳

Dermot O'Brien emphasised to me that what always amazed him was Vincent's total attention to detail. "He would leave absolutely nothing to chance. Martin Molony was riding a lot in England at the time Vincent was using his talents at every available opportunity. He became very friendly with Bob Turnell. On one occasion Bob and Martin's brother, Tim came over for a spell of shooting. I was with them in the hotel in Mallow one evening at dinner and we were detailing for Bob Turnell the exactitude that Vincent brought to his training methods. Bob threw his hands in the air and remarked, 'If I had to do all that, I wouldn't consider it worth the price in the pressure it would mean, no matter how much success it brought. '

"For Vincent all the bits and pieces had to fit in. You might end up concluding that the finished job was perfect but you would have failed to notice how the small details – so patiently observed – all added up to the achievement of that perfection.

"Later that attention to detail would reveal itself again in the way he put cotton wool plugs in The Minstrel's ears when he feared the colt might be upset by all the pre-race hustle and bustle of Derby Day at Epsom".

Incidentally, it was Newmarket trainer, John Gosden, then assistant at Ballydoyle, who was detailed to go to the start to take out the plugs. "So you had the marvellous sight of the little Minstrel and big John pulling out the plugs at the start of the Derby", recalled Jacqueline O'Brien with a smile.

Dermot O'Brien noted that Vincent never spared expense where his horses were concerned. "The cheap ones got the same treatment as those that were bought big at Keeneland. He was always terribly caring where the horses under his care were concerned. There was always the additional consideration, of course, in the case of the top Flat horses that you could be talking about potential sires, whose eventual value would run into millions of pounds. That too created an additional burden".

So Vincent, as Jacqueline noted, was prepared to search globally for top-quality oats and hay and didn't mind the cost when he got what he wanted. He elicited the advice of experts in various countries about the best method to feed. Feeding was an integral part of his whole approach to the preparation of his charges for the big targets.

"Vincent always planned and worked for the big occasions – small races did not interest him – and, in planning a programme for a horse, he worked backwards from the main event. His whole career on the Flat was geared towards making top stallions. The selection of yearlings and their training was always with this in mind", was how Jacqueline put it in a contribution to the *Racing Post* on the occasion of Vincent's retirement from training in November, '94.

I remember standing with him on the gallops at Ballydoyle on a mild, overcast March Monday morning in 1987, four days before he celebrated his 70th birthday, as he supervised his string of about 60 thoroughbreds, his son Charles beside him.

Vincent instantly recognised every horse on the gallop – even before it had topped the rising ground – and reeled off, professionally and authoritatively, the pros and cons of each of them, right down to the lead horse. He talked about their breeding, about the way the three-year-olds of this 1987 season had performed as two-year-olds, whether he was satisfied or disappointed and his hopes in each individual case for the season ahead. "That's a Kris... that's a Northern Dancer... that's a Be My Guest, the best looker he bred so far... that's a Nijinsky two-year-old looking very well... that's a filly called Music and Dance... we paid five million for the mare when she was carrying her... ".

He mentions "five million" in a matter-of-fact way as a man in the foreign exchange department of some bank might refer to that sum being transferred from one businessman's account to another. But then when you have put colts like Nijinsky and The Minstrel and Alleged through your hands – colts whose stud value reached astronomical figures – you are no longer surprised at the mention of a million or even five.

What stirred him, I concluded, was Classic potential revealed on the gallops and especially when the sophisticated electric timing apparatus of the modern era confirmed what the eye had told him.

Vincent, as we have seen, was always an innovator. Way back in his Churchtown days he had a gallop that was a replica of the uphill climb from the last at Cheltenham. No way was a Festival challenger of his going to be caught out by the hill.

And no way either was a colt heading for the Epsom Derby going to have his prospects ruined by failure to handle the gradients in the swing around Tattenham Corner. One of the most wonderful sights of all at Ballydoyle, I always felt, was the gallop that in its own way reproduced Epsom where he left such a lasting imprint.

On that morning over a decade ago now, he showed me the boxes lined with rubber – so that no valuable colt or filly could get cast in its box. The padding in each box had an aero material in it to protect the horses. And he had special material also outside the stables to prevent slipping. Extra staff were detailed to watch areas in the yard and on the working grounds where it was feared there could be accidents.

The gallops, in fact, set standards that made him the envy of others worldwide, though the shrewd ones came to learn from The Master. He was the first to make all-weather gallops and trainers like Barry Hills and Guy Harwood arrived from England to study them being used. Aidan O'Brien, who succeeded him as Master of Ballydoyle, said to me one day that he was working horses on gallops, apart from the main ones, that other trainers would be happy to have as the sole training grounds for their charges.

Yes, the blue bloods in Vincent's stable were treated in a manner that 'royalty' deserved. But the totally professional approach did not end there. In days of high security, he did not believe in closing off the world outside completely to the horses in his care. The half doors allowed them to look out and Vincent believed that it enabled them to satisfy their curiosity. "You may not believe it but I know from my experience with horses that they want to know what's going on outside their own box", he said to me. The boxes were very spacious by any modern standard. This was achieved by converting three into two to make them more comfortable and luxurious.

There were many other ways in which the total attention to detail manifested itself. In a tour of the stables, your eye was immediately caught by the starting stalls in the big barn where the two-year-olds were given plenty of practice at coming out smoothly – and there was even background music to soothe the nerves of the highly-strung fretting ones. Was I correct in hearing that they normally preferred classical to pop?

Nothing was left to chance in what I concluded was one of the most efficiently-run stables in the world.

Back to Dermot O'Brien, who stressed that Vincent had the knack from the very outset of growing with the challenges that he came to face. "He always kept his sights high. Indeed, he kept aiming higher and higher".

Aubrey Brabazon, who had such a highly-successful relationship riding for Vincent, leading to some of the most memorable triumphs at Cheltenham, said: "For me the No. 1 attribute that put Vincent ahead of all others as a trainer was thoroughness. I remember in the era when horses were brought to race meetings in primitive-looking trailers, Vincent would see to it that he always had a spare one standing by in case of a breakdown. He was never caught out.

"Also, where he had runners in important chasing and hurdle events, he saw to it that he alerted a jockey to be on hand and ready, in case his No. 1 choice had a fall in an earlier event and could not take the mount."

Aubrey added that the more he reflected back on those days, the more he became convinced that from the very outset Vincent was ahead of the field in the "sheer professionalism he displayed".

In a majority of cases the men who passed through Churchtown and Ballydoyle did not end simply being run-of-the-mill journeymen. It was akin to attending one of the great universities of the horse and his 'college' left an indelible mark on all who passed its portals. Men found something in working with The Master.

The names spring easily to mind: Christy Kinane, Danny Kinane, Tony Redmond, Jimmy Gordon, David Murray Smith, Paddy Norris and later his son, Robert, Michael Kauntze, John Gosden, Michael Dickinson, Dhruba Selvaratnam and Vincent's own sons, David and Charles who were assistant trainers to him. All gained the confidence to go out and set up on their own and each and every one of them remembers his spell with Vincent in a special way – and with gratitude for what he acquired.

Twenty years after the year of The Minstrel – he was assistant trainer then at Ballydoyle – John Gosden had reason to privately thank Vincent O'Brien for all that he had learned when operating under his wing as he welcomed back Benny The Dip into the winner's enclosure at Epsom after the colt by Silver Hawk (a son of Roberto) had given him his first Derby triumph. Silver Hawk himself had been third in the 1982 Derby behind Golden Fleece – so the links, direct and indirect, with Vincent O'Brien were there for all to see.

It was an emotional day for John Gosden, not just because Willie Ryan's mount, Benny The Dip (named after a villainous New York pick-pocket of Damon Runyon's imagination) had held off the gallant grey, Silver Patriarch (ridden by Pat Eddery) in a photo-finish but because he could not but remember his father in his moment of singular triumph. "This is for my father," Gosden said. "He trained Charlottown as a two-year-old and then had to stand and watch him win the Derby. He died soon afterwards."

'Towser' Gosden was a wonderful old trainer who fell ill and was compelled to hand the horse on to another trainer, Gordon Smyth, who saddled him to win in 1966.

John Gosden added: "My father did a lot of work with Gordon Smyth but he had given up because he had become ill and didn't think he could do justice to the horses. He stood in the winner's circle that Derby Day in '66 but it was a devoid feeling. All I can say to him if he is up there and looking down is, 'We finally did it'."

Jacqueline O'Brien was at Epsom to congratulate John Gosden. Beforehand, she, of course, was hoping that English 2,000 Guineas winner, Entrepreneur (the mount of Michael Kinane), would win in the colours of Sue Magnier, wife of John Magnier, boss of Coolmore, where Sadler's Wells, sire of the odds-on favourite stands, of course; with five representatives in the Derby line-up it didn't seem possible that Sadler's Wells could be prevented from providing his first Epsom Derby winner. Such are the vagaries of racing and breeding.

The articulate 46-year-old John Gosden had trained for nine years in California where, as Rodney Masters pointed out in the *Racing Post* on the Monday after his Derby success, he more than held his own with giants of the American scene like D. Wayne Lukas and Charlie (The Bald Eagle) Whittingham. His first runner at the Breeders' Cup, Robert Sangster's Royal Heroine, won the 1984 Mile and both she and Bates Motel scooped Eclipse Awards. Ask around Santa Anita and Hollywood Park and the professionals will tell you that Gosden was a fine trainer and a popular one, throughout all his time there. Then he was head-hunted by Sheikh Mohammed and, after two years, he was persuaded to return to Britain. He arrived at Stanley House at the end of 1988.

Dubai's Minister of Defence, who owns the stables, is also responsible for 80 per cent of the inmates but, ironically, when Gosden finally won the Blue Riband it was not with a Maktoum colt, but one owned by a 72-year-old small-time breeder from Ohio, the wheel-chair-bound Landon Knight, a great friend of the Newmarket trainer.

John Gosden had learned in his days in Ballydoyle that the road to success at the very top of this game can be a slow one. He knew too that it was a game that tames lions. He set himself a programme of four, five or even six years.

He was deeply hurt by the heavy criticism levelled at him in the early part of 1996 that he was an under-achiever but he came back first in the latter half of '96 with a magnificent St. Leger triumph with Shantou, his first British Classic, and then silenced his critics completely on Derby Day '97 at Epsom. "There are so many ups and downs in this game that you learn to be pretty hard inside, especially when you have already had one Derby snatched from your grasp as happened when Lammtarra caught Tamure in 1995," he said.

As Benny The Dip held off Silver Patriarch in that heart-stopping finish, John Gosden was able to reflect back on Lester Piggott bringing it off on The Minstrel and those epic 'Arc' triumphs on Alleged.

At the time of Vincent O'Brien's retirement, he said to Julian Muscat in a *Racing Post* interview that the word 'genius' had, of course, been cheapened through being bandied about too much. "But there was no doubt about it applying to Vincent. And he would have achieved it all no matter when he was born."

Gosden put a special spotlight on Vincent's commercial instincts. "You could never underestimate his business acumen. It took courage to invest in the Northern Dancers at a time when everyone else was still persevering with the proven European stallions. Northern Dancer fascinated him; that horse's progeny allowed Vincent, a shy man, to express himself through them.

"He was so astute. I remember the days it took to syndicate The Minstrel. Vincent realised the importance of the deal, how it would open up a whole new market. It was a tense time. We daren't as much as say 'boo' around the yard."

Referring specifically to Vincent's eye at the sales, John Gosden concluded: "You only have to look at what he did at the 1988 Keeneland July Sales to recognise his judgement of yearlings. He went all the way there and came back with one horse which cost him $3.5 million. And that was Royal Academy. He would never mess about with a horse that didn't have a proper pedigree."

✳   ✳   ✳

Michael Dickinson, talking to me at the Keeneland July Sales one day, said: "It was very flattering for me when I had the first five home in the Gold Cup in 1983, Bregawn's year, that comparisons were drawn with some of Vincent's outstanding achievements in the National Hunt arena. I know I would never have pulled off that record without all the knowledge I acquired at Ballydoyle and so indirectly Vincent left his special mark on that particular achievement of mine.

"From the time I first began to learn about racehorses, I looked up to him like a God. I read all about the big races he had won. Then later, when I was riding over the jumps, I wrote to him asking him if he could give me a job for the summer, as I wanted to further my education. Initially, my approach didn't succeed as he wrote back to say he had no vacancy at that time. I persevered and it was one of my proudest moments when eventually I passed through the gates at Ballydoyle. I spent two summer, 1973 and 1974, working there – two of the happiest years I have ever enjoyed. And also the most informative. I was made to feel that I was one of the family, and I will always be grateful to Vincent and Jacqueline for that ".

Michael Dickinson, who would depart for the States to set up as a trainer at Fairhill, Florida (the breach with Robert Sangster and the bitter departure from Manton being something he preferred not to talk about) summed up what he saw as placing Vincent O'Brien on a pedestal apart: "He did not make mistakes. Everything was so well organised at Ballydoyle, from the boxes to the gallops themselves, that you were talking about sheer perfection, a perfection that was stunning.

"His knowledge of horses, of breeding, was immense – overwhelming, in fact – and when it came to an eye for picking potential champions, few if any could match him. From my own experience there, I would say that the 'Ballydoyle way' got the very best out of a horse – if it had the ability".

That tribute of Michael Dickinson sums it up in a nutshell – yes, Vincent "The Perfectionist".

At the 1997 Dubai World Cup I had the pleasure of meeting 46-year-old Dhruba Selvaratnam who had been an assistant trainer at Ballydoyle from 1980 to 1990 – the decade when Brian Molony was also there as an assistant. Born and brought up in Sri Lanka, he is married to an Irish girl, Marian and the couple have two children.

Racing has always been in his blood and both his father and grandfather were successful trainers. Indeed, his grandfather began to train in 1912 as part of the Royal Ceylon Mounted Police.

Dhruba got his big break in 1990 when he was offered the job of private trainer to Sheikh Ahmed bin Rashi Al Maktoum. He accepted and travelled to Dubai to take up this challenging position. He soon made his mark in the UAE, winning the Trainers' Championship in two successive seasons. His first title came in 1992-'93 when he scored 34 victories. The following season he finished on 61 wins. In 1994-'95 he was fourth and in 1995-'96 the battle for the crown went right down to the wire with Selvaratnam finishing runner-up with 57 successes.

During the summer of 1995 he travelled three horses to Belmont Park where they were based for two months.

Those who passed through the portals of Ballydoyle in Vincent O'Brien's time acquired the ability to think big and to aim for the highest targets.

Vincent has had every reason to feel proud of how his 'pupils' have upheld the honour of their alma mater.

5

The
Jockeys

Vincent said frankly to me one day while we sat conversing in the sun lounge at Ballydoyle: "I always went for top jockeys". His approach was that if he felt he had the material to win big prizes – over the jumps or on the Flat – he was not going to miss out by not having the right rider up.

He picked Bryan Marshall and Pat Taaffe, both superb horsemen, for his three Grand National winners. He had Aubrey Brabazon, a jockey with a wonderful pair of hands, versatile enough to ride with the best on the Flat as well as over the jumps, to win the Gold Cup three times on Cottage Rake and the Champion Hurdle twice on Hatton's Grace. Tim Molony was on Hatton's Grace when the gelding won the Champion Hurdle for the third time and this fine horseman rode Vincent's fourth Gold Cup winner, Knock Hard.

Of course, he utilised the immense talents of Martin Molony and, as with Lester Piggott, it went far deeper than a trainer-jockey relationship in the normal sense. Vincent respected Martin so much that he never gave him instructions as he didn't have to give Piggott instructions. And friendship blossomed in both instances, born, I like to think, out of genius, matching genius and a totality of professionalism.

"A wonderful horseman" was how Vincent described Martin Molony to me, making the point that he was totally dedicated to his profession. Elaborating, he said that Martin had developed the style of a Flat jockey in a finish and, therefore, could ride a powerful finish at the end of a chase or hurdle race. It gave him a distinct advantage over many of his contemporaries. Like his brother, Tim he was fearless. "We were always great friends apart from our professional association. In fact, there was a strong and lasting friendship between our two families", added Vincent.

Phonsie O'Brien was riding in the same race – the Munster Chase – at Thurles on Tuesday, September 18th, 1951 when Martin Molony's career was abruptly ended at the age of 26 through the fall of the 4-6 favourite, Bursary, who had won at Tralee six days earlier. Martin suffered a fractured skull and lay at death's door for a week in Thurles Hospital, the racing world holding its collective breath waiting for bulletins on his progress.

Phonsie went to see him every day in hospital. "The waiting was awful, as we wondered would he pull through. Our two families were so close, you know. We were so glad when eventually we learned that he was out of danger".

Vincent O'Brien struck up a tremendous partnership also with T. P. Burns, son of 'The Scotsman', Tommy Burns. T. P. rode five of the ten Gloucestershire Hurdle winners and won the Irish Derby and English St. Leger on Ballymoss.

T. P. rode a lot for the stable over a period of nearly twenty years and then was assistant trainer for seven years before joining Dermot Weld in the same capacity. Recalling those five Gloucestershire Hurdle winners, he told me: "They were all gambled on without exception. You knew the money was down. When there is gambling, there is always pressure. You felt the pressure. And, believe me, the pressure was far greater then, far more intense than when Vincent was turning out Derby winners for wealthy patrons.

"Vincent didn't give vent to any displays of emotion in victory and likewise he wasn't one of those to apportion blame when a gamble became unstuck. His attitude was: 'It's lost, we'll get it back'. In a word, that day was finished and it was on to the next day", added T. P.

On the domestic front he exploited the talents and vast experience of Liam Ward. Liam rode Nijinsky to victory in the 1970 Irish Derby, won the Oaks on Aurabella (1965) and Gaia (1946) and the Irish St. Leger on White Gloves (1966) and Reindeer (1969).

Christy Roche... Georgie McGrath... Johnny Roe... Declan Gillespie... Tommy Murphy... were others who became associated with Ballydoyle. And Georgie McGrath, who is today a starter with the Emirates Racing Association in Dubai, had the distinction of riding Sadler's Wells to victory in the 1984 Irish 2,000 Guineas.

One could write a chapter on the Australians who came and went in their time – and on their comparative merits.

Vincent engaged 'Scobie' Breasley for Ballymoss when T. P. Burns could not take the ride because of injury and the Man from Wagga Wagga rode him to victory in the 1958 King George VI and Queen Elizabeth Stakes and Prix de l'Arc de Triomphe. Incidentally, when asked who was the greatest trainer he rode for in a career that saw him amass 3,000 winners before he finally retired at 54, 'Scobie' replied with total conviction: "It has got to be Vincent".

Vincent had immense respect for the Australian's superb judgement and tactical brilliance. Two other Australians for whom he had great admiration were Jack Purtell and Garnie Bougoure (Phonsie O'Brien thinks that Bougoure was one of the most artistic jockeys ever associated with Ballydoyle and it was simply amazing how often the verdict went his way in a photo finish).

Vincent himself put it this way to me: "The best Australian jockey could win a race by a neck or half-a-length for you with 7lbs or more in hand. And, of course, they were very good judges of pace".

Looking down the Vincent O'Brien record at the end of this book, you will see two other Australian riders – Neville Sellwood and T. P. ('Pat') Glennon.

When Scobie Breasley could not take the mount on the small, neat and compact Larkspur for Vincent O'Brien in the 1962 Epsom Derby as he was retained by Sir Gordon Richards, he recommended Neville Sellwood. It was the Derby in which seven horses fell, including Hethersett, the favourite. Larkspur's amazing good fortune in avoiding the pile-up was revealed when Neville Sellwood said that the 22-I outsider "passed between the upturned legs of Hethersett". If he had been a big gangling horse, he would almost certainly have been turned over.

Sellwood maintained afterwards that he would have won the race even if there had been no pile-up. However, the weight of informed opinion was that Hethersett, trained by Dick Hern, would almost definitely have triumphed if he had not been brought down and he proved his class by subsequently winning the St. Leger with Larkspur unplaced.

T. P. Glennon was No. 1 jockey to the Ballydoyle stable in 1962 and '63 and later Vincent brought over Jack Purtell, who had won the Melbourne Cup three times. Purtell made a lasting impression on knowledgeable Irish race-readers. He was to win the 1965 English Oaks for the Ballydoyle stable on the 100-7 chance, Long Look. He also won the 1964 Queen Mary Stakes at Royal Ascot on Brassia.

❊   ❊   ❊

Vincent O'Brien and Robert Sangster had the services of Pat Eddery for five years before Arab money saw him start another chapter in his career. Pat had the unenviable task of taking over the mantle of Lester Piggott. He won the Epsom Derby on Golden Fleece (1982), the Irish Derby on El Gran Senor (1984) and Law Society (1985), the Irish St. Leger on Leading Counsel (1985), the Eclipse Stakes on Sadler's Wells (1984) and the English 2,000 Guineas on Lomond (1983) and El Gran Senor (1984).

In fact, Eddery was No. 1 jockey at a time when Classic and big-race successes were still coming the way of the stable and the twilight days had not yet begun to fall. Looking back on his period there, he said: "Those five years riding for a marvellous trainer are five years I will always remember. We got on really well together. I am grateful to him for all the experience I gained. It was invaluable. To sum up, let me put it this way: you get outstanding jockeys and outstanding trainers. Now and then one comes along with a unique gift. Lester Piggott was specially gifted as a jockey and Vincent O'Brien in the same way as a trainer. You cannot express their kind of flair in so many words. They just had the knack of doing the impossible".

The only real setback for Pat Eddery during his sojourn at Ballydoyle was the defeat of El Gran Senor in the 1984 Epsom Derby. He got a terrible roasting from sections of the British media. And I found that it had stung him deeply when initially I asked to interview him about the race. The fierce debates will go on down the decades about that so-near-and-yet-so-far sole reverse for the 'wonder colt' who had won four off-the-reel as a two-year-old and gave such a brilliant performance in winning the English 2,000 Guineas that Capt. Michael Byrne, then Senior Irish Turf Club Handicapper pointed out to me that the colt was "the best miler we have rated in the International Classifications since they were first published in 1977 – the best that I personally have seen as an official handicapper."

Then he added very significantly: "I do not subscribe to the school that criticised Pat Eddery after El Gran Senor's Epsom defeat. The colt went from pulling the proverbial roller two furlongs out to struggling close home. I consider that Pat's skill and judgement got him as close as he did that day".

When the initial storm had abated, Pat Eddery was able to sum it up for me in one seven-word cryptic sentence at Newmarket one day: "If you don't stay, you don't win". And in the final analysis El Gran Senor, though unquestionably the most brilliant miler of his day and probably outstanding also up to ten furlongs could not win up that so-testing final climb to the winning post at Epsom when it came to the crunch in a twelve-furlong Classic that finds them out as only the Derby can.

The Irish Derby was made for him in the sense that it was run exactly to suit him, became a sprint over the final few furlongs and it answered nothing about Epsom.

Naturally, Eddery's critics drew comparisons with Piggott, arguing that Lester would have held up El Gran Senor to the very death and somehow or other managed to win it. But these same critics forgot what Eddery outlined to me – the colt had "so much talent, so much class, so much speed and was so vastly superior, in fact, that he was running all over Al Ralaq, Telios and Claude Monet despite my efforts to keep him covered up to the last possible second. Look, they simply died ahead of me. And when I saw Claude Monet go like the rest, I found myself in front, even before we hit the hill".

And then the punch line: "El Gran Senor didn't stay in that final furlong when Secreto came at him. Never was the old maxim 'if you don't stay, you don't win' borne out as clearly as it was that day at Epsom."

When Eddery had the goods under him in Golden Fleece in 1982, all doubts were dispelled as he won from what seemed an impossible position coming down Tattenham Hill. He had only three horses behind him rounding the Corner, yet such was his acceleration in the straight that he won unchallenged in the end. One of the greatest Derby performances of modern times.

One day in Ballydoyle as he passed the box that had accommodated Golden Fleece, Vincent O'Brien repeated audibly to himself more than once in my presence: "What speed, what speed".

He put the colt up there beside Nijinsky and Sir Ivor and in his home in

Newmarket, Lester Piggott turned to me and observed that a horse he did not ride may well have been the best that Vincent ever trained – better even than Nijinsky and Sir Ivor.

That colt was Golden Fleece, who had not really been extended in winning any of his four races. "If he had not been forced into early retirement after winning the Derby, he could – if we are to go on the speed he showed at Epsom – have been capable of anything", added Lester.

✳   ✳   ✳

After Eddery came the Texan Cash Asmussen. Controversy would follow in his wake. Fierce controversy at times.

He arrived at Ballydoyle at the start of the 1987 season on a two-year contract with Robert Sangster and Vincent O'Brien – and it goes without saying that he arrived to a fanfare of trumpets. He could not have foreseen then that he would be terminating his contract "by mutual agreement" a year earlier than it should have ended.

Cash, then 24, had achieved everything he wanted to achieve in France, where he had been champion twice at that stage and he had become accustomed to hearing the cry "Bravo Cash" or "Allez Cash" as he booted home the winners. The lure of being No. I. jockey to Vincent O'Brien was too good a chance to miss. Then, too, as "a student of the game", he knew he would be joining a great "university" of racing and he did not hide the fact that he wanted to learn from the Master.

The summer of 1987 became the summer of Cash Asmussen's discontent – not with Ireland and its people as a whole but at the "stick" he had to endure at the hands of a vociferous section of the racing public. He also came to be concerned at what he described at the time as "a lot of negative press".

"It got to the stage where I believed these people were playing a sort of game with me. Sure, they could be mad but they were never vicious mad, as you can find them in other countries where racegoers can be far more vocal and objects can even be thrown at jockeys by disgruntled punters. I got the feeling at times that these Irish racegoers were doing it more in a joking manner and, therefore, I was never troubled by any sense of viciousness.

"No, it never did get to the point where I held anything against Irish racegoers as a body or against the Irish generally.

"I love the Irish people as they live for racing. Go into any pub, into any church or any bank and 98 per cent of the people you meet know racing and you're amazed how many know the form book. When people live for racing, it makes a professional feel really good".

Cash's ambition of "riding as many Classic winners as possible" was not realised, though he did win the Irish St. Leger for John Oxx on Eurobird and Oxx, incidentally, never lost faith in him and sings his praises to this day.

Asmussen hit Ballydoyle in a valley period. You might go even further and say that the glory days of the Seventies and early Eighties were past. There was no Sir Ivor, no Nijinsky, no Alleged, nothing of the calibre of The Minstrel in the stable – the kind of champions that Lester had ridden. And neither was there anything to compare with Sadler's Wells, Golden Fleece or El Gran Senor – the kind of class colts that Pat Eddery had the privilege of riding.

Seattle Dancer was the pride of Ballydoyle when Cash arrived – the great hope for Classic glory in 1987. But though Cash won the Derrinstown Stud Derby Trial Stakes and the Windfields Farm Gallinule Stakes on him, he could only finish sixth in the Prix du Jockey Club (French Derby) and later finished second in the Grand Prix de Paris at Longchamp.

Supposing there had been a Nijinsky or a Sir Ivor, a Golden Fleece or an El Gran Senor, would there have been such an intense spotlight put on the defeats the Texan suffered on a few odds-on chances of questionable ability in the final analysis? As great horses make trainers, so jockeys gain from the super champions and ride the crest of the wave with them.

Mention Golden Temple today to any Irish racegoer and he will probably have forgotten that she was trained by Vincent O'Brien. And yet when the Golden Fleece filly, carrying the colours of Stavros Niarchos, failed to land the odds of 4-9 laid on her in a field of seven at the Phoenix Park on Saturday, August 22nd, 1987 it resulted – as Con Power reported in the *Sunday Press* at the time – in "the kind of railing never before handed out to a jockey in this country".

Cash Asmussen dismounted to the strains of "California Here I Come" being sung by one disenchanted punter and there was even the story – maybe apocryphal – that another punter shouted: "You wouldn't ride Kathy Barry" and Cash, who never lost his cool or his wit during all this time, responded in keeping with his jovial character: "Try me!".

You had got to admire the man.

The final irony of his riding in Ireland was that no one ever questioned his integrity. It came down, as in the case of Golden Temple, to whether or not you agreed with the tactics he adopted in races he lost and whether you were satisfied with his record in tight finishes. A glance at the 22 very close finishes that Cash was involved in revealed that he came out best in only six as against being on the losing end in sixteen. And in the case of twelve photo finishes in this overall total of 22 races, he was first in three (one subsequently meriting a disqualification) and failed in nine.

Experienced race readers were critical of Asmussen for lying too much out of his ground at Leopardstown when Golden Temple was at the rear of the field early on and eventually ran on to take second place behind Just Class in a field of seven. They were sharply critical of him at the Park for getting boxed in in such a small field and being forced to come between horses at the crucial moment. Earlier in the season they had been critical of his riding of Seattle Dancer in the Nijinsky colt's opening race of the season at the Park when this Classic hope, starting 4-6 favourite, did not see daylight until too late and failed to beat the I4-I outsider, Reet Petite.

Talking to me later about the controversial defeat of Golden Temple in that August race at the Park, Cash said: "The opening never came when it would have made all the difference between defeat and victory. When the openings come, you're a hero – when they don't, you're a villain. That just goes with the territory".

Then he posed the pertinent question: "What did Golden Temple do afterwards?"

A glance at the records shows that she didn't win a race. Yet it can be argued that she caused Cash's days at Ballydoyle to be numbered, even though, ironically, he finished the '87 season with 62 winners, coming second to Michael Kinane (86) in the Irish Flat Jockeys Championship and his percentage of winners to rides while in Ireland outstripped his career percentage.

*   *   *

Vincent O'Brien kept his feelings to himself when he felt a jockey had ridden a bad race. Jacqueline has gone on record to state: "He would be mad, of course and I would say: 'Why don't you tell him he came too soon', or whatever the problem was. Vincent had no interest in teaching jockeys and would respond to me: 'If he doesn't know what he did wrong, I'm not going to start telling him'."

Northern Ireland-born John Reid took over the mantle of Cash Asmussen at Ballydoyle. He was in the saddle twice on Golden Temple in 1968 and each time she was beaten. Reid was a competent rider, judged to be much more than a mere journeyman jockey when he linked up with the Vincent O'Brien stable. For one thing, it was felt that he wasn't going to lose races from a position where they should be won. There were even those who expected that he would deliver at a level far better than Asmussen.

Frankly, however, he was at Ballydoyle like Cash at lean times compared with the heady days and the establishment of Classic Thoroughbreds did nothing in the final analysis to create another glory era.

There was an awful lot riding on the 1990 Irish 2,000 Guineas for Classic Thoroughbreds when Royal Academy took on Tirol, which had earlier won the English 2,000 Guineas. Also in the line-up was the Francois Boutin-trained Machiavellian, which had started 6-4 favourite at Newmarket and was now strongly fancied by connections to reverse the placings with Tirol, owned by Cork meat baron, John Horgan.

But Horgan would say to me later that he had feared Royal Academy more than Machiavellian – and he was proved right. Reports during the week beforehand that Royal Academy had done an outstanding gallop were reflected in the strong support the colt received in the betting , and he started at 4-1 with Tirol 5-2 favourite and Machiavellian at 9-4, having opened at 7-4.

Vincent O'Brien, aware of Royal Academy's stamina limitations, told John Reid that he did not mind how long he held up the colt, he would not blame him if he got beat. Royal Academy had the rest of the field beaten when he led briefly inside the last furlong – but he could not repel the late surge of Tirol and Pat Eddery. It was either going to be a case of Royal Academy winning on the line or not at all.

The combination of the Horgans, who were estimated to have hit the English layers for a cool £500,000 in winning bets on Tirol's success in the Newmarket Guineas, and shrewd Wiltshire-based trainer, Richard Hannon had done it again.

Vincent O'Brien and his wife Jacqueline ventured nothing in public but privately their disappointment was very deep and friends claimed that they were both convinced that if Royal Academy could have been held up a little longer, he would have won.

When you reflect on the different jockeys who have been associated with Ballydoyle down the decades, it all gets back to Lester in the end. In fact, it was Vincent, as we shall see, who induced Piggott to come out of retirement at the age of 54 and like Maria Callas and Tito Gobbi in one last great flourish in TOSCA, they produced their own *tour de force* at Belmont Park, New York on October 27th, 1990 when Royal Academy, under a powerful ride from Lester, won the Breeders' Cup Mile (Turf).

For Piggott it was a special moment, a very special moment and for Vincent, unable to be there because of a bout of flu but watching the race on television back home in Ballydoyle, it was the crowning moment of a career that had extended over half-a-century. And to have done it on the other side of the Atlantic in the highly-competitive setting of Breeders Cup Day made it all the more momentous and satisfying.

Lester Piggott wins at Epsom on Be My Guest (son of Northern Dancer), a top Coolmore sire year after year. In 1996 his son Pentire had Ascot Gold Cup winner, Classic Cliche and Derby winner, Shaamit behind him when winning the King George.

6

The Ultimate Partnership

It was the ultimate partnership. In fact, it was the most successful and unique trainer-jockey relationship in the history of Flat racing. From the 1966 season when he rode Valoris to victory in the Oaks – his first Classic winner for the Ballydoyle stable – to 1990 when he won the Breeders Cup Mile (Turf) on Royal Academy at Belmont Park, New York, Lester Piggott made the racing world marvel at the heights he reached on horses trained by Vincent O'Brien.

They were the most-feared duo when it came to the Epsom Derby, winning four in a decade through Sir Ivor (1968), Nijinsky (1970), Roberto (1972) and The Minstrel (1977) but the other Classics also fell to them. And nothing matched the level of achievement when the Prix de l'Arc de Triomphe was won two years running by Alleged (1977 and '78). The tactical genius that Piggott showed in '77 when he decided, because of a slow early pace, to go on – even though Vincent had advised him against making the running – represents one of the the finest displays of jockeyship in this event in modern times. It was a classic instance of Piggott winning from in front and, entering the straight that day, he was in total command and, of course, he knew that the racehorse under him was a veritable machine at his best.

One must not forget either Piggott riding four of the Fabulous Six winners that Vincent O'Brien turned out at Royal Ascot in 1975. It became seven for O'Brien in that memorable week if you take in Guillaume Tell's triumph in the Churchill Stakes at the Heath meeting on the Saturday.

No other jockey but Piggott would have won at Epsom on Roberto and The Minstrel. Piggott brought Roberto home a winner by the tip of a nostril in one of the most dramatic finishes ever to an Epsom Derby. There is no need to dwell on the controversy that stemmed from Piggott's liberal use of the whip. He has admitted that if he did the business in similar fashion under the whip guidelines operating today, he would almost definitely have been stood down for a lengthy period.

Vincent wasn't complaining and neither was owner John Galbreath. They both saw the colt in the stables shortly after the race and reported that he was in excellent form.

Roberto became locked in a desperate battle with Rheingold (Ernie Johnson), who was on the outside and became so unbalanced because of the camber of the track that he kept leaning in on the O'Brien-trained colt. Already bumped by Penland Firth before his challenge died, Roberto now received some additional bumps from Rheingold who was ahead by a neck inside the final furlong. It was then that Piggott got down to ride perhaps his most powerful and strongest finish ever and his admirers were unanimous that it was his strength that lifted Roberto to victory over a better stayer (Rheingold would win the Prix de l'Arc de Triomphe the following year for Barry Hills with Lester in the saddle).

If the photo finish verdict had gone to Rheingold, he would almost definitely have been disqualified in the lengthy Stewards' Inquiry that inevitably followed.

Lester Piggott again didn't spare the whip as he got The Minstrel home by a neck over Hot Grove in the 1977 Epsom Derby. It was an epic duel between Lester and Willie Carson over the final two furlongs. Piggott knew that Hot Grove would stay every inch of the twelve furlongs as he had won the Chester Vase on the colt in May. In the final analysis, however, it was the courage of The Minstrel allied to the sheer power of his rider in the finish that landed a fifth Epsom Derby for Vincent O'Brien and gave Lester his eighth (he would go on to make it nine in 1983 through Teenoso).

＊　　＊　　＊

I remember Piggott saying to me at lunch in his Newmarket home one day that the jockey who makes excuses in defeat in a Classic has probably only himself to blame as often as not. In the after-race press conferences at Epsom or the Curragh I never once heard Lester making an excuse when defeat was his lot. He would simply say that he had his mount in a position to deliver the final challenge and he would then shrug his shoulders and indicate that it wasn't good enough. Never saying that he got boxed in because if he got boxed in, the fault would be his, especially if you had one with the speed of a Sir Ivor or a Nijinsky.

There was never any question that these two would triumph at Epsom. Sir Ivor's acceleration was awesome as he cut down Connaught in the last 300 yards. From a position of being four lengths behind one moment, he was soon on level terms and on his way to a scintillating victory and Connaught's rider, Sandy Barclay, who was only 19 then, could only remark ruefully later: "It was just our fellow's misfortune to be foaled in the same year as Sir Ivor". Then he came up with the immortal quote: "Sir Ivor is the most brilliant horse I have seen – in all my nineteen years!."

Lester Piggott described Nijinsky as "an exceptional colt" from the time he won the Dewhurst Stakes on him at Newmarket in 1969. "Because he was a big horse, you noticed him more than the others. When he galloped beside other horses, he made them look like selling platers. Yes, I knew he was special from the very outset", was how Lester put it to me.

Nijinsky dwarfed his rivals in the parade ring at Newmarket before the 1970 English 2,000 Guineas and dwarfed them in the race itself which he won with the authority of a real champion. Some breeding purists thought he would have stamina limitations in getting the final two furlongs at Epsom as his sire, Northern Dancer had failed to stay the mile-and-a-half of the Belmont Stakes but Piggott himself was fully confident that Nijinsky would get the trip. He saw only one danger – the French colt Gyr – and decided that his tactics would be to concentrate on riding a race to beat the Gallic challenger. Etienne Pollet had actually put off retiring for a year in the hope that his impressive looking chestnut would give him a second Epsom Derby triumph to supplement that of the peerless Sea Bird II in 1965.

It turned out exactly as Piggott had believed it would. Gyr went into the lead two furlongs out but, once Lester showed Nijinsky the whip (he didn't have to use it this time as he had done on Roberto and The Minstrel), the colt produced an irresistible surge to go right away and beat Gyr by two-and-a-half lengths with Stinto a further three lengths away third (the form was franked when Gyr went on to an easy victory in the Grand Prix de St. Cloud).

✳   ✳   ✳

Lester Piggott won acclaim – and rightly so – for his Epsom Derby victories. But he came in for a lot of stick in the media when he lost on Alleged in the 1977 St. Leger to the Oaks winner, Dunfermline and again when he failed to win the 1977 Prix de l'Arc de Triomphe on Nijinsky.

Piggott did not flinch when I questioned him about that short-head defeat in the 'Arc' – the most controversial and widely-debated defeat of his entire career.

He was not in the least perturbed by the theories advanced in various books about the issue that (1) he had asked Nijinsky to do too much by forcing the colt to make his run from too far back; (2) he lost the race through over-confidence as he assumed that Nijinsky, with his great turn of pace, could pick up those in front of him immediately the button was pressed and (3) when he hit Nijinsky with the whip, the horse swerved left with fatal consequences.

Looking back without emotion to that first Sunday in October '70, Lester discounted all the theories that had made him seem to be the villain of the piece.

"Nijinsky got very worked up beforehand and the situation wasn't helped by the fact that the paddock at Longchamp was crowded with camera crews. One Japanese crew seemed to be only interested in Nijinsky and they even stuck a microphone under the horse's mouth – as if he would give them an exclusive interview! Gerry Gallagher, Vincent's Travelling Head Man tried his hardest to protect the colt but the camera crews were not going to be deterred. By the time I went to get up into the saddle, Nijinsky was sweating freely and in such an excited state that I was distinctly worried. He had already used up a lot of energy.

"Nijinsky didn't really go in the first part of the race, though I remember clearly what Vincent had said when we had a discussion on the phone in the count-down to the race. We had agreed that I should lie up, Vincent making the point that few horses left with a deal of ground to make up in the short straight at Longchamp went on to triumph in the Arc. And he feared also that in a race like this where the field really 'goes' all the way, beaten horses would be coming back on Nijinsky, creating the distinct possibility that he might be obstructed by a sudden wall in front of him when making his run.

"Now I found that I could not lay up as I had done in previous races. The pace was reasonable enough. There was nothing crazy about it. But I could feel Nijinsky struggling a bit under me in those early stages.

"I decided then not to rush him, to let him settle in order to see if he would come to himself and at the crucial stage of the race give me that 'feel' I had always got from him on his great days. When we turned into the straight he was further behind than I would have wished. I had the choice of going in for the rails or else I could eliminate any danger of getting boxed in by moving to the outside. With four horses blocking the path on the inside as I began my finishing run, I had no option but to switch to the outside, thus losing some ground.

"Now Nijinsky was moving at last and I reckoned we had a chance of winning, even though Yves St. Martin and Sassafras were still in front on the rails and we had a deal of ground to make up. I was certainly not as far off the leaders as was inferred by some commentators later. Nijinsky in his Epsom Derby form would have easily cut down any of those in front of him. As it was, we got a nose in front of Sassafras with about a hundred yards to go. I felt I was going to win, though Nijinsky didn't go away as he had done at Epsom.

"Just about thirty yards from the post, Nijinsky swerved to his left for no reason at all. It was not because I showed him the whip, as some have claimed. He had never done it before in all the races in which I had ridden him.

"I did not have time to change my whip to the other hand. He only had to keep a straight line to win it. That sudden swerve cost him the race – but only by the narrowest of margin."

"I know beyond any shadow of doubt that I would have won it but for Nijinsky reacting as he did with the post within sight and the race at his mercy. Everything else does not matter. The fact that I got in front of Sassafras one hundred yards from the post proves that Nijinsky had the beating of the French colt – even though patently not at his best that day", Piggott summed up.

Lester is convinced now in retrospect that the bout of ringworm weakened him greatly and affected his training schedule. Most important of all, it resulted in Nijinsky going for the St. Leger on a rather rushed preparation. That he reckoned was the root cause of the fatal swerve that ultimately lost him his unbeaten record and led in turn to the disastrous decision to go for the Champion Stakes to try and erase the Longchamp defeat.

As Phonsie O'Brien put it: "Charlie Engelhard knew he was dying and he wanted to see Nijinsky complete the Triple Crown by winning the Leger. Vincent wanted to miss out on the Doncaster Classic. His aim was to give the colt all the time he needed after the bout of ringworm before going for the primary objective, the Arc de Triomphe. But Engelhard wanted to have his way – and, as his time in this life was limited, Vincent gave him his way".

Nijinsky completed the Triple Crown by taking the Leger – the first horse to win the three colts' Classics since Bahram in 1935 – but Lester Piggott said unhesitatingly: "Frankly, I was disappointed with his running at Doncaster. Perhaps afterwards we may have thought he needed the race, but certainly I wasn't too happy with him. Looking back on it now, there seems little doubt that the ringworm had left its mark and that race, instead of bringing him on, saw him unable to go through with it at the critical point – through no fault of his own – in the Arc. "

Vincent O'Brien revealed that Nijinsky lost close on 30 pounds after the St. Leger (Nashwan, in contrast, lost only 4lbs for his exertions in adding the Coral-Eclipse Stakes to the English 2,000 Guineas and Epsom Derby triumphs in 1989. His trainer, Major Dick Hern reported that you would not be surprised if a horse lost up to 20 lbs after such a race. But certainly not 30 lbs).

In hindsight Nijinsky should never have run at Doncaster, even though the temptation to see him complete the Triple Crown was very great, especially for his owner.

✳   ✳   ✳

Such was the impact made by Alleged's eight-lengths' win in the Great Voltigeur at York in 1977 that it seemed unthinkable that he would be beaten in the St. Leger, for which he started 4-7. Lester Piggott took up the running entering the straight but Willie Carson on the Queen's Oaks winner, Dunfermline caught Alleged inside the final quarter mile and scored a sensational victory.

Piggott was criticised for taking it up far too early on Alleged and becoming, in effect, a sitting duck for Carson's late challenge. But Lester's response to his critics was that he employed exactly the same tactics as at York when Alleged produced such a burst of acceleration in the straight that he left his field for dead. He concluded that on St. Leger Day Dunfermline touched a peak of brilliance that meant she was not going to be denied – though she couldn't reproduce it on the day of the Prix de l'Arc when she had to be content with fourth place behind Alleged.

Lester Piggott had always this communion of minds with Vincent O'Brien that meant the two invariably discussed things on a basis of equality, man-to-man, before and after each race and no one valued Lester's opinion more than Vincent. Jacqueline O'Brien said: "Vincent could always hear what Lester said no matter how softly or indistinctly – because he wanted to hear it. "

Lester's daughter, Tracy, now a successful member of the RTE Television racing team, said: "To see the two together was always rather strange as they seemed to say nothing, and yet you could see that there was an almost enviable mental intimacy between these two fascinating individuals".

At the time Vincent retired from training at the end of the 1994 Flat season, Tracy summed up his partnership with her father thus: "There was one common denominator – an invisible, but obvious link, that I have never been able to put my finger on, between Vincent and Lester. Maybe it was just one of those unfathomable mysteries of brilliance and genius. We have come to the end of an era. But history will never let it be forgotten".

Piggott himself said to me: "Once Vincent was satisfied that I knew a horse, especially after I had ridden it, he would not bother me with instructions. Yes, we would, of course, discuss things in a general way. When he had a jockey riding for him all the time and had built up a special relationship with that rider, it wasn't his way to give too many orders. And that was the way I liked it".

Piggott heading for Ballydoyle early on in each new Flat season to ride the three-year-olds considered to be out of the top drawer and the two-year-olds geared for big things was always a very significant moment as his assessment was viewed as crucial by Vincent. Indeed, there was no finer illustration of his judgement than when he came over to ride Manitoulin, who looked like being Vincent's second string in the Epsom Derby in the year of Roberto (originally to have been ridden by Bill Williamson). Piggott concluded after riding Manitoulin in a gallop that he wasn't a patch on Roberto. It's history now how Williamson was jocked off Roberto by his owner, the American millionaire, John Galbreath and Lester got the ride at Epsom.

Ironically, though, tensions arose from time to time between Vincent and Lester on the gallops at Ballydoyle.

Some who were close to Vincent at Ballydoyle have said to me that Lester operated to his own "agenda" at times. Piggott has gone on record to admit that it led to "strain" that the Master of Ballydoyle felt that when he rode work he endeavoured to find out how good the horse was rather than adhering to instructions.

Lester in a gallop could drop eight lengths behind and then press the button to assess what speed the horse under him had and this could upset Vincent who might deem it far too early to be putting a potential Classic or Group winner under that kind of test. In that situation Lester would have been expected to jump off with the others and go a nice steady gallop and not take matters into his own hands.

Pat Eddery was far easier to control and the same tensions never arose between him and Vincent.

*   *   *

Vincent O'Brien made the point in the *Irish Independent* interview with Tom McGuirk in 1988 that Lester was already established before he rode for him – "but when I saw him I was determined to have him".

Asked if there was one quality in Piggott that he would put above all others, he replied: "Lester had an extraordinary will to win... often it was simply his determination that found the extra yards when it mattered. It was something I had too, and it made us very similar and it cemented our friendship."

It was Vincent who induced Lester to come out of retirement in 1990. Tuesday, October 23rd of that year saw Piggott ride four horses for Vincent at the Curragh and win on all four of them – Legal Profession, Fairy Folk, Classic Minstrel and Passer-By.

When Lester produced that brilliant late surge in the Breeders' Cup Mile to go by the grey Itsallgreektomest and Corey Nakatani a few yards from the line, the judgement Vincent had shown a quarter of a century earlier when he put his faith in Piggott to win the English Oaks on Valoris was fully vindicated.

Yes, the ultimate crowning moment of glory for the ultimate trainer-jockey partnership.

Vincent O'Brien was winning the National Stakes for the 14th time when Lester Piggott scored for him on El Prado in 1991 from Nordic Brief (No. 3) and Mekong. (Picture: Ed Byrne)

7

When Nijinsky Might Have Died

On the eve of the 1970 Epsom Derby the shadow fell over the O'Brien camp momentarily that the great Nijinsky might fall victim to a fatal bout of colic. It is an extraordinary story how the colt recovered quickly enough to take his place in the line-up for the Classic and justify in brilliant style the confidence reposed in him.

Nothing, I feel, in his career as a trainer illustrated better Vincent O'Brien's total command in a crisis than the manner in which he personally oversaw everything in relation to Nijinsky from the moment he was whisked out of Ballydoyle for Sandown racecourse to ensure firstly that he would not be hit by the cough that had afflicted a number of horses in the stable.

Vincent was fortunate that he had at the time in assistant trainer Michael Kauntze a man he trusted completely. If Vincent in those critical days was the Commander-in-Chief then Kauntze could have been likened to his front-line General. The two worked in total unison. In this team-work at the highest level you saw again that facet of Vincent's character and make-up that enabled him to delegate. And because he was able to delegate, he could take the overall view and not be encumbered with small details that could have clouded his judgement, for it was essential that he should plot every move and see to it that things were executed exactly as he wanted them to be executed.

Michael Kauntze remembers as if it was only yesterday the moment, about a week before the Derby, when Vincent O'Brien gave him the order to get Nijinsky out of Ballydoyle after one or two horses had started to cough. "When do you want us to leave?", asked Kauntze of the Master of Ballydoyle. "Now", came the firm response.

"So a horse-box was got ready and we left at about two o'clock in the morning for Shannon Airport and Nijinsky was flown from there to England and duly taken on to Sandown racecourse", said Kauntze. "The whole operation was clouded in the strictest secrecy. Nobody outside the stable knew that the colt had left Ballydoyle. When members of the media rang up and asked about Nijinsky's well-being, the girls answering the phone had instructions to give nothing away."

Meanwhile, Johnny Brabston, Nijinsky's regular work-rider, was putting the colt through his paces at Sandown. "We were up around 5.30 or 6 o'clock", recalled Michael Kauntze. "We had the racecourse to ourselves. Vincent had arranged matters with the management that they would co-operate fully in maintaining the strictest cloak of secrecy. And they did.

"Each day I would report to Vincent how Nijinsky had gone at work. I would report everything down to the minutest detail. That was the way he wanted it.

"Then we learned that there were sales at Sandown on the Monday of Epsom Derby week. I asked when the first people would begin to arrive. I was told as early as 7 a.m. I immediately informed Vincent and it was agreed that we would have Nijinsky out of Sandown and stabled at Epsom well before anyone reached the Esher course for the sales.

"We were up at 4 a.m. and Nijinsky had his final spin on the Sandown track before heading for Epsom at 6 o'clock. So smoothly did everything go that if anyone had seen him that morning at Epsom they would have concluded that he had come directly from Ballydoyle. "

✳   ✳   ✳

Nijinsky had what Vincent O'Brien described to me as "a problem with his insides – he got colic very easily".

That, in fact, was the reason why "it was necessary to really keep him going all the time" and why he had five races as a two-year-old, winning all of them, including the Railway, Anglesey, Beresford and Dewhurst Stakes.

Now 24 hours before the Epsom Derby was due to be run the colic problem reared its head again.

Michael Kauntze recalled: "Johnny Brabston had worked Nijinsky on the course, bringing him down the hill and around Tattenham Corner. He seemed perfectly okay then. However, later in the day at evening stables we noticed he was in some discomfort and was tending to sweat.

"We informed Vincent right away. He in turn rang his vet, Bob Griffin and reported the symptoms to him, expressing his own view from long experience that it seemed to him that the colt had a slight touch of colic.

"Both Bob and Vincent agreed that there was no way he could be injected so close to the race. If the worse came to the worse, he would have to be withdrawn and the dream of completing the Two Thousand Guineas – Derby double would have gone by the board."

Meanwhile, by now Vincent had arrived in England from Ballydoyle and, as was his custom in the count-down to every Epsom Derby, he stayed in the RAC Country Club about a mile from the course but it still gave him the privacy he always preferred. You might say that the Commander-in-Chief was now in his forward post. (In fact, an illustration of how much he was in command is revealed by the fact that when Nijinsky was stabled at Sandown, Vincent arrived at 3.30 a.m. one morning telling Michael Kauntze he could not sleep as he wanted to be certain that the security operation around the colt was spot-on.)

The Epsom vet was contacted. "We knew that his on-the-spot examination would be vital", said Michael Kauntze.

Riboprince had accompanied Nijinsky to England, the plan being that this colt, who had been second to Approval in the Dante Stakes, would go on to France and contest the French Derby the following Sunday (Riboprince, rated 117 by the Timeform experts compared with 138 for Nijinsky, would finish 6th at Chantilly, beaten nine lengths behind Yves St. Martin's mount, Sassafras, who subsequently, of course, would win the 'Arc' that same season).

If Nijinksy had been withdrawn, Riboprince would have by-passed the French Derby and become instead the Ballydoyle replacement in the Epsom Classic.

"The Epsom vet was convinced to begin with that it was Riboprince he was being asked to examine", said Michael Kauntze. "Then I put him on his honour and informed him that the problem was with Nijinsky. I can still see the look of shock, indeed horror, on his face.

"The agony of waiting while the vet was carrying out his examination was overwhelming. The thought raced through my mind that if it was a fatal bout of colic, what then? I could only pray and hope for the best.

"Happily, the vet told me that it was just 'a minor colic' and then he advised that Nijinksy must be made eat and eat as much as possible. And his favourite food – if that would encourage him to eat up.

"We knew he was partial to carrots and we coated these in oats. Amazingly, he took to the 'dish' immediately. We fed him carrot by carrot through the night for six hours. Once he began to eat, we had a great feeling of relief and somehow felt that the worst was over.

"The Epsom vet rang up during the night to ask us how things were going. He came back early in the morning and, after a quick examination, reported that 'he looks fine to me now'.

"Vincent, who was in attendance to talk to the vet on his return, was able to breathe easily again. In fact, every one of us who had been close to Nijinsky during the crisis breathed a great sigh of relief. It would have hit us terribly if the colic had forced his withdrawal, especially when we regarded him as a certainty to win, granted he got normal luck in running. If Vincent O'Brien had issued a statement to the media immediately Nijinsky contracted the twinge of colic and it had hit the evening papers, it would have thrown the ante-post market into total confusion. The big bookmakers had very heavy liabilities. Betting would have been suspended automatically. In the circumstances Vincent would have been on a hiding to nothing. Supposing then, on the attack of colic being overcome, he had been forced to retract his earlier statement, it might well have been construed in a totally wrong manner, especially if Nijinsky won – as he did. In hindsight, it can be seen that Vincent was very wise not to rush his fences but to hold fire until he was absolutely certain as to whether or not Nijinsky could take his place in the field."

On the morning of the Derby Nijinsky had a light canter. Vincent O'Brien was always of the belief that a canter like that was good for a horse. It put it in the right frame of mind for the task ahead and often it would think that its task for the day was done and it would help in settling a horse.

After the Guineas, for which he started 4-7 (the shortest odds-on favourite since Colombo in 1934) and beat Yellow God going away by two-and-a-half lengths, Lester Piggott told Vincent O'Brien that he could have taken the opposition at any time he chose. Piggott, in fact, was of the opinion that Nijinsky had the acceleration to win the King's Stand Stakes.

Michael Kauntze was convinced that Nijinsky was an exceptionally fast colt who stayed well enough to win at twelve furlongs. In a word, he could get a trip and at the same time produce a brilliant turn of foot at the moment that mattered.

The stiff Curragh twelve furlongs presented no problem to Nijinsky as he took the Irish Derby in scintillating style in the hands of Liam Ward by three lengths and then gave what Kauntze considered the greatest performance of his career in winning the King George from an outstanding field that included Blakeney, the 1969 Epsom Derby winner, Hogarth, the Italian Derby winner of '68, Karabas, winner of the 1969 Washington International, Crepellana, the 1969 French Oaks and Caliban, the Coronation Cup winner.

Lester Piggott was actually easing him at the finish and he would go on record later to state "the colt was never better than he was that day".

It represented, in Michael Kauntze's view, one of Vincent O'Brien's greatest achievements in a career glistening with glorious achievements to produce Nijinsky in the kind of form that saw him demolish the opposition in the King George.

"Vincent knew now, as we all knew at Ballydoyle, that the Prix de l'Arc de Triomphe was well within Nijinsky's scope – that what he had done against older horses at Ascot, he could also do with the same authority at Longchamp. We never thought he would be beaten after Ascot where his performance was comparable with Sea Bird's 'Arc' triumph. We all believed that he would go straight to the 'Arc' and that victory in that race would represent the crowning seal before he went to stud".

No one at Ballydoyle could have foreseen the evolving events that would result in Nijinsky bidding for the St. Leger on a rushed preparation and as a result subsequently losing his unbeaten record in the 'Arc' and then going out on an embarrassing note in the Champion Stakes.

*   *   *

Looking back on the bout of ringworm that Nijinsky contracted after the King George, Michael Kauntze said that it was the worst case he saw in a lifetime with horses. "He lost all his hair not just down the sides but around his whole belly area. If you put a girth on him there was blood everywhere. We could not put a night rug on him either because it would make him so

THE DADDY OF THEM ALL . . . Lester Piggott on his comeback at 54 years of age shows all his old power as he drives Dr Tony O'Reilly's Passer-By to victory to complete his four-timer at the Curragh on 23 October 1990. (Picture: Irish Independent.)

Silhoutted against the sun, Lester Piggott returns to the winner's enclosure after riding Defendant to victory in the Kerry EBF Maiden at Killarney on Monday evening, July 15, 1991 and (below) a smiling Lester in the winner's enclosure with his good friend, Finbarr Slattery after victory of Defendant. (Pictures: Caroline Norris.)

Lester Piggott in happy mood after winning the Irish 2,000 Guineas on Rodrigo de Triano in May, 1992 and (below) Piggott and Vincent O'Brien, the ultimate professionals, in the weighroom at the Curragh on Saturday, May 25, 1991, after Lester had ridden Sportsworld to victory in the Conrad Silver Race for three-year-olds. (Pictures: Caroline Norris.)

Lester Piggott captured in this fine shot by Jacqueline O'Brien on the gallops at Ballydoyle in the mid-Seventies.

BARN TALK . . . Lester and Vincent look ahead to the challenge the Classics will bring, especially the Epsom Derby in the era when challengers from Ballydoyle played such a dominant role. (Picture: Jacqueline O'Brien.)

Nijinsky (Lester Piggott) being led in by his owner Charles Englehard after winning the 1970 Epsom Derby and (below) Nijinsky (wearing noseband) on outside sweeping around Tattenham Corner with Gyr (Bill Williamson) immediately behind on the way to victory.

Alleged, with Piggott in the saddle suffers the only defeat of his career when failing to Dunfermline (Willie Carson) in the 1977 English St. Leger and (bottom) Law Society (Pat Eddery) wins the Chester Vase on his way to victory in the 1985 Irish Derby.

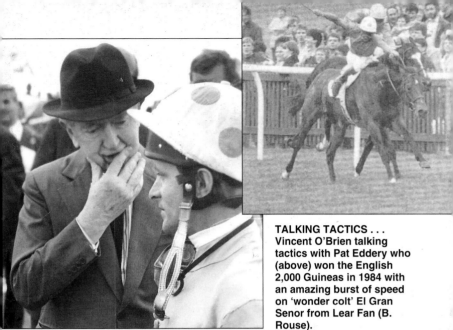

TALKING TACTICS . . . Vincent O'Brien talking tactics with Pat Eddery who (above) won the English 2,000 Guineas in 1984 with an amazing burst of speed on 'wonder colt' El Gran Senor from Lear Fan (B. Rouse).

Right: Ed Byrne captures the pulsating drama of the 1984 Epsom Derby as Secreto (Christy Roche) on left wins by a short head in a photo finish from El Gran Senor (Pat Eddery).

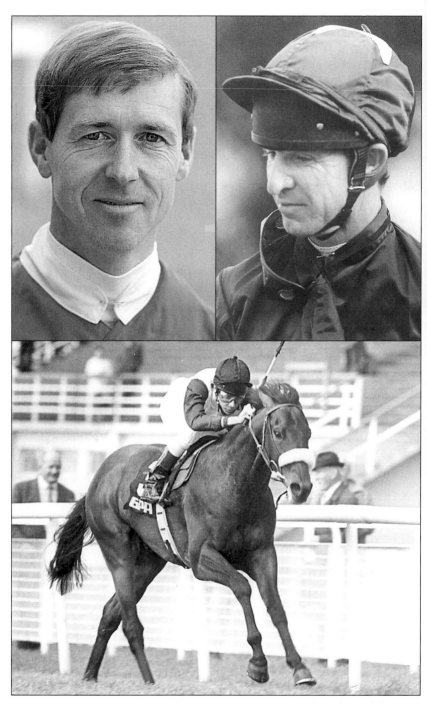

Down-born John Reid (top left) and Christy Roche who were both attached in their time to Ballydoyle and (below) the American Cash Asmussen, who succeeded Pat Eddery as No. 1 stable jockey, winning the National Stakes on Caerwent in 1987.

itchy. He was terribly irritable. He simply could not be ridden while he was in that state. "

Now it was the great wish of Charles Engelhard to be remembered not alone as "the man who owned Nijinsky" but to be immortalised as "the man who owned the first Triple Crown winner since Bahram" (Bahram had won the three colts' Classics in 1935).

Vincent O'Brien was proud to number Charles Engelhard among his owners and Phonsie, who doesn't suffer shams easily – even if they have millions in the bank and a private jet – could talk with affection about "my friend Charlie" as he recalled the fabulous Nijinsky days. Michael Kauntze said of him that he was one of the finest gentlemen he met during his days at Ballydoyle and he recalled Engelhard sitting in his special chair reeling off with a knowledge that was profound details of horses in his ownership or that had impressed him in particular races.

He was a classic member of the American Establishment, having graduated from Princeton University and seen service as a bomber pilot with the rank of Captain in the Second World War. His immense wealth was made out of minerals. He represented the American President at the Independence Day ceremonies in Gabon in 1962 and again at the Coronation of Pope Paul VI in 1963 after the death of Pope John XXIII.

The right clubs, the right restaurants, the right hotels were his natural milieu, and yet he had that easy zest for life, that *joie de vivre* that made him love the funny side of things. On the day that Nijinsky won the Irish Sweeps Derby at the Curragh, Charlie Engelhard's wide frame almost filled one end of the VIP presentation stand. The rains came down as Anna McGrath, wife of Paddy McGrath, was presenting him with the winning owner's trophy in the form of a chalice and Engelhard came up with the classic throwaway remark: "If this goes on much longer, the water in this chalice will turn into wine!".

His racing interests stretched from the United States to Ireland and Britain and South Africa. Apart from Nijinsky, his familiar colours of green, yellow sleeves and scarlet cap were carried with distinction over a decade – the Seventies – by Classic winners like Indiana, winner of the 1964 English St. Leger; Ribocco, winner of the 1967 Irish Derby and English St. Leger and other good horses of the calibre of Ribofilio, Romulus and Habitat.

Charles Engelhard was only 54 when he died in 1971 – the year after Nijinsky had left an indelible imprint on racing history. He had battled unsuccessfully with a weight problem (because of injuries he had suffered to his legs in a crash-landing while in the U.S. Airforce, he was unable to take exercise and was constantly in pain). Indeed, the legacy of those war-time injuries was that he had to accept that the normality of his life physically would be affected for the rest of his life.

It would have been difficult to say "No" when to all intents and purposes he made it his last request as an owner that Nijinsky be aimed at completing the Triple Crown. In any other circumstance Vincent O'Brien would have dug in his heels and even more so in this instance when he realised how much the ringworm had affected the colt. But Engelhard was granted his final wish.

In the St. Leger Nijinsky had a length to spare over Meadowville at the finish and some commentators concluded that he had scored with something in hand but Lester Piggott confided to Michael Kauntze afterwards: "I could not have won by another inch.

It can be argued that Nijinsky would have needed a race before the 'Arc' in an era when staged racecourse gallops after racing were not the norm. However, if Vincent had decided that this was necessary, there is no doubt whatsoever that he would have given the colt a much easier task than he had at Doncaster. It would simply have been a pipeopener for Longchamp.

❋　　❋　　❋

Michael Kauntze is adamant that four factors contributed to Nijinsky's defeat at Longchamp. "Any three of them would have greatly affected his performance on the day but when you combined the four together and took into account also the mark the Doncaster Classic had left on him, you realised what a task he was facing and what a true champion he was to fail in the end by only a head", he stressed.

Firstly, being a very highly-strung colt, he got upset in the paddock at all the attention focused on him. It had to be remembered that the Longchamp paddock is like an amphitheatre with the crowds thronging the tiered viewing area seemingly pressing in on the horses. "There was plenty of noise that day", Michael Kauntze recalled, "and apart from the special attention he received from the Japanese television crew, Nijinsky was never going to be left alone for a moment. It got to him in the end. He got very worked up and was a lather of sweat".

The second major factor, according to Kauntze, was the draw. Nijinksy was drawn on the outside. "We were all dismayed when we heard the draw as we knew that those drawn on the inside are always the best favoured runners in the Arc. ".

The third vital factor was the manner in which Nijinsky got stopped when making his run. "At Longchamp you have this little straight before the turning into the main straight. It was then that Lester went to make his run but got checked by four horses in front of him and he lost momentum at the crucial stage. He had no option but to pull to the outside, losing ground in the process. By the time he got him going again, Yves St. Martin on Sassafras was heading for home on the rails".

The fourth factor and the deciding one was the swerve. "I was down at the start that day and got into the starter's car as the field left the stalls", Kauntze recalled. "I had a perfect head-on view as Sassafras and Nijinsky battled it out in the final stages. I can still see Sassafras on the rails and Nijinsky coming up the middle of the course to challenge him. The next thing I saw was Nijinsky swerving – a sudden violent swerve, as I recall it – and that was when Lester picked up his stick in his right hand and showed it to him, though I know Lester was emphatic afterwards that this did not cause the swerve as some claimed. At that moment his unbeaten record was gone, as it enabled Yves St. Martin to get Sassafras's nose in front on the line".

In thirteen races over two seasons, Nijinsky was never out of the frame. The final record would read: won – eleven; second – two.

He had been named, of course, after the Russian ballet dancer, Vaslav Nijinsky, who won a supreme place among male dancers when brought by Diaghilev to Paris and London before the First World War, especially for his spell-binding performances in *Les Sylphides, Spectre de las Rose* and *L'Apres-midi d'un* Faune.

Nijinsky – that is the colt – had given spell-binding performances also in winning the English 2,000 Guineas, the Epsom Derby and most of all in the King George.

Charles Engelard became known on both sides of the Atlantic through a champion of champions carrying his colours, and the videos that Nijinsky created outlive the mundane question, which might interest some, of how much Charlie left when he passed on and his widow, June dispersed the once-proud racing empire. He was known as the "Platinum King" but he said that when he died he would be remembered "as the guy who owned Nijinsky."

No finer milestone than that.

Tommy Murphy, Assistant Trainer today to Aidan O'Brian, the new Master of Ballydoyle, winning the 1977 Irish 1,000 Guineas on Lady Capulet for Vincent O'Brien from Bold Fantasy (C. Roche) and Lady Mere (L. Piggott).

8

The Halcyon Days

Brian Molony, who was assistant trainer to Vincent O'Brien for almost a decade in the Eighties, remembers most of all the halcyon days of 1982-'83 and '84 – the seasons that produced Golden Fleece, Sadler's Wells, Lomond, Caerleon, Solford and El Gran Senor and a dominance of the major two-year-old events on the domestic front that was awesome.

There were no more than 38 to 40 horses at Ballydoyle in those golden seasons, he noted. "Yet for sheer class and the emergence of colts that left a lasting imprint in the annals of racing and breeding it was an exceptional time. I will always feel privileged that I was part of the team working hand-in-hand with Vincent as the Group winners flowed from what you might describe as the Ballydoyle conveyor belt."

Brian Molony, who today is Manager of the Blackhall Stud, part of the Kildangan complex, said that one of Vincent O'Brien's finest training feats was the manner in which he prepared Golden Fleece for the one primary target – the Epsom Derby of 1982 – and delivered him to triumph in such amazing fashion and in such an exceptional time that he had to be be rated one of the best Derby winners of modern times. One must never forget either how he won it. "Pat Eddery had been wrongly criticised for El Gran Senor's defeat in the 1984 Derby when the colt didn't get the distance. But by all the accepted theories on where a horse should be placed coming round Tattenham Corner, Golden Fleece should have been out of the reckoning on Derby Day '82 as he was three from last at that point and on the wide outside. Yet such was the acceleration he produced in the final furlong that he won unchallenged in the end."

Golden Fleece had been bought at the Keeneland Sales in July, 1980 for $775,000, making him one of the ten most expensive purchases in the world of that same year. On breeding alone he was a potential champion in the making. For not alone was he a son of Nijinsky but he was out of the American mare Exotic Treat, who traced back to Rare Perfume and the legendary Jaipur and her own daughter, What A Treat was the champion filly in the United States in 1965 and, most important of all, had proved herself well capable of getting twelve furlongs in the highest class.

But Brian Molony pointed out that while Golden Fleece was an imposing and rangy racehorse – an advertisement, in fact, for his sire – he was not the toughest or soundest of colts. "In addition he showed an aversion to going into stalls. I remember how we would walk him again and again into the stalls each afternoon to try and get him accustomed to them."

Vincent O'Brien knew from an early point in Golden Fleece's two-year-old career, according to Molony, that "this was one horse he was going to train for one day and everything else would be secondary to that aim".

Big and backward, he was given all the time he needed. It was mid-September '81 before he had his first race in public – the Oldbawn Maiden over a mile at Leopardstown. Second approaching the straight, he led two furlongs out and Pat Eddery eased him before the finish as he won by two-and-a-half lengths from Assert, who came out three weeks later and won the Beresford Stakes by four lengths.

"We all realised after the Leopardstown success and from what he was revealing in work on the gallops that Golden Fleece was something special in the making. Vincent was too long around horses, however, to suddenly go over the top in enthusiasm. But I knew that his intuition was telling him that, all going well, this one promised to be his greatest Derby winner since Nijinsky."

Golden Fleece opened his three-year-old career by easily winning the Sean Graham Ballymoss Stakes at the Curragh and then added the Nijinsky Stakes at Leopardstown.

So taking in the Epsom Derby of '82, he ran only four times – and was never once extended in winning.

Brian Molony argued that the colt's performance in victory on Derby Day '82 had to be viewed as all the more incredible when one reflected on the fact that "we discovered that he had a dirty nose after the race".

In a spin on the course the morning before the Derby, he had coughed a few times. Indeed, there was a distinct possibility that he might not run. He didn't cough again that day, even though Vincent, with his attention to detail, had posted a man specially outside the colt's box to listen for the tell-tale sound.

Golden Fleece duly lined up for the Classic and Robert Sangster, in whose colours he ran, believes that "only 70 per cent of his best" was seen that day at Epsom. If that was the case, then the question naturally follows: How great in actual fact was this colt?.

✳   ✳   ✳

Brian Molony views the winning of the 1983 Prix Du Jockey Club (French Derby) with Caerleon, subsequently to become an outstanding success at stud, as yet another of Vincent O'Brien's finer achievements as a trainer.

Caerleon, unlike the strapping Golden Fleece, was a compact son of Nijinsky, bought at the Keeneland Sales in '81 for $800,000. He won his two races as a two-year-old, the Tyros Stakes at the Curragh in June and the Anglesey Stakes over the same course in August '82. But Brian Molony noted that he always had dodgy feet and this meant that Vincent had to exercise infinite patience in bringing him along.

Starting at 4-7, he was unplaced in the Ballymoss Stakes in his first outing as a three-year-old and was then second to stable-companion Solford at the Phoenix Park at the end of May in a ten furlongs race, losing by three-parts-of-a-length, though it was noted that he was running on well at the finish.

Solford, also by Nijinsky, had been unbeaten in his two runs as a two-year-old and at that point looked to some pundits to have the brighter future.

However, as with Golden Fleece on Derby Day '82, Vincent O'Brien had Caerleon tuned to perfection for Chantilly on Sunday, June 5th, '83. Carrying the colours of Robert Sangster, he was strongly opposed in the market. The French would not hear of Cash Asmussen's mount L'Emigrant being beaten by the challenger from Ballydoyle. But Caerleon, getting a brilliant ride from Pat Eddery, won easily by three lengths with Lester Piggott third on Esprit Du Nord.

Incidentally, Solford would win the Prix du Lys (Group 3) at Chantilly on the following Sunday. Yes, a time of rich pickings for Ballydoyle.

Caerleon caught a tarter when beaten by three lengths by the Michael Stoute-trained, Shareef Dancer (wearing the colours of Sheikh Maktoum al-Maktoum) in the Irish Sweeps Derby. But from the point of his future stud career it was very significant that two lengths behind him in third place was the Epsom Derby winner, Teenoso.

He was going well in the King George VI and Queen Elizabeth Stakes, for which he started 9-4 favourite, when he lost both front shoes and was virtually tailed off.

Vincent O'Brien was always convinced that he was better over ten furlongs than twelve, so now he sent him for the Benson and Hedges Gold Cup at York. An inspired decision, as it evolved.

His judgement was once again fully vindicated when Caerleon, again under a brilliantly-judged ride by Pat Eddery and showing great courage in a heart-stopping battle over the last two furlongs, held the powerful challenge of Hot Touch (Steve Cauthen) by a neck.

The Benson and Hedges Gold Cup success capped a memorable few weeks for Ballydoyle as Solford had taken the Eclipse Stakes at Sandown and the season would close on a very satisfactory note for the three-year-olds when Salmon Leap (a son of Northern Dancer), who had earlier that year won the Derrinstown Stud Derby Trial Stakes and the Pacemaker International Whitehall Stakes, finished fifth in the Prix de l'Arc de Triomphe.

Salmon Leap (Pat Eddery) had started at 11-2 in the Epsom Derby but, after being hampered two furlongs out, he had to be content with fourth place. Vincent engaged the American ace, Willie Shoemaker for English

2,000 Guineas and Irish 2,000 Guineas runner-up, Lomond, who was never a factor, finishing sixteenth.

Lomond, having won the Gladness Stakes on his reappearance as a three-year-old, caused a 9-1 upset at Newmarket. He was so wonderfully bred – being by Northern Dancer out of Seattle Slew's dam, My Charmer – that he needed to win only the one Classic, the English 2,000 Guineas, to justify standing him at stud at Coolmore. Incidentally, he ran only once after the Epsom Derby, starting favourite for the Sussex Stakes at Goodwood, in which he finished seventh.

✳ ✳ ✳

In a season that brought so many memorable victories across the board and which saw El Gran Senor win the Dewhurst Stakes – Vincent's seventh success in this most prestigious of juvenile events – it might seem very surprising on the face of it that 1983 was barren as far as Royal Ascot was concerned.

But Brian Molony explained to me that Vincent invariably resisted running at Royal Ascot his best juveniles – the ones he already had in mind for Classic campaigns as three-year-olds. "You could count on the fingers of one hand the top-notch two-year-olds he ran at the 'Royal' meeting in the Eighties."

And yet, according to Brian Molony, there was an anomaly in this as Vincent liked to be represented in the two-year-olds races at Royal Ascot – in a way he felt that he should – and, therefore, ran a few juveniles there that couldn't be mentioned in the same class as Golden Fleece, Salmon Leap or Solford. For example, Magic Mirror, which won the Norfolk Stakes at the 1984 Royal Ascot meeting, had scored in a Listed event at the Phoenix Park on its second outing. He was never destined for greatness as an older horse. "Again it was a tribute to Vincent's uncanny ability to get the very best out of the horses in his charge that he could win a race like the Norfolk Stakes with one that couldn't live with El Gran Senor".

Brian Molony argued that Vincent would under no circumstance sacrifice a horse's three-year-old career for the sake of success on the juvenile plane – if that meant going against the carefully devised programme he had planned. "You have got to see it also against the background that he was in the business of the making of stallions. Everything was geared to this in the case of horses of the calibre of Golden Fleece, Sadler's Wells, Lomond, Caerleon and El Gran Senor. The stakes he was playing for were very high and you might say that every time he went all in, he was going after a very big pot".

✳ ✳ ✳

Sadler's Wells never ran at Royal Ascot. Indeed, as in the case of Golden Fleece, Vincent O'Brien showed the Master's touch in the way he held him back and did not produce the son of Northern Dancer (out of Fairy Bridge) until September 17th, 1983 at Leopardstown. Starting at 1-2 the colt won the General Assembly Maiden over seven furlongs by six lengths in the hands of Pat Eddery. He followed this up by taking the mile Beresford Stakes by the same margin at the Curragh.

Imagine having El Gran Senor and Sadler's Wells in your stable as three-year-olds in the same season.

It was no disgrace for Sadler's Wells to be beaten by two lengths by El Gran Senor as both colts made their reappearance at the Curragh in the Gladness Stakes on April 14, 1984. After El Gran Senor had won the English 2,000 Guineas in the style of the 'wonder colt' he had been dubbed, Sadler's Wells took the Irish 2,000 Guineas by a neck from the highly-regarded French colt, Procida with Secreto one-and-a-half lengths further away third.

Sadler's Wells would go on to fail by just one-and-a-half lengths to Darshaan in the Prix Du Jockey Club (French Derby) with Rainbow Quest third, then won the Eclipse Stakes by a neck from Time Charter and was runner-up to Teenoso in the King George with 6-4 favourite, Time Charter fourth. He was fourth in the Benson and Hedges Gold Cup.

Brian Molony recalled that Vincent O'Brien remarked to him after the York race that it was in all probability Sadler's Wells last run.

"I mentioned to him that someone – maybe it was Pat Eddery or one of the work riders – had said to me that Sadler's Wells appeared to go better right-handed than left. Vincent fell silent for a moment. I could see that he was thinking. I realised later that my remark had sunk in when he decided to run Sadler's Wells in the Phoenix Champion Stakes.

"It was run over the right-handed track at the Park and Sadler's Wells, showing that he liked the switch from going left-handed, resisted the challenge of Seattle Song to win by three-quarters-of-a-length."

The final race of his career was the Prix de l'Arc de Triomphe in which he finished eighth behind Sagace, Northern Truck and All Along.

Praised by Robert Sangster as the best of Northern Dancer's sons, he had run nine times in all as a three-year-old, winning four times and being runner-up three times. No tougher or more courageous horse had come under Vincent's charge and it was not surprising really that he should be valued at £20 million when put to stud to stand at Coolmore.

His fee then was £125,000 and close on fifteen years on, such was the level of his achievement as the world's leading sire of Stakes winners (19 in 1996 alone) that it still stood at £100,000. He had been champion sire in Great Britain and Ireland for five consecutive years, a 20th century record.

The victory of his son, Yalaietanee in the 1997 Greenham Stakes marked (according to Tony Morris in the *Racing Post* of April 22, 1997) two notable landmarks in the perennial champion sire's amazing career – his 50th individual Pattern winner and his 100th Pattern success.

"Sadler's Wells now stands level with his sire, Northern Dancer, on the score of Pattern wins and eighth behind all-time leader Habitat", continued Tony Morris. "And he has now equalled Habitat's record for individual

Pattern winners, having forged clear of Mill Reef and Riverman last year (1996) in terms of Group 1 victories."

It was only a matter of time, concluded Morris, before Sadler's Wells became a clear leader in all departments. "That time may well come in 1997."

Even though he had not – up to 1997 – sired an Epsom Derby winner, nor yet an English Classic-winning colt, nor a Graded winner on dirt in the United States, he had proved himself, wrote Tony Morris, "the European sire par excellence".

Sadler's Wells got eight individual Pattern winners from his first crop of 55, and a remarkable 12 Pattern or Graded winners from 59 foals in his fifth crop.

Tony Morris summed up: "The plain fact is, you cannot help but admire Sadler's Wells. He earned his chances, first through an exemplary racing career, then through the instant success achieved by his early runners".

Andrew Caulfield in his Breeding Column in *The Sporting Life* of Tuesday, January 21, 1997 assessed how European-based sires fared in the 1996 International Classifications and under the heading "Sadler's Wells Still Well Clear", noted that the pride of Coolmore had for the second year in succession set new record figures, with his astounding total of 30 qualifiers being one better than the previous year. Of course, his total had to be set against the "ammunition" he had at his disposal in that breeders still clamoured to send him mares, despite the size of his fee (Rainbow Quest, for example, had only half of Sadler's Wells ammunition). "But even allowing for the fact that his crops for 1992, '93 and '94 averaged over 100 foals per crop, his 30 qualifiers still represented an exceptional achievement", wrote Caulfield, who added: "Caerleon had another good year with 15 qualifiers" (incidentally, the qualifiers had to be Group-class performers).

Caerleon, in fact, produced five Group 1 winners in 1996, including Lady Carla, winner of the Epsom Oaks and Fusaichi Concorde, winner of the Japanese Derby.

If Vincent O'Brien had trained no other top-class colts in the Eighties but Sadler's Wells and Caerleon, the stallion careers of this duo alone would have given him a lasting place in the world of breeding.

But for a trainer who was a maker of stallions, two did not suffice. He also provided the Coolmore complex with Lomond, El Gran Senor and Golden Fleece in those halcyon days of the early Eighties.

✳   ✳   ✳

Brian Molony said that no one ever dictated to Vincent when it came to laying out the programme for each horse in his charge.

"He might use his charm in getting millionaires to send him horses to train or provide the money for the buying of yearlings at Keeneland and other yearling sales. But no owner, irrespective of the millions he had in the bank, would ever lay down the law to Vincent on when or where a horse carrying his colours should run, though Vincent, of course, would be fully conscious of the wishes of individual owners and would endeavour to meet them – if it did not affect the future of a colt or filly, especially one in the Classic mould.

"I remember well when American millionaire Bob Fluor, part-owner of Alleged, indicated to Vincent that he was coming over from California in a private jet with a party, including members of his family and another partner in the horse, millionairess Shirley Taylor to see the colt bidding for the Irish Derby. He was looking forward to seeing him carrying his colours to victory.

"There were no ifs and buts about it. This man was used to getting his way. An American trainer in the same position as Vincent would probably have caved in to his demands. But Vincent was convinced that Alleged would not act in the firm ground that appeared almost certain to prevail on Irish Derby Day '77. Alleged was withdrawn and the end result was that he won the Prix de l'Arc de Triomphe later that season and made it two back-to-back the following year."

Vincent O'Brien was essentially a loner, according to Brian Molony, who came to know him better than most over a period of ten years. It was the loner in him that was happy fishing along his favourite stretch of the Blackwater River. It was the loner in him that spurned the social round. He was never a great mixer in the way that his brother, Phonsie mixed readily in gracing the racing and golfing circles.

"In all the time I was assistant trainer to him, I don't recall ever having a social conversation as such with him", said Brian. "It just wasn't Vincent's way – after purely business matters had been dealt with – to sit back and chat informally, to let the veil down so to speak.

"He lived horses and lived for them. He lived breeding matters and lived pedigrees. Few, if any, could match his knowledge of pedigrees. He was unique in that respect.

"He did not like confrontation. In a way, I was a go-between himself and the staff. He was a hard task-master and had that ruthless edge that is essential, I believe, if you are to succeed at the top in the racing jungle. He didn't suffer slackness or falling-down on the job. He set the very highest standards himself and expected others to meet those same rigid standards. So if someone failed down the line, I would be the instrument to convey his displeasure and ensure that it did not happen again. It rarely if ever happened again.

"You knew you were working in a stable that housed horses of the very highest class – horses of the calibre of El Gran Senor, Golden Fleece and Sadler's Wells to name but three of the super-stars that were there during my time. Everything was pitched at an Everest peak and you were one of the privileged ones to be there in a golden era.

"Now that the Camelot days are part of the history of racing, we can appreciate them all the more and be glad that we were a part of them", he added.

9

The Method

John Reid, who succeeded Cash Asmussen as No. 1 jockey at
Ballydoyle in 1988, has advanced the theory that Vincent O'Brien's
genius was that he was a man of inspiration.
Others who worked for him have talked also about the "inspiration factor"
– that rather than having a method that could be clearly and concisely set
down on paper as Ben Hogan, Jack Nicklaus and Nick Faldo, to name but
three, set out their approach to the golf swing, Vincent was intuitive and
innovative and, as Phonsie has put it, he had this tremendous attention to
detail – "from the moment he got up to the moment he went to bed, detail
was everything".

When Tiger Woods pulverised the opposition in winning the 1997
Masters as Augusta, Georgia, the golf writers zoned in on the perfection of
his swing. But a perfect swing comprises different components all brought
together in such a balanced manner that to the naked eye the ease with
which it is executed makes us wonder why we can't do the same off our
club handicaps.

To argue then that Vincent O'Brien's genius was founded to an extent on
the "inspiration factor" alone is rather too simplistic. It overlooks the
essentials that marked him out not alone as special but as one who brought
to his profession qualities that by any standard were unique.

One has got to remember that he differed from others in that he was
much, much more than a great trainer. As his son-in-law John Magnier put
it: "He was on a plane apart when it came to breeding matters. Vincent
could compete with anyone in buying on looks alone. He could, I am
certain, pick a potential winner, even a future champion without even
looking at the pedigree.

"But he always took the view that the yearlings you really go after must
have a pedigree to match their looks and conformation. If they don't have a
pedigree, it's unlikely they will prove attractive as sires to breeders, who
place tremendous importance on the genetic bank. In fact, it's rare in the
world of breeding that those put to stud that fail to answer the cruel

demands of the genetic bank will emerge as top sires".

So in all assessments of Vincent O'Brien, it can never be overlooked that he was training with an eye – in the case of the colts – to making stallions. The targets were set with this ultimate goal always in mind. And in the case of horses like Nijinsky, The Minstrel, Alleged and El Gran Senor the programme in the case of each was geared to eventually planting the flag on the highest peak, so to speak, in the knowledge that the pay-off at the end of the line would make it all worthwhile.

Vincent O'Brien had the ability to concentrate to the exclusion of all else on training the horses in his care. Another essential was the ability to keep on learning and assimilating knowledge even when he had arrived at the stage that he had acquired an almost God-like stature as a trainer in the eyes of racing followers in Ireland and Britain and much further afield.

He was hard on himself and expected all those working for him to rise to the standards that he set.

T. P. Burns, who was his assistant for seven years, said that Vincent's insight was phenomenal, his patience quite extraordinary. It meant nothing to him to earmark a horse in his charge for a target a year ahead, maybe even longer. It was no trouble to him to put away a horse when he was going for bigger things. He was ahead of his time all the time, yes, a step ahead of the others. When he was dominating the Gloucestershire Hurdle at Cheltenham over a decade, he brought to a fine art what was required to win that race. It was like winning the Epsom Derby over a succession of seasons, and probably harder in a way, because you had to pick out a particular type of horse and then you never knew what you would run up against in a hurdle race of this kind.

"Vincent wasn't going to allow the big gambles at Cheltenham to go astray because his challengers could not jump. He took infinite patience in teaching them. One of the greatest attributes of all of a Vincent O'Brien-trained horse in the National Hunt races, especially hurdle races, was that they could jump. They would invariably gain that vital length in jumping. The only horse of Vincent's I ever fell on was Stroller and that was not his own fault".

T. P. Burns noted also that he was "always amazed at the way Vincent seemed to know everything about the opposition in each particular race. He could read how a race would go in advance in uncanny fashion".

"Having ensured that you were acquainted with the horses you rode for him, he didn't burden you with a book of instructions once he had come to trust your judgement and professional skill. It was a pleasure to ride for him, as he was a true professional himself always".

In the case of his assistant trainers – and John Gosden and Michael Kauntze were two others who held that post at Ballydoyle – Vincent once he trusted someone, left that person to get on with the job. "He expected you to know your business and see to it that there would be no slip-ups", said T. P. Burns. "You were on your honour. There could be no messing. His demands were pretty high. He expected you to keep up with them. The standards he set others, he maintained himself. There was no place in his set-up if you could not meet these standards".

✳   ✳   ✳

Michael Kauntze, talking to me over lunch in Dublin one day in May '97, looked back over his years in Ballydoyle – the Golden Age of Nijinsky, Roberto and other top colts.

Life there, he quickly discovered, was regimented and built around one man. "You had to learn to get into Vincent's way of things. He was a tough man to work with but, provided you did the work he expected of you, it was fine. He was very definite too in the the way he wanted the work to go.

"You have got to remember that he was handling top horses nearly all the time – horses that were being prepared for Classic and Group races. Therefore, things were pitched very high – at the highest level imaginable.

"When Kooyonga started out as a three-year-old I asked myself: 'How would Vincent have dealt with this filly?' That was perhaps the finest tribute that I could have paid him – endeavouring, in effect, to get into his mind. Kooyonga had been a better than average two-year-old but I knew she still had about 10lbs to find if she was to graduate to Classic standard. After she had won her opening race of the '91 season, I was able to give racing journalists, who asked me about future plans, not only her next race but her next three races – the English 1,000 Guineas, the Irish 1,000 Guineas and the Coronation Stakes. That was the way Vincent always planned things – looking beyond the next immediate target to the entire programme for a potential champion."

When Kooyonga duly won the Irish 1,000 Guineas and the Coronation Stakes in the hands of Warren O'Connor, Kauntze knew in his heart that the knowledge he had acquired at Ballydoyle had proved invaluable from the moment he took up training.

One of Kauntze's tasks at Ballydoyle was to prepare the OUTLINE list of work for the next day. Vincent would then study it and change it and sometimes it looked like a school essay after the teacher had written all over it. One of Kauntze's proudest possessions is a list of horses and riders for the next day's work with just a solitary tick at the bottom. "Yes, I'm very proud of that", he repeated.

"When Vincent's horses worked, they worked", Michael Kauntze went on to explain as he went deeper into the O'Brien Method. "He was tough on the horses and at times it seemed to be a case of the survival of the fittest. But it was his belief that a good horse could take training.

"He was able to assess to a tee the requirements of every individual horse. He gave the two-year-olds as much time as they needed. But once they came on stream and looked useful, he did not refrain from running them.

"It was Vincent's philosophy that if you could not train to win in six days, you would not do so in seven. So they weren't worked on Sunday mornings unless they were running early on in the week or mid-week.

63

"I would say that he was influenced to an extent by American theories and he could even use American terminology in his designation of what he wanted a horse to do in a piece of work."

George McGrath agreed with T. P. Burns and Michael Kauntze that Vincent set very rigid standards and demanded also total loyalty to the stable. Once you joined Ballydoyle, you were expected to make it your life. In the case of a rider who might feel that he could pick up outside rides if he were able to divide his services between a number of different trainers, it wasn't always the ideal situation – but you had to understand the terms when you worked at Ballydoyle. The quality of the horses there in the peak days meant that Vincent had to know that all his staff were on hand when he wanted them.

Pinpointing one of the facets that showed Vincent's total attention to detail, George McGrath told me: "When you rode two-year-olds at work, Vincent would jot down afterwards in a special pad your conclusions on each individual, especially in the case of those that hadn't as yet seen a racecourse. He was meticulous in this respect. I remember once saying to him that such a two-year-old would be best over seven furlongs. Vincent ran him in a six-furlong race and he won. He reminded me that I had suggested seven. My response was that I had concluded that he definitely needed more than five."

Vincent's son, Charles, who was Assistant to his father for six years before setting up on his own in County Kildare, revealed to me that one of the reasons why middle-distance horses were not tested beyond seven furlongs or a mile was that the gallops at Ballydoyle were very severe and brought the most out of a horse.

"The really top-class middle-distance horses had a sprinter's pace over three furlongs," he noted. "For example, The Minstrel worked with the brilliant sprinter, Godswalk who won the King's Stand Stakes in 1977. And he was under very little pressure to stay with him."

He went on to stress that, in his view, much of his father's success stemmed from the way he knew the strengths and weaknesses of every horse in his charge. "He played to the strengths and knew exactly how to cope with the weaknesses. He always endeavoured to keep the number of horses in the stable down to manageable proportions, so that he could give them the kind of individual attention that he believed was the route to success."

Charles said that when his father started out in Churchtown and during his initial days in Ballydoyle, he was what one could describe as "a hands-on trainer" in that he did most of the important tasks himself. But later he became a "hands-off trainer", delegating most of the routine work in the stable to people he had total faith in, so that he could concentrate on the broad canvass.

Brian Molony told me that what he came to realise most of all from his days as Assistant Trainer to Vincent O'Brien was his ability to delegate." I don't think anyone could equal him in this respect," he said. "But you have got to remember that when he delegated, he delegated to lieutenants that he trusted completely. Into that category came people like Maurice O'Callaghan, Danny O'Sullivan and Bill Fogarty. Those of us who had the privilege of working in the stable would all like to think that we had Vincent's trust also."

Brian Molony agreed with Charles that Vincent graduated from being a hands-on trainer to a hands-off trainer.

"He did not need to be, nor did he want to be, bogged down with the day-to-day details. So a lot of the preparatory work that is necessary before the horses actually go out on the gallops was already done before Vincent made his appearance and thus he was able to give his undivided attention to each horse and what he saw as the essential requirements in work procedures for the day.

"You might say that everyone in a position of authority under Vincent thought that he was running the show. It was Vincent's gift that he could inspire, that he could bring the best out of people. He didn't want the members of his back-up team to be nonentities or automans, so to speak. He wanted them to contribute, to express their thoughts, to offer suggestions, to be involved. He took everything on board like the Captain of a ship. While everything revolved around him, he was in total command, always at the helm."

*   *   *

Today there is a tendency to divide Vincent O'Brien's career into two distinct phases – the jumping phase and the phase from 1959 when he was solely a Flat trainer. But it has got to be remembered that from 1943 to 1959, a span of 16 years, he pursued a dual role and that extended to over 20 years if you take in the period when he was assistant to his father.

Horses like Hatton's Grace, Cottage Rake and Knock Hard are a trio who will be remembered mainly for their feats over the jumps but Vincent O'Brien knew that they had the speed that could be utilised on the Flat. Hatton's Grace won the Irish Cesarewith two years running (1949 and '50) and also the Irish Lincolnshire in the hands of Martin Molony while Cottage Rake won the Irish Cesarewitch (1947) and the Naas November Handicap (1946) and Knock Hard the Irish Lincolnshire (1950).

You could say that these races should have been the preserve of men who made their living solely from the Flat.

How did he do it?

"I suppose it was a question of developing an individual horse's confidence. That was the basis of it – to have him enjoying his work and enjoying his racing", he told Alan Byrne in the course of a *Racing Post* interview in November '94.

Otherwise the horses, he said, were exercised in much the same way as those trained by his rivals, with the possible exception that his charges did some sharper, quicker work.

The Vincent O'Brien training method evolved gradually, not through any deliberate study or analysis but by learning from others and plotting his own course.

"Going through life I have always been a good listener", he said. "I remember in the Forties Sydney McGregor, an Englishman who was one of my first owners (he owned Good Days) gave me some good advice. He said 'you must listen to even the silliest fellow because he may say something interesting or useful'. And I have always followed that".

Vincent O'Brien, amazingly enough, applied the same system to working his three Grand Nationals winners – Early Mist, Royal Tan and Quare Times – as to the other jumpers in his stable. And they jumped the same schooling fences. "I didn't believe in building replica Aintree fences because once they got to a racecourse horses, I knew, tended to get wound up and thus were much more alert, so they would usually make much more effort and concentrate more than they would at home.

"If you built a fence like Becher's Brook at home, the danger, I felt, was that they would dig their toes in approaching it and their courage would consequently become impaired".

Bryan Marshall, who rode Early Mist to victory in the 1953 Aintree Grand National, was impressed by Vincent's "thoroughness" and by the way he missed out on no single detail of a race in his preparation. For example, he asked Marshall to come over to Ballydoyle to ride Early Mist in a gallop – his first acquaintance with the gelding. Vincent did not want Bryan to go into the Aintree race without assessing for himself how he should ride Early Mist. Marshall was delighted with the way the eight-year-old went in the gallop and was happy afterwards that his jumping was good enough to see him safely around Aintree.

He deliberately rode him at speed into a few fences in the course of the gallop, then pulled back half a length behind the leader at another and Early Mist negotiated the obstacle without trouble and even jumped to the front again.

Marshall expressed his optimism and enthusiasm afterwards to Vincent O'Brien, who, however, showed his customary caution. This caution stemmed not alone from his doubts he still entertained about Early Mist's ability to jump the course but also from the fact that the horse's preparation had been short and hurried as he had been sidelined with a splint that led to his being fired for the trouble (a job carried out by Bob Griffin, the veterinary surgeon, whose close links with Vincent O'Brien and his family went right back to the time of Dan O'Brien).

The night before the Grand National in '53 Vincent O'Brien brought Bryan Marshall up to his suite in the Adelphi Hotel in Liverpool where he had a slow-motion movie projector. He went through a number of previous Nationals and showed Bryan the mistakes that had been made, what to avoid, where to stay, where to go.

'Mincemeat' Joe Griffin, who owned both Early Mist and Royal Tan before the crash came, was in the room that evening and later he would reflect: "I will say one thing about Vincent O'Brien – he is a master of his own art".

Incidentally, Joe Griffin could have become the owner of a third Grand National winner. Vincent O'Brien came to him after Royal Tan had won the 1954 National and said, 'I'll sell you the winner of next year's Grand National for £2,500'.

The horse that 'Mincemeat' was being offered was Quare Times, who in 1955 became Vincent O'Brien's third successive winner of the Aintree race.

'Mincemeat' would always regret that one missed opportunity in his life, for it would have seen him become the only owner in racing history to have won the National three years running and making it more remarkable still, he would have done it with three different horses. "What a marvellous trainer this man was that he could tell me within a couple of hours of winning one National that he would sell me the winner of the following year's race", said Joe Griffin twenty years later.

*　　*　　*

Already we have seen that Vincent O'Brien was prepared to show infinite patience as he set long-term targets for his charges and in the case of two-year-olds that he believed had the potential to be champions, he could wait and wait and wait. "He would never run a two-year-old which he thought would be better for time", said Jacqueline. "He must really have tested the patience of the owners".

But then Nijinsky might not have come to anything if he had been trained elsewhere and didn't have the benefit of such fine work riders as Johnny Brabston and Danny O'Sullivan. As Jacqueline noted: "He was very difficult initially as a two-year-old and only time, great care and excellent work-riders got him right".

Michael Kauntze when he became assistant trainer in 1968 (he would be at Ballydoyle until 1973) actually took over from Vincent's brother, Dermot, who was part and parcel of the stable set-up for 23 years – a man who stayed out of the central limelight but who had a tremendous input into Vincent's success story. In the final analysis, Dermot, having been through the mill for over two decades, took the easy route out and set up as a breeder. One could only take that intensity of pressure for so long.

Michael Kauntze recalls that Dermot took him out to dinner and gave him some of advice he would not easily forget. "I hope that you have the good fortune not to have a good horse in your first year".

But, of course, Kauntze was there for twelve Classic winners and he quickly came to realise what Dermot meant when he made that remark to him over dinner. Engraved in his mind is the moment that Nijinsky arrived at Ballydoyle – standing 16 and a quarter hands high. "He was a very big, strong, precocious yearling, which is why he was so good as a two-year-old. I remember waiting to go into the ring at Newmarket (for the Dewhurst) and somebody said the horse wouldn't look out of place if he were parading for the novices' hurdle at Cheltenham".

"Life was quite considerably harder when there was a good horse", Michael Kauntze noted. "Vincent worried just as any other trainer worried, because of his tremendous attention to detail. Things would get tenser and tenser leading up to a big race. Because he had such an agile mind, he was always thinking of things and saying: 'Have you done this, have you done that?

"He never raised his voice, he wasn't a demonstrative man from that point of view, but you just knew something was wrong".

❋   ❋   ❋

One final quality that contributed immensely to Vincent O'Brien being able to stay at the top for half-a-century was his capacity, as John Magnier put it, "to take a beating better than any man I know in this business. "

"If it is a sign of greatness to be able to lose, then I can only say that he was always a terrific loser", John went on. "If something went wrong and he ascertained that it wasn't any fault of his, or anyone else closely associated with a particular situation, then he would put defeat out of his mind and go out the next day as if it never happened. Give him the worst possible news and you discovered that he was fully capable of taking it on the chin. You ended up feeling sorry for yourself as he told you 'not to worry'.

"You have to have guts to take it as a trainer and breeder at the level at which Vincent operated throughout his career. His brother, Dermot said of him once that whatever was inside the man could only be likened to four Rolls-Royce engines rolled into one".

No apter description than that...

Dr. Tony O'Reilly, who had horses in training with Vincent O'Brien and his wife Chryss, who has an outstanding knowledge of breeding matters. They are pictured at Leopardstown on Heinz '57' Phoenix Stakes Day.

10

The Speed Factor

Speed... speed and more speed. There is little doubt that one of the key factors that Vincent O'Brien brought to the way he trained his horses was the enormous emphasis he put on speed.

You reflect on the brilliant burst of acceleration Sir Ivor produced to cut down Connaught and win going away in the 1968 Epsom Derby. You reflect on the pulverising speed of Golden Fleece in the 1982 Derby as he came from last to first to win in awesome style in the end and you reflect too on the lasting impact left by El Gran Senor as he took the 1984 English 2,000 Guineas.

The mind goes back also to the two-year-olds who hit the headlines for Ballydoyle, especially at Royal Ascot and to the sprinters who left footprints on racing's sands of time in events like the King's Stand Stakes, the Cork and Orrery Stakes and the July Cup. Speed was the essence.

Cash Asmussen remembers the speed work from his days as No. 1 jockey at Ballydoyle. The Texan came in for criticism for giving his mounts a lot to do but he affirmed in a *Racing Post* interview with Julian Muscat in November '94: "If I could have changed one thing while I was there, I would have ridden his horses from even further back in their races. I was amazed at some of the short work he put into them at home.

"In retrospect, with that speed, I could have got them to relax better away from the pace and they would still have found plenty in a finish".

Michael Kauntze, Assistant Trainer from 1968 to '73, noted that Vincent placed great store in what Phil Bull, the founder of *Timeform* indicated to him in a letter and that was that a horse's best distance was 'the trip he can get while going at optimum speed'.

"So Vincent was always convinced that if a horse stayed, he stayed. You could not teach one to stay. It was either built to get a trip or was bred with the necessary stamina in its make-up.

"You very rarely saw a horse worked beyond seven furlongs. There was, in fact, very little difference between the work given to a seven-furlong horse and a mile-and-a-half horse. Generally, they were worked up to a mile maximum. But Vincent was uncanny in the way he could bring a horse to its peak on the days that mattered. And this was because he had planned its progamme with total exactitude and he wasn't just thinking of one single target ahead or the immediate one.

"Vincent Rossiter was invaluable as a work rider in the Ballydoyle set-up, as he was a very good judge of pace from in front. For that reason he invariably set the pace in the key gallops. Johnny Brabston and Danny O'Sullivan were other vital cogs in the machine on the gallops. Yes, Rossiter, Johnny Brabston and O'Sullivan were men with no flash about them but they knew exactly what was required of them and I repeat once again that Nijinsky would never have developed into a champion of champions but for their contribution on the gallops, especially in his two-year-old season when he posed immense problems".

Vincent had come to appreciate, according to Michael Kauntze, that if a horse got the mile at the Curragh in a true-run race of Classic or Group standard, in particular, then he would get at the very least ten furlongs anywhere else and if he was a colt in the class of Nijinsky or The Minstrel, he had every prospect of getting the Epsom Derby trip. Vincent didn't doubt that Nijinsky would have the stamina to triumph at Epsom.

However, he was able to accept the defeat of El Gran Senor in the Epsom Derby in philosophical fashion because he knew that the colt didn't really have the requisite stamina to last home up the hill when put under pressure by Secreto in the climactic punishing battle.

Michael Kauntze revealed to me that Vincent O'Brien had a penchant at times for working sprinters on their own, though more often than not they would be as lead horses and school-masters for the two-year-olds. He believed that if you had top sprinters working with each other in gallops, they could take it out of each other as naturally they would want to stay ahead.

✳   ✳   ✳

Brian Molony, like Michael Kauntze, got real insights into the speed factor in the Ballydoyle operation during the Eighties when two of the fastest colts of all emerged in Golden Fleece and El Gran Senor.

Vincent realised that the best of the Northern Dancers, as later the best of the Nijinskys, had brilliant speed but he came to know also that this had to be balanced against the temperamental factor. So oftentimes the training was geared to ensuring that a colt of exceptional ability was brought along in such a way that it peaked on the days that Vincent had set as the primary target and it might be just one ultimate target as happened in the case of Golden Fleece, with everything building up to Epsom Derby Day '82.

The Northern Dancer colt, The Minstrel had shown brilliant speed as a two-year-old, culminating in an authoritative win in the Dewhurst Stakes of 1977. But he was beaten into third place in the English 2,000 Guineas and had to settle for runner-up position behind Pampapaul in the Irish equivalent. Now the fear that he would not, after all, get the Derby distance seemed to have been confirmed. Amazingly, Lester Piggott conveyed to Vincent O'Brien that if he ran him at Epsom, he would ride him and he predicted further that as long as the going came up good to firm, he would win.

Brian Molony said that while The Minstrel had the speed to go with sprinters like Godswalk and Marinsky on the gallops at home, he needed a mile-and-a-half to show his best, as was shown in the Epsom Derby, the Irish Derby and the King George VI and Queen Elizabeth Stakes.

Colts like Alleged and Golden Fleece, however, were not worked with the sprinters. Golden Fleece was such a big, rangy horse that his forte was in producing an awesome turn of speed at the climactic stage of a twelve furlong race as he left the opposition for dead in the Epsom Derby.

"Training horses can be a boring business and it's not as exciting as it is often painted to be by some writers", said Brian Molony. "It can be all about routine and organisation. The way Vincent differed was the infinite patience he exercised in the case of certain horses in his charge, in his ability to give them time.

"We have seen how he was prepared to forego running a two-year-old he regarded as special at Royal Ascot because he had bigger targets in mind for its three-year-old season.

"And yet he got the optimum out of colts and fillies that he knew were not destined for greatness as three-year-olds. You have only to glance down the records of two-year-olds events on the domestic front in the Seventies and Eighties in particular, to understand what I mean and also to see how great was the dominance he exerted – events like the Railway Stakes, Anglesey Stakes, National Stakes, Beresford Stakes and the Birdcatcher Stakes.

"A number of the winners would not figure in any debate on the lasting merits of the great horses that passed through Vincent's hands, yet his genius lay in delivering them to win important events in their own right. It reached a point that other trainers were afraid to take him on because they believed that nearly everything out of Ballydoyle was a world-beater when that was not always the case."

Brian Molony stressed that Vincent as the maker of stallions saw the vital need of getting the crucial black type after a two-year-old's name where a two-year-old could be produced without being rushed or if it was in the category that it could run in a number of races without leaving any mark. The Dewhurst Stakes, for example, was one of the most prestigious events of all and success in this, Vincent knew, could be enough in the case of a beautifully-bred colt to assure its future at stud.

Thus Storm Bird's victory in the 1980 Dewhurst Stakes was the key ultimately, allied to his breeding, that ensured that he commanded the amazing figure of $24 million – even though he failed to win a race as a three year-old. Nijinsky (1969), The Minstrel (1976) and El Gran Senor (1983) all won the Dewhurst Stakes as a prelude to what was to follow in their three-year-old careers. Vincent had seen to it that they had the essential winning bracket to put them on the road – with their breeding – to be assured a place at stud.

Brian Molony presented the very interesting argument that it did not always follow that because a colt was good enough to triumph in the Dewhurst – and even win that race impressively – that he could be seen as a likely winner of the English 2,000 Guineas the following season.

"It can be quite a rush to get a horse ready for the Guineas from the time he is pulled out as a three-year-old and few emulate what Entrepreneur did in 1997 in taking this Classic without a prior run," he said. "A lot of factors can upset a colt's preparation and then, most important of all, not all train on, including some that look like veritable flying machines as juveniles".

✳   ✳   ✳

Molony said that after Nijinsky and The Minstrel, it was inevitable that there would be a lot of hype surrounding anything out of Ballydoyle that looked to have the credentials to win the English 2,000 Guineas or Epsom Derby. The ante-post layers in preparing their winter prices on the Classics, were naturally very wary of the 'talking horses' in Vincent's care and it was inevitable that a colt could be made favourite and even a very warm favourite, without full cognisance being taken of traits in its character. The punters, for their part, were often only too eager to rush in blindly and it could lead inevitably to fingers being badly burned.

Try My Best, the 1977 Dewhurst Stakes winner, was a case in point. A bay colt by Northern Dancer out of Sex Appeal by Buckpasser, he represented the best of American blood. Those who were at Leopardstown on Saturday, September 27, '77 and saw Try My Best win the Larkspur Stakes by six lengths knew that they were looking at an exceptional speedster. And that faith was fully justified when he went to Newmarket and beat Sexton Blake by one-and-a-half lengths.

Lester Piggott said as he dismounted after the Dewhurst: "This colt is without doubt the best two-year-old we have seen this season. He will have no trouble in getting the Rowley Mile."

Robert Sangster saw him not alone as a Guineas hope but as a potential Derby winner.

Vincent O'Brien himself predicted: "I do not see why he should not develop into another Nijinsky."

Millionaire Dublin property tycoon, 27-years-old Patrick Gallagher (later to end up in Belfast's Crumlin Jail for a time after the collapse of Merchant Banking), evaluated Try My Best at £2 million on his achievement in emerging the undisputed juvenile champion of the 1977 season and decided to lay out at least £500,000 to buy a quarter share in him. He was to purchase that share eventually for £750,000.

It was an investment, which at the moment it was clinched, looked like paying off very handsomely indeed. And yet there was an insurance factor in the breeding potential – irrespective of what the future held in the Classics – that you would not always have in a big business deal.

The fall-back position was that even if this 'wonder' colt disappointed in the 2,000 Guineas and Epsom Derby – and Patrick Gallagher took full cognisance of this in his calculations – the value would still remain at £2 million on Try My Best's two-year-old performances.

Patrick Gallagher later categorically rejected suggestions that he was an innocent abroad when he paid £750,000 for a quarter share in a colt that had to win at least one Classic before he could hope to realise any profit on his investment. "Let me put it on record that the way the Syndicate (comprising Robert Sangster, Simon Fraser, Danny Schwartz, John Magnier and Vincent O'Brien) treated me in clinching the deal was exceptionally good," he said. "The worst that could happen was balanced against the best that Try My Best could achieve as a three-year-old. In the world of big business you are gambling all the time. You are gambling in setting up new companies, in going into property deals and you have to learn to steel yourself against disaster."

A decade on from when Patrick Gallagher said this to me his empire had collapsed and he knew what it was like to spend hours alone in a cell... contemplating the might-have-beens.

In that golden spring of '78, in the count-down to the English 2,000 Guineas Patrick Gallagher, standing 6ft 4ins tall and bestriding the Dublin property scene like a colossus, was already planning the victory party to celebrate what he was convinced by then would be a sweeping initial Classic success for Try My Best. And what a champagne party it was going to be.

"I estimated that victory in the Guineas would increase the colt's value to £4 million straightaway," he told me over a drink in a St. Stephen's Green hostelry when he was still in the days of wine and roses. "And I calculated that if he had taken the Epsom Derby as well, his value would have jumped to £7 million, possibly £8 million.

"After that you had the Irish Derby and if he had maintained an unbeaten record, the sky was the limit. I saw him as the finest colt since Nijinsky. Remember, The Minstrel did not win the English 2,000 Guineas prior to taking the Epsom Derby and Irish Derby and then the King George and we know the price tag he was to achieve."

Later after the stunning defeat of Try My Best, men would remember how the flamboyant financier and racehorse owner had hired a private jet to bring a party of family members and friends over for the race and a London night-spot had been booked in advance to continue the festivities after the champagne corks had first been set popping at Newmarket itself.

The build-up to the 1978 Guineas was immense and there was an air of expectation in racing circles both in Ireland and Britain that had not been experienced since Nijinsky opened his bid for the Triple Crown here in 1970.

Disquieting rumours had emanated that all was not well with the colt and instead of starting at odds-on, in keeping with his tremendous reputation, Try My Best was easy to back at even-money on the day. Did the bookies know something that the ordinary punter was not aware of?

Try My Best broke well enough from the stalls in the swampy conditions but at no stage held out any hope of reaching a challenging position. When asked to quicken by Lester Piggott shortly after half-way, he drifted left-handed, found nothing under pressure and dropped steadily back through the field – to finish a dismal last of nineteen.

Thus the colt that had cost 185,000 guineas as a yearling was unplaced behind the 28-1 outsider Roland Garden, which cost only 3,200 guineas as a yearling.

"Come on Vincent, it's brandy time," was the immortal comment from Patrick Gallagher in that shattering moment and he added: "Risks are taken every day. Some come off, some don't. You can't sit around crying when they fail to come off."

So the party went ahead anyway, even if lacking the heady effervescence that would have marked it if the colt had triumphed in the manner expected of him.

Gallagher sold back his share at a reduced figure to the Syndicate, deciding to cut his losses rather than endeavour to get back exactly what he had invested in the colt.

The Guineas form was too bad to be true. Was it the heavy going? Was it a virus? Or could Try My Best have been got at?

The famous English professional punter, the late Alex Bird argued in his autobiography that Try My Best was 'got at' the same as Gorytus before the 1983 Dewhurst Stakes.

Vincent O'Brien, when I questioned him in the summer of 1992 on that point, rejected the 'got at' theory but he had no doubt on one point: "The colt was sickening when he ran in the Guineas – he must have been; otherwise he could not have run as badly as that. He was listless and had lost a lot of weight after the race."

Brian Molony also rejected out of hand the 'got at' theory. It is his belief that it was simply an instance of a flying two-year-old not training on.

Try My Best did not run again. He was retired to stud – and thus it became one of the great unanswered questions whether he would have won the Epsom Derby if he had gone to post running in the form he had displayed the previous season.

Vincent O'Brien explained to me the reason for the decision: "After the Guineas I had to give him a rest and when I started to do a bit with him, I found he didn't stand up to anything. I decided then we should retire him."

✳   ✳   ✳

Danzatore, following three scintillating wins as a two-year-old, including a six-lengths victory in the Beresford Stakes was installed winter favourite for the English 2,000 guineas of 1983.

But while he was by Northern Dancer, he was out of Shake A Leg and Brian Molony noted that there was "a kink" on the dam side of the family,

"On looks you could not fault him and he had tucks of ability as he proved in those three wins as a two-year-old. He did not have the heart, however, to make a decent racehorse as a three-year-old," said Brian.

"Vincent was tempted to run him in the Dewhurst but decided in the final analysis to nurture him in the hope that he would go on to even greater things the following season.

"I suppose if he had run in the Dewhurst it might have toughened him up. But then who knows... it was yet another depressing instance of a very highly regarded juvenile with a lot of potential simply not making it as a three-year-old."

There was no greater example of hype getting out of hand like a prairie fire – with Ballydoyle in no way responsible – than the case of Apalachee back in 1973-'74. This giant two-year-old of the long, ground-devouring stride was by Round Table and the fanfares began to sound immediately after he had won the Lee Stakes on his debut in the colours of John Mulcahy in August '73. They sounded even louder when he took the Observer Gold Cup in easy fashion.

Lester Piggott, however, entertained doubts on the score of Apalachee's inability to quicken in the manner of a Sir Ivor or Nijinsky. It was a question of overwhelming the opposition rather than killing them off with a sabre-like thrust represented by the kind of blinding speed that Sir Ivor produced at the climax of the 1968 Epsom Derby.

But still he wintered well and the hype really spilled over when he dismissed with commendable authority an excellent field in the Gladness Stakes.

But those who had gone in head down to back him ante-post for the 2,000 Guineas after the Observer Gold Cup and the many more who could not wait to get on after his triumph in the Gladness tended to overlook how impressive the Francois Boutin-trained Nonoalco had been in winning the Prix de la Salamandre at Longchamp and didn't seem to want to know about the credentials of Giacometti. In a word they were caught up in a wave of euphoria and not surprisingly Apalachee was installed 4-9 favourite – even though ominous rumours were circulating that there was something wrong with his wind.

When asked the question by Lester, Apalachee produced nothing and there were no excuses as he finished third behind Nonoalco (Yves St. Martin) and Giacometti.

Sadly, there wasn't even the alibi that he had made a noise. Hope did not die there and then and it looked as if he might become a challenger at Epsom. But a crucial gallop left Vincent in little doubt that he would not get the twelve furlongs. Again there was speculation that he might revert to a mile and go for the St. James's Palace Stakes at Royal Ascot.

This plan too was shelved. He did not run again, being retired to stud to stand at the Gainesway Farm in Kentucky.

Compounding the failure of Apalachee in that 1974 season was the manner in which Cellini also failed to train on, though in his case the hype was nothing like that which surrounded the first-named colt.

Cellini too was by Round Table and, after winning the National Stakes, he established himself as a Classic prospect by taking the 1973 Dewhurst Stakes, Lester Piggott having the mount on both occasions. At that point Vincent O'Brien's concern was to ensure that Cellini and Apalachee would avoid taking each other on. When Cellini came out in '74 to win the Vauxhall Trial Stakes at the Phoenix Park and then the Tetrarch Stakes at the Curragh, there was every reason for the hope to be entertained that the two-pronged attack on the English and Irish 2,000 Guineas by Apalachee and Cellini would bring a Classic double for Ballydoyle. So much for those hopes.

Apalachee, as we have seen, turned out to be a dismal failure while Cellini could only finish third at the Curragh behind the Seamus McGrath-trained Furry Glen, a 10-1 chance ridden by George McGrath. Later Cellini again disappointed when only runner-up in the St. James's Palace Stakes at Royal Ascot. He too was retired to Kentucky to the Gainsway Stud.

*   *   *

Finally, in the list of two-year-olds that failed to train on, Monteverdi proved as big a disappointment as Apalachee. He had it on looks and being by Lyphard, was a grandson of Northern Dancer. Furthermore, he took the route to possible stardom as a three-year-old by following in the footsteps of Nijinsky and The Minstrel in winning the Dewhurst Stakes in 1979 in the hands of Lester Piggott.

But the manner in which he swerved ominously in the final furlong of that race, before Piggott managed to straighten him out again with a crack of his whip, had to leave a serious question mark over him. But still the ante-post layers not alone made him winter favourite for the 1980 English 2,000 Guineas but for the Epsom Derby. At that stage he was unbeaten in his three races.

When he could only finish second on his reappearance in the Vauxhall Trial Stakes at the Phoenix Park, it didn't materially affect the hype surrounding him as it was felt that he was not suited by the soft going that day but the bubble burst when again he could only finish runner-up in the Greenham Stakes at Newbury.

Those who had backed him to win the English 2,000 Guineas had to tear up their dockets when he was re-routed to the Irish equivalent. The fact had to be faced at the same time that he wasn't in love with racing. The fitting of blinkers didn't boost confidence in any way.

The worst fears were realised when he finished fifth to the P. J. 'Darkie' Prendergast-trained Nikoli, the mount of Christy Roche. Lester Piggott related in his autobiography *Lester* how he was so annoyed with the colt for not trying at all that, on dismounting, he exclaimed to Vincent O'Brien in the hearing of some race-writers: "He's useless."

The comment was picked up and publicised widely and, even Piggott himself admitted, that it couldn't have helped in efforts to keep a high value on Monteverdi as a stud prospect, bearing in mind his unbeaten record as a juvenile. To question a horse's courage so openly and bluntly in public went beyond the diplomatic bounds.

Piggott accepted that Vincent was truly gifted in the way he could gain the maximum when it came to achieving the highest possible value for a colt at stud and, of course, John Magnier invariably played a key role in the inter-play of negotiations. Nothing will ever match the $24 million attained for Storm Bird.

But then in addition Alleged (bought originally by Robert Sangster for $120,000) was syndicated for $13 million while The Minstrel (bought at Keeneland for $200,000) was syndicated for $9 million.

Golden Fleece had an overall value of $30 million when retired to stud at Coolmore after his Epsom Derby triumph in 1982.

Before he contested the 1984 Epsom Derby the value of El Gran Senor was put at a mind-boggling $80 million.

So the failure of colts like Apalachee, Danzatore, Cellini and Monteverdi to realise as three-year-olds the potential they revealed as juveniles had to be balanced against the overall strike rate Vincent O'Brien achieved and the amazingly-successful syndication deals that were concluded. Certainly Robert Sangster wasn't complaining.

It has got to be remembered that Vincent O'Brien was gambling on horseflesh as others gambled on shares or on futures on the financial markets. He never said anything other than that it was a high-risk business and not one for the faint-hearted. When he went into the ring to bid at Keeneland or at any of the other major yearling sales, he was putting his eye and his judgement on the line and you had to have courage and nerves of steel to last in this jungle.

His son Charles, who was invariably at his shoulders at the sales in the period when he was Assistant Trainer, said that both in the racing sphere and in the bloodstock arena his father was "a very, very good loser" and was never one to dwell on setbacks. In fact, he had a penchant for springing back and adding further to his list of achievements.

❊   ❊   ❊

It can never be overlooked that a key ingredient in Vincent O'Brien's most notable successes over the jumps was the speed factor. Never was it better illustrated than in Cottage Rake's first Gold Cup triumph in 1948. 'The Rake' was practically an outsider, starting at 10-1 while Happy Home, carrying the colours of Miss Dorothy Paget and with Martin Molony in the saddle, was all the rage with the punters.

Vincent O'Brien was standing down at the last fence as Happy Home and Cottage Rake rose to it together. Men who were there that day and who know what horsemanship is all about, still talk in awe of the way Martin Molony drove Happy Home into it hoping that he could make the then inexperienced Cottage Rake stand off too far and either fall or make a bad mistake.

Happy Home came out of it in front – gaining a length to a length-and-a-half with one of the most fearless jumps Martin Molony had ever essayed. "But Cottage Rake beat my one for speed in the run to the finish", said Martin factually. The verdict was one-and-a-half lengths.

Ironically, Martin Molony told me that he considered that the best race he had ever ridden over jumps. "God gave me great courage", he said simply, no doubt thinking inwardly of the manner in which he powered Happy Home into the last at the end of an unforgettable duel over the last mile. "I doubt if any one of us would have ridden at it with such sheer guts and gusto as Martin did that day", was Aubrey's tribute.

When Aubrey Brabazon passed away in the autumn of 1996 at the age of 70 it was fitting that Martin Molony should speak at his graveside, noting that he would have won more than one Gold Cup were it not that he had to give second best to 'The Brab' in awesome battles that have passed into history.

The speed factor was crucial also in Hatton's Grace lowering the colours of National Spirit when the Vic Smith-trained gelding was seeking to complete a three-timer in the 1949 Champion Hurdle. And it was the ingredient that saw him go on and win again in 1950 and '51.

Yes, it was finishing pace from the last that meant everything in Hatton's Grace's case, as his speed from the last also contributed so much to Cottage Rake taking the Gold Cup three years running.

Aidan O'Brien, the new Master of Ballydoyle (left) with Jim Bolger, who played a vital role in putting him on the road to a record-breaking career as a trainer.

11

The
Grand Vision

The Grand Vision was based on the bedrock of Vincent's eye picking out yearlings that would make potential Classic and Group winners. It afforded the public the opportunity to invest in the Master of Ballydoyle – or, more correctly, in Classic Thoroughbreds which was launched in Dublin in 1987 as a bloodstock investment company, with Vincent O'Brien, John Magnier and Robert Sangster three of the key promoter-directors.

Punters could now get in on the glamorous end of racing's big action. It was ideal for the small man in that the shares were priced at 30p each. The dream, of course, was that one of the yearlings purchased at the sales in the States and in Europe – or a few of them – might graduate as three-year-olds into the Nijinsky, Sir Ivor or The Minstrel class and be syndicated in deals that would make the gamble well worthwhile.

Quite of a number of the yearlings were the progeny of sires that had originally been trained at Ballydoyle – stallions like Be My Guest, El Gran Senor, Alleged, Northern Dancer and The Minstrel. Naturally, hopes were very high at the outset – so high, in fact, that when the company was enlarged with a one-for-two rights issue, no difficulty was found in reaching the target figure.

The story of the death of a dream represents a classic instance of the might-have-beens. It can be argued that if Saratogan had won the 1989 English 2,000 Guineas – when the shares touched a high of 41p on the Thursday of that week – all might have been different. As it was his failure at Newmarket and again in the Irish 2,000 Guineas, coupled with the subsequent failure of Classic Secret and an injury to the highly-regarded sprinting prospect, Puissance, in the count-down to Royal Ascot, resulted in the shares dropping dramatically to 16p and when the company was wound up, they stood at a dismal 3.5p

Royal Academy's success in the 1990 Breeders' Cup Mile (Turf) at Belmont Park came too late to save the company. But, more important, matters were very bad in Kentucky at the time with famous stud farms up for sale and others heavily in debt. Where Royal Academy might well have been syndicated for a figure close to $20 million dollars, if he had won the inaugural running of the Breeders Cup Mile in 1984, he was now sent to Coolmore with a value on his head of $3.5 million. This was actually the sum that had been paid for him when Vincent won his famous duel with D. Wayne Lukas at the Keeneland Sales in July 1988.

The real tragedy of the failure of Classic Thoroughbreds lay in the fact that it was going to deter investors from getting involved in any such major venture in the bloodstock arena again. On the other hand if it had succeeded it would have opened up new vistas and Irish racing and the Irish breeding industry would have gained much in the process.

From the very outset Vincent O'Brien had emphasised that investors in Classic Thoroughbreds were going into a high-risk business. If many went in in the hope of a quick "killing", then the Master of Ballydoyle was warning them against seeing gold at the end of the rainbow. If anyone got his fingers caught in the wringer, at least he had to admit that he had been warned.

Vincent O'Brien, as Chairman, staked nearly £1 million in the company and in that respect was putting his own reputation firmly on the line. The steely courage he showed in going $1 million above the original maximum he had set himself in the battle to acquire the colt by Nijinsky out of Crimson Saint (who would be named Royal Academy) was amply justified in the memorable Belmont Park triumph in the hands of Lester Piggott and the success Royal Academy has since become as a stallion. It proved that the eye of the Master was in no way dimmed even at 71.

* * *

Classic Thoroughbreds was the brainchild of Vincent O'Brien, Robert Sangster and John Magnier with a vital input also at the consultation and planning stage by financier, Dermot Desmond, a close friend and golfing companion of John Magnier. Dr Michael Smurfit, head of the multi-million Smurfit Group and Chairman at the time of the Irish Racing Board, was brought on board to add that vital "heavyweight" image that would influence the financial institutions. Also recruited was beef baron, John Horgan of Cork.

It was set up as a £10 million company. The break-down of that initial float saw roughly £3 million earmarked for the promoter-directors, £5 million taken up by the financial institutions and the remaining £2 million offered to the public, all of whom had the option of increasing holdings by 50 per cent by June 1988.

Promoter-directors John Magnier, Michael Smurfit and Robert Sangster each invested £600,000 while John Horgan put in £250,000. Cash Asmussen (61,250 shares), Bob Lanigan (55,000) and Dermot Desmond (50,000) also showed their faith in the venture while Vincent's son, Charles (61,500) and his daughters, Jane Myerscough (61,500) and Elizabeth McClory (61,500) were listed too in the media as investors.

With a one-for-two rights issue, the company was enlarged by a further £5.7 million in mid-1988, with the express purpose of providing the finance for yearling purchases in the 1988 season. So in all close on £16 million was invested.

It's easy I know to be wise after the event. I remember, after the fall, sitting one day in his office on the Grand Parade in Cork with John Horgan talking to him for my book *The High Rollers of The Turf* about the coups landed with Tirol in the English 2,000 Guineas and Irish 2,000 Guineas when the subject turned to Classic Thoroughbreds. John was able to take on the chin the loss of the bulk of the £250,000 that he put into the company. I put it to him to him that the point had been made by insiders to me that there could have been a few fall-back positions to avoid a total wash-out.

In cold retrospect he was inclined to agree that at the outset all the eggs should not have been put into the one basket – that is solely into the buying of yearlings. Instead of splashing out £7.6 million on yearlings in the first year, half of this money might have gone into something of a more gilt-edged nature, certainly into a venture that did not carry the same high-risk factor. A sum of £3.8 million might have been invested in taking an interest in stallions in a link-up with Coolmore, using its immense expertise and know-how and world-wide contacts. It was money that would not have gone down the drain and it would have been there as a nest-egg should matters not materialise on the primary plane.

My own belief is that consideration might also have been given to looking at potential stars in the National Hunt arena. The small investors would have been thrilled if the company had come up with the winner of a major event at Cheltenham. The outlay in acquiring a few animals, already proven and entered for the Festival meeting, would have been nothing like the outlay required on yearlings bred on the lines to make Classic or Group winners. To ease the burden on Vincent himself a trainer or two with proven track records in the National Hunt arena and a successful strike rate at Cheltenham could have been brought on board the 'Classic' ship to go after potential stars and train them.

Again that would have represented a safety net giving encouragement to the small investors while they waited for singular success on the higher plane on the Flat. It can be argued that too much was reposed at the outset on a make-or-break policy that the batch of yearlings purchased at the sales would produce Classic winners.

The counter-argument, of course, to all that is that the investors in Classic Thoroughbreds, from the big men to the small men, were basically investing in the uncanny eye and judgment Vincent O'Brien had shown in picking out potential Classic winners when he went to the yearling sales. They wanted to have a direct stake in his judgement. And it was for that very reason that it was named specifically "Classic Thoroughbreds". In the final analysis you couldn't escape the conclusion that it was going to stand or fall ultimately on whether the yearlings it bought would click or not. Sadly, outside of Royal Academy hopes were never really realised.

The cold statistics tell their own story. Before the close of 1987, £7.6 million had been spent on the yearling portfolio. The company started the 1988 season with interests in 38 juveniles (29 colts and 9 fillies) in training at Ballydoyle. At the close of the first season's racing, 23 of them had been out, providing 9 winners of 12 races. In 1988 Classic Thoroughbreds acquired an interest in a further 16 yearlings – 12 colts and four fillies.

So you could say that out of 54 yearlings, Royal Academy is the one that will always spring to mind whenever 'Classic' is mentioned. In a Quiz who could readily name any of the others outside of Saratogan perhaps?

*   *   *

Brian Molony, who was Assistant Trainer at the time of the birth of Classic Thoroughbreds and lived through the nightmare of its failure, holds very firm views on the venture.

He contended that, to begin with, far less horses should have been purchased in the first year of operation. Noting that the company started the 1988 season with interests in 38 juveniles and that already £7.6 million had been spent, he argued that it might have been wiser to have purchased no more than half that number of colts and fillies.

Vincent found himself at 70 over-seeing the training of over 80 horses where he had become accustomed to having no more than 38 to 40 in the peak days of the early Eighties. In a way it was asking too much of him.

Brian Molony said that the biggest burden Vincent felt on his shoulders was in trying to make a success of Classic Thoroughbreds for all the small investors who had put their faith in him. "He felt it very much and nothing, I think, affected him as deeply than the eventual failure of the 'Classic' venture. You see, he knew that the big investors could take it in comparison to their overall wealth but, reflecting on his own days starting out in Churchtown, he saw that thousands of ordinary people had backed his judgement and his ability to pick out yearlings who might eventually become Classic winners and graduate to being successful stallions."

Molony maintains, in cold retrospect, that Saratogan was over-hyped and his failure in the 1989 English 2,000 Guineas was a terrible blow. This allied to the subsequent failure of Classic Secret and an injury to the highly-regarded sprinting prospect, Puissance in the count-down to Royal Ascot were further cruel blows at the very time when the company needed all the luck that was going.

Summing up, he said that if it had been decided at the outset to diversify in a stallion venture or to put a certain amount of money into the National Hunt sphere, it would not really have complied with the basic concept behind the establishment of 'Classic' in the first instance. "The whole approach was to buy yearlings in the Royal Academy mould. If it had happened that one like him had been acquired the first year – better still even two or three – the story would have been far, far different. It only goes to show that there is no more high-risk business in the world

FACES OF THE MASTER . . . Vincent O'Brien (top left) pictured before the start of the 1986 Flat season and (top right) Ed Byrne's study taken during his final years as a trainer and (bottom) Caroline Norris's picture of Vincent (with Jacqueline) at the Curragh just before he announced his retirement at the end of the 1994 season.

Clashganniff House, Churchtown, Co. Cork, where Vincent O'Brien was born on April 9, 1917. Noel O'Brien, his wife, Margaret and family live there today.

Vincent's parents, Dan and Kathleen (left) pictured at Clashganniff House.

The rolling acres within sight of Clashganniff House over which Vincent O'Brien exercised his horses when he was establishing himself as a trainer.

Vincent O'Brien, King of Cheltenham in the late Forties and Fifties made a return visit in March '95 after a number of decades to the scene of his great triumphs. He was guest of honour at a lunch on Gold Cup Day and was acclaimed by well-wishers when he entered the parade ring after the big race. (Picture: Bernard Parkin.)

Vincent O'Brien and Jacqueline with Martin Lynch after he had ridden Nick The Brief to victory in the 1990 Vincent O'Brien Gold Chase (now the Hennessy Cognac Gold Coup Chase) at Leopardstown. (Picture: Caroline Norris.)

Martin Molony (right) rated one of the greatest jockeys of all time and (centre) showing what a brilliant horseman he was over the jumps and (bottom) T. P. Burns, left and Aubrey Brabazon (right), pictured chatting with "Mouse" Morris on his last visit to the Cheltenham Festival meeting.

Vincent O'Brien and Pat Taaffe at a reception to announce details of the inaugural Vincent O'Brien Gold Cup in 1987 and (bottom) Pat Taaffe captured memorably in this picture from the Taaffe family album as he leads over the Canal Turn on Quare Times in the 1955 Aintree Grand National.

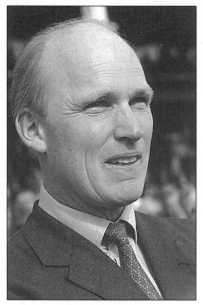

A quartet who graduated from the Ballydoyle academy (clockwise from left): John Gosden, Michael Kauntze, Curragh vet, Robert Norris (assistant trainer and also vet at the Ballydoyle stable) and Michael Dickinson who acknowleges that he would never have trained the first five home in the 1983 Gold Cup but for all the knowledge he acquired at Ballydoyle.

Michael O'Hehir, the commentator for Vincent O'Brien's most notable triumphs over the jumps and on the Flat; Brough Scott, who saw Vincent O'Brien as a genius with horses; and (bottom) Sir Peter O'Sullivan, who retired as The Voice of BBC Racing at the end of the 1997 Flat season, with his successor Jim McGrath, left. (Picture: Colin Turner.)

Lester Piggott in a memorable gathering with friends in the Royal Hotel in Tipperary town on the evening in Oct. 1990, he rode against Jonjo O'Neill (beside him in picture) in a charity race at Tipperary racecourse. Also pictured are (back row from left), Andy Lacey, proprietor Royal Hotel, Timmy Hyde, Arthur Pierce, John O'Neill, London (face partially covered), Tommy Murphy and Tommy Stack. At front with arms aloft is Frank O'Neill, London.

Vincent Rossiter, left, and Gerry Gallagher, right (back to camera), two great and valued servants of the Ballydoyle stable join Tracy Piggott (centre) as she chats with Lester on the evening in July '91, when he drew a record attendance at Killarney races.

than going out and investing in yearlings with an eye to purchasing Classic winners," he said.

Charles O'Brien agreed with Brian Molony that too much was spent on yearlings the first year, for it meant that if there was not one like Royal Academy among the first batch, it didn't leave a lot in the kitty for purchases in the succeeding years. While a case might be presented for investment in the National Hunt sphere to keep the interest of investors alive during the winter months, he again agreed with Brian Molony that the company had been established with one basic aim – and that was to buy yearlings with an eye to coming up with Classic winners and successful stallions. Anything else would have been secondary or supplementary to this basic aim. In a word, 'Classic' was going to stand or fall on the success of the policy being pursued. Unfortunately, Royal Academy came too late.

The company had been valued before Saratogan's English 2,000 Guineas failure at £23.67 million at the peak 41p-a-share price. It was estimated that the asset value would have been increased by an equivalent of £4 million if the El Gran Senor colt had triumphed at Newmarket (Classic Thoroughbreds owned 50 per cent of Saratogan). Bloodstock experts were even predicting that Saratogan's value would reach $12 million if he won. His failure to even reach a place (he actually finished ninth in a field of fourteen) was a blow from which Classic Thoroughbreds never really recovered.

I must admit that I even caught the Saratogan 'bug' myself on a visit to Ballydoyle. I caught it even worse when I sat in the sitting-room of Phonsie O'Brien's home beside the village of Kilsheelan in South Tipperary and he did not hide his enthusiasm for the prospects of the El Gran Senor colt.

Then when I arrived in Newmarket for the race and met Lester Piggott in his home, I realised that he too was inflicted with the bug after his contact with the Master of Ballydoyle. I was beginning to think that the ante-post bet I had on Saratogan at nice odds was one I would certainly be collecting on.

On the Friday in Newmarket, the gallop-watchers convinced me that Major Dick Hern had one to be seriously reckoned with in Nashwan, so I had no hesitation in laying off to save my stake on Saratogan. The confidence of the connections of Nashwan was not misplaced. The Blushing Groom colt won readily enough and by Derby Day he would be 5-4 favourite to complete the double which he duly did in the style of a real champion.

The final irony was that Classic Thoroughbreds did not have the money in 1990 or '91 to purchase yearlings. One could have wept in 1991 at the fact that if the £7.6 million spent in 1987 – just four years beforehand – had been available then, more than one colt of the calibre of Royal Academy might have been purchased much, much cheaper. As was pointed out in the invaluable book *Horsetrader* (which tells the absorbing story of Robert Sangster and the ups and downs of the thoroughbred market globally) the highest-priced lot at the Tattersall's Highflyer sales at Newmarket in '91 went for £380,000 compared with the £2.4 million paid in 1982. The gross at Keeneland fell drastically the same year. "The eternal spring of Kentucky was over".

Vincent O'Brien could be forgiven for privately wishing that he was hitting the yearling sales that same year with the resources at his back that 'Classic' had in its first two years of operation.

Again the might-have-beens...

*　　*　　*

In a desperate bid to save Classic Thoroughbreds from extinction, drastic cost-cutting measures were undertaken. Vincent O'Brien voluntarily agreed to reduce by 50 per cent his training fees for the horses in his care.

But in the end it was all to no avail.

An Extraordinary General Meeting was held in the Berkeley Court Hotel in August '91 that effectively brought the curtain down on what Dr Michael Smurfit described as "this noble and unique experiment".

"After three disastrous years we have come to the conclusion that enough is enough", said Dr Smurfit. "The underpinning of values, by purchasing only top-quality horses, does not occur – due to the unprecedented decline in the value of thoroughbreds these past three years. It is a decline which unfortunately continues... There is little point in proceeding with the purchase of any further horses".

There was still a seven-figure sum in the bank and some of the one hundred shareholders who turned up for the meeting were adamant that the company should "keep racing until the last penny was gone". It was even advocated that 'Classic' switch to a policy of buying National Hunt horses.

The axe, however, came down and the money in the bank was distributed among the shareholders. I recall getting a cheque for the small investment I made with a friend!

The big men of the calibre of Dr Michael Smurfit, Robert Sangster, Vincent O'Brien and John Magnier were not seriously hurt by the sad collapse. Similarly none of the small investors who staked sums ranging from £300 to £500 and even £1,000, were going to be forced to sell their homes in the wake of the shares plunging to the proverbial 'buttons'.

In a word, most of those who went in did so at their own depth and I didn't hear any stories of people jumping from high windows in the mini-crash that followed Saratogan's defeat at Newmarket.

Classic Thoroughbreds arrived on the bloodstock scene at the wrong time. The Maktoum brothers of Dubai and other oil-rich Sheikhs had the ammunition in the money sense to win the battles and, indeed, the war if it came to that against any battalions ranged against them when they set their minds on acquiring what they really wanted.

The one occasion they stayed out of the front-line trenches, Vincent O'Brien was successful in acquiring the bay Nijinsky colt at the Keeneland Sales in July, 1988 that would be named Royal Academy.

But even then, as we have seen, he had to go to $3.5 million to beat off the challenge of Californian trainer, D. Wayne Lukas who had arrived in Lexington, Kentucky with no less than $15 million to spend. O'Brien spread Classic's risk in the colt by allowing Robert Sangster to take a quarter share.

The reason the Arabs stayed out of the bidding was that they had their fingers burned previously when acquiring a yearling that had a pedigree similar to Royal Academy's. But Vincent O'Brien was not going to be deterred once he became convinced that the colt had something of "the look of eagles" that he spotted in his sire when he first set eyes on him.

He saw it in Nijinsky and in Royal Academy but, unfortunately, for Classic Thoroughbreds you do not find colts with that look every day of the week.

And therein lies the gamble in investing in thoroughbreds... even those that are bred in the purple.

The Old National School in Churchtown, (now the Community Hall), where Vincent O'Brien started his schooldays on Monday, 13 September 1920.

The class of 1923. Vincent O'Brien (*ringed*) is in the second row from the back, and his teacher, Tom Tierney, the principal, is at the extreme left. It was he who said of Vincent, "This lad is something different".

PART TWO

SHAPING THE MAN

12

Steeped In Racing Lore

Vincent O'Brien was shaped for manhood and for his destiny as a racehorse trainer in country steeped in racing lore and renowned not alone for the horses it produced, but for the natural horsemen who hailed from the area.

He grew up to know all about Cahirmee Fair, held in Buttevent about the third week of July each year and once the greatest in Europe, lasting about a week where now it only lasts a day. It reputedly dates back to the time of King Brian Boru, who drove the Danes out of Ireland at the Battle of Clontarf in 1014.

It was said that each cavalry battle on the Continent meant money for the farmer-breeders of the area. However, once the dragoon and hussar regiments switched to tanks, that outlet dried up like a spent oil-well.

According to local legend, the 600 gallant horses of the Light Brigade had left their farms to clatter into Buttevant to be sold at the Cahirmee Fair. And earlier still, they will tell you, the pride of the Fair was a horse which eventually became famous as Marengo, Napoleon's favourite white charger.

Con O'Brien, "The Bard of Ballyhea", who was "a bit of a genius in his own way" and who was related to Vincent O'Brien from another side of the family, was inspired to write a ballad about Cahirmee Fair – and the sadness of its fall. He described "the sunshine blazing down on all, on dealers great and blockers small" and "jarveys steering through the throng, with passengers the whole day long" and the hotels packed day and night "with money flying left and right".

A magazine correspondent who visited the Fair when it was still in all its glory described how "knots of horses trot along the road in a cloud of limestone dust, with drovers whooping behind". She wrote also of sharp eyes watching the hunters, the cobs and the Connemara ponies streaming past the cross-roads at the edge of the town and the signpost to Mallow...and the vagrant horse-dealers "whose caravans are parked in a line along the verge of the Limerick road".

Buttevant publican, Tony O'Neill, for long a friend of the O'Brien family and a storehouse of knowledge on the history of the area, recalled that this area gave the word 'steeplechase' to National Hunt racing.

The O'Brien homestead in Clasganniff, looking east to the Ballyhoura mountains, lies three miles from the steeple of St. John's Church in Castlelands, Buttevant.

In 1752 two local gentlemen, Cornelius O'Callaghan and Edmund Blake, took part in what is accepted as the first steeplechase on record. The race was "to settle a bet of a hog's head of wine".

A line of country was selected and then an objective set, towards which the contestants would race. What was more suitable and more easy to see in the distance than the steeple of a church?.

Messrs O'Callaghan and Blake raced over four-and-a-half miles of country from Buttevant Church to the St. Leger Church in Doneraile. And because it was from steeple to steeple, it gave rise to the word "steeplechase" in the racing vernacular to this day.

The challenge was won by O'Callaghan, who was a direct descendent, on the mother's side, of W. A. (Billy) McLernon, a leading amateur rider.

Two hundred years on from the first recorded steeplechase, it was decided to stage a repeat. The original race, as we have seen, had been from Buttevant to Doneraile but the historic renewal on April 23rd, 1954 was staged from Doneraile to Buttevant. John Huston, a great supporter of the Hunt in the West of Ireland, was one of those who competed.

The race was won on a horse called Baypark II by P. P. Hogan who was later to play such a significant role in the fortunes of Robert Sangster. Willie O'Brien, a nephew of Jackie O'Brien, was second and Billy McLernon third, Brian Mclernon fourth and John Twomey fifth. The field comprised thirty participants.

In P. P. Hogan's home in Rathcannon, I was shown the imposing Tostal trophy which he received for his victory.

✳   ✳   ✳

They are proud in Buttevant and Churchtown of the outstanding jockeys who have direct links with this area of County Cork. Jack Moylan rode for Dan O'Brien and later for Vincent and his daughter married Jimmy Eddery, Pat Eddery's father.

Jimmy 'Corky' Mullane, who had the most perfect 'sit' of any jockey of his era on a two-year-old, was born near Buttevant and in time was to ride as first jockey to the powerful Paddy 'Darkie' Prendergast stable.

The Duhallow Pony Club was the nursery for outstanding jump jockeys like Jonjo O'Neill and Brendan Powell. Jonjo's birthplace, Castletownroche, is just 15 miles from Buttevant.

Michael Collins, father of Curragh trainer, Con Collins, trained with a commendable strike rate at Springfort House (now a well-known restaurant outside Buttevant). Con was actually born there. Incidentally, Michael Collins helped lay out the original Mallow racetrack. He subsequently moved to the Curragh, trained for Joe McGrath and won the Irish Triple Crown with Windsor Slipper.

The Churchtown area became renowned for the Classic horses it produced. Loch Lomond, which was trained by the legendary J. J. Parkinson at Maddenstown Lodge to win the 1919 Irish Derby, was bred here. And exactly 60 years later that tradition was maintained when Dickens Hill, which was bred at the Flannery's Egmont Stud, finished second to Troy in the Epsom Derby (1979) and was runner-up to the same colt in the Irish Derby.

You cannot escape the conclusion then that Vincent O'Brien was reared in an atmosphere permeated with a love of horses and racing, also with following the hounds and with shooting and fishing in their respective seasons.

Vincent knew "almost from the cradle", as they say in Munster, how to sit astride a pony and later a hunter. He remembers – before he actually began following the hunt in the formal manner – going out with young friends of his and experiencing the sheer exhilaration of jumping ditches – "and it was such fine expansive country that we never had to jump the same ditch twice", he told me.

His brother, Dermot recalled winter days when Vincent and himself along with "three excellent lads", Ned Fitzgerald, Danny O'Sullivan and Maurice O'Callaghan (the latter two later to become valued employees of Vincent's) schooled point-to-pointers again across that magnificent country-side. "It was marvellous", said Dermot. "I can never forget the wonderful memories left by those days as we went, maybe four miles, over natural jumping country. It meant that horses just had to jump. It was better and more exacting than any hunt. Vincent loved it like the rest of us".

Locals who remember Vincent from those days recall him as "a good rider – a natural in the saddle".

He wore the traditional black jacket as he hunted with the famous Dashing Duhallows, actually the oldest hunt in Ireland. At the time when Charles Edward Louis Casimer, commonly called "The Young Pretender", was raising the standard in Scotland, Mr Henry Wrixton of Ballygibbon kept a pack of hounds. It is on record that the Wrixton family hunted in 1745 and a button was found later with the inscription "Duhallow Hunt – Revived, 1880".

The Churchtown area is equally renowned for shooting and fishing, pastimes which had always been accepted as an integral part of life in the O'Brien family and which Vincent would come to indulge with notable expertise.

Forty-eight years after Vincent O'Brien sent over Cottage Rake from Churchtown to win the first of three successive Gold Cups, Fergie Sutherland challenged successfully for the Blue Riband of chasing with Imperial Call from his Killinardrish stable, near Carrigadrohid and created the mother of all victory parties in Fergie's 'local', The Angler's Rest.

Before he was forced after passing his 59th birthday to give up hunting because the knee in his good leg was beginning to give him trouble, Fergie Sutherland (who had the lower part of his left leg blown off by a land-mine in the Korean War) hunted with the Duhallows, with the Muskerry and the Aghabullogues, and as each had a different day, he had ample opportunities to indulge the great passion of his life. Of course, he is a passionate and expert field sportsman also – extending to game shooting in season while out of season he keeps his eye in by making the clay pigeons his target in summer. Talking to Fergie, it's easy to imagine him out after the snipe. He will readily educate you, if you so desire it, into the intricacies of 'the drive' and acquiring the know-how to assess where the snipe are likely to go.

The country around Lombardstown, near Mallow has been put firmly on the racing map in recent years by Eugene O'Sullivan. He won the Christies Foxhunters Chase at the 1991 Cheltenham Festival meeting with Lovely Citizen and I remember still the connections linking arms in the winner's enclosure as they sang the Cork anthem "The Banks Of My Own Lovely Lee". Then in 1996 the Boys from Lombardstown had reason to sing "The Bould Thady Quill" with gusto in the aftermath of the Eugene O'Sullivan-trained Another Excuse winning the Midlands Grand National by eleven lengths at odds of 14/1 with Mallow-born Brendan Powell in the saddle (John Thomas Gleeson, poet, scholar and patriot composed this famous ballad and there is a plaque to his memory at the Gleeson Community Centre near Lahern Cross).

Eugene O'Sullivan, who is married, incidentally, to Fiona Meehan, sister of Lambourn trainer, Brian Meehan, doesn't mind admitting that he was inspired by the story of Vincent O'Brien starting on his own as a trainer at the age of 26 – after the death of his father, Dan – from his Churchtown base in 1943 and inexorably climbing the ladder to conquer every peak it was possible to conquer. You don't have to travel far from Lombardstown to reach Clashganniff House where Noel O'Brien and his wife, Margaret and family reside today. There is a close affinity and friendship between the O'Briens and the O'Sullivans and Noel has sent horses to Eugene to train. No matter where you turn in this country of the horse, the legacy left by Vincent O'Brien during his sojourn in Churchtown dominates the scene in a strange way. The achievements that have inspired Eugene O'Sullivan will continue to inspire others in the emerging generations as we reach the new Millennium – and beyond.

*   *   *

Vincent O'Brien grew up in a happy household like any normal lad in a country area. It did not matter whether the lads who went to school with you were the sons of labourers or farmers, you played with them in the school yard and you played with them after school. Ireland in is rural heartlands, in its towns, has always been unique in the sense that its national schools and its secondary schools, too, provide the platform for all classes to mingle and 'townies' learn how to mix with their 'country cousins'. And that is why the born politicians, products of this same school system, display the common touch and amaze visitors with the way they can so readily win a response from their 'constituents', whether it is in the street, the pub or at some race meeting.

County Cork being one of the great traditional strongholds of Ireland's national game of hurling – equivalent to what cricket is to England – it was inevitable that Vincent O'Brien should play the game at school.

A former school-mate of his, Danny Fisher told me: "After school we would play hurling in a field in front of Vincent's house. He was a great hurler. I think he could have gone on to win All-Ireland honours with Cork if he had kept at it".

Dan Flynn, another school-mate of his, concurred as did Jimmy O'Sullivan, who would later work for the O'Brien stable and whose brother, Danny was an outstanding work rider initially and later Head Lad. "I remember Vincent as a very good hurler especially when there were matches between Clashganniff and Churchtown", said Jimmy. "He had a great eye and a great shot", said Jack Murphy, whose brother Bill was in the same class as Vincent.

The goalposts can still be seen from Clashganniff House in the field where these friendly matches took place.

Vincent had started going to school when Ireland was in the throes of the War for Independence, brought to a whole new public globally through Neil Jordan's widely-acclaimed film *Michael Collins,* the biggest box-office money-spinner ever to hit the screens in Ireland. County Cork, which gave Collins to 'The Cause' and which was ultimately the scene of his tragic death at Bael na mBlath, was a hotbed of guerilla warfare against the regular British units and the Black and Tans, who did not always observe the letter, or even the spirit of the Geneva Convention.

"I remember on my way home from school, we would hear the sound of one of the Crossley tenders carrying a unit of the Black and Tans and we would hide behind some ditch until they had passed by; we would lie there in fear, our hearts stopping at the thought that if they spotted us they might begin firing indiscriminately", Vincent recalled.

13

'A Thorough Gentleman, A Pure Old Toff'

Dan O'Brien was photographed at Limerick on a November day in 1940 – the 7th to be exact – leading in his own horse Hallowment which he trained to win the bumper. The successful rider was Vincent – his first winning ride as an amateur.

In the photo Dan is in cap and overcoat (reaching down well below the knees as was the fashion of the times) and he also sported that day the inevitable tweeds. Tweeds were his special fancy. He also had quite a selection of the shirts that were so popular in his day – the ones with the studs and a few collars. "There could be great difficulty in getting those collars on", his daughter Pauline recalled.

Dan O'Brien was listed in the 1893 *Munster Directory* with eight others in the section under the heading "Churchtown-Gentlemen and Clergy". The Directory had a separate section for those listed as "farmers" solely.

Yet on the day that Vincent started school in the old National School in Churchtown (now a Community Hall) his father, when signing the School Register, gave his profession as "farmer".

But then Dan O'Brien was a down-to-earth personality, with no airs and graces – a man of the people in every sense of the term. "A thorough gentleman, a pure old toff," was how Tony O'Neill of Buttevant described him to me.

Tall and well-built, he carried himself in the local community with that quiet dignity that made him extremely popular. Then, too, he was a man with a keen sense of humour, a wonderful mimic and he had a remarkable fund of stories.

The theatre and music – light opera especially – meant a great deal to him, and he would never miss a presentation by one of Ireland's best-ever and most popular comedians, Jimmy O'Dea, at the old Cork Opera House. It's a building long since gone but it helped create the operatic tradition for which the City by the Lee became famous (local tenors in the gods would show in the interval of an operatic production how "La donna e mobile" really should be sung).

92

Dan O'Brien never drove himself. His son, Donal would be seen at the wheel of the maroon-coloured, fluid-drive, bull-nosed Dodge. Whenever there was a good show in the southern capital that attracted him, the big Dodge would be on its way and friends in Buttevant would be heard to remark: "There's Dan off again to the theatre".

"Yes, Father had a great ear for music", said Pauline. "If you hummed a tune he didn't know, he would be able to get it within a few minutes on the piano or on the melodeon which was his pride and joy. Mother, too, was very good at the piano, so there was always the sound of music in our house. And when the piano wasn't being played or the melodeon, Father would put on a John McCormack record or a Gracie Fields record, like 'The Biggest Aspidistra in the World' and hum it to himself or sing it aloud with real gusto. How he loved those old records.

"Nothing gave him more pleasure than the magnificent voice of John McCormack. Whenever there was an opportunity of listening to him in concert in Cork, he would be there. He deeply admired McCormack's singular rendering of appealing Irish numbers like 'The Bard of Armagh', 'I Hear You Calling Me', 'Mother Machree', 'Kathleen Mavourneen' and 'Macushla'. He cherished his 78s and they were played over and over again".

Dan O'Brien and John McCormack became friends, probably through the famous tenor's interest in racing (he actually owned a number of indifferent horses at one stage and dissipated quite a deal of his money on the Sport of Kings but then McCormack was earning such vast fees by the money values of today that he could be forgiven for indulging in this passion). When his schedule permitted him to do so, he would go racing on the Metropolitan circuit, particularly at the Curragh. Dan was generous in giving tips when he fancied one of his own and, no doubt, put his friend on to a winner or two.

✳   ✳   ✳

Dan O'Brien was born in Clashganniff House, where the family had farmed before him.

His first wife, Helena died at 36 on October 28th, 1914 as she was giving birth to her fifth child in an upstairs room. The Duhalllows were hunting in the Churchtown area. The baying hounds entered the front field and Dan O'Brien came out and quietly told the Whip that there had been a death in the family. The hunt was immediately called off.

Dan married again – in March, 1916 – at the age of 47 to his late wife's first cousin, Kathleen Toomey. Kathleen was no stranger to Clashganniff House. She and Helena had been close. Indeed, Helena put her on her honour that if anything ever happened to her, then she must play her part in helping to see the family through difficult times.

There had been four boys by Dan's first marriage – Donal, John, Ignatius and James.

Vincent was the eldest of four children of the second marriage – three boys (Dermot and Phonsie the other two) and a girl Pauline, who married John Fogarty, a businessman and a member of a well-known County Wicklow family. She died of cancer some years ago. A 6-handicap golfer in her day and a Junior All-Ireland champion, she had a wonderful vivacious and effervescent personality and in this respect was very like Phonsie.

Vincent O'Brien was born in Clashganniff House on April 9th, 1917.

The weather is reputed to have been very unseasonal when he was christened in Churchtown. "I often heard them say at home that the snow was hedge-high the day Vincent was brought to St. Nicholas's Church", recalled Dermot.

He was given the names "Michael Vincent" – thus the "M.V." – and in the baptismal records still extant, the parents are listed as "Daniel O'Brien" and "Kathleen M. Toomey".

Clashganniff House is within walking distance – not more than half a mile – of the village of Churchtown, which today has a population of 450, though there are 1,300 people in the combined parish of Churchtown-Liscarroll.

Churchtown is proud to claim that it was the birthplace of Dr. Barry Edmond O'Meara, who was the doctor to Napoleon on St. Helena. A noted Irish poet of the first half of the eighteenth century, one Seán Clárach MacDomhnaill, also hailed from the village, while the family of Maeve Binchy, today an international best-selling novelist and *Irish Times* columnist, came from the area.

The village has a butcher's shop, Gaffney's (Vincent O'Brien was their biggest customer when training here) and one pub, O'Brien's (no relation of Vincent). Up to some years ago it had another pub in O'Sullivan's (formerly Flannery's). O'Brien's pub, in typical Irish style, used at one stage combine a supermart and Tom could be seen selling rashers, sausages and black pudding in one half of it, while his brother Pat was pulling a creamy pint within hailing distance in the bar section. They had a successful racehorse which Tom trained and it was aptly named Ask Pat, because when someone in the supermart didn't know the price of something, the reaction automatically was to shout across and "ask Pat". Now O'Brien's is run as a pub only.

Once the village had three pubs but O'Keeffe's, which shared the glory days when Cottage Rake came back to a victory parade, first in Buttevant and then in Churchtown after that first Gold Cup win in 1948, no longer serves spirits, beer or stout.

The old-timers still remember the bonfires blazing and, as Jimmy O'Sullivan put it to me, "Churchtown being drunk dry" and Vincent O'Brien "being carried shoulder-high round the village" as they acclaimed him for his first big Cheltenham Festival triumph.

They remember how Frank Vickerman, the owner of Cottage Rake – "a very generous man" – went round the pubs in advance and told them to stock up and that he would meet the bill. They remember "nine barrels of stout out on the street" being tapped to cater for the hundreds who gathered in the village to join in the celebrations, which went on into the early hours of the morning. And they remember, too, how Frank Vickerman and his wife, Constance, went to the old National School with the original owner of Cottage Rake, Dr "Otto" Vaughan of Mallow and Vincent O'Brien and, after dispensing "gallons of sweets", they signed the school register, as did Vincent and Dr Vaughan. The Vickermans' entry can still be read today: "Our visit has given us great pleasure… the essays written on Cottage Rake were really excellent".

* * *

It was on Monday, September 13th, 1920 that Vincent O'Brien started his schooling in Churchtown. Clashganniff, the townland from which he hailed, means "The Sandy Furrow" – great land for rearing horses and training them because of its special limestone qualities.

The fathers of most of the children attending the old National School were listed as "labourers" or "farmers". Labourers dominated – a sign of the depressed times when Ireland was in the middle of the War for Independence and the affluent Sixties were a long way away as yet.

School photographs were taken by a photographer doing the rounds on his bicycle. He would stand his box camera on the familiar tripod and vanish momentarily behind "the bag" as he snapped a group picture. The group picture would probably cost 6d but if a boy could promise to bring an extra 6d the next day, the photographer would oblige by taking him and his brother, where there were two members of the one family in a school. Vincent and Dermot knew that their father could afford that extra 6d, so a picture of the two of them together during their school days was taken for posterity.

Vincent was captured in the second row from the back in the group photograph of the Class of 1923. Tom Tierney, the School Principal, who is at the extreme left of the print, went on record to state: "This lad is something different".

You wonder what he saw. Perhaps with that sixth sense he realised that the Hand of Destiny would steer this kid on a course that would ensure that he didn't take the emigrant ship to England but that in time all the pieces would come together on the jig-saw and he would go right to the top of the ladder in his chosen profession.

Confirmation day is always a day to remember for Catholic boys and girls in Ireland. In the old days it was the day when most boys got long trousers and then they did the rounds and received "presents" from relatives and from neighbours and friends. The traditions persist to this day – though they do not wait until Confirmation day to get into long trousers.

Vincent O'Brien was confirmed with his school pals of around the same age on May 9th, 1928. He was rather young, however, at eleven for Confirmation. He had the honour of being confirmed by Bishop Robert Browne, who had won distinction as President of Maynooth College.

As a youth Vincent went everywhere with his father – to races, to sales and round the country to various farms looking for young stock to make hunters, point-to-pointers and chasers. Vincent would smile later when he recalled for me that once he had the audacity in the hearing of grown-ups to advise his father quite seriously against buying a particular animal in a field because of something he had spotted about its forelegs. He was already on the road, without realising it, to Lexington and the Keeneland Sales – half a century before he made the initial onslaught with 'The Syndicate' in 1975.

He would never forget the debt he owed his father for introducing him so young to the world of the judgement of horseflesh – for helping him acquire "an eye" that can be acquired in no university or any seat of learning but only in the hard school of experience.

When Dan O'Brien wrote "farmer" in the school register in Churchtown as his profession, he was being true to the extent that he raised dry stock on his farm at Clashganniff. But really horses were his life. He trained and raced them for the pleasure of it. His main interest was picking out good horses and breaking them. He put all types through his hands, from good-class Flat horses to jumpers and hunters.

One of the best was the useful Flat handicapper, Holy Fooks, named after a famous local character who had lived back in the last century around Kanturk. When fighting a duel on horseback one day, he rattled a seasoned pig's bladder which had lead in it in the face of his adversary. It made such a horrible sound that it frightened the opponent's horse. He turned tail and as he ran for his life, Holy Fooks could be heard exclaiming: "Come back you coward!". Holy Fooks – the horse that is – was sold to Florrie Burke to go jumping and was afterwards ridden to victory by Joe Canty in the 1924 Galway Hurdle.

"My father belonged to an era of sportsmen", said Phonsie O'Brien. "The thing he loved most of all was going to the races, seeing his horses run and meeting his friends. He loved the day out and his group of friends looked on a race meeting as a chance to entertain each other. They were not in the horses for money – you had sportsmen and their horses. My father particularly loved going to Killarney because, in addition to the races, he could stay down there and play cards. He would sometimes play all night, buying drinks most generously for his friends, though he did not drink himself. "

"Father liked nothing better in life than a game of cards with his friends", recalled Pauline. "The games they played generally were nap, poker or '45'. They would adjourn to the drawing room and at midnight Mother would make tea for them. Father could drink tea till the cows came home. He never drank alcohol. His favourite drink was grapefruit juice. He would take a large glass of this when playing cards. He poured the whiskey as lavishly as if it was grapefruit juice. I remember the laughter and the repartee emanating from the drawing-room as the drinks had their effect. Yes, I remember those times as very good times, very happy times. Our parents gave us a lot of love."

Vincent would have been brought up then to see a game of cards as one of the accepted means of finding relaxation with friends in the pre-television era. Indeed, it was unthinkable not to be able to join in playing a hand if asked. He was shaped by the things that were part and parcel of the household in which he was reared.

Later on in life he found relaxation from the fierce pressures of training Derby winners of the calibre of Sir Ivor, Nijinsky and The Minstrel in poker sessions at Ballydoyle with owners and friends. He could hold his own with the best and the man who gave away nothing about his feelings when viewing yearlings in the barn area at Keeneland, for example, before "going to war" when the bidding commenced, certainly revealed nothing in his face if he had three Queens in his hand. If Vincent thought that someone would add to the cut and thrust of the occasion, he wasn't averse to laying on the helicopter to whisk him to 'the school' for the evening.

✳   ✳   ✳

Vincent came to love – and identify with – the special atmosphere surrounding race meetings in Ireland as he did the rounds with his father. Life was horses. In fact, he might have adapted the immortal words of Oscar Wilde – "Art is the only serious thing in the world" – to read: "Horses are the only serious thing in the world".

Imagine him then at his father's shoulder as they arrived at Leopardstown or the Curragh and the fruit-sellers showing their special affection for Dan as they exclaimed, "Ah, Mr O'Brien it's yourself – what is goin' to win today? We will keep the best fruit for you". Of course, he would blurt out a tip if he expected one of his own to win. Whether he won or lost, it didn't greatly affect his outlook or his personality. "There's always a next time", summed up his philosophy in defeat. There was no better loser ever.

Dan O'Brien, without knowing it, was passing on the same philosophy to his son – shaping him for days when defeat meant much, much more on the High Sierras he was riding as the Master of Ballydoyle than at the level at which his father performed. The manner in which he took the defeat of 'wonder colt' El Gran Senor in the 1984 Epsom Derby – his only defeat – would have made old Dan proud of him.

Dan O'Brien was a superstitious man when it came to racing. "He hated to see a ginger-haired woman if he was on his way to the races and had a fancied runner", Pauline recalled. "If one of the horses got beaten and he had seen a ginger-haired woman that morning, he would put it down to the ill-luck she brought".

There is a story that became something of a legend in Irish racing circles that it was because his father was broken by the bookmakers that Vincent set out to exact his revenge on them by landing some of the most spectacular and carefully-planned coups in the history of the Turf. I put the question straight to Vincent himself and he flatly refuted it. "If my father had £5 on a horse, he would consider that a big amount".

97

Dan O'Brien had money when fellow farmers in the area were forced to sell off their cattle in order to meet their rates bills. They went to the fair knowing in their hearts that they could not bring the animals home again. They had to take what was offered . Vincent had seen it happen when accompanying his father to fairs and it left an indelible imprint on his mind. "The tariff walls that the British Government put up against us during the Economic War meant a very bad situation", he recalled. "I remember seeing big bullocks weighing maybe 10 to 12 hundredweights being sold for 10s. And calves for five bob. The skins and hides were worth more than the animals themselves. They skinned them on the spot and threw the carcasses over the hedge".

Tony O'Neill recalled a farmer in the area failing to dispose of a two-year-old bullock at Buttevant Fair and then selling it for the price of a good round of drinks by today's standards to a few men who played a hand of poker for it. "They sportingly let him sit in and dealt him a hand but he didn't succeed in winning back the bullock. He was content, however, to have got something for the animal and a game of cards into the bargain before he went home to his wife and family".

Vincent O'Brien was shaped for manhood in an era when the boom days of the latter half of the Nineties for the Irish economy represented something way beyond the horizon and talk of the Euro was more distant still. Survival in the Economic War was all that mattered for many in the rural heartlands.

Vincent was shaped also, as he accompanied his father to the races, to point-to-point meetings and to fairs, for the freedom of open spaces, for the smell of the grass in the early morning as the horses were galloped and the sound of jackdaws in the trees... and the exhilaration that came with following the hunt.

The bonds between Father and son went deep.

'Mincemeat Joe' Griffin in his prime (at left) threw fabulous parties at the Adelphi Hotel in Liverpool and also made it open house in the bars in Cashel, County Tipperary after the Aintree Grand National triumphs of his horses Early Mist and Royal Tan. He won a small fortune in bets on Early Mist.

14

The 'Prison' Of Formal Schooling

Vincent O'Brien, on his own admission, hated the confines of the schoolroom. "I almost felt as if I was in prison", he said. He stalled at leaving home for Mungret College in County Limerick unless Dermot went with him.

"I was three years younger than Vincent", Dermot recalled. "He was twelve the day we departed from Churchtown in 1929. There were a lot of tears that day, as Vincent was very close to his father. Tim Molony, Martin's brother, sat in the same desk beside me in Mungret." Tim, who died in September 1989, would later ride Hatton's Grace to victory for Vincent in the 1951 Champion Hurdle and power Knock Hard to a memorable triumph in the 1953 Gold Cup.

Looking back on that unhappy sojourn in Mungret, Vincent told me: "I longed for the day when I could feel again the air in my lungs on the farm in Churchtown. I wanted very much also to be with my father and the horses, going to point-to-points and, of course, following the hunt".

Ironically, Dan O'Brien would not have had the money to send Vincent and Dermot to Mungret or get through the Economic War, that meant such days of hardship for Irish farmers in the Thirties, had he not received a legacy from America in 1929 – the same year as his two eldest sons went to Mungret. It amounted to £30,000, equivalent to over £900,000 today.

He could have – if he had so desired – bought up all the land that was for sale in the Churchtown-Buttevant area and much further afield. He was not, however, a grasping man and treasured very much the popularity he enjoyed in the community. Perhaps if he had bought an extra farm specially for Vincent, it would have saved the first son of his second marriage a deal of mental torment as he pondered where his future lay once the lands of Clashganniff House passed to his eldest step-brothers, Donal and John (Donal subsequently sold his interest to John). Under the marriage settlement when he married a second time, Dan O'Brien had agreed that the farm should pass on his death to Donal and John.

Denis Gaffney, the local butcher in Churchtown, told me that he often heard his father speak of the day when Dan O'Brien arrived from Clashganniff House and in a room off the shop showed him a cheque for £17,000. That would seem to indicate that Dan did not get the whole £30,000 in one lump sum but that the rest of it came later. And there were even suggestions that he would have got more from the will if he had gone to the States to collect it personally, and that a portion of what he was bequeathed was in stocks and shares and could have got caught up in the Wall Street crash.

The money from America arrived at a most timely juncture for Dan O'Brien. While others in the neighbourhood and in Ireland generally were on the bread-line and even below it, he was able to live quite comfortably. And there is ample evidence to show that he liked the life of a gentleman farmer-cum-trainer. He kept a good staff and paid them well and also fed them well. However, he was not a born manager where money matters were concerned and, certainly, but for the legacy, he would have been in serious difficulties financially.

Being a great family man, it would have shattered him if he could not have provided for his family in a proper manner. More so as his wife had delicate health all her life. She chose to stay as much as possible in the background and yet was a wonderful mother to her children.

"Frail, gentle and retiring but of a very sweet and endearing disposition", was how Pauline described her. "She was always there to help us when he needed her, so wise, so far-seeing and so full of love for us all, especially my step-brothers. Each night after the evening meal she would see to it that we all knelt down and said the Family Rosary (and the trimmings). This was never overlooked, never once forgotten, never set aside".

Pauline added: "When Vincent married, Mother moved from Ballydoyle to a house – 'Windswept' – which the family procured for her in Clonmel. She was great to make visits to members of the family and we would go to Clonmel and stay with her. Even though her health was never good, she out-lived Father by thirty years".

Dan O'Brien released Vincent from the "prison" of formal schooling when he was fifteen, which meant that he only spent two years in Mungret College. But he had to serve his apprenticeship and was sent to Fred Clarke's training establishment at Leopardstown, Foxrock, County Dublin, pursuing at night school the studies he missed out on leaving college. He became a proficient amateur rider, riding at point-to-points and also under both Rules and entering the winner's enclosure three times.

Martin Molony recalled riding on the same afternoon when Vincent O'Brien had the mount on Knight's Crest in a bumper race at Rathkeale, County Limerick. Rathkeale had a track in those days in the early part of the Second World War. Martin Molony actually rode his first hurdle winner there in 1942 on a horse called Prince John, scoring by a short head from Mrs Peg Watt's Border Knight, ridden by Willie O'Grady, father of Edward O'Grady.

*　　*　　*

In time Vincent graduated to becoming Assistant Trainer to his father. In fact, he held this position for seven years before going out on his own when his father died.

He became very familiar with the point-to-point circuit and also with the meetings styled today as the "Festival Round".

The means of transporting horses then was a far cry from what it is today.

Jimmy O'Sullivan recalled going with Vincent with three horses to the now-defunct Miltown-Malbay track in County Clare. At Ennis they switched to the West Clare line made famous in the Percy French song ("Are ye right there, Michael, are ye right?") and, because of the narrow gauge, they had to put the horses into cattle wagons. The journey was not wasted, as two of the horses won. Timmy Hyde's father, the late Tim Hyde, was the successful rider. Vincent got accustomed to being away from home for four or five days for these Festival meetings. Nowadays, Curragh-based trainers will drive to Galway and back each day and even do the same in the case of Killarney, Tralee and Listowel.

It is amazing that racing was maintained in Ireland during the period of the Second World War, considering the difficulties that had to be overcome with petrol rationing. Turf-burning trains were excruciatingly slow but at least they provided a means of transport in days when any vehicles on the roads were only operating under special permit and coupons for petrol, as in the case of tea, were like gold dust (some enterprising bookies had hit on the formula of getting petrol for the burial of a close relative out of town when, in fact, it meant that a group of them were utilising the one car to get to a country race meeting!).

On the other side of the coin, the days of the Emergency – as the period of the Second World War was known in Ireland – had a relaxed ease and pleasantness that left Martin Molony with some of his happiest memories, especially when riding in picturesque Killarney.

"We used to travel in a horse-drawn caravan as it was the only available means of transport. My brother, Tim, also travelled in the caravan along with neighbours, the late Ned Hartigan and the late Henry O'Brien (no relation of Dan O'Brien but a great friend and loved by all the children). There were no autos on the road and little traffic of any kind, so the horse could be given his head to go about his business.

"We used to occupy the many hours of the journey by playing solo, both going and coming back to home at Rathmore, near Croom, County Limerick. Usually we would stop at Castleisland overnight and continue on to Killarney the following morning for the races.

"One of my great memories of the Killarney races was in 1949. On the day prior to the start of the Festival meeting, Michael O'Hehir placed in his newspaper column a tip for punters, admonishing all those who planned to have a flutter to back each and every one of my rides at the meeting. During the three-day meeting I was fortunate to have five winners and four seconds from ten rides, making Michael a pretty fair prognosticator.

"After racing, many very enjoyable evenings were spent in the Great Southern Hotel listening and dancing to the band of the late Major Watt".

✳   ✳   ✳

In the late Thirties, Dan O'Brien mated his mare Golden Meter with Vesington Star. Out of these matings came three excellent handicappers, Astrometer, Astrologer and Astronomic who, between them, won fourteen races on the Flat from 5 furlongs to 2 miles, not all of them in his ownership.

Astrometer would win the Irish Cesarewitch while Astrologer, when owned by Jimmy McVey, gave John Oxx his first big handicap success in the 1943 Irish Cambridgeshire.

It is Astrometer, however, that would be remembered most of all… and also a horse named Solford.

This duo would become key factors in helping shape Vincent O'Brien into a master of the perfectly-planned coup in a major handicap event in an era when he couldn't have kept his head above water without hitting the bookies.

Storm Bird, one of Vincent O'Brien's shrewdest Keeneland selections at $1 million, pictured winning the 1980 Larkspur Stakes in the hands of Steve Cauthen. He was sold for $24 million. Storm Bird ran in the colours of Robert Sangster.

15

The Bookies Never Suspected!

T he bookies never suspected for one moment. In fact, they were caught with their pants down not just once but twice. And all because they had not come as yet to fear the name "M. V. O'Brien" as they would in later years.

You could forgive them in a way for being off guard when Solford won the Irish Cambridgeshire in 1938 and Astrometer the Irish Cesarewitch in 1941. For the name on the card on both occasions as the trainer of each of these horses was "Dan O'Brien". Normally, too, the big rails bookies would see these important back-end handicaps going to one of the big-name Curragh trainers and certainly not to a small stable in County Cork.

What they failed to spot was that Vincent O'Brien was the guiding genius behind the bringing off of the Autumn Double by Dan O'Brien.

If they had spotted it, they would never have quoted 20/1 Drybob and 20/1 Good Days when they completed the Autumn Double for Vincent himself in 1944 when he was 27 and now a trainer in his own right.

Vincent was only 21 when he helped lay out Solford for the assault on the 1938 Irish Cambridgeshire from his father's Churchtown base. In his planning, he displayed the infinite patience that would be his hallmark in later years when he realised that there was something special under his care.

Solford was an unbroken three-year-old bay (by Soldennis out of the Swynford mare, Margaret Beaufort) when purchased by Dan O'Brien from his breeder, Jack Hartigan of County Limerick. From the outset he showed distinct promise, winning three races on the Flat at four and five, but then he broke down when, with Vincent in the saddle, he started 2-7 favourite in a field of three for the Fermoy Plate at Mallow on June 17th, 1936 and was beaten four lengths by the 8-1 outsider, Owen Mor.

Vincent was behind the decision to give Solford time. He was off the course for the entire following season. On his return he won over hurdles at Naas in March 1938 and was then trained specifically for the Flat, the Cambridgeshire at the back-end being the long-term target. He ran up a sequence of six wins and, not surprisingly, was allotted 9st 9lbs in the Cambridgeshire.

Ridden by Jack Moylan, he carried this burden to a length victory over Ajar in a field of fifteen with Seedling, the 3-1 favourite unplaced.

Vincent was prepared to stay in the background and let his father enjoy the limelight – and there was no prouder man in the whole of Ireland than Dan O'Brien. Not surprisingly, the *Cork Examiner* (now *The Examiner*) gave headline treatment to this success by a "local" trainer.

There was even a ballad composed about Solford's triumph and one verse went:

I'll raise my glass to Moylan
May his glory ever shine
To Solford and his owner
The genial Dan O'Brien
And I won't forget the trainer
Whenever I relate
How Solford won the 'Cambershire' of '38.

That impressive Cambridgeshire success immediately resulted in the cheque books being brought out and Solford was purchased by Curragh trainer Charlie Rogers on behalf of Miss Dorothy Paget, who put him into training with Owen Anthony at Letcombe Bassett, near Wantage. Solford fell in the lead at the last flight in the 1939 Champion Hurdle but atoned by winning it in 1940.

At home in Churchtown, Vincent O'Brien had reason to be proud of his role in the making of Solford as a champion-to-be.

* * *

Vincent could not be described at this stage by any stretch of the imagination as a horse dealer. In fact, in order to get some ready cash he dealt in greyhounds. Generally, he bred them himself and sold them to England. At one point he was happy to have negotiated the sale of three to one Englishman.

"But when the Second World War broke out, the three greyhounds were returned to me", Vincent recalled. "The bottom fell out of the export trade and it actually ceased altogether, so that I was stuck with these greyhounds on my hands. I finally managed to sell one for £8 but, after waiting two years to get paid, I accepted an offer of £4 on the advice of my solicitor, who was David Nagle's father. It was all I had in the world.

"I put every penny of it on a grey mare called White Squirrel by Grey Squirrel. Actually, she was not a thoroughbred but a three-quarter bred, so she did not figure in the Stud Book".

Vincent had been schooling this mare for point-to-points and in a way it was the first horse he ever actually trained himself – and prepared for a gamble. Initially, his hope was that she would win a point-to-point but when foot-and-mouth disease broke out in the spring of 1941 all fixtures were cancelled. It was when the mare showed up particularly well with Flat horses in his father's string that Vincent decided that White Squirrel might have a future in racing and decided to go for "a touch".

The race he chose was the Sportsman's Plate – a bumper at Clonmel on May 8th, 1941, and, with a field of 27 runners, a good betting event was assured. Vincent decided that he would ride her himself.

A close friend of his had accompanied Vincent to the Powerstown Park meeting. Vincent's father, if he thought one of his horses had a chance of winning, loved nothing better than to tell all his friends about it. For that very reason, Vincent made up his mind that his best hope of getting a good price to his money was to wait until he got to the race meeting itself before advising his father to have a flutter. Before the bookmakers had formed a market on the bumper, he told his friend to go to his father and tell him that he should have a bet on the mare. "My father, who wasn't a gambler, gave my friend a tenner and he got on at 20-1. Of course, that started a rush and I had to be content with the 10-1 my friend took to my £4 bet".

White Squirrel duly beat her 27 rivals to win by a comfortable one-and-a-half lengths. "I was thrilled that we had been successful with my first gamble and it was the one that got me started", he said.

What was of deep significance about that gamble was that from that moment on he trusted his own judgement far more than previously and was prepared to back it to the hilt.

There was still though no question of him starting up on his own. He was content to continue as assistant to his father.

Happy also to allow his father again take the spotlight centre-stage when later that year – 1941 – Astrometer won the Irish Cesarewitch carrying 7st 6lbs in a field of 25. Ridden by Robin Hardwidge, he won by a short head from Bold Maid. Willie Howard rode the unplaced 4-1 favourite, Tom Mix.

So in the three years between 1938 and '41 Vincent had combined with his father in a famous double and was prepared for the assault to bring off the Autumn Double in 1944 when he was only in his second year as a trainer on his own.

That was a year after his father died and in restrospect Vincent regretted that the bid to win the 1943 Irish Lincoln did not result in a final singular triumph for his father as a trainer but then he realised that you can't win them all.

Astrologer was Dan O'Brien's representative that day at the Curragh. Again Jack Moylan was up. There was a field of 26. Astrologer went under by half-a-length to Foamcrest, trained by Cecil Brabazon and ridden by Tommy Burns, T.P's father.

It was a tremendously-exciting finish and Pauline remembered her father remarking: "If Astrologer had stuck out his tongue he'd have won".

"After the race, Father gathered all his friends around him and invited them upstairs to the Owners and Trainers", she continued. "I remember that Henry O'Brien from Fedamore, his bosom pal, was there, also the Hartys of Patrickswell and the Flannerys. It was such a lovely day, so warm that all the men had taken off their coats very early on during racing. Father did so too, even though he was always extremely careful in such matters after contracting pneumonia twice from wettings he got at fairs. Mother pondered aloud the wisdom of taking off his coat but he laughed and said, 'Now, now, I'm as young as the rest of you'.

"A man came up to him while we were having tea and said that he had very good oats for sale – that he would be putting the oats up for public auction during the following week. He promised to give Father first option. That decided Father in favour of going back home on the train, and leaving Mother to come on with us to Arklow. It was agreed there and then that my husband, John, would be at Kingsbridge (now Heuston Station) to meet him off the train and drive him to Arklow on the following Monday.

"I remember Father gave me an extra kiss before we parted that day at the Curragh. I never thought it would be the last time I would see him. I recall John taking the phone call from Churchtown that fateful Monday morning, and when he put down the phone he was strangely silent for a moment. Then he came to me and said quietly: 'Pauline, I'm afraid I have bad news for you. Your father is dead'.

"Later I heard the full story. Going back from the Curragh he told his friends that he was not in the mood to play cards with them. That was very strange, as he never turned down the chance of a hand of cards. He went to bed that night complaining of feeling cold. Dr Corbett came next day – Sunday – and said he would have to stay in bed. He got the medication that people got in those days for threatened pneumonia but his condition deteriorated rapidly. He died very suddenly late that evening. Penicillin became available the following September.

"Instead of there being a great reunion in Arklow, we found ourselves heading for Churchtown and the funeral. We were all so sad, especially after he had seemed so full of life at the Curragh on that glorious Saturday afternoon".

✻   ✻   ✻

Vincent O'Brien reached a critical point in his life with the passing of his father on May 6th, 1943. He was then 26. The family farm had passed to his step-brother, Donal, and all the horses that had been trained by Dan O'Brien were sold off. Vincent was at his wit's end contemplating what to do, though naturally he wanted more than anything else to be a full-time trainer.

If you are a believer in the destiny that shapes our ends, then you will understand that events can happen at one point in time that may well have a profound influence on a person's life some years later. In a word, time in the accepted sense has no bearing on the movement of one's star in the hands of one's Maker. Some may see it as pure chance, others will invariably find deeper, even spiritual elements.

In Vincent O'Brien's case, it was amazing how Fate decreed certain happenings that resulted in his realising his ambition and pursuing his chosen career when he might have had no other option but to take the emigrant ship to England.

Frank Vickerman, a native of Stroud in Gloucestershire decided to switch his wool business from Yorkshire to Dublin. Jackie O'Brien, who combined farming with his wool business in the Fermoy area of County Cork, became his principal agent in the South of Ireland. Now Jackie was a born character, moving at ease in racing circles and it was only natural that he should become part of the Vincent O'Brien set-up. Indeed, the first time O'Brien horses were transported by plane from Shannon to Bristol for the 1949 Cheltenham Festival meeting, Phonsie O'Brien recalls that Jackie "came along for the fun and 'the craic'".

"He had a face like Barry Fitzgerald", said Phonsie. "The last memory I have of him is of walking into the bar of the Grand Hotel in Fermoy and there was the bould Jackie sitting up on a high stool and a terrier on another stool beside him – with a cigar stuck in its mouth".

Hunting and going to point-to-point meetings represented for him part of the very essence of life. But at the same time he was an excellent judge of horseflesh and kept some point-to-pointers himself. One he picked out – China Cottage – won the Champion Hunters' Chase at Mullacurry with P. P. Hogan in the saddle and P. P. recalled for me: "You'd think he had won the Cheltenham Gold Cup, he was so full of himself after that success as an owner. I was happy to ride for him any time he asked, as there was no finer or more generous character".

Frank Vickerman's son, Brian, was serving with the British Army in the desert campaign against Rommel in North Africa. Frank, who at that stage was not into racing himself, thought it would be nice to give him a few horses as a welcoming-home present.

Jackie O'Brien had purchased six yearlings at give-away prices by today's standards, the reason being that the bottom had fallen out of the export market for Irish horses once racing was badly affected in Britain for the period of the War and the Cheltenham Festival meeting was suspended in 1942.

Sadly, Brian Vickerman never did return from North Africa. He died of malaria.

It was revealed to me in Churchtown in the summer of '97 that Vincent O'Brien, then at his wits end as to where he should turn to make a living, even contemplated for a time setting up as a butcher in Buttevant. There is, of course, no confirmation of this but it shows that he could easily have been lost to the training profession.

Jackie O'Brien suggested to Frank Vickerman that he give at least a couple of the yearlings to Vincent O'Brien to train. Vincent's budding talent was known to the wool agent from Fermoy, for he was a judge not only of horseflesh but also of trainers and jockeys.

Thus Vincent was approached by Jackie O'Brien at Limerick Junction races in September of 1943 and asked if he would like to train a few horses for Frank Vickerman.

"I had no doubt about training as the career I should pursue once Jackie (O'Brien) made that approach to me", said Vincent as he recalled what was perhaps one of the most fateful moments of all in his life.

But the movement of his star in the hands of his Maker did not end there.

Frank Vickerman, in fact, was to become the man who would help put Vincent on the map not just on the domestic front but at Cheltenham. The year it all started was 1944.

But first in 1943 as he started out on his own as a trainer, Vincent sent out only one runner – and it was a winner. Oversway, running in his own name and with Noel Sleator in the saddle, took the Elton Plate, a nine-furlong Flat race worth £74 at Limerick Junction by one-and-a-half lengths from Galway Girl. The winner was returned at 6-1. Oversway was sold by Vincent to Archie Willis, who sent him to the Curragh to be trained by Aubrey Brabazon's father, Cecil.

✳   ✳   ✳

Now in 1944 at the age of 27 Vincent – an unknown really – made the big-name Curragh trainers rub their eyes in astonishment and at the same time landed his first important betting coup as a public trainer in his own right when he sent out the winners of the Irish Autumn Double – Drybob and Good Days.

Drybob (Morny Wing), starting at 20-1, actually dead-heated with Dawross (Jimmy Eddery) in the Cambridgeshire. That was on October 7th at the Curragh. Then on November 4th Good Days, with Morny Wing again in the saddle, beat Free Trade, the 6-1 favourite, by a neck to win the Cesarewitch at odds of 20-1(the race had been transferred to the Phoenix Park from the Curragh).

Vincent did not have the resources to have a good old-fashioned tilt at the ring himself on Drybob and Good Days but he advised Frank Vickerman that both horses were ready to run for their lives. Frank had £10 each-way at odds of 800-1 the double.

Looking back over a half-a-century later, Vincent said: "There was a part of me that found it difficult to believe that such a double could come off. So I modestly said to myself, 'I'll have £2 each way'".

If Drybob had won outright instead of dead-heating, Frank Vickerman's winnings would have come to £10,000 and Vincent's to £2,000. In the end they had to settle for £5,000 and £1,000 respectively. Yes, that dead-heat in the Cambridgeshire made a lot of difference, as the odds were halved. Few at the Curragh and at the Phoenix Park on Cambridgeshire Day and Cesarewitch Day in '44 were aware that Vincent O'Brien was repeating with Drybob and Good Days what he had through his father already achieved with Solford and Astrometer. The bookies, as we have seen, never realised it. They concluded that it was then that the "unknown" from out of Churchtown had arrived when, in fact, he had been there before and "done" it. Those who caught the full blast of Vickerman's tilt at the double saw it in their satchels!

Now Vincent had got the nest-egg that would make a world of difference to him (when you realise that £2 a week was the starting salary for a junior reporter on a provincial paper in 1950, you will see that the £1,000 that he netted in his bet on the double was a lot of bread in 1944).

More important still, it was out of the £5,000 he netted that Frank Vickerman acquired Cottage Rake in due course and started the cycle that would see Vincent become the "King" of Cheltenham for well over a decade.

The victory of Solford under 9st 9lbs in the 1938 Irish Cambridgeshire had proved to Vincent that a good horse can shoulder weight and still win and in the case of Astrometer's Irish Cesarewitch triumph in 1941, he learned that a three-year-old could win against older horses in a big field in a handicap.

In 1950 Hatton's Grace would win the Irish Cesarwewitch with 10st. and the same season Knock Hard put up an excellent weight-carrying performance when taking the Irish Lincolnshire.

Always Vincent was learning and putting what he learned to good account later.

In between Drybob dead-heating for the Irish Cambridgeshire and Good Days winning the Irish Cesarewitch, Vincent sent out Wren Boy from Churchtown on October 12th, 1944 to gain his first success under National Hunt Rules by taking a hurdle race at Limerick Junction worth £74. The owner of the winner was W. J. Gleeson.

Aubrey Brabazon was in the saddle when Vincent won his first steeplechase on June 14, 1945 with Panay in the Templemore Plate at Thurles. The owner of Panay was given as "Mr D. G. B. O'Brien" but in reality it was Frank Vickerman (it was possible then to register an assumed name with the Turf Club). By the time Cottage Rake became his property, he was proud to be listed as the owner of this champion chaser.

✳   ✳   ✳

Vincent was able to start on his own as a trainer without acquiring the land for gallops and incurring the cost of building stables as his step-brother Donal rented the gallops and boxes at Churchtown to him that had been utilised by Dan. Later Vincent would rent extra land from the Lynch family of Cregane.

Donal and Vincent got on very well together. The Emergency saw both of them joining the Local Defence Force (LDF), Ireland's equivalent of the Home Guard in Britain. Dermot was in the Army, a Lieutenant serving in County Kerry – "You could say I went to university in Kerry", he said with a smile.

"For the Emergency I was in the Waterville area, guarding the cable station on Valentia. The late Bill Shanks was a comrade-in-arms and close friend of mine. They were great days".

Vincent encouraged those working in the stables – Danny O'Sullivan and his brother, Jimmy, and Maurice O'Callaghan – to do their bit for Ireland, as the saying went. Eamon de Valera as Taoiseach (Prime Minister) had decided on a policy of neutrality and got the full backing of the people in the General Elections during the period of the Second World War. The Opposition Parties in the Dail also supported the Republic's neutral stance, though quietly behind the scenes Dev bent over backwards to facilitate Britain in several ways and in days of a heavily-censored press no one was any the wiser (for example, if a British pilot had to make a forced landing on the Republic's territory or eject himself from his plane, he was spirited over the Border and back to Britain whereas a German pilot in similar circumstances ended up behind bars for the duration).

The LDF were willing to "die for flag and country", if needs be, though the means at their disposal and at the disposal of the regular Army also were pathetic when viewed beside the might of the German Army. It would have been like an elephant stamping on a mouse. Jack Murphy of Churchtown, who was in the LDF with his brother, Bill, said that they had only six rifles between the whole unit. He laughed when he recalled "Lord Haw Haw" saying one night that when Hitler was finished with Churchill, he would "deal with de Valera's cabbage garden".

The stories that grew up around the LDF were made for music hall comedians, as with the Home Guard. I recall my old Editor on the *Tipperary Star,* Bill Myles telling of a group of new recruits being addressed in a packed hall in some rural town one night and a chap in the back row suddenly shouting out: "When are ye giving out the boots!".

Vincent O'Brien, in his brown LDF uniform, would have learned from Sergeant Flaherty of the regular Army how to throw a hand grenade – "A big moment when we were shown how to pull out the pin", said Jack Murphy. Jimmy O'Sullivan recalled the big manoeuvres that were held at one stage involving both the Army and LDF. "I remember the 'enemy' advancing and we were told that if they crossed Mallow bridge, we were beaten".

On another occasion, a plane crash-landed in a field that was used as gallops by Vincent O'Brien. "John Sheehy and myself, dressed in our LDF outfits, guarded the plane through the night until regular Irish Army personnel arrived at around 6.30 a.m. We didn't ride work at all that day", said Jimmy.

Jimmy recalled the days of compulsory tillage, the shortage of tea and sugar, the rationing coupons. "It was all brown bread, mostly coffee, very little tea, though most people preferred tea to coffee. There were even clothes coupons but you had plenty of those as there was no rush to buy new clothes then. You could hardly get a cigarette for love nor money and people improvised making their own".

A hurling tournament for fifteen suitlengths brought out a fervour and a passion in the competing teams that would have done justice to the battle for the All-Ireland title itself. But then how many hurlers could have afforded a new suit in that era.

Those enjoying the benefits of the current boom days for the Irish economy who think nothing of paying £400 to £500 and more in one of the "in" places in Dublin for a suit will never understand what it was like back in the Emergency.

But before the advent of television and before package holidays in the sun became the norm, people learned how to entertain themselves. And in the very simplicity of life, there was an enjoyment derived that those who have become slaves to "the box" and to the video era will never find.

Always one for the open spaces, Vincent O'Brien loved nothing better than to go out shooting in season. Jimmy O'Sullivan remembers carrying the bag. "Vincent was a great shot", he said simply.

"Yes, a wonderful natural shot", Dermot concurred – and he was speaking from experience as he often went out with Vincent.

It was a great area for duck, snipe, pheasant, woodcock. The pheasant season opened on November 1st, the duck season on September 1st. It was said of Vincent that he was adept at bagging a pair – that is of snipe, the true test of a great shot.

Vincent also loved fishing and it suited admirably that part of him that loved to be alone. Early on he fished the Awbeg – trout and pike – but later he had his favourite stretches along the Blackwater, wonderful for salmon fishing. "I would say that fishing has always been his favourite pastime", said Dermot. "He trained himself to cut himself off from the pressures of training and he discovered early on that there was no better way of doing it than indulging in a day's fishing".

Later, of course, he would discover golf and this was another way – an outstanding way – of cutting himself off from pressure. As he passed the milestone of his 80th birthday in April '97, he was still getting in nine holes every day.

Following the hunt was an integral part of life for him almost from the cradle. He hunted with his father and his friends and he continued to hunt in County Tipperary when he moved to Ballydoyle. A day out hunting was always special.

When Vincent became the Master of Ballydoyle, when his great triumphs as a Flat trainer brought a mystique around him that put him on a plane apart, when his name was known globally, it was difficult for many people to imagine that in his Churchtown days, he was very much an ordinary chap who merged easily into the local community. It was the natural thing to do that he should join the LDF. It was the natural thing to play cards in the long winter evenings, get involved in a "25" drive maybe for a turkey at Christmas or in poker sessions with friends. The rich melodious sound of Cork voices around the card table, as the banter and the craic evolved with each passing hand, identified the warmth of friendship, a cameraderie that was special.

Hatton's Grace (No. 4) coming at the last to beat National Spirit (inside) in the 1950 Champion Hurdle, with Martin Molony on the extreme left challenging on Harlech. *Below:* Aubrey Brabazon returns to an Irish roar as Mrs Moya Keogh leads in Hatton's Grace, with Vincent O'Brien directly behind wearing hat. To Moya Keogh's right (wearing a hat) is her husband Harry. The crowds did not compare then with the overwhelming emotional scenes in the amphitheatre-style winner's enclosure engendered by the epic triumphs of Dawn Run (Gold Cup, 1986), Danoli (Sun Alliance Novices Hurdle, 1994) and Imperial Call (Gold Cup '96).

PART THREE

MASTER OF THE JUMPS

16

"Begod 'Tis Cottage Rake!"

The year 1945 was to be in many ways the most fateful in Vincent O'Brien's life. It was the year that Dr Timoty 'Otto' Vaughan of Mallow approached him and asked him to train Cottage Rake for him. Dr Vaughan had acquired the horse from his brother, Dick, who bred him at his Hunting Hall Stud in County Cork.

'The Rake' might well have been sold before he ever arrived at the Churchtown stable but fortunately for Vincent he was brought back to Mallow, the good Doctor having failed to dispose of him at Goff's Sales (then held in Ballsbridge).

Cottage Rake was a six-year-old when he came under Vincent's wing in '45. 'Otto' Vaughan appeared to be of the state of mind that once he had won a bumper (amateur Flat race) or maiden hurdle, the horse would be put on the market again. Vincent sent Cottage Rake to Limerick on December 27th, 1945 where he won the County Maiden Hurdle with consummate ease at 10-1, ridden by Danny O'Sullivan, following this up by taking a bumper (Corinthian Maiden Plate) at Leopardstown in February, 1946 with P.P. Hogan in the saddle.

Dr Vaughan was very anxious to cash in after these two unbeaten runs. Thwarted more than once by veterinary reports on the horse, he was convinced that someone would be prepared to take a chance. It was now Vincent's job to find a prospective buyer, who would be willing to leave Cottage Rake with him. He realised after the impressive Leopardstown win that he had a potential champion on his hands – a horse that could put him on an entirely new plane.

And he realised, too, that Cottage Rake was bred to go right to the top. For one thing he was by the outstanding sire of jumpers, Cottage. And, secondly, there was Stella blood in his veins on the dam's (Hartingo) side and Vincent, with his expert knowledge of breeding, knew that Stella was a foundation mare who had to transmit class.

Vincent now turned to Frank Vickerman, who still retained happy memories of the Drybob/Good Days Irish Autumn Double coup, and he agreed to purchase the horse. He made out a cheque for £1,000 to Dr Vaughan as a down payment, only to get word from Vincent that another veterinary examination had revealed a minor problem of rheumatism in the shoulder. Frank Vickerman decided to cancel the cheque but then learned that Dr Vaughan had already cashed it.

"So Frank Vickerman had no option but to take the horse. Could anything have been as fortunate as that?", mused Vincent aloud.

✳　　✳　　✳

Cottage Rake was Vincent O'Brien's first-ever challenger at Cheltenham and he was the horse that started the golden era for him that made him 'King' of the Festival meeting for a decade. He was the horse too that put him firmly on the map with racing followers in Britain. Suddenly, they began to recognise a unique talent. It was no longer a case of Vincent remarking, as he did after his father's death five years early, "Nobody knows me".

Understandably he was tense and very uptight on Gold Cup Day '48. So taught, in fact, that he actually said to Aubrey Brabazon, who had no ride in the race before the Gold Cup, that he was going to the bar to have a brandy, adding "I think I could do with one".

"Normally Vincent would never take a drink like that before a race", recalled Aubrey. "So you can imagine how he must have felt when he decided to try and ease his tension with a stiff brandy".

Vincent viewed the climax of the race from down at the final fence. He saw Happy Home in the hands of Martin Molony and Cottage Rake, with Aubrey Brabazon in the saddle rise to it together. He saw Happy Home come away a length to a length-and-a-half in front after the awesome manner in which Martin Molony drove him into it. With no racecourse commentary in those days, he could only guess from the tumult and the shouting that it was a terrific battle up the hill to the line and he could only hope that Cottage Rake's finishing speed had enabled him to get up.

His heart was in his mouth as he made his way back to the stands. "It was when I saw Aubrey touching his cap to acknowledge the cheers of the crowd that I knew we had pulled it off".

Aubrey Brabazon was immortalised in a ballad of the period just as the balladeers would sing of Dawn Run's never-to-be-forgotten Gold Cup triumph 38 years later and Peter O'Sullivan-style commentaries on how the gallant mare got up to win became the order at gatherings of racing folk.

Aubrey's up, the money's down,
The frightened bookies quake,
"Come on, me lads, and give a cheer,
Begod 'tis Cottage Rake!"

Aubrey showed me the menu from Dublin's famous Jammet's Restaurant (long since gone) where the celebratory dinner was held on Easter Monday night, March 29th, 1948. The opening course was appropriately styled "Le

Saumon Fumé Churchtown" and this was followed by "Le Pottage Vincent". The main dish was a choice between "Les Paupiettes de Sole Cheltenham" and "Les Pouissins à la Rake garnis".

They drank Moet et Chandon 1938 and the toasts were to "Ireland", "The Horse", "The Trainer" and "The Jockey". On the back of the menu they listed "The Rake's Progress" to that first Cheltenham Gold Cup win on March 4th, 1948. Among the autographs on "The Brab's" menu was that of Vincent O'Brien.

The 1948 race marked the first pulsating Cheltenham duel in Aubrey Brabazon's *mano a mano* with Martin Molony – two outstandingly gifted horsemen and two jockeys who did not have to use the whip to get that winning drive from their mounts, either over the jumps or on the Flat.

Martin Molony always rode long because it came natural to him to ride that way and Vincent O'Brien unhesitatingly referred admiringly to his power in a finish. Vincent had nothing but the highest admiration also for the supreme touch, the superb control he exercised with his hands and the horseman's brain of Aubrey Brabazon. Martin and Aubrey were horsemen through and through.

Cottage Rake took the Emblem Handicap Chase under 12st 7lbs at Manchester and the King George VI Chase at Kempton on his way to winning the 1949 Gold Cup by two lengths from Cool Customer, who, in the hands of P.J. (Joe) Murphy – later to suffer fatal injuries in a fall in a chase – had looked all over the winner as he led going into the last. Again it was that brilliant burst of finishing speed that won it for 'The Rake.'

He had a very tough race, having recovered just in time from a bout of equine flu. This setback would definitely have prevented him taking his place in the field had not Gold Cup Day been lost during the Festival meeting because of frost. The race was postponed for four weeks. The extra month provided the precious time for Vincent O'Brien to ensure that Cottage Rake was fit enough to do himself justice.

When Cottage Rake completed the three-timer by winning the Gold Cup again in 1950, it was his most convincing victory of all. He won pulling up by ten lengths.

"Knowing the horse's terrific acceleration, I took a big gamble that day and it came off", recalled Aubrey Brabazon." Again, Martin Molony, this time on Lord Bicester's Finnure, represented the main danger. Finnure had beaten us in the King George at Kempton and I considered that I had not ridden a clever race that day and must use different tactics next time.

"I decided that the best thing to do was to turn on the speed at the most unlikely place – namely, rounding the sharp turn before the last regulation at the top of the hill. Luck was on my side. Martin's horse made a mistake just then and, aided by the downhill slope, my mount flew for about 100 yards to go ten lengths in front.

"Perhaps Finnure did not like the rather slow gallop early on or Cheltenham did not suit him quite as well as Kempton. In the final analysis, Cottage Rake had it over all opposition once it came to the last at

Cheltenham and over three memorable seasons his finishing speed proved the trump card."

✳   ✳   ✳

How good was Cottage Rake? Certainly not as great as Golden Miller or Arkle but, in the opinion of T.P. Burns, he had still to be rated "a great chaser". T.P. posed the question: "How many horses have won three successive Gold Cups?".

Vincent O'Brien himself ranked him with Prince Regent, Golden Miller and Arkle as "the greatest winners of the Gold Cup". He argued that he had more speed than Golden Miller, Prince Regent or Arkle – the speed that enabled him to win the Naas November Handicap over twelve furlongs when still a novice chaser and also the Irish Cesarewitch.

However, Aubrey Brabazon would only rate Cottage Rake third – after Golden Miller (five Gold Cup triumphs from 1932-'36) and Arkle (three successive victories from 1964-'66).

Martin Molony contended that Cottage Rake could not give weight away like Prince Regent or Arkle. "Prince Regent was able to win handicaps with 12st 7lbs on his back and was conceding 42lbs to Knight's Crest when I rode my mother's horse to a length victory in the 1944 Irish Grand National. Likewise he was giving away 24lbs to Lovely Cottage when beaten into third place in the 1946 Aintree Grand National".

Martin went on to stress that Arkle could carry welter weights to victory. "I remember meeting the trainer of The Brasher, a good chaser, before the 1965 Whitbread Chase. The Brasher was carrying 10st and his trainer was confident he would run a very good race and even entertained hopes of beating Arkle at the weights, as Arkle was carrying 12st 7lbs. But though The Brasher looked to be there with a very good chance at the last, Arkle suddenly sprinted away and won handsomely, despite the concession of 35lbs".

There is little doubt that but for the intervention of the Second World War, Prince Regent would have won three-in-a-row and could well have completed a five-timer. The Tom Dreaper-trained gelding was actually eleven when he won the Gold Cup by five lengths in 1946 with Tim Hyde in the saddle. Supposing he arrived in 1942, the year he won the Irish Grand National under 12st 7lbs – what then? Yes, he could have won the Cup from 1942 to 1946, equalling Golden Miller's record.

In any assessment of Cottage Rake, it must not be overlooked that Silver Fame, named by Martin Molony as "the greatest chaser I rode", could not beat Vincent O'Brien's charge at levels. And 'The Rake' beat Silver Fame in the Emblem Chase in 1948 conceding 5lbs.

Silver Fame was a splendidly bold chestnut who won 26 races during his career. He took the Gold Cup as a twelve-year-old in 1951 when he did not have to contend with Cottage Rake, Martin Molony guiding him to a short-head win over Greenogue.

Cottage Rake was buried in McCarthy's field in Fermoy, the field to which he retired when he developed tendon trouble after finishing fourth under 12st 7lbs in the 1950 Irish Grand National.

Vincent O'Brien expressed regret that some kind of commemorative stone was not erected where Cottage Rake was buried. The idea of erecting a bronze of the great chaser was mooted after the third of his Gold Cup triumphs but it never came to fruition. Aubrey Brabazon was sent a poem by Ellen Sheehan of Mallow titled simply "Cottage Rake" and it captures the reason why in witty fashion:

In memory of this gallant steed
A figure of bronze was planned
To stand outside Mallow Station
But the project was duly banned
"A horse would be out of place"
Said a Councillor at the time
"Might even be disrespectful;
To the nearby Marian Shrine"
The Rake's sponsor most indignant
Full of impatience and remose
Shouted "Since when did the Virgin Mary
Take umbrage to a horse"

Yet the bronze was never placed
To the matchless Cottage Rake
Who took the Gold Cup at Cheltenham
Three times without a break.

❋ ❋ ❋

Vincent O'Brien won his fourth Gold Cup when Knock Hard, the horse with the doubtful heart, triumphed in 1953 in the colours of Mrs Moya Keogh. Martin Molony, if his career had not been summarily ended by that fall at Thurles in 1951 would almost certainly have been on him. As it was, the ride went to his brother, Tim, who according to Nat McNabb "conjured victory from the impossible".

Knock Hard was never a natural chaser, never really in love with the game but once he jumped the last he had the speed of a Flat horse to carry him to success, though, of course, he could never rank in the same league as Cottage Rake.

Vincent remembers him, however, with a special fondness for the gambles he landed, such as the Irish Lincolnshire in 1950 and the Coventry Plate win at Wolverhampton in 1952, at a time when the stable needed to gamble successfully.

Knock Hard, a 5-1 chance, was cantering under Phonsie O'Brien when he fell two out in the 1952 Gold Cup, the year that Miss Dorothy Paget's Mont

Tremblant won at 8-1 for Fulke Walwyn and Dave Dick (Freebooter, the 1950 Grand National winner started favourite).

The money lost by the connections of the Ballydoyle stable through that costly fall was recouped with interest the following year when Knock Hard made amends at 11-2 – but those with weak hearts and high blood pressure certainly suffered and had reason to be grateful for the brilliant riding of Tim Molony.

Knock Hard faced a field that included the 1950 winner, Mont Tremblant; also Teal, who would win the Aintree Grand National in 1952; E.S.B, who would win at Aintree in 1956; Halloween, the mount of Fred Winter; Mariner's Log; Galloway Braes and Rose Park.

"I viewed the race with Vincent and Jacqueline", said Nat McNabb. "There was fog about that day and, as they started down the hill, I could make out Mont Tremblant, Rose Park and Galloway Braes dominating events at the head of the field. Knock Hard had dropped right back. We were mystified. He seemed out of it at that point. Tim Molony was driving him. Suddenly, the horse started to pick up and came from a seemingly hopeless position to be there with a chance at the last. The odds, however, were still very much against him winning".

Vincent O'Brien took up the story: "Knock Hard produced his best leap at the last and, seeing that there were no more fences in front of him, decided to put his head down and run. He stormed up the hill and had five lengths to spare at the finishing post over Halloween, who had come through beaten horses from a long way back. It was an incredible performance".

Knock Hard never recaptured the glory of that day and failed to win in ten further outings before his retirement, Vincent accepting that there was a sad falling-away in form. He failed to figure in the first three in the 1954 Gold Cup when starting at 9-4.

Knock Hard (Tim Molony) winning the 1953 Gold Cup with Mont Tremblant (Dave Dick), left, fourth and Galloway Braes (Bert Morrow) third.

17

Hats Off To
Hatton's Grace

Martin Molony expressed no doubt about it whatsoever. Hatton's Grace was unquestionably the best hurdler he rode, though he was not on him when he won the Champion Hurdle three years in succession (1948-'50). Martin noted that "Hatton's Grace proved his versatility by winning the Irish Cesarewitch two years running (1949-'50) and also the Irish Lincoln (1949)".

If Frank Vickerman was a key figure in helping to put Vincent O'Brien on the Cheltenham map through Cottage Rake, the Keoghs, Harry and Moya boosted Vincent's reputation still further when they decided to switch three horses – Hatton's Grace, Royal Tan and Castledermot – from Barney Nugent to the Churchtown stable. Knock Hard would follow later.

Harry Keogh was in the manufacturing business in Dublin and Hatton's Grace ran in his wife's colours. Initially, this versatile performer who would retire with eighteen victories under his belt (twelve National Hunt successes and six on the Flat) was owned in partnership with Colonel Dan Corry of the Irish Army jumping team, who had acquired him from John Kirwan, the County Kilkenny trainer (Kirwan had bought him as a yearling for 18 guineas from his breeder, J.W.A. Harris of the Victor Stud, County Tipperary).

Vincent O'Brien told Harry and Moya Keogh that he would only take Hatton's Grace, Royal Tan and Castledermot on condition that they would not see a racecourse for quite some time. "I recall Vincent saying that he was prepared to wait a year with the trio, if necessary", said Mrs Keogh.

"Vincent was determined that he would be given time to build up the horses we sent him. He wanted to do his own thing. It was in the summer of 1948 that the horses were sent to him and he did not let us see them until October. Vincent's patience was tremendous and, of course, it paid off handsomely".

Hatton's Grace did not see a racecourse for five months and had just two outings in 1949 before he won the Champion Hurdle for the first time.

Small and most unimposing, he was an eight-year-old when he joined

Vincent O'Brien in the summer of 1948. It was an outstanding feat of training by Vincent to turn him out to win his first Champion Hurdle at the age of nine and maintain his appetite for the game so well that he completed the three-timer at eleven and meanwhile also had some notable wins in big handicaps on the Flat.

✳   ✳   ✳

National Spirit had won the Champion Hurdle two years running when Vincent sent Hatton's Grace over to take on the Vic Smith-trained gelding. Just as Desert Orchid would become four decades later, National Spirit was a great favourite with the racing public in Britain and was a very warm order to complete the hat-trick. On the face of it, Hatton's Grace hardly inspired confidence to be the one to dethrone the champion, as he had been unplaced at 20-1 in the previous year's Champion Hurdle when ridden by Martin Molony.

"Hatton's Grace was with Barney Nugent then", recalled Nat McNabb. "He had won at the Leopardstown Christmas meeting and then a handicap hurdle at Naas and was showing such good form at home that Barney Nugent decided to let him take his chance at Cheltenham.

"Because of a strike, it was not possible to send him over by plane. He had to go by boat, from Rosslare to Fishguard, and was housed in a shed for three days before he resumed his journey to Cheltenham. He didn't eat up, which wasn't surprising after what he had been through. He finished fifth or sixth and I said to myself, 'if he can put up a performance like that after hardly eating for three days, then he must win the Champion Hurdle next year'. My mind was made up there and then".

Nat McNabb went on to recall that when the horses entered the parade ring before the 1949 Champion Hurdle many people who had not taken much note of Hatton's Grace before that were turned completely off him. He drifted out to 16-1 in the betting before coming back to start at 100-7. "In fact, he was rather miserable looking compared to National Spirit, a fine big horse. And if the English thought National Spirit was a certainty to complete the three-timer, they were entitled to think so on his performances in the two previous runnings of the race".

Significantly, however, even though Hatton's Grace had been unplaced in his opening run of the season at Naas, he had later won the Rathcoole Handicap Hurdle under 12st 7lbs at the same course. It was a month before the Champion Hurdle and he started at 7-4.

"They told us we'd never beat National Spirit", recalled Vincent O'Brien, even though some critics were saying that at the age of eight, National Spirit was getting a bit old. Against that Hatton's Grace was a year older and not many were prepared to back him to win a Champion Hurdle at that stage of his career. Hatton's Grace, showing real pace from the last flight, won easily by six lengths.

The following year he started at 5-2 and this time National Spirit, in blinkers, led him to the last flight but made a bad mistake and Hatton's

Grace came away to display again a fine burst of finishing speed, winning by one-and-a-half lengths from Harlech, ridden by Martin Molony.

Aubrey Brabazon was the successful jockey in 1949 and '50. In 1951 Tim Molony was in the saddle. National Spirit again led into the last but blundered in an exact replica of the previous year's error, allowing Hatton's Grace through to win by five lengths from the French horse Pyrrhus III in the very heavy going.

✳　　✳　　✳

Less than a month after winning his first Champion Hurdle, Vincent O'Brien had the inspiration to have a go at the Irish Lincoln with Hatton's Grace – something very few trainers would contemplate doing. Vincent, however, knew the capabilities of Mrs Keogh's horse and knew also that even with 9st. he was a betting proposition. The O'Brien stable got good odds to their money and eventually Hatton's Grace came down to 6-1. He fully justified Vincent's confidence.

The jockey who had the ride was Morny Wing, one of the best Flat riders in an era marked by tremendous competition between a clutch of jockeys of exceptional quality. Morny Wing (22 Irish Classics), Tommy Burns (21), Joe Canty (17) and Martin Quirke (9) proved beyond any shadow of doubt that they were men for the big occasion.

Wing, who excelled on two-year-olds, hailed from Yorkshire and served his apprenticeship in England. He fell in love with Ireland and never went back. Six victories in the Irish Derby on Ballyheron, Waygood, Rock Star, Rosewell, Windsor Slipper and Bright News helping to cement the relationship.

Having hit the bookies hard with that successful gamble on Hatton's Grace in the 1949 Irish Lincoln, Vincent O'Brien went for another major coup on Knock Hard in the Irish Cesarewitch later that year. Ironically, Martin Molony on Hatton's Grace foiled it when he won against the expectations of the stable, carrying 9st 2lbs.

Martin Molony tends to play it down. "I got a marvellous run on the inside. That horse had courage".

But it was generally reckoned to have been one of his greatest-ever finishes on the Flat as he won by a short head from Penny On The Jack (to which Hatton's Grace was conceding 36lbs) and a neck from Pelorus (getting 35 lbs).

"We had worked Knock Hard at home with Hatton's Grace and he had pulverised him for speed, so we knew we had something to go to war with", recalled Vincent O'Brien, who noted that in the race itself Knock Hard would be meeting Hatton's Grace on 10lbs better terms than in the gallop.

And Phonsie added: "We concluded that Knock Hard was a stone-cold certainty if held up to make the best use of his acceleration in the final furlong".

But Hatton's Grace was one of those horses who didn't give of his best on the gallops. He was a different animal entirely on a racecourse.

There was a famous council of war at the Jockey Hall restaurant on the Curragh at lunch-time on the day of the race – Vincent, Dermot and Phonsie gathering with Harry Keogh and Dermot McDowell (a great friend of the Keoghs) and Nat McNabb and Bob Mulrooney, the duo Vincent entrusted to get the money on.

The tactical plan decided over lunch was that they would first go in on Hatton's Grace in order to put out the price on Knock Hard. And they were going to make sure that those who always had tabs on Bob Mulrooney and Nat McNabb would be left in no doubt that Hatton's Grace was the one the stable was on.

The overall strategy worked like a dream. Hatton's Grace came down to 3-1 as Knock Hard eased to 6-1, to 7-1 and even to 10-1 on some boards.

Then as Vincent's trusted lieutenants "went to war", Nat McNabb and Bob Mulrooney in the van, the bookies were overwhelmed with the rush of money on Knock Hard, whose price came down to evens while now Hatton's Grace drifted out to 8-1.

"Vincent's instructions to Bert Holmes were not to hit the front on Knock Hard until inside the final furlong", recalled Nat McNabb. "The horse, however, was going so easily turning into the straight that Holmes let him go on. Hatton's Grace was a terrific stayer and he caught Knock Hard, who was actually beaten out of a place in the end."

Five months later Vincent O'Brien recouped the losses on Knock Hard with a brilliantly-executed stroke. And he showed tremendous shrewdness in the way he outwitted the bookies. He ran Knock Hard in a novice chase at Naas – which he won, incidentally – a fortnight before the Irish Lincoln. Frankly, as Vincent himself said, the aim was "to get a better price about the horse in the Lincoln". How many would believe that a horse that ran in a novice chase would win the Lincoln carrying 8st 12lbs?

✳   ✳   ✳

Vincent O'Brien could easily have made it four Champion Hurdles – as he made it four Gold Cups.

Stroller was heavily supported down to 7-2 to win the 1956 Champion Hurdle, despite the fact that the Ryan Price-trained Clair Soleil, the 5-2 favourite was unbeaten in England (having won twice in France). T.P. Burns said to me that this was the race that left him with the proudest memory of all of his days associated with Vincent O'Brien – even though defeat was his lot in the end.

The two fought out a truly magnificent duel to the third last hurdle after the flattering Price Charlemagne (Bryan Marshall) had cracked. T.P. brought Stroller upsides the favourite. Fred Winter, however, riding like a man possessed, responded by getting a superb leap out of Clair Soleil. Burns was almost level again going into the second last. Again Clair Soleil came away in front and was half-a-length up as they came to the ultimate flight. Now T.P., calling upon all his experience, settled Stroller for a supreme effort and got back some of the lost ground. But it was Clair Soleil that landed first on the Flat.

The Cotswolds echoed to the sustained roar of the crowd. Sixty yards from the post T.P. had brought Stroller level and the odds then were on Vincent O'Brien's charge coming out on top. However, the superior stamina of Clair Soleil proved the deciding factor and he came again to win – by only a head, with Cruachain third.

Little wonder then that Stroller was all the rage with the Irish contingent the following year. He was backed from 3-1 to 2-1 favouritism. There was no pace early on and the field was tightly bunched at the top of the hill. Then as the runners bore left for the swing towards home, Stroller was badly baulked and three out was caught by that swinging hurdle, slipped up on landing and was deemed in the records to have fallen, when the story might have been an entirely different one if Lady Fortune was smiling on him on the day.

The race, incidentally, went to the 100-9 shot, Doorknocker, carrying the colours of Clifford Nicholson, and he had been trained by Paddy Sleator before going to W. Hall's stable.

The winning jockey was Harry Sprague who had the mount on Stroller when he was pulled out again two days later to run in the Spa Hurdle (3 miles) with 12st 5lbs on the his back, T.P. Burns was on the other representative from the Vincent O'Brien stable, Lucky Dome, carrying 11st 2lbs and on the face of it much better in on the handicap.

Tipperary vet, D.J. O'Keeffe was with a group of friends, including Jim Blake from Golden, a great friend of Vincent's, who was drowned while on holidays in Tangiers trying to save someone who had got into difficulties (in the Vincent O'Brien section in the museum at Leopardstown one can see the famous picture of Vincent, Martin Molony and Jim Blake together on an Alpine holiday, all three wearing dark sun glasses).

"Jim Blake had it from the horse's mouth that Lucky Dome was the one," recalled D.J. O'Keeffe. "We were having a bad meeting, having backed a clatter of losers including Stroller in the 'Champion' and Sam Brownthorn in the Gold Cup; he was runner-up, with Toss Taaffe riding, to the favourite Limber Hill. So we went for a touch on Lucky Dome to get out.

"Having done the business, I toured around the betting ring and noted that Stroller had suddenly come down from 5-1 to 7-2 while Lucky Dome, which had opened at 5-2, had drifted out to 3-1 and then 4-1. I went back to my friends to tell them but was told not to worry – their information was correct.

"Harry Sprague got up in the last stride to win by a short head from Kilkilogue from the Bobby Patton stable – with Lucky Dome two lengths further away third. Lucky Dome may have been the one on the book and the one that was fancied as the O'Brien horses headed for Cheltenham that year but on the day Stroller, despite his weight, certainly proved the right one and made ample amends for those two Champion Hurdle defeats."

Incidentally, Stroller was owned by Harry Lane, whose colours had been carried to victory in the 1952 Grand National by Teal.

✳   ✳   ✳

In later years when the racing writers set Vincent O'Brien's record in the Gold Cup and Champion Hurdle side-by-side with his brilliant strike rate in the Classics and other major events on the Flat, it tended to overshadow how phenomenal was his dominance of the Gloucestershire Hurdle at the Festival meeting. It overshadowed too the fact that his 23 victories (including Cottage's Rake's second Gold Cup, which was not run at the Festival meeting) were achieved in just twelve years up to his decision to disperse all his National Hunt horses after Cheltenham 1959.

You have got to remember also that the Irish contingent looked to him to deliver and backed the fancied runners from his stable with the kind of confidence that ruled out any day of reckoning.

Already we have seen that he had ten victories in all in the Gloucestershire Hurdle (taking in the two legs) in the period 1952-'59. Vincent O'Brien named Saffron Tartan (winner of Division Two in 1957) as the best of his winners of this race and T.P. Burns said of him: "He was the best of them all, the finest novice that ever left the stable; he had the rest of the field stone cold from the top of the hill and beat Predominate as if he was a selling plater."

It is hardly surprising that both Vincent and T.P. Burns should rate Saffron Tartan so highly when one reflects on this horse's subsequent achievements and also those of the horse he pulverised, namely Predominate. When Vincent switched from training jumpers to concentrating completely on the Flat, Saffron Tartan was sent to Don Butchers, who trained him to win the 1961 Gold Cup in the hands of Fred Winter from the 1960 victor, Pas Seul, and Mandarin. And Mandarin was the winner in 1962 from Fortria and Duke Of York.

Predominate, for his part, was second in the Cesarewitch, won the Queen Alexandra Stakes, the Goodwood Stakes three years running and climaxed his career by taking the Goodwood Cup at nine. In all, the gelding won fourteen races worth over £17,000 in prize-money and he had the distinction of winning at Goodwood four years running.

From the moment Vincent began to make his mark at Cheltenham, the build-up of pressure in the stable at the turn of each New Year was awesome. "Cheltenhamitis" was how Dermot and Phonsie described it.

"No stone was left unturned in the count-down to Cheltenham to ensure that failure could not be laid at the door of human error," said Dermot. "Vincent was totally analytical in his approach to every facet of getting the horses ready for their particular races and he knew, of course, that the money would be going on them – big money – and in his mind there was no place for excuses once he believed that he had the material for the job. That is why the pressure was intense, terribly so.

"Vincent would be pretty uptight as his mind became totally fixed on the Festival meeting. Everything was geared to it. And, remember, to lift a race valued £8,000 meant winning a prize worth many times that amount today.

"There were no prizes in Ireland to compare with the Cheltenham events. Cheltenham also presented the opportunity for good old-fashioned tilts at the ring, before the English bookmakers came to really fear Vincent and began to quote very short prices – ridiculous at times – about some of the Festival challengers, especially in the Gloucestershire Hurdle. We really made money the first year Cottage Rake won the Gold Cup at 10-1 and also when Hatton's Grace, in 1949, took the first of his three successive Champion Hurdles at 100-7 (we had backed him, of course, ante-post at much longer odds than the S.P. price)."

Dermot recalled William Hill saying to Vincent and himself once: "Never back odds-on, boys. Always try and get a price to your money."

William Hill was not aware when he said that of the fact that Vincent had got a price to his money when he landed his first gamble at Clonmel on White Squirrel and when he brought off the Irish autumn double with Drybob and Good Days. In the days when he had to gamble to survive, no one could match Vincent in laying out a horse to win the race that was set as the primary target. And no one was better either at making the bookmakers reel as the ring hummed with the action as Vincent's trusted "lieutenants" moved in swiftly along the rails.

The greatest legacy Vincent left from those High Noon days at Cheltenham was his cementing of the aura that would subsequently surround the Festival meeting with the coming of each March. But we must not overlook either the roles of Tom Dreaper and Dan Moore in the forging of the special links the Irish have with the Festival meeting and why it was inevitable that it would grow and grow.

You have only to recall the great chasers that Dreaper sent over – Fortria, Flyingbolt, Fort Leney, Ben Stack and, of course, Prince Regent and the greatest of them all, Arkle. And Dan Moore challenging with L'Escargot, Tied Cottage and Inkslinger and paving the way for what his son, Arthur would achieve later.

These were the trail-blazers, these the men who left indelible footprints on the Cheltenham scene.

And subsequently Vincent O'Brien and P.J. 'Darkie' Prendergast would become trail-blazers on the Flat, pitching at the highest targets in England and proving that they were masters of their profession.

But when I walk each March through the gates of Prestbury Park and when I see the great green spread of the Cheltenham course, almost taking one's breath away with its majestic sweep, I cannot but reflect on the 1948-'59 era when Vincent O'Brien was the man the bookies feared most of all, when the boys who put up in The Plough and other hotels followed him fearlessly by day and talked of his genius over the cards at night in the long journeys into dawn. And because at heart the bulk of Irish racing followers are lovers of the jumping game, they view that time as special – special for what it created but special most of all for the excitement of onslaughts that rocked the ring and in the delivery there was a satisfaction that comes better still when it's Cheltenham.

18

'Mincemeat' Joe's Odyssy

'**M**incemeat' Joe Griffin never believed in doing things small. Whether it was in the Adelphi Hotel in Liverpool, on the boat back to Dublin or in the homecoming celebrations under the Rock of Cashel, he set a standard with his victory parties that would never be matched by any owner of a Grand National winner.

"Life's wonderful", he had told the world when at 36 he was styled the "Irish Mincemeat King" and his Redbreast Preserving Company was on the crest of the wave, turning over up to £2 million a year in exports – and that at the time was a lot of money coming into the country for a small exporter.

"Money for me is for spending and for making people happy", he asserted. "I have made a lot of people happy".

You can say that again!

When Early Mist won the 1953 Grand National, Joe gave up to £10,000 (more than the stake money at the time) in presents to the trainer, jockey and handlers of the horse and sent a dozen bottles of champagne into the jockeys' room. The mother-of-all-parties in the Adelphi cost £1,500, the Dublin Bay prawns being specially flown in for the occasion from the Irish capital and the asparagus from France to supplement the smoked salmon and turtle soup. "Bring on the champagne", he said – and they certainly did.

It was drinks all the way on the boat back with Joe making it a free bar for everyone and the hangers-on had a ball of a time. Later after the fall, he would say "I should have chosen my friends more carefully", but then he added "but I have no regrets about spending the money".

Those who had the good fortune to be there remember to this day the celebrations in Cashel when Early Mist came home in 1953 and Royal Tan the following year.

'Mincemeat' Joe went up on to the ledge between Davern's pub and Gannon's draper's shop (now The Man's Shop, owned by the renowned personality in the greyhound world, Pat Dalton) and announced: "The drinks are on me."

He indicated that he would pick up the tab in every pub in town. Naturally in '53 some of the pubs were rather wary of the offer but all those who took it up got paid down to the last penny the following week.

In 1954 every pub in town wanted to get in on the act and people came from far and near once word got around that 'Mincemeat' Joe was putting out the boat. It was certainly a night to remember as they sang and danced in the streets and saw the dawn coming up over The Rock.

But none of the publicans got paid that year as Joe's star was already on the way down. He would end up in the bankruptcy courts, suffer the heartbreak of the bailiffs going to Ballydoyle and impounding his horses, including Royal Tan and watch helplessly as all his other possessions – even down to his racing binoculars – were taken from him. Even his two Grand National trophies – gold cups each weighing 50 ounces – would be auctioned in Dublin.

However, in the days of wine and roses when the C.B.S. Flute & Tin Whistle Band led the victory parade into Cashel, 'Mincemeat' Joe, out there in front with Royal Tan, was the hero of the moment. Frank Gannon remembers how Bro Nolan had special sashes made for all the members of the Band – "30 or 40 or us".

"I remember how we walked behind the horse instead of ahead of him to ensure that we wouldn't frighten him with the sound of our tin whistles. I remember the bonfires blazing on the hills.

"I remember Joe Griffin making his victory speech from the very same ledge from which Dev had spoken during an election campaign. Joe would have seen the humour in that, he was such a born character. He got a tremendous reception from the crowd. What I remember most of all is that I drank 34 bottles of club orange and lemon and we were over the moon as it was all thanks to Joe."

Perhaps 'Mincemeat' Joe's proudest moment of all was when Early Mist was accorded a civic reception on his return to Dublin. Thousands turned out to watch as the horse was paraded through O'Connell Street to the Mansion House, where the Lord Mayor, Andy Clerkin, officiated. It culminated in the gelding receiving a pat on the neck from the Lord Mayor as Joe posed for photographs. (There was even an Early Mist chocolate bar specially produced showing the horse – circled – jumping the last at Aintree).

To be acclaimed like that by his native Dubliners represented the scaling of an Everest peak for 'Mincemeat' Joe, who was unquestionably one of the most colourful characters ever to hit the racing scene. He was small and stocky with twinkling eyes, the direct opposite of the archetype business tycoon, but with a sharp brain and that native Dublin cunning that made him see a good business opportunity. In the food shortages that persisted after the Second World War, the English hankered for 'goodies' that were taken for granted in Ireland. "Joe, we haven't seen mince pies for years," an English friend remarked to him. His mind immediately began to tick over.

He bought on "tick" from the Greek Government a £100,000 shipload of dry fruit, a cancelled order from a British grocery chain. He used the fruit in mince pies and sold the product in jars to the same British grocers for

£200,000. It was easy to pay the Greek Government on the resultant profit. Joe was on his way.

His wife, Peggy blended in perfectly to the new world that Joe had discovered and every minute of which he lived to the full and relished – as if the tap from which the finance was coming would never run dry. "When you have, as we had, profits running in the region of £1,000 a day, money doesn't mean anything. It loses its value and you just spend and spend," he would recall later.

But the accountancy methods were unorthodox to say the least. There was no control really. One of the most bizarre disclosures during the bankruptcy trial was that a cheque drawn on the company for £5,565 and entered in the ledger under the heading "raw materials" was actually for the purchase of Early Mist.

Yet, after his passing at the age of 75 in January, 1992 – buried in London, where he was living then, unsung and unknown by the younger generation – the heading over my obituary notice in the *Sunday Independent,* carried with a photo of Joe's smiling face, read: "Death Of Legendary Horse Owner".

We forgot then the humiliation of the nightmare of his two-year grilling in the bankruptcy courts that haunted him for the remainder of his life, the jailing first for contempt and then another term, twelve months this time, in Mountjoy Prison, where he claimed, with that natural wit that never deserted him, that he was "Lord of the Manor" and had been put in charge of the kitchen and the cooking, adding: "When I was leaving the officer in charge said to me: 'Joe, I hope you won't come back but if you do, you'll come straight down here to the kitchen because you're the best cook we ever had!'".

We remembered only that in the period 1950 to 1953 he achieved what members of the aristocracy and money barons had spent their lives and fortunes trying to achieve and yet failed to realise. He won the Aintree Grand National not just once but twice and could have had a third if he had taken the advice of Vincent O'Brien and purchased Quare Times when it was offered to him – and granted his fortunes had not taken a plunge in the meantime.

For example, the year that Joe Griffin won with Early Mist, Lord Bicester, owner of some of the finest chasers in the history of National Hunt racing, was then 86 and had been trying unsuccessfully for fourteen years to win the National – and he was still not giving up hope. And, ironically, on the death of J. V. Rank, whose lifetime's ambition it had been to win this race and whose time ran out just too soon, Early Mist was bought at the dispersal sale of the Rank horses by Vincent O'Brien on behalf of Joe Griffin for £5,300.

In three short years, 'Mincemeat' Joe won £65,000 in stake money alone on his horses and winning bets brought that figure well beyond the £100,000 mark. Multiply it by ten and you can quickly calculate that he was in the millionaire class as a successful owner.

❋   ❋   ❋

Just as later, he would show an uncanny eye for picking out yearlings that would make potential Classic winners, Vincent O'Brien had few peers when it came to knowing exactly the type of horse required to tackle the Aintree fences in an era when they presented a much greater challenge than is the case today. It could NEVER be regarded as sheer luck that he won the National three years running with three different horses. After Royal Tan had won the race in 1954, he said to "Mincemeat' Joe Griffin: "I'll sell you the winner of next year's Grand National for £2,500."

Just imagine that – Joe was being offered Quare Times twelve months before the gelding triumphed at Aintree and Vincent had enough confidence in his own judgement to lay it on the line that the gelding would win.

There is little doubt that Vincent could have added another Grand National winner to his list had he been allowed to follow his own professional instincts and put a professional jockey of his choice up on Royal Tan in 1951 rather than his brother Phonsie.

Vincent had purchased Royal Tan (by the sire Tartan, belonging to the Carroll family and standing not far from Cashel at the time) from the late Ben Dunne Snr. of Dunnes Stores for the Keoghs. There was a lot of confidence behind the horse to win the 1950 National Hunt Chase and he was backed down to 9-2. Phonsie O'Brien had the mount.

But Royal Tan overjumped and fell at the very first fence. Phonsie was almost in tears when he came in and the Keoghs were sorry for him as he was very young at the time. When it came to the Aintree Grand National the following year, Harry Keogh remembered Phonsie's discomforture at Cheltenham and said to Vincent O'Brien that he should give the mount to his brother.

The Keoghs were among his most loyal owners and Phonsie had won on Royal Tan at Leopardstown in February '51, before finishing second in the Irish Grand National in the count-down to Aintree. In the final analysis, Vincent went against his better judgment and bowed to the Keoghs' wishes in allowing his brother to take the ride.

It was only the second time in his training career that sentiment over-ruled cold professional considerations. The other occasion, as we have seen, was when Charles Engelhard got his way in the case of his horse Nijinsky and Vincent allowed the colt to contest the St. Leger after only recently recovering from a bout of ring-worm. In both instances it back-fired.

Royal Tan was only seven when he contested the National for the first time in 1951. He started at 22-1 in a field of 36 and 34 of the runners would fail to complete the course after a disastrous and highly-controversial start that led to havoc at the first fence.

Approaching the second last fence the race rested between Royal Tan and Nickel Coin. These were now the only two horses left standing. Bar a fall they had to finish first and second. Phonsie O'Brien looked across at Johnny Bullock and called to him: "What's that you're riding?"

"Nickel Coin", Bullock shouted back. "Your goose is cooked, Johnny", said Phonsie, who recalled: "I was going so easily that there was no way I could see us getting beat."

"We strode on to the last fence. I knew I could go on ahead of him at that point if I wished but I remembered Vincent's instructions – 'Don't jump the last in front if you can avoid it'. Vincent's theory was that with that long run-in at Aintree, you would be in front for too long if you took the lead before the last. Later events would prove that Royal Tan was a horse that hated to be dictated to, though he was very clever, highly intelligent, in fact. In retrospect, I believe now that if I had kicked on and let him do his own thing, it might have been all so different.

"He just made a goddam mistake at the last, after jumping all the earlier fences without trouble. That was it in a nutshell, nothing less, nothing more", added Phonsie with a shrug of his shoulders.

But a lot of ink has been used since 1951 in probing the whys and wherefores of Royal Tan's so-near-and-yet-so far failure to lift the National. Vincent's own view of that fatal last-fence blunder is that when Phonsie gave Royal Tan a kick with his heels going into the jump, the horse seemed to resent it. He hit the top of the fence and came right down on his nose. Amazingly, he did not topple over and Phonsie, at the same time, managed to stay in the saddle.

Meanwhile, Nickel Coin and Johnny Bullock, having safely negotiated the last, galloped home to a bloodless victory. But it shows how far superior Royal Tan was that, despite being almost on the floor, he still got to within six lengths of the winner at the finish. How much would he have won by if he had jumped the last as he did in 1954?

The following year, with Phonsie O'Brien again riding, he once more blundered at the last when lying third and having every chance. His head went right down to the ground but he managed to struggle back to his feet. This time, however, Phonsie was pitched out of the saddle, so Royal Tan is recorded as a faller in the '52 race won by Teal.

✻   ✻   ✻

After Bryan Marshall had won the 1953 National on Early Mist for Joe Griffin, 'Mincemeat' would naturally contemplate no one else for Royal Tan in 1954.

Again with that thoroughness, that meticulous attention to detail that others might overlook, Vincent arranged a school for Royal Tan at Gowran Park after racing. Vincent, Dermot and Phonsie had a council of war and it was agreed to impress upon Bryan Marshall that he must not adopt forceful tactics but leave Royal Tan do his own thing.

It was in the Gowran Park school that Marshall discovered the way to ride the horse. "It was to leave him alone. He objected very much to being driven."

Twenty fell in the field of 29 in the 1954 National and Marshall knew he was within sight of victory at the last. "Everything, I knew, rested now on his not blundering as on previous occasions. By allowing him to jump it rather than kicking him into it, he sailed over and I sighed with relief – no more fences to go, so I really got down to riding him then," recalled Marshall.

It was Tudor Line who blundered at the last. He recovered, however, to come from the elbow with a sustained challenge and it was to develop into one of the most memorable and pulsating finishes in the history of the race. Tudor Line (10st 7lbs) had exactly a stone advantage over Royal Tan and was also a year younger and it seemed that George Slack on the outside would get the better of the dramatic struggle to the line. However, Bryan Marshall held on to win by a neck.

Royal Tan was a ten-year-old when he finally won it. Reflecting back to 1951, there is a case to argue that he could have set up an Aintree record to put him on par with Red Rum.

In the 1955 National George Slack jumped into the lead three out on Tudor Line, making a death or glory bid to wear down the easily-running Quare Times but, as Michael O'Hehir reported in the *Sunday Independent,* "the one who appeared to be worn down was Tudor Line himself".

As George Slack put it afterwards: "I thought I would get Quare Times off his feet but when I moved up I saw that Pat Taaffe was not in the least worried – and I knew that was that."

Once over the last fence, Quare Times (bred in County Tipperary by the late Phil Sweeney at his Orwell Stud, near Thurles) raced away to a 12-lengths victory in conditions that were so bad that the water jump was cut out.

Pat Taaffe, later on in his career when he became associated with Arkle, winner of three successive Gold Cups (1964-'66) on this peerless chaser superb, regretted very much that Anne, Duchess of Westminster would not allow the gelding to take his chance in the Aintree Grand National. She was so devoted to Arkle that she was terrified of him being injured through no fault of his own.

Taaffe expressed the view to me that Arkle would have had no problem adapting to the Aintree fences and was certain that he would have triumphed in the National.

Incidentally, the great Tom Dreaper, Arkle's trainer, found it hard for a long time, according to Taaffe, to bring himself to concede that there could be any horse better than Prince Regent. "In the end, however, he remarked to me quietly one day: 'I suppose, Pat, I have to admit that I have trained none greater than Arkle'".

When I discussed with Vincent O'Brien his assessment of his three Grand National winners, he had no hesitation in coming down in favour of Royal Tan. "For me Royal Tan was the best jumper I ever had", he said with emphasis. "A really clever horse – so smart, in fact, that he would never allow anyone to dictate to him. Early Mist had to be asked but Royal Tan was a natural when it came to jumping fences and he took to them like a cat. If you ask me which was the classier of the two, I would have to say Early

Mist but again, let me repeat, there was no comparison between them in the pure art of jumping. Early Mist was never a natural jumper and that is why he had to have a master jockey on his back like Bryan Marshall. Royal Tan had it over Early Mist – by a clear margin", said Vincent.

On Quare Times, he said that he was "a free-running, free-jumping horse and he suited Pat Taaffe to perfection. They were an ideal partnership together."

✳   ✳   ✳

By the time he won his first Aintree Grand National in 1953, Vincent O'Brien had already been installed in Ballydoyle since the Spring of '51. When Hatton's Grace returned to Ireland after winning his third successive Champion Hurdle on Tuesday, March 6, '51, the horse was not taken back to the Churchtown stables in County Cork. Indeed, while Vincent was at the Festival meeting, the training establishment was being moved to the new quarters near Cashel and in the shadow of Slievenamon.

The marriage settlement – when Vincent O'Brien's father, Dan married again after the death of his first wife during child-birth – decreed the inevitability of the move to Ballydoyle. Vincent was renting the gallops and boxes from his step-brother Donal and had rented extra land from the Lynch family. The only way that he could have remained on in Churchtown was if Donal had sold the family homestead and lands to him and bought another farm. But in the Irish way of things, it is extremely difficult for an eldest son to sell his birthright. Donal could not bring himself to do it. Vincent understood his feelings.

Dermot and Vincent went scouting. They must have looked at twenty-four different places before they finally opted for the house and lands that would become Ballydoyle. "I remember so vividly the day we came up the avenue and saw the old Georgian farmhouse and the 180 to 200 acres going with it. We both looked at each other and we knew without a word being exchanged : 'This is it'," Dermot recalled.

"There was an immediate feeling about the place that captured us. I know we were both looking for the same thing. We had seen so many places that disappointed in one way or another. It wasn't possible to say exactly in so many words the moment we reached our silent decision but, even before the bulldozers got to work to prepare the gallops, we could picture it as it would be – the place of our dreams with the Knockmealdowns, the Comeraghs and Slievenamon forming the ideal backdrop to close on 200 acres in Ireland's Golden Vale".

Dermot made it clear that a move to the Curragh was never a serious option in Vincent's or, indeed, his own mind. "No, I can tell you truthfully that Vincent never wanted to go the Curragh. As he put it to me at the time – there was too much light. By that he meant that it was too open, too flat. Like riding a bicycle on a straight road that seemed to go for ever, or across a desert like the Sahara into nothingness. Vincent would like a few bends on the road, or put another way, he couldn't contemplate public gallops that had no undulations and neither could he contemplate living in an area where you couldn't see a hill around you," said Dermot.

So Vincent decided to open his own gallops to his own vision of things. He would fence in the area under his control. He would have an operation that carried on from Churchtown, expanding on what he had created there and yet not losing that distinct individuality that was a hallmark of his whole approach from the beginning. In time Ballydoyle would become a model of everyone's idea of what a modern stable should be.

The Ballydoyle set-up that would inspire so many laudatory articles lay a long way ahead on the day that Vincent walked into the Munster and Leinster Bank (now absorbed into Allied Irish banks) in Cork and asked for a substantial loan to buy the house and lands that was to comprise his new training establishment. The same bank had facilitated him when he was going out on his own in far more modest circumstances in Churchtown after the death of his father in 1943. He would never forget the help he received when he needed it most and to this day has kept an account in the same branch.

The house and lands were acquired from the Sadlier family, who had owned a lot of land in the Cashel area at the turn of the century. The member of the family with whom Vincent concluded the deal was Miss Daisy Sadlier who was living then on the farm with her invalid mother. She was finding it too much to look after the farm and wanted out. People in the area remember her driving around in her flaming red convertible sports car.

The money garnered from successful gambles, in particular the ante-post coups on Cottage Rake and Hatton's Grace, and Alberoni with Aubrey Brabazon up winning the Leopardstown Handicap Hurdle under 10st 2lbs in July 1950, plus the loan from the bank, enabled Ballydoyle to be purchased for £17,000.

Frank Gannon noted that it was big money at the time as the best business site in Cashel sold for £1,200.

He noted that the arrival of Vincent at Ballydoyle was a great boon to the area. "It was like an industry, employing in time 50 to 60 personnel, rising to 85 by the end of the Eighties."

Vincent had an account with the draper's shop run by Frank Gannon's father, Bill. "Lads would come in from Ballydoyle to be fitted out in our shop and my father was paid promptly every three months. We regarded the Ballydoyle account as special."

It was a time of great poverty in the area and Frank Gannon said that he saw sights that could have been right out of Frank McCourt's bestseller, *Angela's Ashes,* about his childhood days in Limerick. One memory lives with Frank Gannon to this day – it was of coming along the road into Cashel one day and seeing the brilliant student who was second to him in the class in the Christian Brothers School working with a gang tarring the road. "There were so few job opportunities that it was either that for him or taking the boat to England or emigrating to the States", he said. "So many went away against their will. It was terrible."

∗   ∗   ∗

Dermot, Vincent's assistant, Maurice O'Callaghan, the faithful headman for 30 years, Danny O'Sullivan, an outstanding schooling rider – they all moved to Ballydoyle. The kernel of the team that had known such success already under Vincent's inspired captaincy remained together. However, Jimmy Gordon, who was another of Vincent's trusted employees in Churchtown, stayed put as Mai, the girl that he would marry, had a grocery shop-cum-drapery in Churchtown and he was also thinking of setting up as a trainer himself.

"To say 'No' to Vincent was the hardest thing I ever had to say in my life", Jimmy recalled. "I had known very happy times working in the Churchtown stable and I knew I could never repay Vincent for all the knowledge I acquired in those years."

The 280 acres in Ballydoyle would in time be expanded to over 600 and the boxes that had housed such champions as Cottage Rake and Hatton's Grace became absorbed into new offices. The new special features that could not have been contemplated in the spring of 1951 included by the end of the Eighties a complete veterinary station, a computerised health system for the horses, gallops that were not put out of action by inclement weather and an isolation area where thoroughbreds aimed at big prizes could be isolated from those that might be suddenly hit by a virus.

Before Vincent actually made the move from Churchtown, Phonsie had spent months helping to supervise the task of preparing the new gallops. It was back-breaking work. Vincent remembers that it was simply a case of transforming ordinary farm land, which up to then had been used for tillage or grazing, into gallops. "It was a long haul, a terribly long haul and I wouldn't like to be starting out on it again," he said.

He was fortunate to have the dedicated support of Dermot and Phonsie. There was a tremendous affinity between the three. Without that affinity, without the total loyalty forthcoming from Dermot and Phonsie, I do not think that Vincent could have made the transition so successfully and neither could he have survived the crisis that hit him when he had his licence withdrawn for a year over "The Chamour Affair", which is dealt with in Chapter 23.

Phonsie, who was a successful trainer in his own right, took over at Ballydoyle during the days of suspension, ensuring continuity where otherwise there might have been a complete shut-down.

Dermot was also an invaluable cog in the Ballydoyle machine. In fact, it could never have operated as smoothly as it did without his self-effacing but cool, authoritative presence. The fact that he had served in the Irish Army had enabled him to acquire the ability to handle men.

It did not matter one iota to Dermot if the writers put the spotlight on

Vincent. A lesser man might have become jealous of his brother. Not so Dermot. They represented a powerful duo together, the perfect foils for each other – just as Phonsie, with his outgoing personality, complimented them both. Yes, they were like "The Three Musketeeers" – all for one and one for all.

Eventually, Dermot decided to get out of the heat of the kitchen, having borne intense pressure at the very highest level for close on three decades. It was a mutual parting with Vincent as he set up on his own in the Derrygrath Stud, near Cahir, County Tipperary. Bringing all the knowledge that he had acquired over the years to the breeding of horses, he enjoyed some singular successes. From his outstanding mare, Driella, he bred Seskin Bridge, Commeragh King and two other winners. Another daughter, Derrynaflan got injured and did not win but bred Suir Run, for whom Dermot got 43,000 guineas at Goffs Derby Sale in 1987. Unfortunately, he was killed in England in a hurdle race when there was a tremendous amount of money on him.

BETTER ONE DAY AS A LION THAN ONE HUNDRED YEARS AS A LAMB

This was the title that Raymond Smith gave to his last racing book and it was based on the motto by which his friend, the late Jack (Treetop) Straus, World Poker Champion in 1982, had lived. Tom Foley and Fergie Sutherland have proved the motto to the hilt through the exploits of Danoli and Imperial Call respectively. The epic moments are graphically captured by the author.

But others too in recent seasons have lived days of a lion, like Edward O'Grady, Arthur Moore, Adrian Maguire, Charlie Swan, Normal Williamson, Mick Fitzgerald, Dermot Weld, Jim Bolger, John Oxx, Aidan O'Brien, Michael Kinane and Christy Roche.

It's a book for those who glory in the courage of the men in silks and in the talent and genius of the trainers who make the champion horses. Not overlooked either are the exploits of the big-time gamblers of our time.

It retails at only £9.95 and is available from Easons bookshops and other leading bookshops in Dublin, Cork, Limerick, Galway and Belfast. Autographed copies for £10 (including postage) direct from the publishers: Sporting Books Publishers, 4, Sycamore Road, Mount Merrion, County Dublin.

THE EYE OF THE MASTER... Vincent O'Brien puts his glasses on the field and his reading of races was vital to his assessment of the quality of the opposition facing his charges.

PART FOUR

KING OF THE FLAT

19

Why Lester Opts
For Sir Ivor

Over lunch one day in his Newmarket home, Lester Piggott made the point to me that lasting judgements on a horse's greatness can only be made on the calibre of the opposition it beats.

And for that reason he put Sir Ivor ahead of Nijinsky when I asked him to choose between two of the greatest of Vincent O'Brien's six Epsom Derby winners.

Piggott, of course, found it extremely difficult to desert Nijinsky in favour of Sir Ivor – describing the 1970 Derby winner as "a brilliant horse, probably on his day one of the most brilliant I have ever ridden".

But the basis of his argument was that "Nijinsky's season as a three-year-old was not, to my mind, a good year. The horses racing against him were not as good as those that opposed Sir Ivor. I have always felt that Sir Ivor beat a super colt in Petingo (outstanding winner of the Craven Stakes) in the Guineas. In the Derby he mastered Remand and Laureate in a few strides and then when I asked him the question, he produced a brilliant surge of finishing speed to leave Connaught literally standing and, remember, Connaught that same season won the King Edward VII Stakes and then the Prince of Wales Stakes two years running (1969 and 1970) and the Eclipse Stakes as a five-year-old in 1970."

The scintillating 1968 Epsom Derby triumph allied to superb victory in the Grand Criterium the previous October represented two of the principal reasons why Lester went so far as to give Sir Ivor the accolade of being, in fact, the best horse he ever rode.

In very heavy going at Longchamp – conditions that one would have imagined would have been all against him – Sir Ivor dismissed with the authority of a true champion a field replete with winners – and outstanding winners at that. He had three lengths to spare over Pola Bella who had won the Criterium des Maisons Laffitte (beating Cabhurst, subsequently top of the French Free Handicap).

Piggott blamed Sir Ivor's defeat in the 1968 Eclipse Stakes at Sandown on the very firm going – "yet he kept on up the hill to be only narrowly beaten by Royal Palace and Taj Dewan. Royal Palace had won the Derby the previous year and took the King George VI and Queen Elizabeth Stakes in 1968."

Developing his argument on Sir Ivor's greatness, Lester said that in the Champion Stakes at Newmarket over his best distance of ten furlongs, the colt was much too good for Taj Dewan, which had run within a pound of Royal Palace in the Eclipse. "So again on a comparison of form, Sir Ivor comes very well out of that race."

He went on: "In the Prix de l'Arc de Triomphe, Sir Ivor was beaten into second place by a really outstanding colt in Vaguely Noble, who had too much staying power for him over the Longchamp twelve furlongs in soft going (Vaguely Noble had won the Observer Gold Cup by seven lengths as a two-year-old and, even though he held no Classic engagements, he made a then record public auction price for a thoroughbred of 136,000 gns – an investment fully rewarded when he took the Prix de l'Arc de Triomphe)."

"I knew after the Champion Stakes that Sir Ivor would win the Washington International and I said so to Vincent", said Piggott. "It looked at one point that snow might cause a postponement of the race but it cleared, leaving the going very heavy. The ground was terrible. Hock deep, in fact. I had to save him as much as possible. I knew that it was the only way he would get the trip in that going. My tactics were to get him as relaxed as possible, conserving everything for a sharp late run.

"As we swung into the short straight, still lying fourth behind the leader, many people must have thought that it was impossible for Sir Ivor to win from that position. I did not go for the race until the last possible moment and when I pressed the button, it was all over in a few strides. I feel certain that I would have won by 100 yards if the ground had not been soft.

"Behind Sir Ivor that day were two high-class American-trained horses in Czar Alexander and Fort Marcy, second and third respectively, with the French-trained Carmarthen fourth, while the English Oaks winner of that year, La Laguna (trained by Francois Boutin in France), was fifth and Azincourt from the Argentine seventh."

✻   ✻   ✻

It was in the Grand Criterium (8 furlongs) that Lester Piggott sat on Sir Ivor for the first time and told Vincent O'Brien afterwards that he thought he was something special. But he had already won three juvenile events in Ireland, including the prestigious National Stakes. Amazingly enough, he was only fourth on his racecourse debut in the Tyros Stakes (6 furlongs) at the Curragh but Liam Ward predicted confidently to the Master of Ballydoyle that those who had finished ahead of him that July day would never do so again.

Sir Ivor was a big handsome bay colt bred in the United States by Mrs Alice Headley Bell, a descendent of the legendary hunter, Daniel Boone. By Sir Gaylord, he was out of a good winning mare in Attica (by Mr Trouble), who traced back to the Aga Khan's Mahmoud, while his grand-dam was second in the Kentucky Derby and had excellent winning form to her credit.

He carried the colours of the American Ambassador to Ireland, Raymond Guest, who had the inspiration in a quiet moment in the Embassy – as he was flicking through the catalogue for the forthcoming Keeneland Sales – to put a call through to his friend 'Bull' Hancock of Claiborne Farm, one of America's best judges of horseflesh. The Ambassador fancied on breeding just two horses in the 600 lots and instructed 'Bull' Hancock to buy whichever of the two he thought was the better. Thus Hancock secured Sir Ivor for $42,000.

Raymond Guest struck a fabulous bet on the 1968 Epsom Derby – before Sir Ivor won the National Stakes in '67. He got a friend who knew William Hill to tell this most famous and fearless of bookmakers to quote a price about each of the three horses that the Ambassador had entered for the '68 Derby. Hill readily offered 100-1 about each of them.

"I expected Sir Ivor to win the National Stakes so it was essential to get in before that race", recalled Raymond Guest. I had £500 each-way at 100-1 on Sir Ivor and soon afterwards he won the National Stakes and then followed up by taking the Grand Criterium. Owing to the American tax laws I only kept about £16,000 out of total winnings of £62,500."

The bookmakers never recovered their money from Raymond Guest over Sir Ivor. He announced in June '68 that he did not intend to have another bet.

In the Timeform ratings of Vincent O'Brien's Best Flat Horses, Sir Ivor got a rating of 135 along with The Minstrel whereas Nijinsky and Alleged both hit a mark of 138 with Ballymoss and El Gran Senor on 136 each.

John Randall argued in the *Racing Post* that Sir Ivor would not be a contender for the title of Vincent O'Brien's greatest horse were it not for the opinion of both the trainer and Lester Piggott. And Randall noted that Piggott had gone on record to state that Sir Ivor was the best horse he had ever ridden.

"But Sir Ivor's claims to that exalted status are weakened by two awkward facts", according to Randall. "First, although he looked a great horse in the 1968 Derby, he lost his next four races; and second, he was three lengths runner-up to Vaguely Noble in the Arc, beaten apparently on merit. Even if he was better at ten furlongs, a truly great horse would have finished closer."

John Randall maintained that most professionals, if asked to name the greatest Flat horse trained at Ballydoyle, would come down in favour of Nijinsky – because he won the Triple Crown – or Alleged by virtue of being a dual Arc winner.

Randall went on to claim that when discussing champions over a period of decades, "the most objective means of comparison are Timeform ratings, and on that scale Nijinsky and Alleged were the best Flat horses Vincent O'Brien ever trained".

But I would contend myself that the flaw in Randall's argument is exposed by the rating of 137 that Apalachee won – putting him ahead of Ballymoss, El Gran Senor, Sir Ivor and The Minstrel. That rating was on two-year-old performances alone and, granted, he was a highly-impressive winner of the Observer Gold Cup (now the Racing Post Trophy), his rating putting him third to Windy City (142) and the filly Star of India (138). But, as we have already seen, he failed dismally to train on as a three-year-old and, even John Randall acknowledges, that it showed that there is a big difference between potential and actual achievement. It would be a slur then on the achievements of Ballymoss, El Gran Senor, Sir Ivor and The Minstrel to mention Apalachee in the same breath as them simply because he commanded a Timeform rating of 137. The case rests.

I have mentioned earlier in this book that Lester Piggott went on the record over our luncheon conversation in his home to state that a horse he did not ride might well have been the best to have passed through Vincent O'Brien's hands. "I believe that Golden Fleece could have been the best horse that Vincent ever trained – better even than Nijinsky and Sir Ivor", said Piggott. "Few horses win the Epsom Derby from the position he won it from. Yet, although he was last coming down Tattenham Hill and had only three horses behind him as they rounded the Corner, he showed such phenomenal acceleration in the straight that he won unchallenged in the end.

"You cannot overlook either the time he recorded that day. It was the fastest by a Derby winner since electric timing was introduced in 1964. Though Mahmoud's Derby winning time in 1936 was slightly better, they had to rely on hand-timing then. There has to be a question mark, therefore, over that record holding up to modern scrutiny."

Lester said that Golden Fleece had not really been extended in winning any of his four races. "If he had not been forced into early retirement after winning the Derby, he could – if we are to go on the speed he showed at Epsom – have been capable of anything."

Where does Vincent O'Brien himself stand in the debate on the comparative merits of Sir Ivor, Nijinsky and Golden Fleece?

There was a stage – before Golden Fleece's Epsom Derby triumph in 1982 – when he placed Sir Ivor and Nijinsky firmly at the top of his Derby winners. He found it extremely difficult to separate the pair of them. He inclined towards Nijinsky on the score of sheer brilliance on the days of his greatest successes as a three-year-old, in particular the Epsom Derby win and also victory in the King George and Queen Elizabeth Stakes. And yet for the acceleration he showed on Epsom Derby Day and for his courage in the mud in the Washington International at the end of a terribly long and exacting season, that took in nine races in all, Vincent had to put Sir Ivor right up there with Nijinsky – on the score of durability as much as any other quality.

But later he would acknowledge that on his performance in winning the '82 Epsom Derby, there was none faster than Golden Fleece.

So in the final analysis, Vincent coupled Golden Fleece with Sir Ivor and

Vincent O'Brien and his wife Jacqueline at Royal Ascot '93, the day Vincent won the Cork and Orrery Stakes with College Chapel, his last winner at the Royal Ascot meeting.

Jacqueline in conversation at Royal Ascot '97 with well-known County Tipperary personality Mattie Ryan, a great worker for charitable causes.

Vincent O'Brien, there as a spectator this time, brings the eye of knowledge and experience to studying the card at Royal Ascot '97. (Pictures: Bernard Parkin.)

THOROUGHBREWED

Aidan and Anne Marie O'Brien, Sue Magnier, Dr. Tim Mahony, Chairman of Lexus Ireland, Michael Tabor and Christy Roche at the presentation of prizes at the Curragh after Desert King has won the 1997 Lexus Irish 2,000 Guineas.

John Magnier, the boss of Coolmore (left) and Michael Tabor, who form a powerful duo in the bloodstock world today and who have made a major impact at the yearling sales globally, in happy mood after Desert King's triumph, above inset. (Pictures: Caroline Norris.)

A victory salute from veteran big-race jockey, Christy Roche and a smile from Aidan O'Brien with lad Kevin Power giving Desert King a victory pat after the colt had reproduced his brilliant Guineas form in taking the Budweiser Irish Derby.

Christy Roche brings all his experience of the big occasion into play as he powers Desert King to victory in the Budweiser Irish Derby over Dr Johnson (John Murtagh), trained by Vincent O'Brien's son Charles who was seeking to land a first Classic. (Pictures: Caroline Norris.)

Aidan O'Brien holds aloft the magnificent Budweiser Crystal trophy as he receives the congratulations of President Mary Robinson (right) and Bill McNulty, Managing Director, Anheuser-Busch European Trade following Desert King's victory in the 1997 Budweiser Irish Derby.

American Ambassador Jean Kennedy Smith (left) warmly acclaims Sue Magnier and Michael Tabor who shared in the memorable success of Desert King. Also pictured is Doreen Tabor.

TOGETHERNESS . . . David and Catherine O'Brien with their children (from left) Robert, Charles, Andrew and Alexandra and Charlie (the dog) in front of Chateau Vignelaure in Provence. (Picture: Remy Le Morvan.)

David O'Brien and John O'Byrne, Proprietor of Dobbin's Restaurant in Dublin, taste the first of the new wines of the season.

Sue Magnier, looking resplendent in a white outfit, leads in Harbour Master (Christy Roche) after he had won the Coventry Stakes at Royal Ascot '97. Tommy Murphy, assistant trainer at Ballydoyle shares in the moment of triumph.

Aidan O'Brien has reason to pat Harbour Master who became his first Royal Ascot winner. It's a proud day too for Aidan's wife, Anne Marie and for Tommy Murphy, right. (Pictures: Bernard Parkin.)

THE STAR

STARFORM

YOUR NO. 1 RACING PULLOUT EVERY SATURDAY

ALL YOUR TOP TIPSTERS

TED WALSH

KIERAN O'CONNELL

TRACE PIGGO

Nijinsky – the 'Magnificent Three' in a hand of six Epsom Derby winners in the twenty-year period 1962-'82. Few could cavil with that. It is deciding in what order the three would finish if contesting the same Derby under ideal conditions that must undoubtedly bring sharply-differing opinions from racing enthusiasts.

The debate will go on down the decades.

✳   ✳   ✳

Ballymoss was the first great Flat champion that Vincent O'Brien put through his hands. In the year – 1958 – that Ballymoss won the King George VI and Queen Elizabeth Stakes and Prix de l'Arc de Triomphe, to join other great champions who had done likewise, namely Ribot, Mill Reef and Dancing Brave, the Master of Ballydoyle also had in his charge Gladness, who achieved a rating of 131 when she won the Ascot Gold Cup the same season.

Enter now John McShain, who was to exercise as big an influence on Vincent O'Brien's progress up the ladder to achieving real international fame as a Flat trainer as Frank Vickerman (owner of Cottage Rake when he won three successive Gold Cups) did in the National Hunt sphere.

John McShain was no ordinary American millionaire categorised as of Irish decent (no less than 40 million Americans claim Irish blood in their veins). He became one of the biggest and most respected building contractors in the States, and was responsible for building the Pentagon and restoring the White House. He was 90 when he passed away at his residence, Killarney House, Killarney in September, 1989. For 28 years his wife Mary and himself had used Killarney House as a summer residence but they lived there permanently for the years immediately preceding John McShain's death. He had come to love playing the Killarney golf course (now more than one course) and equally he loved to fish the famous lakes. He invariably attended the Killarney July Festival race meeting and sponsored the John McShain Handicap.

For racing enthusiasts around the globe, this American multi-millionaire went into history as the owner of Ballymoss and the man who acquired Gladness on the advice of Vincent O'Brien.

The Hinge of Fate once again stepped in to favour Vincent O'Brien in the manner in which he met John McShain. And the man who made it all possible was an English lawyer, Hedley Nicholson from Yorkshire who was a great racing enthusiast and a keen admirer of Vincent O'Brien. On being introduced to the Master of Ballydoyle, he formed an immediate friendship with him.

The biggest twist of Fate of all occurred when James Turner (later Lord Turner), President of the National Farmers' Union asked Nicholson to look after John McShain when he arrived for the Tattersalls September Sales, staged at Doncaster during the St. Leger meeting (Turner had met McShain in the States when leading a visiting group of farmers and was anxious to

141

repay the hospitality shown the group in a hotel in Philadelphia owned by McShain).

So all the pieces on the board came together in a perfect jig-saw that resulted in McShain meeting Vincent O'Brien through Hedley Nicholson and asking him to buy a batch of yearlings for him. Some of those purchased went to the States, where McShain had 35 horses in training. One of the others was Ballymoss.

Vincent paid 4,500 guineas for Ballymoss (by Mossborough), sent to the Sales by Richard Ball, who had a small stud farm in County Dublin and was known affectionately as 'The Poet', as he once published a book of poetry. He had the distinction of breeding dual Aintree Grand National winner, Reynoldstown, as well as the Lincolnshire winner, Babur and Star King, who, renamed Star Kingdom, became a top sire in Australia.

Ballymoss, slow to mature, only won one out of four races as a two-year-old – a seven furlong event at Leopardstown – and failed again in his first race as a three-year-old (the Madrid Free Handicap at the Curragh). But there was an explanation for the latter defeat as T.P. Burns was able to tell Vincent O'Brien that he did not act in the heavy going.

He was allowed off at 20-1 in the Trigo Stakes a month later with John Power in the saddle and Gladness (T.P. Burns) was the stable hotpot at 11-10. But the top-of-the-ground conditions were all against the mare whereas Ballymoss at last got the going that would reveal him in an entirely new light. And in victory he was eminently suited by the twelve furlongs.

A stone bruise in his foot curtailed his preparation for the Epsom Derby and in the circumstances he put in an amazing performance in the hands of T.P. Burns to finish only one-and-a-half lengths behind Crepello, who recorded a very fast time. Both Vincent O'Brien and T.P. Burns were convinced that if it was at the Curragh on Irish Derby Day that Ballymoss had been meeting Crepello, he would have beaten him. Epsom came three weeks too soon.

Ballymoss gained due compensation in the Irish Derby justifying odds of 4-9 as he slammed Hindu Festival (Rae Johnstone) by four lengths and then went on to win the English St. Leger at odds of 8-1 after being runner-up in the Great Voltigeur at York on going which T.P. Burns described as like wet peat moss" and his prospects were not helped either by an arduous boat journey (for the St. Leger Vincent sent him over by chartered plane). He had the distinction that day at Doncaster of becoming Vincent's first English Classic winner.

He finished the 1957 season by being unplaced in the Champion Stakes.

✳   ✳   ✳

"It was as a four-year-old that Ballymoss really came into his own", noted Vincent O'Brien's brother, Dermot, adding: "He was one hell of a horse".

He actually failed only once in five outings in 1958 and that was when he finished second in the Ormonde Stakes at Chester – his first race of the season.

Then followed his four major victories in the Coronation Cup, Eclipse Stakes, King George VI and Queen Elizabeth Stakes and the Prix de l'Arc de Triomphe. Scobie Breasley was in the saddle for all four. The ease with which he justified 7-4 favouritism in the King George put him on a new plane and he confirmed his greatness at Longchamps.

Vincent O'Brien again showed his professional approach by sending both Gladness and Ballymoss to Ascot. "I had made up my mind that I would challenge for the King George with Ballymoss if he got the conditions to his liking – that is firm going – but Gladness would run if it came up soft", Vincent revealed to me. "The going was not just firm but very hard so I did not have to think twice before deciding that Ballymoss would be our challenger."

Gladness had contested the Ascot Gold Cup earlier that summer and, with Lester Piggott in the saddle, won at 3-1, and then went on to land the odds of 1-2 in the Goodwood Cup, again with Lester taking the mount.

Perhaps her finest victory of all and the one that set the seal on her reputation was her shouldering of 9st 7lbs to a sweeping seven-lengths triumph in the Ebor Handicap at York. William Hill said that it was unquestionably "the greatest performance" that he had ever seen in a competitive handicap race of this kind. Hill knew his racing. And, of course, Lester was seen at his scintillating best.

The Last Hurrah for the gallant mare came in the King George the following season (1959). Her fetlocks had been fired and she had recovered from tendon trouble. Bob Griffin, Vincent's trusted vet, told him that this would be the last bridge – and both did not want to go a bridge too far.

Because of her leg ailments, it was impossible to give her the kind of preparation that Vincent would have liked but she ran the gamest of races in taking runner-up position to Alcide, the Alycidon colt who, after being 'nobbled' before the 1958 Epsom Derby from which he had to be withdrawn, duly won the St. Leger in smashing style by eight lengths and failed by inches in the Ascot Gold Cup the following season. So Gladness after all did not achieve the supreme accolade by winning the King George, as Ballymoss had done in 1958.

On being retired to stud, Ballymoss sired one outstanding colt in Royal Palace, who won the English 2,000 Guineas and Epsom Derby in 1967 and the following season took the Coronation Cup, Eclipse Stakes and the King George. Gladness bred four winners, including Glad One, runner-up to La Laguna in the 1968 English Oaks and third the same season to Celina in the Irish Oaks.

The mating of Ballymoss with a mare commanding Gladness's record seemed the perfect "match". The Ballymoss-Gladness matings did not produce the super champion some might have anticipated.

Merry Mate (winner of the 1966 Irish Oaks for John Oxx) and Ballyjoy were the offspring – no world-beaters, it has to be admitted, on the international plane.

The achievements of Ballymoss and Gladness on the racecourse stand the test of time and are part of the early years of greatness of Vincent O'Brien as a trainer who was still on the "dual mandate", mixing the Flat with National Hunt.

It was early in November 1958 when the announcement came that Vincent was to give up training 'over the sticks'. While he was in the States supervising Ballymoss's preparation for the Washington International at Laurel Park (the colt finished an unlucky third after losing a lot of ground in an unfortunate incident when Orsini bounced back off the hedge and then there was further scrimmaging on the back stretch), his brother and assistant, Dermot confirmed at Liverpool the "no more jumpers" decision.

Quick Approach, trained by Vincent, had won the November Hurdle by eight lengths. "I don't expect we shall have a runner under these rules at Aintree again", said Dermot. "Quick Approach and Fine Point come up for sale at Newmarket in December. After Cheltenham in March I anticipate that Vincent will give up the jumpers altogether."

True to what Dermot had predicted, Vincent had his last Cheltenham runners at the 1959 Festival meeting. York Fair won Division One of the Gloucestershire Hurdle and Courts Appeal was second to Albergo in Division Two. Both were ridden by T.P. Burns.

The curtain thus came down on one phase of Vincent's career.

Just three years on Larkspur, in the colours of Raymond Guest, won Vincent his first Epsom Derby but, on cold analysis, he has to be viewed as the poorest of the sextet. He doesn't gain inclusion in the Timeform ratings of Vincent's Best Flat Horses. However, he had the distinction of being a trail-blazer and in the ensuing two decades the Master of Ballydoyle would land the Blue Riband five more times and he would be hailed the "King" of Epsom where previously he had been acclaimed as the "King "of Cheltenham and Aintree.

The Moment of Triumph... The Minstrel (Lester Piggott) is led in after winning the 1977 Irish Derby.

20

The Assault on Keeneland

"**L**ife is about timing" Robert Sangster said to me over coffee one morning in the lounge of the Berkeley Court Hotel in Dublin. The timing was just right when he became involved with Vincent O'Brien and John Magnier as the main partners in 'The Syndicate', which would change the face of breeding internationally when the first grand assault was made on the Keeneland Select Yearling Sale in July,1975.

And Sangster became involved also in the creation of the world-renowned Coolmore Stud complex that spreads its tentacles today to the Ashford Stud in Kentucky and Down Under to Coolmore Australia and which has perhaps the most influential role of any stud in bloodstock developments on a global scale. The dynamism and vision of John Magnier can never be under-estimated in any analysis of the spectacular rise and rise of Coolmore and neither can the genius of Vincent O'Brien himself.

Looking back twenty-two years, as I write this chapter in Rosslare, in the summer of '97, looking out over the sweep of the strand to the Harbour over to my right as one of the ferries steams away on its latest run, it's hard to believe that so much should have evolved so quickly from the moment of destiny when, as Robert Sangster recalled for me, "John Magnier and myself went to see Vincent. It was the day that we virtually put 'The Syndicate' together".

But prior to that moment in time they had hit on the inspired idea of "making our own stallions", again as Sangster explained. A three-year plan was decided upon. But first there was the amalgamation of the studs to form a corporate entity, a type of structure that was to become a blueprint of its kind in the breeding world.

In the mid-Seventies Robert Sangster had already "been in horses" for about five years and had acquired a property near Macclesfield in Cheshire that would eventually become the Swettenham Stud.

The challenge was now there: could he go into racing and breeding on a big scale and make it pay? The fateful year was 1974 – the first year of stallion involvement on his part.

On Budweiser Irish Derby Day '97 John Magnier stood in the winner's enclosure after 'talking horse', King of Kings had won his second successive race as a juvenile, surrounded by a circle of Irish and English racing writers noting his every word. Later he would see Irish 2,000 Guineas winner, Desert King, owned jointly by wife, Sue and Michael Tabor take the Derby from Dr Johnson in the joint ownership of Sue and her father, Vincent O'Brien and trained by Charles.

John Magnier and Michael Tabor had become two of the biggest players at the yearling sales. They were in the business of the making of stallions. The wheel had come full circle for John Magnier since 1975 but now because of his immense achievements and the position attained by Coolmore and its flagship sire, Sadler's Wells – not to mention the other successful stallions it offered the breeding world, like Caerleon, Danehill, Royal Academy, El Gran Senor and Storm Bird – he had become a charismatic figure – a man who worked hard and yet could set aside the pressures of being at the helm of a global concern to get involved in tremendous battles on the golf course along with his close friends J. P. McManus and Dermot Desmond.

And he could relax in January in his holiday home in Barbados and play in the Robert Sangster Pro-Am Golf Classic that brought leading professionals and renowned personalities in the racing and breeding worlds together and the action was in keeping with the outsize characters who graced the scene.

Life for John Magnier was a high-stakes game no matter what he was involved in but I have always been amazed at the urbane manner in which he seemed to be able to carry the pressure with such aplomb – as if he could stand aloof from it all looking down, giving off an air of authority and control in keeping with his dress and cool cigars. A world figure who takes centre-stage easily, as if like Laurence Olivier he was born to that role.

He has certainly come a long way in just over two decades from the time that he was boss of the 300-acre Grange Stud near Fermoy where his father had stood the great National Hunt sire, Cottage (died in 1942). John had also founded Castle Hyde Stud in 1971 and together with Robert Sangster he would be involved in Sandville Stud.

Meanwhile the original Coolmore Stud, a few miles north of Fethard in South Tipperary, was owned by Tim Vigors, renowned internationally both as a horseman and as a bloodstock agent who thought big and went in big when he wanted to acquire a horse.

John Magnier and Robert Sangster, having joined forces to purchase two horses, Green God and Deep Diver, and then a third, Sun Prince, concluded that they were having to get involved in a lot of competition with other breeders – Tim Rogers of Airlie Stud, for example, and the bloodstock agents acting for big international interests. They were even competing with studs on their own doorstep.

It did not seem to John and Robert, or to Vincent O'Brien either, to be the correct way to continue. Why should studs that had much in common bid against one another when they could bid together – all for one and one for all? Why not a pooling of resources?

Thus did Tim Vigors come on board and Coolmore Stud became a member of Coolmore, Castle Hyde and Associated Stud Farms, a title which confirmed the link of the Magnier family in the new venture. Grange and Sandville were also in the new company's title, and so too was Beeches Stud, owned by Robert McCarthy and situated across the Tipperary border at Tallow, County Waterford.

Soon two more studs had been incorporated into the complex, Longfield and Thomastown Castle.

✻　　✻　　✻

Before 'The Syndicate' hit Keeneland for the first time, they had an initial venture – often forgotten nowadays – when they bought Boone's Cabin, which was in training at the time with Vincent O'Brien. "He had won the Wokingham Stakes in 1975 with Lester in the saddle", recalled Robert Sangster. "He did not quite make it as a stallion and was later sent to Australia where he did moderately well. Through Tim Rogers, I acquired a share in Blood Royal, winner of the Queen's Vase at Ascot in 1975, with Lester again riding.

"I remember that the decision was taken with Tim Rogers to merge share ownerships in certain unbeaten two-year-olds we purchased in order to avoid clashing head-on for the same animals but we never did manage to get our two syndicates together".

As time went on other people joined – and left – 'The Syndicate' but the "Big Three" stayed together. Glancing back through some of the names is akin to flipping through the pages of "Who's Who" – Charles St. George, the Lloyds insurance broker whose name will always be associated with 1973 Dewhurst Stakes winner, Cellini; Alan Clore, son of immensely-wealthy financier Sir Charles Clore, who had seen his Valoris, trained by Vincent O'Brien win the English Oaks in 1966; Simon Fraser of the Scottish Clan Fraser who was proud to tell his friends that Vincent O'Brien trained for him; Irish-born millionaire Jack Mulcahy, who came to identify Killarney as home, though much of his life had been spent in the States; Walter Haefner, owner of the Moyglare Stud and great patron of Irish racing and breeding; the very wealthy Californian tycoon, Danny Schwartz and Greek shipping magnate Stavros Niarchos.

Vincent O'Brien, John Magnier and Robert Sangster knew when they started on their three-year plan in '75 that buying some of the best yearling colts, put up either privately or at public auction in Europe and the United States, could not of itself be guaranteed to throw up a top-class horse. However, if there was even one, the resultant syndication for stud purposes would more than justify the whole venture. In a word, if you bought a package of five, six or seven in a year and one clicked, the entire operation would be well worth while.

The year 1975 will always stand out as a red-letter one for 'The Syndicate' or 'The Brethren' as they also came to be dubbed. From their first major assault on the Keeneland sales that year, they brought back to Ballydoyle a package of horses that included The Minstrel, Alleged and Artaius. Be My Guest was meanwhile purchased at Goffs.

The invasion of Keeneland that same year was really the turning point. But there were a few inspired purchases at sales in Europe also. Everything they touched over the decade from 1975 to 1984 seemed to turn to gold. Godswalk, Golden Fleece, El Gran Senor, Sadler's Wells – and, of course, while Assert was not bought by Vincent, he won both the French Derby and the Irish Derby for Robert Sangster.

A flood of victories in Europe's top races followed and each champion was stamping himself in the process as a valuable stud property to realise profits from syndication that became the envy of the world in the boom days.

The statue of Be My Guest occupies a proud place inside the entrance to the Coolmore Stud complex. And there is one also at Goffs, where he had been purchased in '75 for a European record price at the time of 127,000 guineas from the Moyglare Stud crop. He was the first of Coolmore's own when he was put to stud in 1978 after a racing career that saw him win three Group races, including the Waterford Crystal Mile.

In 1978 also Godswalk began stud duties at Coolmore. Bought for $61,000 as a yearling, he had proved himself a brilliant sprinter, winning the Norfolk Stakes at Royal Ascot (1976) when trained by Christy Grassick for Patrick Gallagher. He was bought by Ballydoyle during the close season and he won the 1977 King's Stand Stakes when trained by Vincent O'Brien.

But all changed, changed utterly once the emphasis turned to the Northern Dancer blood.

The corner-stone of Vincent's belief lay in the fact that he had seen what Northern Dancer's son, Nijinsky had achieved in the 1969-'70 seasons and he knew that, as the winner of the Kentucky Derby in record time back in 1964, 'Dancer' transmitted exceptional speed to his best sons. More important still, he knew that by buying yearling colts by Northern Dancer and later by Nijinsky, he was purchasing potential stallions as the pedigrees would be right. His basic tenet was that it was no use a colt winning a Classic or other major race if the pedigree did not stand up to the closest scrutiny. Breeders would turn away where they would need no encouragement whatsoever when they had faith in the blood line.

The approach to the Keeneland Sales each year became military-like in the manner in which everything was planned and executed. If Vincent could be said to have been the Supreme Commander like General Eisenhower, then his long-standing friend, the late Tom Cooper of the BBA (Ireland) was a key general in the front lines. He it was who undertook the task of going around the various stud farms in a vast area embracing no less than four States having an initial look at the yearlings who would be offered for sale at Keeneland. He would then send back first-hand reports to Vincent in Ballydoyle, offering his expert viewpoint. And, naturally, because Vincent had such complete faith in him, there was an air of excitement in Ballydoyle and in Coolmore also whenever Tom reported that he had seen something special.

Meanwhile, once Vincent received the catalogues from Lexington for the up-coming Keeneland Select Yearling Sale he immediately went to work pouring over them. He would go back generations through the family of each yearling that had been selected as a possible target for 'The Syndicate'. With his immense knowledge of breeding, garnered from the time he sat on his father's knee back home in Churchtown, he brought to his task a depth of professionalism that no one in the world could surpass. And by the time he was finished, his mind was focussed clearly on the yearlings in the catalogue that he knew he could not let pass without looking at them very, very closely when he arrived in the Bluegrass country of Kentucky itself.

Of course, there were other "generals" also studying the catalogues – John Magnier, for example, and Phonsie O'Brien, both of whom would invariably be at Vincent's side when he toured the barn area at Keeneland. And Robert Sangster would be in close and constant touch with Vincent and John Magnier before the flights to Kentucky were booked.

It was an education in itself, something that left a lasting impression on me, I must admit, to follow Vincent O'Brien and his party as they made their rounds of the barns where the famous American stud farms presented their "wares". Word would have been conveyed beforehand to those in charge when the Master of Ballydoyle would be arriving. If a red carpet was not put out in the literal sense, then he unfailingly got the red-carpet treatment. Because the vendors knew that if he wanted a particular yearling, wanted it very badly, then one purchase could make that July Sale for them.

Infinite patience was shown in bringing out a yearling not just once, but twice, three times and more – if Vincent indicated that he was not satisfied the first time. The very fact of his returning could be an indication that his interest had not died.

"I remember he used to spend a very long time looking at every horse", said bloodstock agent, Joss Collins of the British Bloodstock Agency (London) in an interview with the *Racing Post*. "Some people would have a quick look and walk away if they didn't like a yearling, but Vincent would look for a long time, particularly at those horses with obvious faults".

On arriving at the Keeneland Sales for the first time, you could be forgiven for standing almost in awe at the famous names over the line of boxes for the yearlings in the barn area – Spendthrift Farm; Claiborne Farm; Darby Dan Farm; Calumet Farm. You had only to reflect on the stallions they stood and the reputations forged by the men who founded them or oversaw their advancement to new heights and it was enough to be there to savour the experience both in the sales ring and outside it.

You wondered what passed through Vincent's mind as he stood there looking at a yearling's head – for limitless moments it seemed. You wondered was he looking beyond the eyes trying to find that certain something that would give him the final proof of what he sought to discover. Again this was a facet of the sales themselves that struck one deeply and little wonder that it was caught on canvass for posterity by an artist who understood its lasting significance.

There never seemed to be any respite for Vincent and his trusted "generals" during the days of the Keeneland Sales. Councils-of-war over breakfast and again at lunch and more debates at dinner. Their concentration was total on the task on hand. But then one mistake could cost millions of dollars while an inspired decision could mean the purchase of a yearling that would repay the outlay many, many times over if successful at stud.

✳   ✳   ✳

It was millionaire John A. Mulcahy who, during a long day's fishing on Lough Currane in County Kerry, gave Vincent O'Brien the piece of advice that was to cause a sea-change in what accrued to him in time when he picked out a potential champion at the sales and subsequently trained it to become a Classic winner.

Unlike Charles Engelhard and John Galbreath – American to the core – Mulcahy was Irish natural born, a self-made man who represented the classic example of one who made it right to the top of the ladder from the humblest beginnings. 'Jack' to his friends, he was born in Dungarvan, County Waterford and took the emigrant ship to the United States at the age of 18. He returned a millionaire, having joined Quigley (furnace-making) Corporation and worked his way up to become treasurer and then President and majority stockholder.

Vincent had been introduced to John Mulcahy by the latter's brother, Dan, an old friend of the O'Brien family and attached to the Munster and Leinster Bank (now A.I.B) in Cork, where Vincent had maintained an account since he started training.

Mulcahy had read that Vincent was the top trainer in the world, and wanted to know what rewards there were in it for the trainer, especially when he trained a Classic winner. He was told that all the trainer got was a percentage of the winning prize – that is if he did not gamble.

"I couldn't believe that this man who was known around the globe was getting nothing more than a fee for the expertise he used in picking and training top-class horses", John Mulcahy told journalist Seamus McConville in a contribution to the book *Horse Racing* (edited by Finbarr Slattery).

John Mulcahy, with his experience of how business worked in the States, impressed upon Vincent O'Brien that in future he must ALWAYS get what he called "a slice of the action" whenever he went to the sales and bought a yearling or when, in time, one of the horses he trained to become a Classic winner was syndicated as a stallion. In a word, he must not rely on winning percentages alone. He must become an entrepreneur in his own right.

Mulcahy suggested that Vincent start by pressing for at least a 5 per cent slice of the action in every horse he took into Ballydoyle to train.

"Vincent said he couldn't do that but I told him there was no deal as far as I was concerned unless he did", was how John Mulcahy put it to Seamus McConville.

So a new partnership was born and with it a complete change in Vincent's modus operandi. Already Vincent and "Bull" Hancock of the Claiborne Stud Farm had become close friends, and John Mulcahy, with his shrewd business brain, saw immediately how this could be utilised to translate the philosophy he had expounded to the Master of Ballydoyle into something that would make a highly-significant impact on the racing scene.

The idea simply was that instead of all the Claiborne yearlings being sent to the sales, some of them would be trained by Vincent O'Brien and another percentage in the States (a number running in "Bull" Hancock's own colours and others in his friend Bill Perry's colours). Vincent and his patrons not only got Apalachee and Lisadell in the first lot but also a slice of the action. And one of the most successful horses of all that arrived at Ballydoyle through this concept was Thatch, rated the outstanding miler in Europe in 1973.

Like all owners John Mulcahy had his ups and downs and he regarded it as a "hell of a loss" that Cloonlara, carrying a foal by Northern Dancer, was killed by lightning at Claiborne. He never realised his great ambition to be owner of an Epsom Derby winner. But the influence he had on Vincent O'Brien as a result of that long day's fishing on Lough Currane was in a way more valuable than if he had seen his colours carried to victory at Epsom by a horse trained at Ballydoyle.

*   *   *

The Seventies and early Eighties were highly profitable years for 'The Syndicate'. Hand-in-hand with 'The Syndicate's' dominance of the scene at Keeneland, Robert Sangster was a dominant figure as an owner. In eight Flat seasons up to 1985 he was crowned Britain's leading owner. He had moments that made him the envy of men who had spent their lives – and fortunes – trying to acquire even one Classic winner and with the assistance of Vincent O'Brien as trainer and Lester Piggott as jockey, he knew the glory at the very highest level a number of times.

Then his apparent invincibility was broken. It coincided with the fact that, after Law Society's victory in the Irish Derby in 1985 and Leading Counsel's success in the Irish St. Leger the same year, the only other Classic winner from Ballydoyle for the rest of the Eighties was Dark Lomond's Irish St. Leger win in 1988.

The Maktoum brothers of Dubai arrived on the scene and changed the face of racing internationally and their impact on the sales was also profound as they had the financial muscle to spend as much as $50 million over two days at Keeneland. Sheikh Mohammed became the 'King' and in one season alone (1987) won £1,232,000 in prize money. The same year

Sangster had to be satisfied with third place and £468,000. In 1989 Sheikh Mohammed made a sweep of four Irish Classics. He was the man at the top now in the winning Owners list.

With the recession in the bloodstock industry, headings telling of Sangster and 'The Syndicate' spending small fortunes at Keeneland were replaced by awesome, almost frightening spending by the Maktoum brothers.

But even though the glory days of The Minstrel and Alleged might have been past, Robert Sangster proved that he could survive in one of the toughest businesses of all. As he explained: "When people see headings in the papers 'Sangster on Spending Spree', they think I am only a buyer. I can understand that. But in a way I am my own Chancellor of the Exchequer, seeking all the time to keep the books balanced. What many have never realised is that I sell as well as buy. In 1987 I sold over £22 million worth of bloodstock. I bought less than £1 million that same year".

Some thought he would never sell Vernons when it was linked for so long with the family but he showed that he was not swayed by sentiment when he remarked: "In life everything is for sale except the wife".

"It was an offer I could not refuse", he added, pointing out that it enabled him to clear off about £40 million in loans raised from banking institutions. During the rationalisation programme, he had on his own admission "to reduce quite dramatically my borrowings from the bank".

He did not mind admitting that he had made a mistake in the case of the much-heralded decision to set Michael Dickinson up as his private trainer at Manton. The purchase and modernisation of the 2,3000-acre estate set Sangster back £8 million and the annual running costs totalled £1.5 million. Michael Dickinson in his first year of operation at Manton – 1986 – won only four races worth £13,965.

Some would say that Sangster showed a ruthless edge in getting rid of Michael Dickinson. The outlay, however, had been so heavy that he just could not afford to wait for success. "It was the first time I've ever sacked a trainer", he said. "Looking at it now, he was five years ahead of his time. But what had worked with geldings when Michael was a National Hunt trainer probably upset more highly strung young colts and fillies. I could no longer afford the time for him to perfect his theories".

Eventually his son-in-law Peter Chapple-Hyam took over at Manton and won the Epsom Derby in 1992 with Dr Devious (John Reid), the same colt finishing runner-up to St. Jovite in the Budweiser Irish Derby and then reversing matters at Leopardstown in a photo finish to the Irish Champion Stakes; he also won the English 2,000 Guineas in 1992 with Rodrigo De Triano (Lester Piggott) and the same colt took the Irish equivalent, with Piggott again in the saddle. Chapple-Hyam won the Irish 2,000 Guineas again in successive years, 1994 and '95 with Turtle Island (John Reid) and Spectrum (John Reid). Tommy Stack took the English 1,000 Guineas for Sangster in 1994 with Las Meninas (John Reid).

"It feels good to be back on top again, although, despite what people have said, I've never been down", he said over lunch at London's Carlton Towers

Hotel one day in the Spring of '94 to John Karter of the *Sunday Times.* "I'm not a great believer in luck. I walk under ladders all the time. Racing is a team game and I've surrounded myself with the best players available".

He admitted that it would be impossible for anyone coming into the game today to do what Vincent O'Brien and John Magnier and himself had done. "Maybe it would be possible if you were the Sultan of Brunei!"

He was approaching 60 the day of that interview in '94 and went on record to say "I'm streetwise". Like a streetwise boxer who has been through it all. Ironically, where once he got what he described as "a fantastic adrenalin kick" out of the action in the sales ring and especially in the great duels with the Arab Sheikhs in Keeneland, he reached the point where the Maktoums became his best clients for horses and he has been a guest of Sheikh Mohammed in Dubai more than once.

"You've got to roll with the punches in racing", he told John Karter. "I was never at any stage intimidated by the Maktoums. Even during those Keeneland duels we usually got what we wanted. I didn't see it as an 'us and them' battle. We were always ten years ahead of the game. Making top-class stallions was always the goal of Vincent and John and myself and we were never deflected from that path".

Yes, Robert Sangster has proved himself a Survivor Supreme.

Originally, he had invested heavily in Northern Dancer blood because, as he put it, "that blood will not devalue".

In the all-conquering days when the Triumverate he formed with Vincent O'Brien and Lester Piggott proved invincible on the racecourse, he was happy to exclaim to the world, "Let the pilot do the flying". Little wonder that at the same time he should say of Vincent that he was, beyond doubt, "the best trainer in the world".

✳   ✳   ✳

Before the market crashed in the mid-Eighties, before the "For Sale" signs went up on renowned stud farms in Kentucky and a few even felt the cold winds of bankruptcy, 'The Syndicate' left some memories of frenetic action in the sales ring that have become part and parcel of the history of Keeneland.

One writer described the Select Yearling Sale of July '83 as the occasion "when the world went mad".

Sheikh Mohammed and his team – Michael Osborne invariably at his shoulder, one of his most trusted advisers – now commanded red-carpet treatment as each time they went for a yearling they wanted, you could bet your last dollar on prices going sky-high, if others wanted the same colt or filly.

The very first day Sheikh Mohammed made a winning bid of $2.5 million for a filly by Northern Dancer out of Ballade; it made her the most expensive yearling filly in bloodstock history. Later he paid $1.3 million for a daughter of Alydar, then $4.1 million for a Nijinsky colt out of Belle of

Dodge and $2 million for a Blushing Groom colt out of a daughter of Vaguely Noble.

'The Syndicate' countered by acquiring a Northern Dancer colt out of Desert Vixon for $4.25 million.

It was obvious that the stage was set for a head-to-head battle to the death when Lot 308, the yearling colt by Northern Dancer that was to become better known – or infamous – as Snaafi Dancer was led into the ring.

Colonel Dick Warden, bidding for Sheikh Mohammed, caused D. Wayne Lukas, the famous American trainer, to drop out of the bidding after the $5 million mark had been passed before Joss Collins indicated a bid of $5.4 million for 'The Syndicate'. After that those in the front trenches were carried forward on an emotional tide as one barrier after another was passed... first the $7 million, then the $8 million, next the $9 million and the ring was rocked when Dick Warden nodded a bid of $9.6 million.

But 'The Syndicate' responded with a bid of $10 million to a roar that echoed around the enclosure. It looked all over. Surely there could be no answering call to that.

But this was 1983 and not 1975. Sheikh Mohammed had sat impassively through it all and was still impassive as he gave the green light for the bid he must have known in his heart would break the effort of 'The Syndicate' to acquire a colt Robert Sangster had set his heart on getting.

Dick Warden signalled $10.2 million. It was obvious to 'The Syndicate' members that Sheikh Mohammed was not going to be thwarted. They had to admit defeat.

"We were all mad, I suppose, but that was the time", recalled Joss Collins in the *Racing Post* interview. "It all happened so quickly. Snafi Dancer was quite a big horse and was being sold at a time when Northern Dancer blood couldn't have been hotter."

He recalled the deep sense of disappointment among Vincent O'Brien, Robert Sangster and John Magnier at losing out to that $10.2 million bid. "They were used to getting the best horses and they wanted to continue to do so. With the advent of the Arabs, who came in in such a big way, they couldn't get what they were used to having. Everybody likes to be No. 1 and in that respect maybe they bid higher than they should on that occasion", he said.

That deep sense of disappointment must be set now against the fact that Snaafi Dancer, who was put into training with John Dunlop, never saw a racecourse and subsequently proved almost infertile as a stallion.

If $10.2 million was "madness", the $13.1 million paid for Seattle Dancer in 1985 "seemed to me insane", as Collins put it.

But Collins, who again did the bidding, acknowledged that 'The Syndicate' members "loved this bay colt from the moment they set eyes on him. He was a smashing horse".

By Nijinsky out of My Charmer, he was a half-brother to American Triple Crown winner Seattle Slew and to Robert Sangster's own English 2,000 Guineas winner Lomond.

"He represented everything in the past that had been good to them. The horse had a superb pedigree, everything going for him. It may have been because they realised things were never going to be the same for them again. This was their final dash, the last throw of the dice", said Joss Collins.

Outside of the bidding for Snaffi Dancer, the action created by the sale of Seattle Dancer provided ten of the most hectic minutes ever experienced at Keeneland. In the space of 24 bids Joss Collins would win the day for 'The Syndicate'.

An audible stir, a hum of anticipation as Seattle Dancer is led into the small roped-off ring. There is not an empty seat in the Press Box. Vincent O'Brien sits quietly beside Robert Sangster.

Even the most knowledgeable ones in Lexington on that never-to-be-forgotten July day were hardly prepared – and could never have predicted – the scale and adrenalin-pumping climax to the bidding. When it reached $9.8 million the sense of drama was intense. Excitement mounted in anticipation that the previous world record was about to be shattered. "The Lord loves a cheerful giver", quipped auctioneer Tom Caldwell when the bids went to $10 million. "Hot dog", someone exclaimed, "we're going to get a new world record". Applause broke out when the previous record was passed. Then D. Wayne Lukas bid $13 million and it seemed that he had reached home base.

However, the Sangster team put in a final bid of $13.1 million and Tom Caldwell brought down his hammer to a spontaneous roar.

"I suppose looking back on it now, it might appear crazy to have paid that much money for a yearling when you had no certainty how it would turn out", said Robert Sangster. "We will probably never see that figure reached again in our lifetimes.

"We had Seattle Dancer valued at between $8 million and $15 million. We would have been willing to go as high as $15 million.

The colt had been consigned by Warner L. Jones, Junr. of Hermitage Farm at Goshen in Oldham County, then Chairman of the Board of Churchill Downs. He sold eight yearlings for a total of $19.4 million.

Seattle Dancer was a disappointment on the racecourse considering his looks and his pedigree. He was retired to stud at Ashford Farm, the Kentucky wing of the Coolmore complex.

✳   ✳   ✳

They called it "The Summit In The Desert" and it stirred the imagination of racing around the globe when Vincent O'Brien, Robert Sangster and John Magnier flew out to Dubai in 1985 at the invitation of Sheikh Mohammed and it was caught for posterity by Jacqueline O'Brien in a picture which I carried at the time in colour in the 1985-'86 edition of the *Irish Racing Annual*. When news of the meeting leaked, the media world-wide were immediately posing questions: Was it possible that these men would reach detente on how they would approach the head-on bidding confrontations that had resulted in new record prices being set at the Keeneland Sales when both sides went after a Northern Dancer or Nijinsky colt they wanted? Was it possible that agreement would be reached that would revolutionise facets of the breeding industry?

Vincent O'Brien, John Magnier and Robert Sangster never revealed any details of what was discussed at the Summit. "It was a goodwill tour", was all Sangster would venture later and when Sheikh Mohammed was shown all the press cuttings, he remarked: "I don't know what all the fuss is about. It's no big deal".

"For the truth was, whatever the Kentucky breeders may have thought, this was a purely social visit", concluded Charles Benson, who reported on 'The Summit' for the *Irish Racing Annual*. Still the fascination with the high-powered trip by O'Brien, Sangster and Magnier and the aura surrounding it remained for a long time. No one could deny that it was BIG news in itself that three of the most powerful figures in international racing and bloodstock had flown to Dubai to meet Sheikh Mohammed.

❋　❋　❋

A July day in 1988. I was there in the humid heat of Keeneland when the epilogue was written on Vincent O'Brien's association with the July Select Sale. All eyes were on Lot 269, a Nijinsky colt out of Crimson Saint, as it entered the ring.

When D. Wayne Lukas, who had arrived with $15 million to spend, signalled a bid of $3.4 million with his right hand, it seemed that he had beaten the man the American media had dubbed "The Tipperary Wizard".

But Vincent, immaculate in yellow shirt and white boater, having gone "into the trenches" for this battle, quietly responded with a $3.5 million bid on behalf of Classic Thoroughbreds. He confessed to me afterwards that he would not have gone any higher.

Spotter Pete McCormack from Ontario gave an enquiring glance at D. Wayne Lukas but he signalled this time that he was finished. American racing's Mr Goldfinger had lost out to the Master of Ballydoyle.

The colt was named Royal Academy, who fully vindicated Vincent going all in on his last hand when he won the Breeders' Cup Mile (Turf) at Belmont Park in 1990 with Lester Piggott in the saddle, having earlier that season won the July Cup and lost out in a photo finish in the Irish 2,000 Guineas.

Today he is a successful addition to the Coolmore array of sires. In the 1996 list of Leading Sires of Stakes Winners in Great Britain and Ireland, he was runner-up with a total of seven to Sadlers Wells with nine. His son, Oscar Schindler, carrying the colours of Oliver Lehane, had a memorable '96 season, winning in turn the Ormonde Stakes at Chester, the Hardwicke Stakes at Royal Ascot, the Jefferson Smurfit Memorial Irish St.Leger and he finished third behind the peerless Helissio and Pilsudski in the Prix de l'Arc de Triomphe.

21

Why Golden Fleece Comes Out On Top

Most Flat trainers would be thrilled to have in their stable in the one season a horse capable of winning an Epsom Derby, an Irish Derby and the King George VI and Queen Elizabeth Stakes.

But to have at the same time another colt with the ability to land the Prix de l'Arc de Triomphe indicates a profusion of riches.

Thus is was with Vincent O'Brien in the golden season of 1977 when his nap hand included The Minstrel and Alleged and also Artaius, authoritative winner of the Eclipse Stakes and the Sussex Stakes and Lady Capulet, winner of the Irish 1,000 Guineas on her racecourse debut. It didn't end there. That same season he won the Coventry Stakes at Royal Ascot with Solinus, the King's Stand Stakes with Godswalk and the Hardwicke Stakes with Meneval; the Waterford Crystal Mile at Goodwood with Be My Guest and the Irish St. Leger with Transworld while the very speedy Fairy Bridge emerged as the top-rated filly in Ireland.

The one real disappointment was the potentially-brilliant Sir Ivor filly, Cloonlara, who after being unbeaten in three races as a two-year-old, turned temperamental in her three-year-old season when she started favourite for the English 1,000 Guineas and not alone failed sadly in that event but wasn't led once into the winner's enclosure.

The story of The Minstrel, as we have already seen, was at the outset one of Vincent O'Brien being riven with doubts at the Keeneland Sales in July '75 because the colt was so small in size; secondly, because he had four white stockings and, thirdly, because he was a flashy chestnut and breeding pundits are won't to express sharp reservations about chestnuts on the score of temperament.

But in the end Vincent put all his doubts aside and took the bravest decision in his long career. It was on the ultimate premise that a Northern Dancer did not have to be of the requisite height to be good.

Making his decision all the more amazing in the case of The Minstrel was the fact that he allowed Lyphard – subsequently to make his mark as a miler in France and then as a sire in the States – to be led out of the ring unsold at Newmarket because he judged him to be too small!

It's history now how The Minstrel was acquired for $200,000 and was valued at $9 million when put to stud in the States.

✳   ✳   ✳

Unbeaten in three outings, including the Dewhurst Stakes, as a juvenile and a winner on his debut as a three-year-old in the 2,000 Guineas Trial Stakes at Ascot, The Minstrel could only finish third in the English 2,000 Guineas. He then finished second, beaten a short head by 16-1 shot Pampapaul, in the Irish equivalent, having started favourite in both Classics.

However, Lester Piggott was convinced that The Minstrel had the balance to act on the Epsom course and the courage to emerge victorious if it came to a crunching battle at the death. He had no doubt that if he stayed, he would win the Derby.

Vincent O'Brien, who had been thinking in terms of the St. James's Palace Stakes at Royal Ascot after the defeat in the Irish 2,000 Guineas, agreed to let the colt take his chance at Epsom. With the 9-4 favourite, Blushing Groom, the French 2,000 Guineas winner, failing to stay, Piggott had to call on the last ounce of The Minstrel's courage to get the better of Hot Grove in a desperate struggle in the final two furlongs to win by a neck.

The Minstrel went on to survive an objection – by Frankie Durr, rider of the runner-up Glencoe Lights – after veering over towards the stands in the climactic stages of the Irish Derby. He put the seal on his reputation by beating a top-class field in the King George that included Orange Bay, who had been third the previous year, Bruni, the 1975 English St. Leger winner, Crow, winner of the same race for France the following year in the hands of Yves St. Martin, Crystal Palace, the French Derby winner and Exceller, the Coronation Cup victor.

The Minstrel just prevailed by a head in an epic finish with Orange Bay, with Piggott and Pat Eddery both excelling.

Naturally, Piggott would have loved to have ridden him in the Prix de l'Arc de Triomphe and believed he had all the credentials necessary to win it. But he was whisked out of Ireland in a manner that would have done credit to a James Bond movie well before the first Sunday in October.

The Ballydoyle grapevine got word that the American authorities were about to impose a ban on all horses from Europe because equine metritis was hitting epidemic proportions in the States at the time. The Minstrel beat the ban in the nick of time.

✳   ✳   ✳

The Epsom Derby was never earmarked for Alleged. Vincent O'Brien knew he was a colt who would need time and, furthermore, he was not favoured by top-of-the-ground conditions.

If patience was one of Vincent's greatest attributes, allied to the ability to think ahead to the targets that mattered, then he never exercised these qualities better than in the case of Alleged.

He put him away after he had won the Gallinule Stakes at the Curragh at the end of May, 1977 and did not produce him again in public until the Great Voltigeur Stakes at York on August 17th – a race he won in awesome style on his way to his first victory in the 'Arc'.

The Minstrel, I contend, cannot be put on the same pedestal as Alleged, who only suffered one defeat in ten races and that was when he was second to Dunferminline in the St.Leger of '77, beaten by just one-and-a-half lengths.

Vincent O'Brien kept him in training as a four-year-old with the specific aim of winning a second 'Arc'. The temptation was great to retire him to stud after he had won at Longchamp for the first time. Remember, the odds appeared very much against any horse emulating the great Ribot who had won two 'Arcs' back-to-back in 1955-'56.

But where he had bowed to Charles Engelhard when running Nijinsky in the St. Leger against his better judgement – and that for reasons that were on the plane of a special friendship and feelings for a man whose time on this earth was nearly up – Vincent would not be swayed from his conviction that Alleged should be kept in training. And he had his way.

The Master of Ballydoyle felt that he could pick up the King George VI and Queen Elizabeth Stakes on the way to a second 'Arc' – granted the ground did not come up too firm. But that plan went out the window when Alleged developed a problem in his knees when slightly jarred while winning the Royal Whip at the Curragh. He did not race again until the Prix du Prince d'Orange at Longchamp on September 17, '77. This became, in fact, his one and only preparatory race for the 'Arc'.

Amazingly, he broke the track record for the ten furlongs, even though he had only one race in a year.

It makes one ponder that Alleged could have been a great King George winner that year if he had got the conditions to his liking. And it makes one ponder even further that if the Breeders' Cup was then a feature of the racing calendar, he could certainly have triumphed for Europe. At his peak he was something special.

*　*　*

For that very reason, I put him second to Golden Fleece when I come to place in order my Top Ten among the best colts that Vincent trained over distances beyond sprint distances. In opting for Golden Fleece as my No. 1, I repeat again what Vincent said one day passing the box where he had been housed: "What speed, what speed".

He was thinking, of course, of that pulverising run that brought Golden Fleece from an 'impossible' position coming down Tattenham Hill in the Epsom Derby to win in the end going away.

I know I will come under fire from the admirers of Sir Ivor and Nijinsky for placing Golden Fleece first and Alleged second especially as Alleged did not win a Derby. But in my book two successive 'Arcs' surpass one Derby – irrespective of how that Derby was won.

I will be under fire again for putting Ballymoss ahead of The Minstrel but, if he had not had an interrupted preparation before Epsom, he might well have beaten Crepello in 1957 – the year he won the Irish Derby and English St. Leger and then confirmed his greatness the following season by taking in four successive outings the Coronation Cup, the Eclipse Stakes, the King George VI and Queen Elizabeth Stakes and the Prix de l'Arc de Triomphe.

And I know I will be sharply criticised too for only rating Roberto 8th in my Top Ten. True, after being beaten only half-a-length by the favourite High Top in the English 2,000 Guineas, he won the Epsom Derby in a time (2 mins 36.09 secs.) that was bettered only by Nijinsky in the ten previous Derbys. With the American-based Panamanian rider, Braulio Baeza in the saddle, he led all the way when easily mastering Rheingold and the up-to-then-unbeaten Briagadier Gerard in the Benson and Hedges Gold Cup at York. But some of his form did not compare in any way with the three-year-old achievements of Nijinsky, Sir Ivor or The Minstrel. He was unplaced in the Irish Derby and in the Prix de l'Arc de Triomphe (though, in the case of the 'Arc ,'the pillar-to-post tactics adopted by Baeza – dead against Vincent's instructions – killed any chance of success before the straight was reached. A great pity really when the fast going was all in Roberto's favour).

Kept in training as a four-year-old, he won the Coronation Cup but was unplaced in the King George VI and Queen Elizabeth Stakes.

Roberto, a Hail To Reason colt, ran in the colours of John Galbreath, who was deeply involved in bloodstock and sport generally, being the owner of the Darby Dan Stud Farm in Kentucky and also of the Pittsburg Pirates. He prided himself in his knowledge of sports injuries which was to become a crucial factor in the fierce controversy that developed through the jocking-off of Bill ('Weary Willie') Williamson from Roberto on the eve of the 1972 Epsom Derby.

Briefly, Williamson took a heavy fall at Kempton in the count-down to the Derby, injuring his shoulder. After treatment, he was given the green light to resume riding in advance of Derby Day but Vincent O'Brien got expert opinion to the effect that it was only when Williamson got back in the saddle would it be revealed that he was 100 per cent perfect. Vincent was naturally worried. The upshot was that John Galbreath met the Australian jockey in Claridge's and conveyed to him that he was being replaced by Lester Piggott, though he would receive exactly the same percentage as Lester (that is 10 per cent of £63,735 in the event of Roberto winning).

✳   ✳   ✳

Brian Molony, former assistant trainer at Ballydoyle, has no doubt that El Gran Senor was the best colt Vincent O'Brien ever trained. "I base my opinion on the quality of the field he beat in the 1984 English 2,000 Guineas and what was achieved subsequently by some of those immediately behind him that day at Newmarket."

Lear Fan, the runner-up, beaten two-and-a-half lengths, had won all his outings as a two-year-old and picked up three races in the space of little over a month by an aggregate of nineteen lengths; taking the Fitzroy House Stakes at Newmarket by eight lengths and the Laurent Perrier Champagne Stakes at Doncaster by three lengths respectively.

In fact, he was winter favourite for the 2,000 Guineas and on his reappearance was immensely impressive in the Craven Stakes over the Rowley Mile at Newmarket, giving 5lbs to Rainbow Quest and beating him by a short head. Lear Fan would come back from his comprehensive Guineas defeat by El Gran Senor to take the Prix Jacques le Marois at Deauville by a smashing four lengths and behind him were Siberian Express, the French 2,000 Guineas winner, who started favourite, Mendez, who had been third in the French Classic, also three highly-rated French fillies in Masarika, Speedy Girl and Justicara and two horses with Pattern-race wins in Italy.

Lear Fan, following his victory at Deauville, would finish a close second on going that didn't suit him ideally in the prestigious Prix du Moulin de Longchamp.

Chief Singer, who was third to El Gran Senor in the 2,000 Guineas, had been a most impressive four-lengths winner of the Coventry Stakes at Royal Ascot as a two-year-old and, after he had run inexplicably badly in the July Stakes at Newmarket, he was put away for the rest of the season (several vets were called in to try to get to the bottom of the problem, which seemed to be that while he was sound walking and trotting, he went to pieces when asked to canter).

He made a remarkable recovery from his problem. He would leave a lasting impact in his races subsequent to his defeat by El Gran Senor, the *Timeform* experts in *Racehorses Of 1984* describing him "as versatile a runner as has been seen racing in the best company in Britain since Home Guard over a decade ago". He actually emulated the 1973 feat of the Vincent O'Brien-trained Thatch in taking the St. James's Palace Stakes at Royal Ascot, the July Cup at Newmarket and the Sussex Stakes at Goodwood.

Rainbow Quest, officially ranked the second-best two-year-old of 1983 behind El Gran Senor, had to be content with fourth place in the 2,000 Guineas; the unbeaten Keen who had made such a fine impression at Kempton in April, was no less than twelve-and-a-half lengths behind El Gran Senor in fifth place while Bountiful, who had been fourth in the French 2,000 Guineas, was a well-beaten sixth and the Middle Park Stakes winner, Creag-An-Sgor came in seventh.

Little wonder then that *Racehorses Of 1984* rated it "the best Two

Thousand Guineas run since Brigadier Gerard won from Mill Reef and My Swallow in 1971".

Of El Gran Senor's performance in victory, the *Timeform* experts had this to say: "For superlative merit exemplified in one performance, nothing in the 1984 European season in our view equalled El Gran Senor's brilliant display in the General Accident Two Thousand Guineas. His clear-cut victory over the finest field assembled for the race since Brigadier Gerard's year marked El Gran Senor unmistakably as a colt superior to the general run of Classic winners. He accomplished his task at Newmarket in exemplary style."

Vincent O'Brien announced immediately after the 2,000 Guineas that he would run next in the Epsom Derby. "I believe his Guineas performance to be on a level with Nijinsky's and Sir Ivor's," he said, adding significantly "and many people didn't think *they* would stay". Nijinsky and Sir Ivor were at that point the last two winners of the Guineas to succeed at Epsom.

The Master of Ballydoyle's felt that El Gran Senor's manner of running – "he's much more relaxed than Nijinsky" – would help him stay and also the fact that Buckpasser, the sire of the colt's dam, was regarded in the States as an influence for stamina.

So it came down to the one burning question: Would this 'wonder colt' get the twelve furlongs of the Derby?

It has got to be emphasised here that *Racehorses of 1983* rated his chances of staying a mile-and-a-half in top company as "doubtful".

The argument presented to back up this conclusion was that El Gran Senor's sire, Northern Dancer could not be regarded as a strong influence for stamina – the average distance of races won at three years and upwards by his progeny was around nine and a half furlongs – and none of the offspring of Sex Appeal (the unraced dam of El Gran Senor) had won at the Derby trip. And neither had any of his grandam Best in Show, a Stakes winner at seven furlongs.

The *Timeform* experts concluded then that, while a definite question mark hung over El Gran Senor's ability to win the Derby on breeding, what was in his favour was the fact that he was "a most amenable and placid horse, a perfect ride, which gave him a chance of conserving his stamina and getting further than his pedigree might suggest".

Again, however, the rider was added that few horses capable of a performance over a mile such as El Gran Senor's in the Guineas have also possessed stamina sufficient to enable them to reproduce the same level of performance in the best company over a mile and a half.

✳   ✳   ✳

Brian Molony recalled Vincent's instructions to Pat Eddery on Guineas Day. These instructions were that he (Vincent) did not care when Pat pressed the button and went for victory on a horse he regarded as unbeatable but once he was ahead he must drive El Gran Senor right out to the finishing line.

"You see, El Gran Senor was an unbelievably lazy horse," Brian Molony went on. "Once he hit the front he would feel his task was done and begin looking at the crowds. For that reason it was essential to keep him covered up for as long as possible and unleash him at the point when his brilliant speed would do the business."

Now analysing the Derby defeat, Molony said: "Unfortunately, El Gran Senor was so vastly superior to the rest of the field that they died one by one ahead of him. Pat Eddery had hoped that Claude Monet would last out longer than the rest but he too went like the others, so Eddery was in front two furlongs out.

"Pat had the field stone cold at that point and he gave a glance across at Christy Roche who was working hard on Secreto as he reached a point about a furlong and a half out.

"My own belief is that if Pat had driven him right out there and then, he would have forged sufficient of a lead to withstand Christy Roche's finishing effort on Secreto. The advantage he would have secured, I am convinced, would have been enough for victory.

"I know there are experts who have argued that El Gran Senor did not stay the Epsom Derby distance and Pat Eddery himself quoted the old maxim – 'if you don't stay, you don't win'.

"But it remains one of my greatest regrets from my years in Ballydoyle that El Gran Senor should have lost his unbeaten record by the shortest of short heads in a photo finish. I believe it was tragic that it should have happened to such a brilliant racehorse and, making it all the more tragic, was the fact that before the Derby his value was being put at $80 million – had he triumphed. A group of breeders in the States were willing to buy 50 per cent of him for $40 million – again provided he succeeded in winning the Derby. And the word was that he would have stood in Kentucky at $400,000 a service."

Robert Norris, (son of Paddy Norris), who was an assistant trainer at Ballydoyle and also engaged in a veterinary capacity there, goes along with Brian Molony's view that El Gran Senor was "tops" of all the horses Vincent trained.

In the International Classifications for 1984, he headed the three-year-old ratings on 98 – ahead of Chief Singer (92), Darshaan (91), the French Derby winner, and Sadler's Wells (90) and it is worth noting that his rating was higher than that of Teenoso (95), the 1983 Epsom Derby winner and the King George VI & Queen Elizabeth Stakes winner of '84 and also higher than that of Sagace (93), the Prix de l'Arc de Triomphe winner of '84.

The final word comes from Capt. Michael Byrne, who at the end of 1989 retired as Senior Irish Turf Club Handicapper to be succeeded by Ciaran Kenneally: "El Gran Senor was the best miler we have rated in the International Classifications since they were first published in 1977 – the best I have seen in twenty years as an official handicapper. I do not subscribe to the school that criticised Pat Eddery after El Gran Senor had been beaten at Epsom. The colt went from pulling the proverbial roller two furlongs down to struggling close home. I consider that Pat's skill and judgement got the colt as close as he did that day.

"Winning the Irish Sweeps Derby subsequently proved nothing. It was run exactly to suit El Gran Senor and even the fourth finisher that day, March Song, went on to take advantage of a favourable handicap mark at Dundalk two weeks later.

"To sum up – El Gran Senor was a superb miler, most probably a high-class Group 1 horse at 10 furlongs, but very average in the context of Group 1 at a mile and a half."

Tony Sweeney, one of the most authoritative voices I know on racing, names Nijinsky as the best colt to pass through Vincent O'Brien's hands. "You have got to remember that he was the first horse since Bahram in 1935 to complete the Triple Crown by taking all three colts' Classics and he won the Epsom Derby in record time and also took the Irish Derby and King George VI & Queen Elizabeth Stakes in that 1970 season. I know that the Prix de l'Arc de Triomphe nowadays transcends the St. Leger in international importance but Charles Engelhard, Nijinsky's owner, placed great store on the winning of the Triple Crown and Vincent gave him his wish. No horse since Nijinsky has succeeded in winning it since. So in the 62 years from 1935 to '97 only two horses have achieved the distinction. On his day Nijinsky was an exceptional colt. There were extenuating circumstance for his defeat in the 'Arc' and these have already been well chronicled."

Vincent's son, David said to me from France in the autumn of 1997, that he has no doubt in his mind that Nijinsky was without any question of doubt the greatest colt trained at Ballydoyle. "Brilliant, absolutely brilliant at his best," said David.

Tom MacGinty, who was for thirty years Racing Correspondent of the *Irish Independent* and is today Racing Editor of the *Irish Racing Annual*, has no hesitation in opting for Sir Ivor as the best colt to have been trained by Vincent O'Brien. "I have never seen a horse produce the kind of acceleration in the final furlong that Sir Ivor showed in winning the 1968 Epsom Derby. It was phenomenal."

Sadler's Wells, I might mention here, received a rating of 132 from the *Timeform* experts in *Racehorses of 1984* and it was noted that he was, in terms of prize-money won, by some way the most successful horse to carry the Green and Blue Sangster silks in Europe in 1984. His total earnings in first prize-money for the season came to £384,114 and up to that point only three British or Irish-trained horses - Troy (£404,424). Tolomeo (£400,000) and Shergar (£386,410) - had won more in first prize-money in a single season than Sadler's Wells. "That Sadler's Wells proved capable of showing top-class form at a mile, a mile and a quarter and a mile and a half, and of reproducing his best form in top races run on all types of going from soft to very firm, added greatly to his value, particularly for stud purposes," said *Timeform* experts, who concluded this "beautifully-bred colt has great potential as a stallion." A prediction that was certainly justified - far beyond what anyone could have envisaged at that point in time.

Sadler's Wells then goes ahead of King's Lake (winner of the 1981 Irish 2,000 Guineas and the Sussex Stakes) in my ratings and both keep the 1985 Irish Derby winner, Law Society out of the Top Ten (he would be in eleventh position if we were listing a Top Twenty). By the way, had Law Society won the 1985 Epsom Derby, he would definitely have qualified for the Top Ten; he had the misfortune, as we shall see in the next chapter, to run up against Slip Anchor, as Meadow Court was unlucky to meet Sea Bird II in the 1965 Epsom Derby.

When I come down to the task of putting my Top Ten in order, I cannot help but reflect on the fact that always foremost in Vincent O'Brien's mind, as he planned the two-year-old and three-year-old campaigns for the top colts in his charge, was making the Epsom Derby the ultimate target in every case where a horse had a pedigree that put him in line to land the Blue Riband of Racing on the Flat, for this represented the jackpot in the making-of-stallions policy.

El Gran Senor, despite his brilliance, failed to achieve this goal, granted by the most galling of narrow margins. But he failed none the less.

If I were placing my Top Ten in order, ruling out the Epsom Derby and the twelve-furlong factor, I would have no hesitation in opting for El Gran Senor as No. 1, but I have the Epsom Derby very much in mind as I make my placings. And the international importance also of the Prix de l'Arc de Triomphe.

Here then are my Top Ten in order: 1 – Golden Fleece; 2 – Alleged; 3 – Sir Ivor; 4 – Nijinsky; 5 – Ballymoss; 6 – The Minstrel; 7 – El Gran Senor; 8 – Roberto; 9 – Sadler's Wells; 10 - King's Lake.

✳ ✳ ✳

In any final analysis of the great horses that passed through Vincent O'Brien's hands, you simply cannot escape the fact that Golden Fleece stands out as a colt way above the ordinary – a colt who was capable of going on to unsurpassed heights if he had not been forced to stud earlier than planned. You have only to speculate on how easily he would have won the Irish Derby and with what authority he would have added the King George VI and Queen Elizabeth Stakes and crowned it all by beating the best of the French in the Prix de l'Arc de Triomphe. Yes, the horizons were limitless.

As it was, he was unbeaten as a two-year-old and unbeaten also as a three-year-old. Granted, he had only one outing as a two-year-old, right at the back-end of 1981 but then from the very outset Vincent had set his mind on winning the Epsom Derby with this son of Nijinsky out of a Vaguely Noble mare who had cost $775,000 as a yearling.

(Brian Molony noted that it wasn't possible to train him for the Dewhurst, often a key race in the scheme of things for the special two-year-olds that represented Ballydoyle and Nijinsky, The Minstrel and El Gran Senor all won it and Golden Fleece didn't have the 2,000 Guineas as a primary opening target either in his three-year-old season. It had to be the Epsom Derby and basically his status would stand or fall on that race. Could he be rated 'tops' on the strength of one race? This was, in effect, the question Brian Molony posed.)

It was to be make-or-break time at Epsom on a June day in '82. All the knowledge and experience that Vincent had acquired in the training of five previous winners of the Blue Riband of English racing was poured into ensuring that Golden Fleece got to the starting stalls in the very peak of condition. Then unless something untoward happened, he had the breeding and he had the acceleration to deliver the prize that would recoup with interest – when he was put to stud – the heavy outlay in acquiring him at the Keeneland Sales.

And deliver he did, covering the Derby distance in 2 min 34.27 secs – a record since electrical timing was first utilised in 1964. You have got to see that victory too against the background that ten days before the Derby a swelling developed in his off-hind hock that raised the spectre, as Vincent told me, that he was not quite sound at that point.The trusted Bob Griffin had to bring into play his vast expertise and know-how to rectify the problem. Happily, it didn't prevent Golden Fleece taking his place in the Derby field.

Victory in the Irish Derby looked a formality as the connections of those immediately behind Golden Fleece at Epsom made it clear that they would not throw down the gauntlet to him again at the Curragh. Little wonder that in the opening ante-post lists, his odds were as short as 1-3. Vincent O'Brien, going on the acceleration he had shown at Epsom, was fully confident that he would not alone have won the Curragh Classic but gone on to add the King George and very likely the 'Arc' also to his laurels.

We have seen already how he coughed on the eve of the Epsom Derby and, as Brian Molony revealed, there was a distinct possibility that he might have had to be withdrawn. But he survived the scare. However, winning the Classic so authoritatively and with such sheer brilliance when he wasn't fully himself obviously left its mark – internally if not immediately clear on the surface. Inside a fortnight he was again battling a cold, with Ballydoyle's vet, Demi O'Byrne – nowadays commanding headlines with John Magnier and Michael Tabor at the yearling sales – giving him all the attention that a loving parent would give a sick only son.

Overnight the original next target on the racecourse of the Irish Derby had to be shelved and not long after that it was obvious that the King George was out as well. He had hardly recovered from the cold when a swelling developed in one of his hind legs – a different one this time from that which had given trouble in the count-down to Epsom.

Golden Fleece's golden racing career was over. There was nothing for it but to retire him to stud at Coolmore. Valued at $25 million, he seemed to have a glittering career as a stallion before him but he developed cancer and eighteen months later was dead. A team of top American surgeons had been flown in to operate on him. Initially it seemed that it was a success. But two months had hardly passed when secondaries developed and the heart of a lion that he had shown in coming from last to first with such an awesome sweep at Epsom on a June day in '82 could not save him on a dark February day in '84. "His premature death was a tragedy – a tragedy for Coolmore and for the Irish breeding industry", said his owner Robert Sangster.

It would have been so easy in his case to use the old cliche "we shall not see his like again" as so many used it when Arkle passed away. But racing is the one game where one cannot dwell on the tragedies that can hit great horses – even the greatest.

We can only go on hoping that new champions will be thrown up that we can compare with the peerless ones that left indelible footprints.

Nothing will ever efface the footprints left on racing's sands of time by Golden Fleece on Derby Day '82.

Philip Myerscough, son-in-law of Vincent O'Brien and Chief Executive of Goffs presents the Goffs/Irish Racing Annual Personality of the Year (1996) Award in Irish racing to Fergie Sutherland, trainer of 1996 Gold Cup winner, Imperial Call at a luncheon in Goffs attended by a wide cross-section of personalities from the racing world. (Picture: Peter Mooney)

22

The
Magnificent Six

Nowhere in the world will you find more competitive racing on the Flat than over the four days of the Royal Ascot meeting in June. Yet in 1975 Vincent O'Brien pulled off the phenomenal feat of winning six races from seven runners. And he crowned a memorable Ascot week by taking the Churchill Stakes at the Heath meeting on the Saturday with Guillaume Tell.

Imperial March (Queen Anne Stakes), Swingtime (Cork and Orrery), Gay Fandango (Jersey Stakes), Blood Royal (Queen's Vase), Gallina (Ribbesdale) and Boone's Cabin (Wokingham) were the sextet of winners, with Sir Penfro (Tommy Murphy) finishing 5th in the Hardwicke Stakes.

Four of the winners were ridden by Lester Piggott, with light weights for Imperial March and Swingtime meaning success for Gianfranco Dettori (Frankie Dettori's father) and Willie Carson.

As he read the headlines commanded by the "Magnificent Six", his brother, Phonsie had reason to reflect back exactly a quarter-of-century to another achievement in the period when Vincent was still training in Churchtown and far from being an internationally-known figure when he turned out nine winners with seven horses over the Christmas period 1950.

Vincent took one race at Leopardstown, the Shankill Hurdle, with Hatton's Grace. And he won eight at Limerick with The Beetle (Greenpark Maiden Hurdle), Little Boy Blue (Holiday Handicap Hurdle), Dashing Lady (Mungret Novice Chase), Lucky Dome (Rineanna Plate), Airlift (County Maiden Hurdle), Little Boy Blue (City Handicap Hurdle), Dashing Lady (Thomond Handicap Chase) and Silk Cottage (Southern Plate).

"I rode seven of those winners at Limerick", recalled Phonsie. "I was unable to do the weight on Little Boy Blue in the Holiday Handicap Hurdle and Eddie Kennedy had the ride".

But back to the Royal Ascot bonanza. Vincent O'Brien showed amazing initiative in getting Gay Fandango to the starting stalls for the Jersey Stakes. He was a doubtful runner right up to the week-end before Royal Ascot. He had been hit with sore shins after finishing fourth to Grundy in the Irish 2,000 Guineas.

"The Boss was very keen to get him to Ascot and left no stone unturned", recalled Vincent Rossiter, one of the outstanding work riders at Ballydoyle in a *Racing Post* interview. "I remember he got an acupuncturist from Cork to come up and treat the horse on the Saturday and Sunday.

"We couldn't believe our eyes as we watched him putting pins in Gay Fandango's shins and completing the treatment that an acupuncturist would normally perform on a human being. Frankly, we never thought that we would see a horse getting THE treatment at Ballydoyle. It was a gamble by the Boss and it certainly paid off".

Acupuncturists may now be an accepted part of homeopathic treatment but in 1975 – on humans or on equines – such treatment was unorthodox, in Ireland in particular.

Vincent Rossiter in the same interview noted that it was "another great achievement by the Boss to get Blood Royal to the meeting – not alone win the Queen's Vase".

"The horse suffered from recurring leg trouble and I rode him a lot at work on his own. We covered a lot of ground instead of doing fast work", he added.

Vincent O'Brien invariably chose his Flat jockeys, when Lester Piggott could not do the weight at a meeting like Royal Ascot '75, with all the care and knowledge of individual ability that he had shown earlier in his career when picking his horsemen for the Aintree Grand National.

The choice of Gianfranco Dettori for Imperial March proved an inspired one. "Imperial March was a horse that didn't like being in front too soon," noted Vincent Rossiter. "Gianfranco obeyed the Boss's instructions to a tee, coming fast and late to win in a photo-finish."

Lester Piggott excelled on Gallina and Boone's Cabin. Vincent O'Brien produced the filly Gallina to the very peak of condition for the Ribblesdale that was to prove the one red-letter day in a career that subsequently would see her fail to win another race. Lester had her out like a bullet from the stalls and relishing the fast ground, she streaked home by four lengths.

Boone's Cabin carried 10 stone in the Wokingham Stakes but Piggott's judgement of pace was seldom seen to better advantage as he won with supreme confidence. It was a weight-carrying record for this event.

✳   ✳   ✳

In 1961 Brud Fetherstonhaugh brought three horses to Royal Ascot and all three won – Silver Tor (King's Stand Stakes), Bun Penny (Cork and Orrery Stakes) and Prince Tor (Windsor Castle Stakes).

But Vincent O'Brien's six winners out of seven runners in '75 was not alone unique but incomparable. It must be set against Aidan O'Brien sending ten runners to the 1997 meeting and winning one race, his first Royal Ascot success, in actual fact, with Harbour Master (Christy Roche) in the Coventry Stakes and he was narrowly denied a second winner when Hopping Higgins (Michael Kinane), running for Niall Quinn's Sporting

169

Quest Syndicate failed by a short head in a photo finish to Tippit Boy in the Norfolk Stakes.

It must be set also against Henry Cecil taking nine years up to 1997 to achieve a total of 17 winners from 85 runners and that, as Gary Nutting pointed out in a *Sporting Life* feature in the count-down to Royal Ascot '97, represented a strike rate of 20 per cent. Cecil, the ten-times English Flat champion trainer, had achieved a total of 61 Royal Ascot winners by the end of the '97 meeting – a truly outstanding record for a man who has been at the top of his profession for twenty years.

"I've always loved the meeting," Cecil told Gary Nutting. "But you've got to plan if you're taking it seriously. Occasionally, you can get away with bringing a horse straight from Epsom, but basically it takes months, rather than weeks, of preparation, bringing them along accordingly," added Cecil, who revealed that of the many great moments he had enjoyed at Royal Ascot, the ones that really stood out were the five Gold Cup wins with Le Moss, Ardross (two apiece) and Paean.

Vincent O'Brien had a "bag" of 25 Royal Ascot winners from the time he sent out Adare to win the Jersey Stakes in 1956 to his final flourish in 1993 when he trained College Chapel to win the Cork and Orrery Stakes with Lester Piggott in the saddle.

There is little doubt, in my mind, that Vincent would have added greatly to his tally if he had not wisely decided to by-pass the meeting with some of his best two-year-olds because he was already thinking ahead to their three-year-old careers. Sir Ivor, Nijinsky and Roberto made their racecourse debuts at home in July while The Minstrel, Golden Fleece and El Gran Senor were not produced until the autumn. It was actually November 1st before Alleged saw a racecourse for the first time. The making of stallions invariably resulted in the Epsom Derby being the primary target ahead of all else for the colts and the Dewhurst Stakes was the race that had a way of becoming the launching pad for 2,000 Guineas success, as in the case of Nijinsky, The Minstrel and El Gran Senor, with three other winners of the same race, Try My Best, Monteverdi and Storm Bird failing to train on.

The tumult of applause that greeted Vincent O'Brien as he led College Chapel into the winner's enclosure after the Cork and Orrery Stakes triumph in '93 represented an outpouring of general acclaim and admiration for the Master of Ballydoyle who had graced this racecourse with such distinction over a 35-years span. Inherent in the cheers also was a spontaneous tribute to Lester Piggott, then 57 years of age, who had come out of retirement to renew his partnership with Vincent O'Brien.

*　　*　　*

Vincent loved the challenge that Royal Ascot presented, loved the red-hot competition and got immense personal pleasure in producing contenders to beat the best that Britain and France could put in the field. In the year – 1997 – that Boris Becker said farewell to Wimbledon he was quoted as saying: "This is just 'the place'. It is the most important, the most prestigious, the oldest tournament in the world".

And the immaculate Pete Sampras, the man who beat him in his Last Hurrah match and who went on to land his fourth crown, acknowledged: "This is what the game's all about for us, Boris and I. Wimbledon. The grand slams."

Substitute Royal Ascot for Wimbledon and you get the same aura, the same sense of tradition, that something that transcends the mundane and the ordinary with the extraordinary.

It may seem trite to write it but it's worth repeating – Royal Ascot is to Flat racing what Cheltenham is to National Hunt racing.

I realise from savouring Cheltenham for well over two decades now that on a certain level the two are a world apart, that the twain can never meet. There's no royal enclosure at Cheltenham, none of that exclusivity born of class and a so-formal dress code to accompany it that is anathema in a way to those aficionados of the jump game, Irish and English alike, who have stood shoulder-to-shoulder with me on the grass outside the Arkle Bar watching the climactic moments of another epic Queen Mother Champion Chase, three chasers maybe rising in line and horsemen supreme battling it out to the line. You are content in your winter clothes. The cut and thrust of the chase is all.

Strip it of the top hats and tails for the gentlemen, of the ladies coming out in all their finery and – at times – outlandish displays of headgear, strip it of the top-hatted, green velvet, frock-coated attendants and strip it too of one-and-a-half tons of smoked salmon and as many as 4,500 lobsters being washed down with 50,000 bottles of champagne, with the inevitable strawberries and cream to follow, and it would still stand up there on a pedestal apart as providing the finest four days of Flat racing that you could find anywhere in the world. I am reflecting as I write this chapter on the manner in which the spine-tingling excitement engendered in every fibre of my being as I watched Pat Eddery win the 1997 Gold Cup with a masterly display of wait-and-wait until the death tactics on Celeric, a horse that needed to be ridden that way to win and I am thinking likewise of the congratulations showered on Michael Kinane in the winner's enclosure after he had won the Jersey Stakes on Among Men from what some would have considered beforehand as an 'impossible' draw (like the great jockey he is, he simply 'floated' across to get the rails).

In between races you can savour a Pimm's on the lawn convenient to the parade ring while studying form with your friends. And, as you depart the scene at the end of the day's racing, you can pause awhile and listen to the band, mingling with those who have emerged from the Royal enclosure and from private boxes, others who had lost themselves during racing over their gin and tonics in the conviviality of the Mill Reef and Brigadier Gerard bars. Rub shoulders too with bouncy mini-skirted office-girls and normally-retiring housewives, dressed as they think fit for the annual day-out, having come by rail to make it party time and have a ball, unhindered by the social barriers, knowing they will never have a picnic in front of a Rolls Royce but they represent, one likes to think, the democratic side of an unchanging British institution which, amazing as it may seem, can provide something for everyone.

The band plays on in the sun. The band-master leads the singing of the old favourites, "My Bonnie Lies Over The Ocean", "I'm Forever Blowing Bubbles", "Side By Side", "Knees Up Mother Brown", "Bless Them All", "Daisy, Daisy", "Follow The Band", "London Town", as knots of onlookers, linking arms, sway with the music.

"Only the British have the capacity to create a tradition like this and preserve it", said a friend beside me who later admitted over dinner that he can never escape the lure of Royal Ascot each summer. It's singular, it has its own magic quality and no doubt the pre-race Royal parade down the course will last as long as Royalty lasts.

Royal Ascot needs the sun as Punchestown and Galway become far, far more enjoyable and redolent with atmosphere when the weather is fair and sunny. The rains came down on Gold Cup Day at Royal Ascot '97 and the scene was miserable, disenchanting and limp. Made one want to sing in utter frustration: "When skies are blue…"

※　※　※

Gladness was the greatest Royal Ascot winner that Vincent produced – that gallant mare in the Dawn Run mould who in three successive races in the 1958 season won the Gold Cup and then the Goodwood Cup and the Ebor Handicap, Lester Piggott being the successful jockey on each occasion. Indeed, Piggott began his association with the Ballydoyle stable when he rode Gladness in the Ascot Gold Cup and it was the first – and only – time that Vincent went into detail when giving him his instructions and discussing tactics with him; he even showed him films of all the mare's previous races (subsequently they reached such a communion of minds that it was hardly ever necessary for the Master to 'instruct' the rider he trusted more than anyone else).

It was at York in the Ebor Handicap that Gladness gave Vincent O'Brien one of his greatest moments and made him a very proud man indeed as she won in the proverbial canter by six lengths under 9st 7lbs. And adding to Vincent's pride was the fact that William Hill, one of the most fearless bookies of his day, should, as we have seen already, have described it as "the greatest" performance he had ever seen in a handicap.

Coming up to 40 years from the day Gladness won the Ascot Gold Cup, Vincent and Jacqueline were back to see their son Charles seeking to land the Cork & Orrery Stakes with Burden Of Proof, winner of his two previous races. And this, as we have seen, was the race Vincent had won with College Chapel as he said farewell as a trainer to the Royal Ascot scene in 1993.

Burden Of Proof could only finish seventeenth behind the all-the-way winner, the Barry Hills-trained Royal Applause, backed to 11-2 favouritism and carrying a wealth of "inspired" money (I was told beforehand that this one would not be beaten).

✻   ✻   ✻

The magnificent victory of El Gran Senor in the 1984 English 2,000 Guineas was in a way the last great peak attained by a challenger from Ballydoyle. We did not realise it then but his so-narrow, so-galling defeat in the Epsom Derby marked the beginning of the decline, the setting down of the sun.

True, a glow would linger in the sky for almost another decade – to the day Royal Academy lifted the Breeders Cup Mile (Turf) at Belmont Park, New York in 1990 in the hands of Lester Piggott, who was also The Man at Royal Ascot in 1993 when, as already recounted, Vincent had his last winner at the 'Royal' meeting in College Chapel.

It's worth noting for the record though that Law Society would have provided Vincent O'Brien with a seventh Epsom Derby winner in 1985 but for the misfortune of running up against Slip Anchor; in a way it was the same as that of P.J. 'Darkie' Prendergast's Meadow Court in 1965 when he caught a tarter in the English Derby in the peerless Sea Bird II (rated by Vincent O'Brien as the finest colt he had seen outside of the great horses he trained himself). Both Law Society and Meadow Court gained due compensation by taking the Irish Derby.

Law Society cost $2.7 million at the Keeneland Sales, the highest price fetched by any of Alleged's offspring. The dam Bold Bikini was a six time winner and had foaled six other winners, the best of them being the high-class 1978 two-year-old Strike Your Colours.

Following a winning debut at the Curragh, Law Society won the Anglesey Stakes and the National Stakes before starting a well-backed favourite to give Vincent O'Brien an eighth win in the Dewhurst Stakes. And this despite the fact that he was opposed by highly-rated Mill Reef Stakes winner, Local Suitor and Noblequest, one of the best two-year-olds out of France. Law Society made his effort two furlongs out and got locked in a great battle with Local Suitor and Kala Dancer. It looked as if it would be another day of triumph for Vincent O'Brien when Law Society took the lead inside the last fifty yards but he was caught late and beaten a head by Kala Dancer. If he had not hung somewhat in the final stages, he would have won.

Vincent O'Brien made no bones in predicting that Law Society would have no trouble in staying a mile and a half as a three-year-old and went on record also to state that he was bred to be a Derby colt.

Law Society made his reappearance in the Chester Vase, which Henbit (1980) and Shergar (1981) had won on the way to victory at Epsom and in which Vincent O'Brien had not had a runner since 1972. He impressed when beating Petoski by two-and-a-half lengths.

Vincent O'Brien produced him looking a picture at Epsom. The Henry Cecil-trained Slip Anchor, with Steve Cauthen in the saddle, forged a substantial lead coming down Tattenham Hill. Three furlongs out Law Society went past Supreme Leader and stayed on with all the stamina that one would expect from a son of Alleged. However, he could not peg back Slip Anchor, who had seven lengths to spare at the finish. But Law Society was so much superior to the rest of the field that the third horse home, Damister was six lengths behind him.

Theatrical, seventh at Epsom, and Damister renewed rivalry with 15-8 favourite Law Society at the Curragh and also in the field for the 1985 Irish Derby were Mouktar, easy winner of the French Derby and Group 1 winners, Baillamont and David O'Brien's Triptych, who that season had become the first filly to win the Irish 2,000 Guineas.

Law Society had a rough passage early in the race. Switched to the outside in the straight by Pat Eddery, he made fine headway and with a hundred yards left caught the Dermot Weld-trained Theatrical to win by half-a-length. In the International Classifications for 1985 Law Society got a rating of 90 to 95 for Slip Anchor and 86 for Theatrical.

There were other moments that were significant – moments on the domestic front, in particular, like Leading Counsel taking the Irish St. Leger in 1985 and Dark Lomond winning the race in 1988 – the season that saw Prince Of Birds win the Irish 2,000 Guineas. Challengers from Ballydoyle could still score in the big juvenile events at home but it has got to be admitted that such had been Vincent's strike rate down the years that these victories were taken almost for granted. And, ironically, they were overshadowed too by the fact that the flow of big-race winners in Britain dried up to all intents and purposes after El Gran Senor won the 2,000 Guineas in 1984, the season that saw Sadler's Wells take the Eclipse Stakes and Magic Mirror the Norfolk Stakes. Bluebird was sent over to win the King's Stand Stakes in 1987 with Cash Asmussen in the saddle and Royal Academy won the July Cup in 1990. But the glory days had all but come to an end.

A virus reared its head at a critical juncture to further dampen spirits down Ballydoyle way. A number of highly-regarded juveniles could not make their appearance in 1986, among them Fair Judgement, the Alleged colt out of Mystical Mood, owned by Sheikh Mohammed and Robert Sangster's Entitled, which had an outstanding pedigree, being by Mill Reef out of Lady Capulet, which Vincent had trained to win the Irish 1,000 Guineas in 1977.

Fair Judgement didn't see a racecourse till June '87 when he made a winning debut at the Curragh and in his next outing took the Pacemaker International Stakes (Group 2) at the Phoenix Park but he disappointed subsequently. Entitled ran Don't Forget Me to half-a-length in the Irish 2,000 Guineas of '87, then justified odds of 4-7 in the Desmond Stakes and was beaten a neck by the French-trained Triptych in the Phoenix Champion Stakes.

The old buzz created by seemingly unbeatable two-year-olds was no longer there. The era was past when McCarthy's pub in Fethard hummed with "inspired" gleanings from the gallops that sent men scurrying to the bookies to lay ante-post wagers on events often a year away. That buzz would be evident not just down South Tipperary way. It would carry out from McCarthy's well beyond the borders of Tipperary and once I received a letter from an Irishman working in the hotel business in a South Sea island asking for a copy of the *Irish Racing Annual* carrying Vincent's assessment of his Classic prospects for the following year.

※　　※　　※

It was fitting that Lester Piggott should have come out of retirement in answer to Vincent's urgings to provide the last Grand Flourish.

It all began really on an evening in July, 1990 – Friday 13th to be exact – at Tipperary racecourse. That was the evening when the germ of the idea formed in the mind of Vincent O'Brien that Lester was ready to return to the saddle. It only remained for someone to offer the word of encouragement that would make Piggott take the plunge.

Lester had come over to ride in the Silvermines Veterans Race. There was a certain fun aspect permeating that lovely sunny evening as Piggott on the John Horgan-owned, Edward O'Grady-trained Don Leone was pitted against Jonjo O'Neill on the Jim Bolger-trained Allegorio. The emotions of racegoers were torn between wanting to cheer Lester home and at the same time being eager for a throw-back to that never-to-be-forgotten afternoon at Cheltenham in 1986 when Jonjo O'Neill lifted the Gold Cup on Dawn Run.

As it was, O'Neill came off best by one-and-a-half lengths over Lester, who later relaxed over dinner with a group of friends, including John Magnier, Tommy Stack and Timmy Hyde in the Royal Hotel in Tipperary.

On the Sunday Piggott had to be content with third place behind Chirkpar, ridden for trainer John Oxx by that most accomplished of French jockeys, Yves Saint-Martin with Orbis (G. W. Robinson) in the runner-up position in the John Dennis Veterans Race, staged as part of the Turf Club's bicentenary celebrations.

Now Vincent O'Brien had made up his mind that the moment was ripe to press Lester to ride again professionally. "I noted that evening in Tipperary and again at the Curragh on the Sunday how fit Lester was," said Vincent. "I realised that he was quite up to the task of pitting his experience and skill against the best around and I had no doubt in my mind that if he did decide to come out of retirement, he would have no regrets".

Of course, Lester did not need all that much encouragement to answer the call. There was a certain routine about life at Newmarket, riding out in the mornings as the string, now trained by his wife Susan, went through their paces on the gallops while the afternoons were as often as not spent looking at racing on television. Piggott hankered for the excitement and the challenge of conquering high peaks. It was in his blood. It had been his life as long as he cared to remember. The roar of the crowd was the sweetest music of all to his ears.

There was a biting wind out across the Curragh plain on an October afternoon – three months on from the Veterans Race at the Curragh – when, already having made his mark in the initial stages of his comeback in England, he journeyed over to ride four for Vincent O'Brien and, in addition, he had another booked mount. Yes, I will remember Tuesday, October 23, 1990 as a red-letter day in the Piggott comeback story.

He took the second race, a two-year-old maiden, on Legal Profession, owned by Jacqueline O'Brien, then rode a really brilliant finish as he nursed Denis McCarthy's filly, Fairy Folk (Fairy King-Tripoli) in the last furlong to hold on by a head. He won the third race by a comfortable three-quarters of a length on Classic Minstrel and then a rousing cheer went up from the crowd as he came with a powerful run on Dr Tony O'Reilly's Passer-By to take the last race by two-and-a-half lengths.

The Maestro was showing that he had lost none of his incomparable talent.

The renewal of a great partnership was exciting the racing public and making the turnstiles click merrily. And Vincent was fired up by it and anxious to provide Lester with the "ammunition" to continue to enter the winner's enclosure.

On the Bank Holiday Monday following his four-timer at the Curragh Piggott was back in Ireland, riding at Leopardstown this time. The magic of his name saw the attendance top the 10,000 mark – amazing really for a card that had nothing special on it.

His many admirers were not disappointed. On debutant Judicial Wit, he won the Baileys Mile (2-Y-O) for Vincent O'Brien, scoring by three-quarters of a length from Staunch Friend and Australian rider Ron Quinton.

But the memorable climax to Lester's comeback was his victory on Royal Academy in the Breeders' Cup Mile (Turf) in New York – his sixth success in six rides for Vincent O'Brien. Piggott undoubtedly rode one of the greatest races in a career marked by wonderful Classic and big-race triumphs, as he came with a sustained run to win by a neck.

If the Breeders' Cup triumph was the high-water mark at the backend of the 1990 season, there came an occasion to remember at Killarney on a July evening in 1991 that in a way represented the last acclaimed Act of the O'Brien-Piggott renewed link-up. The memory of that evening is still cherished by every one of the record crowd of 6,000 who flocked to the Kerry track.

Finbarr Slattery, who had announced that he would be retiring as Secretary of this most picturesque of racecourses at the end of '91 and who since then has produced his magnum opus, *Following The Horses* (containing a lifetime's memories of racing days and racing characters), had always had a dream and that was that Piggott would ride some day at Killarney.

A few attempts during Lester's prime had proved abortive because of

Piggott's contractual commitments in Britain and France. Now he was a free agent and agreed to mark Finbarr Slattery's farewell by coming over for the first day of the July Festival meeting. It caught the imagination of the Irish racing public in amazing fashion.

There was drama even before Piggott arrived at the track. The private plane conveying the colourful Barney Curley and himself to Farranfore airstrip had to be diverted because of low cloud to Cork airport. They reached Killarney just before the first race on the card – having got a helping hand from a Garda motor-cycle outrider when getting through Cork's heavy traffic that evening (the Tall Ships extravaganza was on in the Southern capital). Piggott would have his first ride in the third race.

The sombre clouds dispersed and allowed the sun to bathe the majestic setting of the backdrop of the surrounding Kerry mountains. You could sense the calm of the lakes made famous in song. As Piggott took in the scene, someone asked him if had ever ridden in such a beautiful setting and he replied laconically and with a mischievous grin: "I've been to worse!".

The ever-resourceful Finbarr Slattery had posted a blown-up print of a 15-year-old Lester, already a winner, overlooking the scales in the weighing room – just to be sure it caught the eye!

The one missing link that made the scene incomplete was that Vincent O'Brien was in Kentucky for the Keeneland Sales. Charles also. But Charles was by a phone in the Keeneland Sales Ring, awaiting three important calls from one of his father's assistant trainers, Vincent Rossiter. These would come through after Piggott had ridden each of the three booked rides he had for Ballydoyle.

First he swept to a three-lengths win on Defendant in the Kerry EBF Maiden (2-Y-O). A great roar went up from the crowd as he passed the winning post and the cheering redoubled as he entered the winner's enclosure, smiling broadly. "Gosh, you'd think he'd won another Derby!", gasped his beaming daughter Tracy.

This was only the start of a fabulous evening. The crowd had seen Piggott come from behind on Defendant. Now they were to see him wait in front as only he could do it as he stormed to a five-lengths victory on News Headlines in the featured Heineken Handicap. He completed a three-timer for Vincent O'Brien on Classic Trust and like News Headlines this Tate Gallery colt carried the colours of Classic Thoroughbreds.

Charles O'Brien took the last of the calls in the Bluegrass country of Kentucky that confirmed that Lester had scored his third victory on three rides for the Ballydoyle stable and passed on the news to his father. There would be no sudden display of emotion from Vincent, but deep down he would have had reason to reflect that if Lester had been on Royal Academy on the day of the Irish 2,000 Guineas at the Curragh he would have waited and waited – waited until the death and might well have got the verdict over Tirol and Pat Eddery.

❊   ❊   ❊

Before he called it a day at the end of the 1994 season, Vincent O'Brien had only a handful of horses in his charge – around a dozen at most. Why did he hang on so long? Why did he wait until he was into his 77th year to finally call it a day?

"Horses are in his blood. He just liked to go out and see them every day", explained Phonsie O'Brien.

Vincent's own summation was simple and direct: "It's hard to break the habits of years".

After El Gran Senor, he waited and waited for another 'wonder colt' to come, but none came. I put it to Vincent himself that after six Epsom Derby wins, five Irish Derby wins and three Prix de l'Arc de Triomphe successes, allied to all the other big-race wins, perhaps the public had come to expect too much of him?

"It all comes down in the end to the material you have in your hands", he said with emphasis. "You can't turn them into Classic winners if they are not good enough".

"If they are not good enough…" Yes, there was the bottom line. When the horses he put through his hands were good enough, there was no one to equal him in preparing them for the day that mattered.

And no one who could take the pressure like him. He said to me in 1997 that the greatest pressure of all was when you had a colt capable of landing the Epsom Derby and it was a hot favourite like Sir Ivor, Nijinsky or Golden Fleece.

The author, Raymond Smith pictured with Dennis Kennedy, Dr P.J. Hillery, former President and prior to that European Commissioner, Val Dorgan and John McColgan at the launching in Dublin by Dr Hillery of his book of memoirs, _Urbi Et Orbi And All That._

PART FIVE

BATTLES WITH THE TURF CLUB

23

The Wheel Comes Full Circle

T he wheel came full circle from the period in his career which he described as "the dark days" when Vincent O'Brien was elected an Honorary member of the Irish Turf Club in 1997. It was a gesture that touched both Jacqueline and himself very deeply.

Now you might say the curtain had come down finally and irrevocably on all the heart-rending trauma that had stemmed from "The Chamour Affair" of over three-and-a-half decades earlier.

"The worst experience I ever had", was how Vincent had viewed the year when he was deprived of his licence and, not alone that, but Jacqueline and himself and the four children had to leave Ballydoyle while Phonsie took over the reins and ensured that there was continuity at least.

At one stage Vincent decided to quit the game altogether. "He wanted to hear nothing about racing and for months wouldn't even talk about it", Phonsie told me in his home in Kilsheelan in South Tipperary.

But he was persuaded by loyal friends from the ultimate course of action that would have deprived Irish racing and breeding of the man whose achievements in subsequent seasons made such a lasting impact on the global scale. Indeed, at one point there was even speculation as to whether John McShain, one of his millionaire owners, would bring him to the States to train in a private capacity for him. "Vincent O'Brien is a genius in the world of racing. I feel this so strongly that I would be prepared to set him up in America", McShain was quoted as saying at the time.

Europe's loss would certainly have been America's gain.

✳ ✳ ✳

As I write this chapter in the summer of '97, thirty-seven years have passed since Chamour was found to have tested positive after winning an inconsequential race – the Ballysax Plate, a ten-furlong event for maidens on the Curragh card on Wednesday, April 20, 1960. Chamour started 4-6 favourite.

The race in question could never have been used as the medium of a gamble – even if the stable was tilting at the ring then as it did in the old days. Chamour's target was the Irish Derby that same season and it would have been sheer madness to have administered a drug in order to ensure that he would win a maiden race that was not going to make one iota of difference to his value. Die Hard was the colt earmarked for the Epsom Derby.

"My personal gain from Chamour's victory was £20 – ten per cent of the stake", Vincent would say subsequently as he went to see his solicitors on receiving the news of his suspension.

Dope testing had only been recently introduced by the Irish Turf Club. It commenced with the practice of picking 'out of the hat' the name of one winner on each day's card who would be tested for dope. Only samples of sweat and saliva were taken – not urine.

The Turf Club did not have its own facilities and, therefore, relied on the London-based laboratory, Herd and Mundy, who had their headquarters in Weymouth Street. Samples were sent to London by registered post.

The certificate sent back in Chamour's case simply stated that the sample of saliva taken from the colt "contained approximately 1/10,000th grain of an Amphetamine derivative resembling Methylamphetamine". The sweat sample gave 1/5000th on analysis.

No second sample was taken, so once the Turf Club got the findings sent back from London, that in effect was that. There was no basis available to the Stewards for cross-checking with another source before handing down sentence.

No positive identification of the drug it claimed had been found on Chamour was made in the certificate received from London. "You know, one ten thousandth of a grain of something resembling methylamphetamine cost Vincent his licence to train for twelve months", was Phonsie O'Brien's forceful expression of his feelings on the Turf Club's decision. One could only conclude that the certificate was so nebulous in its contents that it should never have become the deciding factor in putting Vincent O'Brien out of racing for a whole year and nearly causing him to quit altogether.

He was originally suspended, in fact, for eighteen months on the strength of this certificate. And, remember, he was allowed no legal representation to help in his defence at the Turf Club hearing. The suspension was later reduced to twelve months. Vincent was prepared to pursue the matter to the very limit to clear his name – both with the Stewards of the Turf Club and through the courts.

Indeed, prior to bringing a High Court action against the Turf Club, he was told privately that if he resorted to legal action, he would never be given a training licence again. As Jacqueline recalled: "Vincent's view was that he didn't care. It was more important to him to have the record put straight. In those days, remember, no one could question a decision by the Stewards. And even if you had lost your livelihood when you felt you had been wrongly accused of doping a horse in your stable, it was still the position that you must not, under any circumstances, contemplate legal proceedings.

"Vincent, however, felt so strongly about wanting to clear his name that he was determined to go right to the brink and over it, if necessary. So he went ahead with his Court action – regardless of the consequences".

Jacqueline was a key figure in the battle waged to clear Vincent's name. Influential figures on a global scale from Britain, to France, Germany and the States were prepared to put their reputations on the line in exposing the flaws in the 'certificate of doping' and proving that its very vagueness made it a document that should never have been used to condemn a man out of hand.

Nothing in the body of expert opinion was as incisive and clear-cut as the report of the Head Analyst at Scotland Yard, Dr L.C. Nicholls, who was highly critical of Mrs Mundy who had performed the tests on the samples taken from Chamour. It wasn't the first complaint he had received in relation to Mrs Mundy.

The crucial point made by Dr Nicholls was that "before it is possible to be dogmatic in saying that there is a foreign substance present which is characteristic of a horse-dope, it is essential, in my opinion, that the substance should be identified beyond reasonable doubt. It is obvious from the certificate supplied that the analyst has not done this in this case and, in fact, says so in the report which implies that an unidentified drug resembling methylamphetamine has been found".

He concluded: "As one constantly giving evidence in criminal cases, I am satisfied that the information given in the certificate might be valuable to an officer investigating a possible crime but it is valueless as definite proof of that crime".

Also very supportive of Vincent O'Brien were Tim Vigors, the famous fighter pilot during the Battle of Britain and an internationally-respected figure in the bloodstock and breeding industry and Dr Francis E. Camps, the British Home Office Pathologist, a recognised expert in Forensic Medicine, who flatly rejected the certificate on the basis that there was no evidence that Chamour had ingested any drug.

Ultimately, the findings assembled from the body of international experts were presented to the Stewards of the Turf Club in printed form as Vincent lodged an appeal for reconsideration of the case. The extraordinary response he received was that if they went back and admitted a mistake, the whole fabric of racing would be damaged. As one of the Stewards put it to Vincent: "The captain must go down with his ship".

And as Jacqueline said: "The Stewards appeared not to know how they could admit the possibility that they were wrong and, therefore, face the blame for their action. So while they reduced the original suspension from eighteen months to a year, they failed, in face of the body of expert international opinion presented to them, to clear Vincent's name."

They felt that the perception of authority in racing was more important than the fate of one person.

✳   ✳   ✳

It was on Friday, May 13,1960 – subsequently to be imprinted in Vincent's mind as "Black Friday" – that the whole world seemed to fall apart in an instant for the Master of Ballydoyle.

Vincent and his brother, Dermot and stable-jockey, the Australian Garnie Bougoure gathered in the Shelbourne Hotel on the afternoon of the Turf Club inquiry. The Turf Club headquarters, now at the Curragh, were centred then in Merrion Square.

The inquiry was conducted by the following Stewards: Joe McGrath, Sir Cecil Stafford-King-Harman and Major Victor McCalmont, then in his forties and later to become Senior Steward. As always with inquiries of this nature, it was held behind closed doors. Only the verdict was made public.

In the official terminology the Stewards were meeting "to hear Mr W.V. O'Brien's explanation of the presence of a drug and stimulant in the samples of saliva and sweat taken from Chamour".

The evidence of 21 witnesses was heard, including veterinary surgeons and a Garda Sergeant. In the official statement, as carried in the *Irish Racing Calendar,* the Stewards expressed themselves "satisfied that a drug or stimulant had been administered to Chamour for the purpose of affecting his speed and/or stamina in the race".

The statement added: "The Stewards of the Turf Club accordingly withdrew Mr O'Brien's licence to train under Rule 102(v), Rules of Racing and declared him a disqualified person under that Rule and under Rule 178 from May 13,1960 until November 1961."

They also disqualified Chamour and placed Timobriol first. As Timbobriol was a stable-companion of Chamour, Vincent O'Brien still got his £20 as his cut of the prize-money. But it was poor consolation as the real effect of the Stewards' announcement sank home. The fact that he had been declared a disqualified person meant that he was not allowed to "enter, run, train or ride a horse in any race at any recognised meeting or enter any racecourse, stand or enclosure".

Though subsequently the Stewards would make it clear in a statement in the *Irish Racing Calendar* that they did not find that Vincent O'Brien "had administered the drug or stimulant or knew of its administration", the fact remained that, as the Rules operated then, he was held responsible as the trainer of Chamour. There and then, the Stewards summarily withdrew his licence to train and disqualified him.

The Rules are different now and a forbidden substance can show up after a test without the axe coming down to deprive a trainer of his livelihood. Of vital importance is the fact that a trainer has the right to have the sample checked. The other great change brought about by the "Chamour Affair" was that the Irish Turf Club appointed their own analyst and no longer left themselves totally dependent on the doping certificate sent back to them from Britain after they had forwarded a sample across the Irish Sea. Every Irish winner would be automatically tested in Ireland.

Most important of all, however, was the decision not to rely solely on analysis of saliva and sweat.The Irish Stewards decided that a sample both of saliva and urine would be taken. Top veterinary experts on both sides of the Irish Sea had come out strongly in favour of this, arguing that it was impossible to decide beyond any shadow of doubt whether a horse had been doped from any analysis of saliva and sweat alone. This did not take cognisance of dilution in the system, whereas in the blood and urine of a horse a drug was secreted and excreted in its entirety.

* * *

The changes wrought by the furore caused by his suspension were in the future. Vincent O'Brien, then only 43, looked suddenly visibly older as the news reached him that evening in the Shelbourne Hotel. The worse aspect of all was that Vincent knew that the decision would mean exile for himself and his wife, Jacqueline and young family from their home, Ballydoyle House, Cashel. They would move to Phonsie's house while Phonsie and his wife and family moved to Ballydoyle.

To the media representatives who crowded into the hotel, he issued the following statement: "The Stewards have withdrawn my trainer's licence and declared me a disqualified person on the grounds that they found evidence of drugs in a routine sweat and saliva test taken from Chamour on April 20, a test to which I knew the horse was liable to be subjected.

"This horse won a £200 maiden race at the Curragh and neither I nor any person associated with the horse had a bet. My personal gain was £20 – ten per cent of the stake. I did not drug this or any other horse. I trust my staff and I have placed the matter in the hands of my solicitors."

Events accelerated quickly. Vincent O'Brien asked the Garda authorities to assist in trying to find the person or persons who doped Chamour. It was reported in the media that Scotland Yard inquiries were being pursued in Ireland "concerning an alleged 'drug ring' in England" and that the same ring might have 'got at' Chamour. Yorkshire businessman F.W. (Walter) Burmann, as the owner of Chamour, offered a £5,000 reward for information leading to the identification or conviction of the persons responsible for doping the colt.

The Turf Club stopped short of ordering that Vincent O'Brien remove all the horses trained by him from the Ballydoyle stables. This allowed his younger brother, Phonsie, to take over the training of the 70-strong string. "He knows my methods, so it will make no difference to the horses", said Vincent. To make the change-over operate as smoothly as possible, Phonsie soon moved the twenty horses he was training at the time from his own stables in South Tipperary to Ballydoyle.

The Turf Club permitted Chamour to continue racing, which surprised some English commentators, who pointed out that in England a horse found to be doped would be automatically barred for life. Chamour impressed when finishing fourth to stable-companion Die Hard in the strongly-contested Trigo Stakes and then won the Gallinule Stakes, his final preparation race before the Irish Derby.

* * *

Irish Derby Day 1960 was to see one of the most significant and extraordinary demonstrations ever witnessed on the occasion of an Irish Classic race at the Curragh. Vincent O'Brien, of course, as a disqualified person, could not attend. He was actually fishing along his favourite stretch of the Blackwater River, listening to the race on the portable radio by his side, as Chamour, in the hands of the artistic Garnie Bougoure, passed the post a length in front of Alcaeus (Ron Hutchinson), runner-up to St. Paddy in the Epsom Derby, with Prince Chamier (T.P. Burns) third.

"We want Vincent, we want Vincent", came the chant from the crowd of 10,000 who had watched the race in sweltering heat. It echoed from the packed enclosures out over the wide expanse of the Curragh plain. These racegoers were venting in no uncertain fashion their feelings about the injustice of the suspension imposed on the Master of Ballydoyle.

First, the scenes were wildly enthusiastic and then they grew in tension as hundreds burst across the course from the infield area to the reserved enclosure and joined the swelling throng already congregated outside the Stewards' room. "Give Vincent back his licence, give it back", they shouted. It was the roar of an angry crowd, the eruption of deep-felt feelings. Men in shirt sleeves in the sun, who had swept across from the 'popular' area of the racecourse, mingled in the swaying crowd with those who had dressed more sedately for a Classic occasion.

But all who had come to idolise Vincent O'Brien for his momentous achievements at Cheltenham and Liverpool could no longer conceal their disappointment at the fact that he was so cruelly denied the honour of being there to see Chamour win a second Irish Derby for him. These racegoers knew that instead of "Trained A.S. O'Brien", the entry in the racecard should have read "Trained M.V. O'Brien".

The crowd surged towards the Stewards' room and for one terrible and very frightening moment it seemed that they would burst into its hallowed precincts. The unthinkable was fortunately avoided.

However, this became the day when the Stewards of the Irish Turf Club came to realise the mood that had been stirred among the Irish racing public. The overwhelming demonstration of the people's will was to contribute in no small way to the reduction of the term of suspension from eighteen months to a year.

Another major contributory factor was the spotlight put in the media on a report that Vincent O'Brien was going to test the Turf Club decision in the Courts.

The Stewards of the Turf Club published a statement in the *Irish Racing Calendar* of Friday, July 20, 1960 completely exonerating Vincent O'Brien of any imputation that he had administered the drug or stimulant, or knew of its administration, adding that any other impression given by the wording of their previous decision was incorrect.

The statement offered a measure of justice but, still, he was a disqualified person unable to pursue his livelihood and unable to set foot on any racecourse in Ireland or Britain.

He was forced to apply to the Stewards to have the suspension reconsidered. On foot of this application, a special meeting of the Stewards was held on November 25, 1960 and it was decided to cut the suspension from eighteen months to twelve.

But why did they not lift the suspension entirely from him? Why did he have to wait until mid-May, 1961 to have his licence to train restored to him?

The trauma of the "Chamour Affair" continued for Vincent O'Brien even after his period in the wilderness ended on Saturday, May 13,1961. There was one final act in the long-drawn-out drama – in the Courts this time.

Vincent O'Brien had sued the Turf Club for libel because the extraordinary bloomer had been made of repeating in the "Races Past Plus Calendar" Volume (Bound) for 1960 mention of the fact that he had been declared a disqualified person under Rule 178 (when in actual fact they had acknowledged publicly that it would have been sufficient to have mentioned only Rule 102 in their original statement).

The libel case was due for hearing in the High Court on Wednesday, July 5,1961 but John A. Costello, for Vincent O'Brien announced that a settlement had been reached. He read an apology from the Stewards in which they said that it was never their intention to blame Mr O'Brien personally during the doping inquiry. They acknowledged that there was no evidence before them upon which such findings could be made.

The Turf Club had to pay all legal costs.

As he left the Court, Vincent O'Brien told reporters: "My only aim was to clear my name. I had no interest in damages. The matter is now closed."

The "Chamour Affair" had wounded him so deeply that I found that thirty years later he did not even like to discuss it. That of itself only re-opened the wounds, causing them to fester again.

He was wont to leave it to Jacqueline to elaborate on the facts, to pinpoint the blatant weaknesses in the doping certificate on which his whole career as a trainer rested in the final analysis.

There came a day at the Curragh in the Nineties when Vincent O'Brien was having a drink with the Stewards after winning a race and Sir Cecil Stafford-King-Harman (one of the three Stewards who warned him off thirty years earlier) extended his hand and said: "O'Brien, I'll forgive you, if you forgive me."

Vincent turned away and left the room. His comment on that moment was: "What had I ever done to them that needed forgiveness? They never lost a night's sleep over us – they tried to ruin me."

✳   ✳   ✳

Six years before "The Chamour Affair", Vincent O'Brien had his licence withdrawn for three months over alleged discrepancy between the English and Irish form of four horses in his charge – Royal Tan, Lucky Dome, Early Mist and Knock Hard.

In fact, it was five days before Royal Tan ran in the 1954 Aintree Grand National that Vincent O'Brien found himself attending the inquiry in Dublin in the old headquarters of the Irish Turf Club in Hume Street and this time it was conducted by the Stewards of the Irish National Hunt Steeplechase Committee with Chief Steward, Pierce Molony (father of the late Dr Paddy Molony and grandfather of Pierce Molony, Secretary/Manager of Thurles Racecourse) in the chair.

Jockeys T.P. Burns, Pat Taaffe, Phonsie O'Brien, P.J. Doyle and Eddie Kennedy were among the witnesses examined along with owners Harry Keogh and Vincent's brother, Dermot. The initial hearing was adjourned to allow two Stipendiary Stewards of the English National Hunt Committee to attend and also jockey Bryan Marshall and owner John A Woods to give evidence.

After the second hearing on March 31st, a statement was issued to the effect that "the Stewards of the INHS Committee could not accept Mr M.V. O'Brien's explanations and when considering what action to take on these findings, the Stewards had before them the fact that Mr M.V. O'Brien had been warned and cautioned on several occasions as to the running of his horses.

"The Stewards under Rule 16(ii) and 104(vii) withdrew his licence to train for three calendar months from April 2,1954."

Vincent, of course, was not allowed then to be legally represented at the hearing by the Stewards.

There is little doubt that more drastic action would have been taken against him but for the fact that Pierce Molony, the Chief Steward had not threatened to resign. In fact, there was even reason to believe that he might have been put out of racing indefinitely.

Vincent was flabbergasted at the Stewards' decision. In a statement he said: "I am completely in the dark as to what, if any, offence I am alleged to have committed. No suggestion was made against the manner in which the horses were ridden in any of their races. In fact, no specific charge of any kind in respect of the running of any of the horses in any of their races has been made".

Dermot O'Brien recalled: "The Stewards first informed Vincent that they were holding an inquiry into all the horses under his care for a period of two years. At the inquiry, they said they had reduced it to four horses. But meanwhile Vincent had to look into all the races in which the horses he trained had run in the previous two years. How could you put together a proper defence when in making their announcement of the inquiry in the first place, the Stewards never mentioned any specific race and, more important still, never pinpointed what actually was the discrepancy in form they were concerned with. That would never happen today.

"Horses are not machines and where particular horses of ours ran badly, perhaps on courses that did not suit them, the Stewards, if we were to take the words 'inconsistent running' strictly at their face value, obviously concluded that the horses in question had not been allowed to run on their merits."

Phonsie O'Brien said that some of the horses did not run well on certain tracks, in fact ran inexplicably badly. "Baldoyle was a very sharp track and several good horses got beat there. Royal Tan and Early Mist, who were essentially National types, could hardly be expected to sparkle at Baldoyle as they did at Aintree. In the case of Lucky Dome and Knock Hard, there were explanations for poor performances they had given before they were successful at Cheltenham. Yet, the Stewards were not happy and seemed to have taken the view that they were deliberately stopped when that was not the case at all".

Getting down to specifics, Dermot O'Brien said that Lucky Dome's victory in the Spa Hurdle at the 1954 Chetenham Festival appeared to be one of the races the Stewards had in mind when they referred to discrepancy between English and Irish form, as Lucky Dome had run badly in his two previous races in Ireland.

There was a clear and valid explanation for those failures, said Dermot. First, he contested a chase at Baldoyle and had baulked and run through the wing of a fence. He returned to the same course for a second-class hurdle event, a 2-mile handicap, with Bryan Marshall up, as he was to have the ride at Cheltenham and Vincent wanted him to get acquainted with the horse. He was allotted 12st 7lbs that day and for a little horse that was a hell of a burden to be asked to shoulder, even though he was a decent animal. Then, too, the distance of two miles was short of his best, as subsequent events would show.

"Any horse we ran that was going to Cheltenham had to run prominently", Dermot explained. "In this case, Lucky Dome would have had to have a hard race even to be third but the Stewards obviously did not see it that way. Lucky Dome clearly remembered his experience at Baldoyle in his previous outing and ran a hopeless race in the handicap hurdle. In fact, Bryan Marshall was very disappointed with him and gave him no chance at Cheltenham. His running was too bad to be true."

While on form it did not seem worthwhile sending him to Cheltenham, John A. Woods loved to have a runner at the Festival meeting and told Vincent to let him take his chance.

Lucky Dome came good over the three miles of the Spa Hurdle and Dermot O'Brien said: "The Stewards of the Irish National Hunt Committee may have felt in the circumstances that they had every reason to ask questions about the unplaced run in the hurdle race at Baldoyle".

✳   ✳   ✳

On the night that Royal Tan came back to Cashel to a tremendous home-coming victory reception after winning the 1954 Aintree Grand National, Mick Davern, the local Dail Deputy (and father of Noel Davern, former Minister for Education and Euro MEP and currently a Deputy and Minister for State in the 28th Dail) hit out in his speech to the very large crowd at the fact that Vincent O'Brien was the subject of a Turf Club inquiry.

He talked of "green-eyed" individuals and his sentiments echoed the feelings of thousands who believed that Vincent was the victim of jealousy because of his outstanding run of success. Dermot did not hide the fact that he too believed that his brother was the victim of "jealousy" and Phonsie maintained that the sweeping indictment mentioning merely alleged discrepancy between the English and Irish form of four horses without one single specific detail being elaborated would never happen today.

The Turf Club Stewards, including Judge W.E. Wylie, "sat in" with the National Hunt Stewards during the inquiry. It was Judge Wylie who introduced the "sit in" as it enabled him to be present at all inquiries. As he was a retired judge, he had ample time on his hands and with his experience on the bench, he tended to dominate the meetings. While ostensibly Pierce Molony as Chief Steward of the INHS Committee was chairing the inquiry into the running of the Vincent O'Brien-trained horses, Judge Wylie may as well have been in the chair as he just took over.

Vincent O'Brien was never to forget a remark Judge Wylie passed to him one evening in the St. Stephen's Green Club (both Vincent and the judge were members). It was at the very time when the Stewards of the Irish Turf Club had met to decide whether they would follow through on a decision of the English Stewards in relation to what became known as "The Blue Sail Affair".

'Mincemeat' Joe Griffin provided the link between Vincent O'Brien and Blue Sail, trained by P.J. 'Darkie' Prendergast. Paddy Prendergast had purchased Blue Sail as a yearling for Joe Griffin for 3,000 guineas. Rae Johnstone had the mount when the colt was unplaced to subsequent Irish 2,000 Guineas winner Tale Of Two Cities in the Railway Plate (over 6 furlongs 63 yards) at the Curragh in September 1954. The following month Tommy Gosling rode him in the Cornwallis Stakes (1 mile) at Ascot and he was gambled on down to 5/2 favouritism, only to lose by a neck to Plainsong.

Despite the defeat, the Ascot Stewards still held an inquiry into what they saw as a discrepancy in form and referred the matter to the Stewards of the English Jockey Club. Their verdict was not to warn Paddy Prendergast off but to tell him that "horses trained by him would not be allowed to run under their Rules and that no entries would be accepted from him".

Normally, such a penalty would have been acted upon right away by the Irish Turf Club but they held their own inquiry on October 23, 1954 and, on the basis of the difference in distance between the two events, came to the conclusion that Paddy Prendergast had no case to answer (this, incidentally, created a historic precedent and one that earned much public support for the Irish Stewards).

Vincent, knowing that Judge Wylie was present at the meeting of the Irish Stewards, asked him if he could give him any news on how Paddy Prendergast had fared (Paddy Prendergast had actually been called to appear before the inquiry).

"We could find no discrepancy there", replied the Judge and then made the remark which left Vincent deeply shaken and which he could never forget: "If it had been me, I'd have warned you off over Knock Hard last January at Leopardstown. He ran like a hairy dog".

Dermot O'Brien has often pondered over the past four decades – when he reflects on the three months' suspension imposed on his brother – why Judge Wylie seemed so deeply concerned about the running of a chaser in an individual race at Leopardstown, why too a man whose principal brief and area of control as a Steward of the Turf Club was the Flat should be so inordinately interested in performances in the National Hunt sector that he should say what he did to Vincent.

Judge Wylie had his own close friends in the National Hunt sector – across the spectrum of owners and trainers – and would be well aware of the envy engendered by Vincent's strike rate both on the domestic front and even more so at Cheltenham and Aintree. He would be aware also of the fact that the consensus was that when Vincent, as a comparative unknown, first hit the headlines from his Churchtown base he would be but a "morning glory" and wither in the frosts of intense competition. Far from it. Once he made the move to Ballydoyle, rather than opting for the Curragh, he continued to dominate the scene to an even more spectacular extent.

Dermot O'Brien came to his own conclusions but intimated to me that he preferred to keep these to himself – and would carry them with him to the grave. On the broader plane, he contended that it was only natural and human that there should be jealousy of Vincent's success, extending even to owners who did not have horses in the stable and to trainers who could not match his strike rate. And, as Vincent at that point, was still winning his biggest prizes in the National Hunt arena, especially in Britain, one could expect that in a country where racing over the jumps meant so much, trainers of National Hunt horses had to be envious.

The Australian Scobie Breasley (left) whose name will always be linked with some of Ballymoss's finest victories and the American Bill Shoemaker (right) who rode Lomond in the 1983 Epsom Derby for Vincent O'Brien.

189

24

Starkey Gives
The 'Harvey Smith' Sign

I t will be remembered as the day at Royal Ascot – Tuesday, June 17,
1981 to be exact – when Greville Starkey on To-Agori-Mou held the
challenge of King's Lake by a neck to win the St. James's Palace Stakes
and then, as he passed the post, he turned round and gave the "Harvey
Smith" sign to Pat Eddery.

Later as he strode by the O'Brien contingent on his way to the scales, he
growled: "Take us on again and we'll beat you again".

To put Starkey's amazing behaviour in perspective, one has got to
remember that he had gone into the Royal Ascot race still bitter and
resentful at the sequence of events that led to To-Agori-Mou first losing the
Irish 2,000 Guineas, then being awarded the race in the Stewards room at
the Curragh, only to lose it as a result of an appeal lodged by King's Lake's
trainer, Vincent O'Brien.

The Nijinsky colt King's Lake, who had finished third on his seasonal
debut to Erins Isle in the Ballymoss Stakes, was effectively a stand-in for
Storm Bird in the Curragh Classic. To-Agori-Mou started 9/10 favourite to
complete the Guineas double by adding this event to his neck victory over
Mattaboy in the English equivalent. King's Lake went off at 5/1 and
Mattaboy at 15/2.

Pat Eddery took up the running on King's Lake two furlongs from home
and was then challenged by To-Agori-Mou. "The two horses seemed to
come close together, but King's Lake rallied well and although Starkey
showed obvious signs of being in difficulty in the last 50 yards, it was hard
to tell what interference, if any, had occurred", reported Tom MacGinty in
the *Sunday Independent*.

Eddery got the better of the dour last furlong struggle to win by a neck,
but an inquiry was promptly announced and Starkey also lodged an
objection.

"The head-on film left the Stewards with little option but to demote
King's Lake", Tom MacGinty went on. "It showed that he came off a
straight line and touched To-Agori-Mou. The latter immediately became

unbalanced and, in rolling, went back on King's Lake, but in my opinion the first and worst offender was Eddery's mount.

"Not everyone agreed and Vincent O'Brien, before he left the track, lodged an appeal against the local Stewards' decision," added MacGinty.

Some close friends of Vincent O'Brien were not happy with Tom MacGinty's reading of the climax of the race and he was contacted by phone after the *Sunday Independent* appeared. However, Tom, whose integrity as a racing journalist could never be questioned, stood by what he had written, even though he had always enjoyed a very good and happy relationship with the Master of Ballydoyle. Their friendship and respect for one another was not affected by that episode.

The official *Irish Racing Calendar* notice on the Curragh inquiry stated that "the Stewards were satisfied that King's Lake had interfered with the chances of To-Agori-Mou and they, therefore, reversed the placings of the two horses, placing To-Agori-Mou first and King's Lake second. They decided to take no action against Eddery".

✳   ✳   ✳

Vincent O'Brien's appeal was heard at the Turf Club's Registry Office on the Curragh on Friday, May 29, '81. The Stewards who heard the appeal were: C. S. Gaisford-St. Lawrence, Lord Killanin and John Byrne.

Evidence was heard from all the Acting Stewards, who had disqualified King's Lake in the immediate aftermath of the Curragh Classic – Major Victor McCalmont (Chairman), Lt. Col. J. Silcock, C. F. Myerscough, Edmund Loder and D. P. Martin (Stewards' Secretary).

Evidence was also heard from E. J. Kelly (Stewards' Secretary), Wally Swinburn, rider of Dance Bid, Stephen Craine, rider of Prince Echo, who had finished third, and Greville Starkey and Pat Eddery and Reg Griffin.

Video recordings of the race were also studied.

The Turf Club was represented by Niall Fennelly S.C., Vincent O'Brien by Niall S. McCarthy S.C. and Guy Harwood by E. M. Walsh S.C.

On the basis of the evidence heard and seen, the Stewards decided that the appeal be upheld and consequently King's Lake was confirmed as the winner of the 1981 Irish 2,000 Guineas and To-Agori-Mou was placed second.

The appeal lasted about ten hours and was the longest ever in the Turf Club's Registry office. Though not the first where legal representatives played a major role, it was notable in that it entrenched the situation where they would become part and parcel of the scene on major occasions like this and unquestionably play a key role. The traditionalists had their own views but there was to be no going back. Nine years on we even had Jim Bolger going to the High Court in a *cause célèbre* – the "Ascho Affair" – seeking to win an order restraining the Turf Club from hearing an appeal against penalties imposed by the Stewards at a Dundalk meeting. And in the count-down to the Budweiser Irish Derby '92 we saw Christy Roche, stable jockey to Jim Bolger at the time, seeking a postponement in the High Court of the 15-day suspension imposed on him for "improper riding" at Naas. The days when the Turf Club Stewards took their decisions on the evidence, with no legal representation for those appearing before them, were gone forever. All was changed.

Major Victor McCalmont, one of the most respected figures in Irish racing, resigned as a member of the Turf Club in the wake of the upholding of Vincent O'Brien's appeal. He subsequently withdrew his resignation. He had the distinction of being a member of the Turf Club and the Jockey Club in his own right and in his time was also an esteemed Senior Steward of the Turf Club.

When To-Agori-Mou defeated King's Lake at Royal Ascot, he was asked if the result had vindicated him? "A lot of people are saying that my position has been vindicated but I say 'No'. What happened at the Curragh on May 16 and today could not vindicate or prove my judgement wrong. They were two separate races", he said.

The capacity crowd at Royal Ascot had cheered to the echo as King's Lake and To-Agori-Mou became locked in their epic battle over the last two furlongs. It was a day of raw passions and deep emotion and Major McCalmont, when asked about Greville Starkey's after-race gesture diplomatically put it down to "the tension that had built up since the Curragh".

But the Ascot Stewards were not prepared to turn the blind eye to it. Starkey was cautioned for his ungentlemanly behaviour and warned that there must be no repetition.

Guy Harwood was more restrained in his obvious pleasure at To-Agori-Mou's triumph and welcomed sportingly the spontaneous congratulations of Vincent O'Brien who was among the first to shake his hand. "I am glad for the horse. He is very tough", said Harwood.

"The general consensus around the unsaddling enclosure", wrote Tom MacGinty in the *Irish Independent,* "was that justice had been done. It is a pity, however, that the real merit of two courageous horses – their merit is highlighted by the fact that the winner broke Brigadier Gerard's track record by .4 of a second – has been overshadowed by all the hullabaloo attached to the Irish Classic".

✳   ✳   ✳

The rivalry between the two colts did not end there. They met again in the Sussex Stakes at Goodwood on July 29, '81 and this time before another massive crowd, who set up a wall of sound as they battled it out in the climactic stages of the mile event, King's Lake, starting at 5/2, getting home by a head from the 11/8 favourite. To-Agori-Mou, urged on by a mighty "English roar" looked to have it as Greville Starkey took the lead at the distance. But Pat Eddery, biding his time to perfection, sliced through the gap as To-Agori Mou and Belmont King, with Lester Piggott in the saddle, drifted apart. There was no bump and there would be no cause for an inquiry. Eddery used his whip to get the response he sought and, no doubt, by the guidelines of today he would have been in trouble but once he took the lead well inside the final furlong, he was not going to be denied and no one was more delighted at the result than John Magnier, who knew deep down that King's Lake's value as a stud property had now rocketed into the multi-million category.

When he did go to stud at Coolmore, he was valued at £8 million but, unlike Sadler's Wells, he failed to make it as a stallion and was eventually exported.

There is little doubt that the hard races he had at Royal Ascot and Goodwood took their toll on King's Lake and on To-Agori-Mou also. Their final showdown meeting was in the Prix Jacques Le Marois at Deauville on August 16, '81. An anti-climax in a way as it was won by an easy five lengths by the outstanding French miler, Northjet with To-Agori-Mou taking runner-up position and King's Lake just a nose behind him in third place.

The durability of King's Lake was shown when he came out in the Joe McGrath Memorial Stakes (1m 2f) at Leopardstown, having had almost a month's rest after Deauville, and beat into fourth place the brilliant Dermot Weld-trained Blue Wind, who had completed a Classic double by winning the English Oaks and Irish Oaks that season. In the Prix de l'Arc De Triomphe – his last race before going to stud – King's Lake finished 11th behind Gold River with Blue Wind 15th.

Two legendary contemporaries of Vincent O'Brien who were trail-blazers like himself, P.J. 'Darkie' Prendergast (left), who trained 22 Royal Ascot winners and Tom Dreaper who turned out 26 Cheltenham Festival winners.

Vincent and Jacqueline on their wedding day in Dublin on Saturday, 29 December 1951.

PART SIX

THE FAMILY MAN

25

The Girl From
Down Under

Jacqueline O'Brien, following the success of her first classic book, *Vincent O'Brien's Great Horses* – produced in collaboration with Ivor Herbert – was asked by the publishers to write a travel book about Ireland. The plan was that it would be illustrated with her own photographs.

That was back in 1984. It seemed a great idea at the time. But then to her horror, she realised how little she knew about the country that had become her home when she married Vincent back in December, 1951. In fact, she was appalled at her ignorance of Ireland.

"When I began thinking about it, the only roads I knew were the ones that led to racecourses", she confessed in the course of an interview with Eileen Battersby in the *Irish Times*. She was only too well aware that the people who live in a place are often less likely to know its history. "The natives are the ones who don't go out looking. Even Vincent, who loves Ireland, actually knew very little about the history and archaeology", she added.

Instead of getting involved in the travel book, Jacqueline O'Brien turned her attention to other projects in the research and writing field. She asked Desmond Guinness to co-write with her a coffee-table book in 1992, titled *Great Irish Houses and Castles*. The photographs were taken by her, of course. Then in 1992 came *Dublin: A Grand Tour,* once again produced in co-operation with Desmond Guinness and this time too the photographs were by Jacqueline O'Brien.

The research she did for both of these works gave her new insights into Ireland's heritage, the history surrounding its great houses and castles and also the traditions created around Georgian Dublin. She noted how hard Desmond Guinness had worked to preserve the buildings of Georgian Dublin and she was happy that the book *Dublin: A Grand Tour* put into lasting perspective what a tragedy it would be if the battle waged by the environmentalists to preserve the aesthetic and the beautiful did not bring concrete results.

The most ambitious project of all undertaken by Jacqueline O'Brien in recent years was *Ancient Ireland* – the book (produced in collaboration with archaeologist Peter Harbison, who co-wrote the text) that came out in 1996 and which effectively traced the course of early Irish history up until the end of the Middle Ages.

Pinpointing the awesome scale of the undertaking, Eileen Battersby noted that it involved "travelling the country, photographing burial grounds, monuments, forts, castles and settlement sites."

But there was much more to it than that. The complex and turbulent history of Ireland, fought out over land ownership, is traced through an emerging civilisation and there is a fascination in seeing through the chapters of the book how the dead were honoured with sophisticated monuments, how the mighty chieftains evoked their strength with massive forts, how, as religion spread, the country-side became dotted with majestic high crosses, the standard of craftsmanship being quite remarkable.

The great castles, as Eileen Battersby noted, were a testimony to the style of life enjoyed by those who occupied them. The Round Towers erected long ago have in quite a number of instances withstood the passage of decades. Jacqueline O'Brien's photographs graphically capture the romantic and almost mystic legacy of ancient times from Doon Fort and Doe Castle, both in County Donegal, to Turoe Stone and Portumna Castle in County Galway, to the Poulnabrone Dolmen in County Clare, photographed against a dark, vaguely menacing sky, to the Dolmen in Proleek, County Louth and not overlooking the timeless and majestic Rock of Cashel.

Jacqueline O'Brien talked of the sense of Gaelic Ireland she garnered from doing that book – "of all those lives lived out so many centuries ago in places which give you such a powerful sense of the past.

She revealed how Vincent had joined her on many photographic trips. "But he is not the ideal assistant. He's an impatient person and doesn't see the point in standing around beside a monument for three hours waiting for the right light. While his patience with horses has always been legendary, I can tell you he's got none for photography."

However, Vincent appeared to have learnt a lot from the books, enjoyed seeing them being put together and gave Jacqueline the best kind of support and encouragement that any husband could give his wife by actually financing each of the three books, *Great Houses And Castles; Dublin: A Grand Tour;* and *Ancient Ireland.*

This support meant that instead of retailing at £45, these books, containing so many colour prints and so expensive to produce in hardback form, could be sold at £30.

Jacqueline O'Brien stressed that she didn't set out to do any of the three books for financial gain. Each, in fact, was a labour of love and each gave her immense personal pleasure and satisfaction, though the effort involved at times was back-breaking. She admitted too that all the time she was only waiting to do the book, *Ancient Ireland: From Prehistory to the Middle Ages* – to give it its full title. It was her "real love" – because she passionately loved the old things. And her reverence for ancient Ireland was very understandable, as Patricia Deevy noted in a *Sunday Independent* feature, because she hailed from a country that was practically "brand new".

*　　*　　*

From the time I first met her, I was amazed at Jacqueline O'Brien's boundless energy and drive and her ability to work on a number of different planes at one and the same time. She has always been happiest when she is busiest and the children will tell you that it has always been her way that she has hardly one major project finished but she goes head first into another; indeed, sometimes the projects would overlap and she would find herself overwhelmed.

It's not surprising then to find on a writing desk in the sitting room in Ballydoyle House an immortal Noel Coward quote: "The only way to enjoy life is to work. Work is more fun than fun".

Jacqueline O'Brien needs no introduction to racing aficionados as a top professional photographer in her own right. In the heady days when a stream of Classic and other big-race winners were being turned out from Ballydoyle, her photographs gained permanency in various books and publications – in *Vincent O'Brien's Great Horses,* of course, in the prestigious annual Timeform publication *Racehorses* and in the *Irish Racing Annual.* No picture of hers made a greater impact or was more widely acclaimed than that of Sheikh Mohammed in Arab dress pictured with his pet falcon, perched on his right hand against a desert background in Dubai. First carried in the *Irish Racing Annual,* it was later reproduced in publications right around the globe.

On press mornings at Ballydoyle, when members of the Irish racing press used gather, maybe in advance of the opening of a new Flat season, to run the rule over leading prospects and discuss the pros and cons with Vincent, Jacqueline would oblige by having photographs, taken on the gallops that morning, ready for them before their departure. Yes, she knew all about deadlines.

It was not long after she got married that she began taking photographs – first as a hobby – because she found horses so beautiful to photograph. She advanced to the point where she went to the College of Technology in Kevin Street to complete the three-year diploma in professional photography (she thinks she was the oldest person ever to have done it – "I must have had about twelve grandchildren at the time"). She came first in her class in the final examination and was awarded the Wiltshire Medal for the best all-round student. That was in 1990.

She carries her trusted Nikon everywhere with her that she feels might create a situation where she might be able to come up with an unusual shot and there is little doubt that she has an eye for capturing something beyond the ordinary and the mundane – like her beautiful shot of the main yard at Ballydoyle, taken from the house on a rare day of snow and reproduced in *Vincent O'Brien's Great Horses.*

Even though she was there with Vincent mainly to enjoy the meeting and renew acquaintanceship with old friends, she still carried her camera with her to Royal Ascot '97. And if Charles had turned out his first winner, you can be certain that she would have caught the victory moments in the winner's enclosure in her own unique fashion.

Some years back there was an exhibition of her photographic work at Arnott's Gallery in Dublin and for the first time many of the general public who would not have seen her prints in racing publications had an opportunity to admire her professionalism.

But the photographs were not confined to racing alone. Also on view were riveting prints resulting from her travels in Tibet, China and other parts of the globe.

She proved in that exhibition, according to a *Sunday Independent* reviewer, that she was equally good on faces as places and for those who had not seen them already, her internationally-acclaimed studies of the inscrutable Lester Piggott made an instant impact.

It was the shots that the public would never see, a look into her personal family album, where the progress of her five children – daughters, Elizabeth, Susan and Jane and sons David and Charles and her much-loved fifteen grandchildren – had been lovingly chronicled that revealed the key to the real Jacqueline O'Brien. She had presided over their triumphs and tribulations and there were those who maintained that Vincent would never have attained such an international reputation without her organisational ability and down-to-earth commonsense.

Incidentally, the proceeds from that exhibition in the Arnott's Gallery, which ran for ten days, went to charity. She has been tireless in her efforts for various charitable causes.

As she has suffered from arthritis herself and has had two hip replacements, she has seen to it that many of the fees that would have fallen due to her for professional work as a racing photographer were paid instead to the Society that helps the victims of arthritis. Very commendable. And yet done quietly without any fanfare of trumpets. Her charitable work in her own locality in County Tipperary also goes unnoticed – by design.

On another plane again she has thrown herself into fund-raising efforts for the Equine Centre outside Naas (of which she was a Governor for almost a decade), as she has a deep conviction that its contribution to the Irish racing and breeding sectors is invaluable. She helped raise a lot of money for this cause.

You might find it very difficult then to imagine how Jacqueline O'Brien could find the time to get involved in Open University courses. But she has made the time.

She regards the Open University as "the most wonderful institution" and she would like to see more and more people avail of it.

After over four decades the story has been well chronicled how Vincent O'Brien met and fell in love with Jacqueline Wittenoom, the girl from Down Under. But it still merits retelling in its essential details.

It happened in 1951, the year that Vincent started training at Ballydoyle. Vincent had travelled to Dublin on a Friday evening with the intention of going racing at the Curragh the following day. An early meal and early to bed was his intention – and some essential work in the morning before setting off for the races.

The Russell Hotel on St. Stephen's Green was then one of Dublin's most famous hotels – more famous in some respects than the Shelbourne (sited on the other side of the Green). If you did not meet some of your racing friends in one of them, then it was odds-on that they could be in the other. The Russell, just down from Iveagh House, which today accommodates the Department of Foreign Affairs, got swallowed up in development as, sadly, the Hibernian Hotel also did.

Vincent decided on a quiet drink before dinner. Then in walked a long-standing friend in Waring Wallis, who was to be an usher at his wedding. He was accompanied by Gerry Annesley. And with the two was a girl, who did not immediately make any particular impression on Vincent. Drinks were ordered all round. Vincent's idea of eating on his own was soon lost in the general conversation about racing.

He joined Waring Wallis and Gerry Annesley and the girl for dinner. "During dinner I just started to look at this girl", he would recall, looking back on that evening many years later.

In that one ten-word sentence he revealed for me how Vincent O'Brien was to be smitten by the chemistry of love before the evening was out.

Strangely enough, Jacqueline was not initially swept off her feet. It was Vincent who made the running. After dinner he accompanied her along with Waring Wallis and Gerry Annesley across the Green to the Shelbourne Hotel. Waring Wallis and Gerry Annesley went to bed early – by the standards of the racing set in those days.

Vincent was left alone with Jacqueline – "and then we got talking". He asked her to accompany him to the races the next day. She agreed and he fixed the time that he would call round from the Russell to collect her. After the last race they joined Aubrey Brabazon for drinks. Aubrey was to be another of the ushers at the wedding.

It could easily have ended with the trip to the Curragh on that day in May, 1951. Jacqueline's leave of absence from her job in the Economics Department of the Central Bank in Sydney was up in July when she was due back in Australia. "I didn't think then that the friendship would come to anything", she recalled. "The time was very short and I was leaving by boat from Southampton. There was no flying in those days, and berths on ships were very scarce – you couldn't cancel and expect to get another berth later so that you could pursue a friendship with a man you had met. So I really thought it would end once I got on the boat".

But Vincent was persistent and insistent. He knew he had met the girl he wanted to marry and, as Jacqueline put it: "By the time I was due to take the boat we had decided to be married and Vincent gave me an engagement ring in Jammet's Restaurant over strawberries and cream. My stay in

Australia was to be a short holiday to say 'goodbye' to my family and friends there".

Vincent's brothers, Dermot and Phonsie, so much part of his racing life, were bestman and groomsman, respectively, at the wedding on Saturday, December 29, 1951 in the University Church on Dublin's St. Stephen's Green.

* * *

Who was this girl who in a way had swept Vincent off his feet in one evening and saw him married before the end of the same year?

She hailed from Perth where her father, the Hon. C. H. Wittenoom was an M.P. and had been Mayor of Albany for almost twenty years. In fact, the Wittenooms were one of the most prominent and oldest families in Western Australia. Jacqueline is fifth generation Australian and can trace her roots to the time when her great-great-grandfather, the Rev. J. B. Wittenoom, brought the first settlers out to Western Australia just after the Napoleonic Wars. She is still today, as she nears a half-a-century living in Ireland, unmistakably Australian and hasn't lost the accent she grew up with in Perth.

The sudden death of his wife resulted in the Rev Wittenoom, who had been a Don at Brasenose College, Oxford and then Headmaster at Newark Grammer School, deciding to emigrate with his five sons and a sister to Australia in 1829. "His wife's death had affected him deeply, so deeply that he wanted to start a completely new life", said Jacqueline. "He applied for the post of Chaplain to the new colony. They were settlers, remember, not convicts. He combined the duties of Chaplain with teaching the children of the settlers. He had to build a church and a school – the first in that part of Australia, laying the bricks himself with the help of his sister."

Jacqueline O'Brien is still today proud to reflect that her great-great-grandfather was one of the pioneers who built Australia. The legacy of service he left was marked by places named after him in Western Australia. His son Charles, incidentally, was an artist and his paintings are the earliest of Perth (no mere coincidence then that Vincent and Jacqueline should name their second son Charles).

Jacqueline's grandfather, Sir Edward Wittenoom, was an explorer in the truest sense of the term and helped open up Central Australia. His brother, Frank and he travelled around on horseback developing big tracts of land in the Murchison district for sheep grazing. Frank Wittenoom started racing in this area in 1880 while Jacqueline recalled that she had a cousin, Langlois Lefroy, who was the President of the Western Australia Turf Club for many years.

Jacqueline caught something of the spirit of the outback during what she described as "a wonderful childhood".

"We lived for half the year on a sheep station in Murchison – 250,000 acres of dry red earth where the sheep ate mulga and salt bush. There was

Sadlers Wells, the pride of Coolmore and the world's leading sire of Stakes winners (19 in 1996 Alone) pictured (above) winning easily on his racecourse debut at Leopardstown in September, 1983. (Picture: Ed Byrne.)

Artaius, one of the amazing package of yearlings brought back from the first assault by 'The Syndicate' on Keeneland in 1975, pictured winning the 1977 Eclipse Stakes, with Lester Piggott in the saddle. (Picture: Ed Byrne.)

Famous American trainer, D. Wayne Lukas chatting at the 1988 Keeneland Sales with Vincent O'Brien, whom he described as "one of the greatest trainers in the history of racing globally". Vincent outbid him by going to $3.5 million for the Nyjinsky colt out of Crimson Saint (right) that was to be named Royal Academy, now standing at Coolmore and one of the leading sires of Stakes winners in Great Britain and Ireland in 1996.

Robert Sangster (left) and John Magnier (right) members of 'The Syndicate' with Vincent O'Brien that dominated the scene at Keeneland from 1975 to the early Eighties. (Pictures: Jacqueline O'Brien, Bernard Parkin and Peter Mooney.)

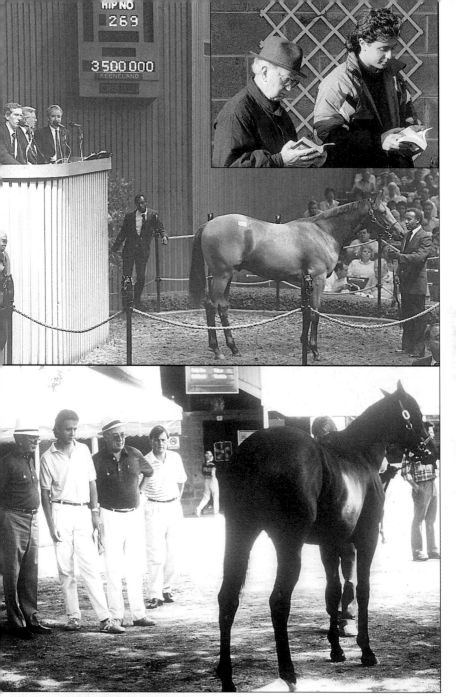

Vincent O'Brien and Charles (inset top) closely studying their catalogues at Goffs Yearling Sales and Charles is beside his father and uncle Phonsie as they look at a yearling in the barn area at Keeneland.

Sheikh Mohammed at the Keeneland Sales with Michael Osborne (left), one of his right-hand men and most trusted advisers, at his side.

Joe Osborne (son of Michael Osborne), left, who manages Sheikh Mohammed's Kildangan Stud and Brian Molony (right), former assistant trainer at Ballydoyle, who manages the Blackhall Stud, a wing of Kildangan.

Dr. Michael Smurfit and Vincent O'Brien at the EGM of Classic Thoroughbreds at which the curtain was brought down on what Dr. Smurfit described as "this noble and unique experiment".

Saratogan, who might have saved Classic Thoroughbreds had he won the 1989 English 2000 Guineas, for that same week the shares touched a high of 41p in anticipation of victory. (Picture: Peter Mooney.)

David O'Brien welcomes another winner in the days when he was scaling the heights as a trainer and (below) his wife Catherine in happy mood too in the winner's enclosure with Aviance, winner of the Heinz "57".

A BRILLIANT PURCHASE . . .

Assert, pictured (right) winning the 1981 Beresford Stakes, was bought for only £16,000. Trained by David O'Brien, he won the Prix du Jockey Club (French Derby) and Irish Derby in 1982 and was then syndicated for $25 million to go to stud in Kentucky.

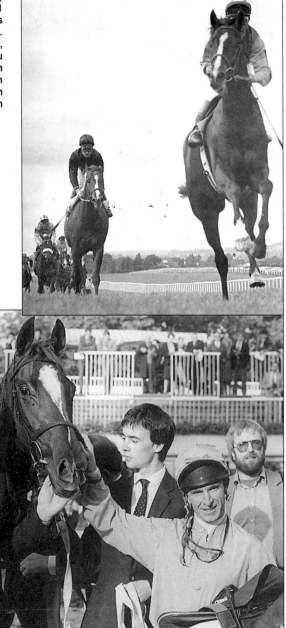

David O'Brien and Christy Roche with the filly Alydar's Best who made a lasting impact as a two-year-old in 1984 by easily winning the Silken Glider Stakes at Leopardstown on her debut and then took the Grand Criterium at Longchamp. (Picture: Ed Byrne.)

Charles O'Brien talks tactics with John Murtagh (left) before he rode Burden of Proof (on outside) to victory over Catch The Blues (C. Roche) in the Weatherbys Ireland Greenlands Stakes at the Curragh in May, '97 (below.)

Christy Roche winning the Ballycullen Stakes in easy style for Charles O'Brien at Leopardstown on Dr Johnson, who in his previous race had been runner-up to Desert King in the Budweiser Irish Derby. (Pictures: Peter Mooney.)

no green grass, but the wool was the finest merino produced. Our nearest neighbours were 30 miles away. My mother had been a school teacher and she saw to it that we were studious and committed to our lessons".

Something of the away-from-it-all call of those childhood days and their special quality can be gleaned as Jacqueline relates how they played with sheep-dogs and pet lambs and baby kangaroos, hunted for emus' eggs, and tormented the young English men who had been sent over to work on the farm – the Jackaroos.

She relates also how school-work had to be mailed to Perth each fortnight for correction. During the summer, the sheep station was too hot. "We lived then in Albany, a town on the south coast."

Once she went to boarding school at 12 to the Irish Loreto Nuns in Perth, she entered an entirely different world – an academic life that would lead on to university and a Degree in Economics, then to two years of research followed by her appointment to the post in the Central Bank in Sydney.

"I was an academic person in those days, very interested in books", she confesses. "I am afraid the horse world didn't mean very much to me, though, as I have said already, my cousin was very prominent in Western Australian racing circles."

Most Australians feel the urge to make a trip to Europe and Jacqueline (known simply as "Jac" at home) was no exception, as she sought to broaden her education. When she decided that Ireland would be part of her itinerary, she could never have guessed that it would change her life.

It was not surprising that Vincent should have been captivated and eventually captured by the girl sitting across the table from him at the dinner in the Russell Hotel. Jacqueline does not like to put any emphasis on it herself nowadays but my research revealed that she was a university beauty queen in Western Australia and some of the photos taken at Ballydoyle in the immediate aftermath of her wedding bear out the striking quality of her looks.

Life was not easy, it has got to be admitted, for an Australian girl of 22 trying to settle down into married life in a country that was totally strange to her. Jacqueline, the academic, who loved classical music, now found herself in a world where the books that dominated were books on breeding rather than economics – a world in which there was no escape from people and she had in a way to become Vincent's protector. "You take the calls, you meet the people", was his approach, she said smilingly – and she did not mind. It was a perfect marriage of contrasting personalities, of opposites. She is outgoing where he is retiring, she is bubbling and effervescent in her outlook and approach where Vincent is happiest staying in the background.

She did not walk into an empire when she arrived initially at Ballydoyle. It was really only beginning to get going. The global image that the stable would acquire in time after the Epsom Derby triumphs, the Prix de l'Arc de Triomphe victories and all the other big-race successes was still quite a long way over the horizon. Vincent was not in a position financially as yet to pay sufficient staff for his wife to concentrate solely on household matters and give all the time she would have liked to give at that point to her beloved gardening.

In Ballydoyle House they had just one furnished room and a bed on bare boards. The day when it would be a model of what an old Georgian dwelling should be, in its own wonderful setting, only came after a lot of back-breaking endeavour.

"I had to learn about horses quickly as we did not have much staff", Jacqueline recalled. "I filled in as assistant, telephonist, secretary – wherever there was work to do. In the early days most communication with owners was done by letter and Vincent and I did most of this together."

She feels that what helped her greatly was the fact that her father was always involved in politics – "so my two brothers and myself were accustomed to public life".

What helped also was the fact that she "found the people in Ireland were very kind and friendly and tolerant of my ignorance of horses and racing".

She admits now, looking back, that the first year in Ballydoyle was the hardest of all. Vincent was racing a lot. And Jacqueline frequently accompanied him. "He'd disappear into the weighroom and I never knew what to do between races because the gaps seemed so long", she told Patricia Deevy in the course of a *Sunday Independent* interview. "It was quite tough before I knew anybody. People used to be so nice to me, but they couldn't go on being nice all day". In that first year she spent a lot of time in the ladies.

The first four children were born very close together. Looking after the children, the gardens, the household and helping out also with the secretarial work meant that she didn't have a minute to herself when she wasn't racing. Fortunately, she was never one for the cocktail circuit ("I don't even drink") and the happiness Vincent and herself found from the outset of their marriage has lasted into the quieter and calmer times they share now that he is retired. And they share those times from Ireland to their holiday homes in Portugal and at Lyford Cay in the Bahamas or when they are in their London apartment.

There is a deep mutual respect between them, a silent communication and understanding that does not always need to be put into words and which is the hallmark of growth in marriages that stand the test of time. She has not only been a wife but a confidante and for someone who knew little or nothing about the Sport of Kings when she first arrived in County Tipperary, she has certainly come a long way in knowledge – knowledge of what is demanded at the very top in the racing world.

Vincent is the first to admit that Jacqueline has been a tremendous influence in his life. When he was striding the High Sierras as a trainer, she was his protection from the many people who would not give him a moment to himself if he was willing to meet the constant demands on time and energy. She was able to separate what was important from what was not – and what demanded his personal attention. She knew exactly when she should say: "I think that better be left to Vincent himself."

Jacqueline showed her resilience, her courage – a resilience and courage worthy of her pioneer ancestors in the aftermath of The Chamour Affair.

"They were our darkest days", she said. "That's when I think I was the greatest help to Vincent."

She still remembers the deep wound and the fierce wrench it represented for them having to leave house and home for the period of the suspension.

Her courage and resilience were again revealed in helping to see her children through times of crisis in their lives.

✳   ✳   ✳

Being the son or daughter of Vincent O'Brien created its own special problems. But then there are those who contend that in this day and age the children of the famous or the very rich may have to pay a price in personal terms for living in the constant shadow of a parent or parents rarely out of the headlines or social columns. In fact, a treadmill can be created that can inevitably catch those who did not bargain for it on the revolving cylinder of an unremitting spotlight. It can plunge one into the whirlpool of party-going and popping champagne corks, of invitations stemming from the aura surrounding the name, into a life that, at times, can take on an unreality that weaves the spell which demands later than one must learn to cope with the legacy stemming from it.

Or you may be asked to pitch things too high in order to emulate and, in the very seeking to emulate and even go one better, you may graft beyond the danger point.

"You couldn't really do very much in public but it would be talked about", said Liz. "You knew you were open to public scrutiny – all the time."

Did she sometimes long to be just the daughter of an ordinary person?

"We knew it couldn't be that way. In a way it was contradictory. We had our own circle of friends and when you are in the middle of something, you cannot see it from the outside. You cannot see yourself in the terms in which others are viewing you."

In this she touched the heart of the matter. The children of Vincent O'Brien may have been acting totally as themselves, being quite ordinary within the family circle, but others outside that circle could not accept them as anything less than the offspring of Ireland's most famous racehorse trainer, an international figure known from London to Kentucky, from Paris to Australia, and all the way back to Ballydoyle. Known, in fact, wherever people followed racing.

David, as we shall see, walked away from it all, from the world of being a top trainer, after turning out the winner of a French Derby, an Irish Derby and an Epsom Derby and today makes wine in his Chateau in France.

Charles, viewed at one stage as the Heir Apparent, the son who was being groomed to take over at the helm at Ballydoyle when Vincent stepped down, chose to set up on his own in County Kildare because he did not want

203

to be encumbered with the pressures that training on the grand scale would mean. He wanted his own operation, his own set number of horses and he wanted to be able to relax as a family man.

I think Charles wisely realised that there could be only one Vincent O'Brien. He would do his own thing, in his own way. To have assumed the mantle of being the new Master of Ballydoyle was not for him in the final analysis.

In a way, he probably took the right decision.

Vincent O'Brien, from his days training in Churchtown, always had a great affection for the Mallow track and fully supported the efforts that saw it re-opened in 1997 as Cork Racecourse with a magnificent new stand. Richard Dunwoody is seen winning the first chase on the new track on Saturday May 17, 1997 on the Jimmy Mangan-trained Stroll Home, later to win the Galway Plate with Paul Carberry in the saddle.

26

David in the Wine Country

It's a far cry from Chantilly on Prix du Jockey Club Day, from Epsom on English Derby Day and the Curragh on Budweiser Irish Derby Day to the wine country in Aix en Provence in the South of France.

A world away now for David O'Brien from the singular achievement of winning the French Derby with Assert, the Irish Derby with the same colt and the English Derby with Secreto – and all before his 30th birthday. Never in the history of racing globally had a trainer made such an impact in such a short time on the Classic scene while still in his twenties.

Christy Roche maintains that when David O'Brien decided to quit training in the autumn of 1988, the profession had lost a genius. "And I do not say that lightly," he added.

"I maintain that if David had not given up training, he would have set records that in time would have had people making comparisons with his father's record.To those who would knock him I would point out that he took a £16,000 colt in Assert and turned him into a dual Derby winner. And he had the courage to take on El Gran Senor, which many thought was unbeatable. His record in a very short spell as a trainer says it all".

David, the private man, who even in his days as a trainer shunned the limelight, gets all the privacy he needs away from the tumult and the roar of the crowds in his Chateau Vignelaure. He is happy with his wife Catherine and their four children Andrew, Robert, Charles and Alexandra to be seen as a wine-maker now where for a time in the Eighties, as he hit the Classic trail, he carried on his shoulders the no-win burden of being viewed as upholding the Dynasty.

In 1984, at the age of 28, he became the youngest man ever to train an Epsom Derby winner when Secreto beat El Gran Senor. He was only 26 when in 1982 he won the French Derby and the Irish Derby with Assert. In 1985 he added to his laurels by taking the Irish 2,000 Guineas with Triptych.

When the announcement of his retirement from training came there was a deep sense of shock and people naturally speculated on the reasons why.

"I had always felt that some day David would walk away from it all," was how Christy Roche put it to me. "An out-and-out gentleman, David was too nice a guy for this game. It was not in him to give owners false hopes. He wasn't prepared to run a horse unless it could do itself justice on the racecourse".

Roche said that David was under pressure right from the very first day as a son of Vincent. He achieved in three short years (1982-84) what most trainers would spend a lifetime trying to achieve.

He wasn't interested in making his name solely by the number of winners he turned out. He had the same attention to detail as his father. And like his father he thought big and aimed big – always. If he could not maintain things at that level, he would judge himself a failure.

After you have won the French, Irish and English Derbys before your 30th birthday, it is difficult to stay with bad horses or horses that do not come up to the mark for various reasons. It was a bad batch of horses that ultimately hastened David's decision to step down.

I remember a Sunday evening back in February '89 when I called to see him. He was living then with Catherine and their three young children – another would be born later – south of Cashel in County Tipperary. There was an intensity about him behind the easy smile, as he relaxed in an armchair, that conveyed to you immediately that he was not one for half-measures, neither was he one for taking the easy route.

He talked about pressure – the pressure that can stem from working fifteen to sixteen-hour long days and how that can take its toll and lead to frustration, particularly if success does not attend your efforts at the pace at which it started.

He admitted that he would wake at night thinking about the horses, about his plans for them, about setbacks they might suffer, about the failure of colts and fillies to realise the potential that seemed to be there – on looks and breeding – when they were bought originally at the yearling sales.

Once he had made up his mind to call it a day, that was it. He was not prepared to go into details, to elaborate, to give long interviews to the media explaining the reasons why. He was not going to get caught up refuting publicly the various theories that sprang from idle racecourse gossip.

He decided to say nothing beyond the bare statement announcing that he was retiring from training and which read: "I have taken the decision for personal reasons, and while it will mean the end of my direct involvement in training, it will in no way diminish my interest in the bloodstock industry, which is so much part of my life."

That was before he went into the wine business, before he became owner early in 1995 of Château Vignelaure, one of the most famouse wine-producing estates of Provence. The estate is run with Rynstone Wines, the group that cmbines the world-wide wine-making interests of Hugh Ryman and Esme Johnstone.

The Château and its surrounding vineyards are located in the wild but beautiful countryside just to the north of the town of Aix-en-Provence in the south-est of France and within striking distance of Marseille and Nice.

The vine has been cultivated here for more than two thousand years. Close to the eastern edge of the vineyard an archeological team has recently unearthed a winery dating from the first century, thought to be one of the largest of the Roman world. It was in the late 'Sixties that Vignelaure took its present form. Under the stewardship of George Brunet (previously owner of the classed growth Château La Lagune in the Médoc) the estate quickly established a fine reputation throughout the world. And Robert Parker, the renowned American wine-critic went on record in his book *Wines of the Rhone Valley and Provence* to note that the Château Vignelaure red is produced from a blend of two great wine grapes, the Cabernet Sauvignon and Syrah, adding: "Vignelaure's wines are elegant expressions of Provencal wine-making at its best." Furthermore, he describes Vignelaure itself as "one of the showpiece properties not only of Provence, but of France".

Today, Château Vignelaure wines find their way all over the globe, being specially popular in Germany and Denmark, also in Canada and with a growing market too in Britain and Ireland. One of the first prestigious restaurants in Dublin to stock Vignelaure was Dobbins and the proprietor, John O'Byrne has built up his own very friendly relationship with David O'Brien. In a word, where once people dining in leading restaurants in the capital city and other centres in Ireland would have been speculating on whether there was another Classic winner about to emerge from David O'Brien's South Tipperary stables, you will find them today talking about the classic quality of the wines he is producing. If ever there was a complete break with one life to become involved in another, this was it.

✳   ✳   ✳

Set aside all the theories and all the speculation on why David O'Brien gave up training and it boiled down to one reason in the end – he did it, as he explained to me, "for family reasons".

In the years he had been training he had devoted himself most of the waking day totally to the horses – to the exclusion of his family with whom he wished to spend more time. David felt that he had to think of Catherine and the children. He was extremely anxious to give time to them.

He had always believed that you were either in something completely or not at all. It was not in him to sit back after the Classic successes he had enjoyed and bask in reflected glory, rest on his laurels and let things run for themselves. He had to maintain the pace, to aim higher, to go after new peaks. Something had to give.

When I talked to him in the autumn of 1997 some weeks before the grapes were harvested, he said he never had any regrets about his decision to make a complete break with training.

One has got to remember that David O'Brien had ten good years, ten wonderful years, in fact, when he knew a lot of success at the highest level. Then the moment came when he realised that it was essential to restore

207

balance in his life and once he made up his mind to quit training, he knew there would be no going back.

"I had ten intensive years," said David, "but increasingly I found owners and their representatives were keen to make plans which were not in the best long-term interests of the horses. I think one reason why Robert Sangster had so much success at Ballydoyle was that he left all decisions completely in the hands of the trainer."

Elaborating, he said it came down ultimately to a question of choosing between family interests and the extraordinary world represented by maintaining a modern training establishment and seeking to ensure a successful strike rate in the races that really mattered. "I was never worried about the work-load. That I could handle. But there was this continuing mental stress which you could never escape. You realised ultimately that you had to choose between your family and the quality of life itself and an occupation which left little time for either.

David O'Brien added: "Within a week of finishing training I was able to break a twenty-year-old smoking habit which had reached the point where I was smoking 80 cigarettes a day. This will show you the sort of stress involved."

"My father had the amazing capacity to handle any kind of pressure and mental stress without it affecting his normal day-to-day life. He is unique in this respect. It was one of the qualities that made him so successful. He could put the setbacks behind him and move on to conquer new peaks. I have always felt that his greatness was revealed to a far greater extent in defeat than it was in victory."

David O'Brien is still involved in the breeding sector, not in a hands-on manner but indirectly through having shares in stallions and mares. He keeps in touch with happenings in racing on the domestic front in Ireland through the *Irish Field* and also knows about major developments globally.

But he does not go racing in France nowadays. Rather he has become something of a soccer aficionado and likes to follow the fortunes of Olympic Marseille and enjoys attending their home fixtures. He also enjoys golf with his three sons who are very keen players.

How would he feel, I asked, if any of his children expressed a desire to go into training in time? Would he discourage it? His quick response was that if this was the life that one of his children desired, he would not put any obstacle in the way; indeed, he would be happy once he knew it would make the child concerned happy in life.

Now in the maturity of his early forties, David O'Brien has found in Provence the kind of life he wanted when he made the announcement that he was retiring from training. He put Catherine and the family first before the desire to scale any further peaks as a trainer and in doing so he got away from the mental stress that was demanding too high a price. There can come a moment in life when a man has got to choose. Methinks David chose wisely.

✳   ✳   ✳

When he began training on his own it was an advantage, David O'Brien told me, to be known, to be introduced to people you had never met before as "the son of Vincent O'Brien". It opened doors, it helped make a lot of contacts, it smoothed the way in a manner that he could not deny.

"But there was pressure created, too, by being Vincent O'Brien's son, through people's expectations being pitched very high and immediately they wondered aloud almost whether I could achieve all that my Father had achieved. On balance, though, I could not complain. I got every chance and the breaks came my way very quickly, much more quickly than anyone of my age could ever expect."

Approaching the end of his very first season as a public trainer – 1981 – when he was still only 25, David O'Brien had saddled more than twenty winners, including winners of Pattern races in Pas de Seul, his first runner in France, Anfield in the Railway Stakes and Ashford Castle Stakes, and Assert in the Beresford Stakes.

David showed that he had acquired his father's eye for picking out "a good one" when he saw Anfield in a field "and I went to the sales determined to have him, no matter what he cost".

In fact, the son of Be My Guest made 53,000 guineas at Goffs and, having won all his three races in Ireland, only lost his unbeaten record in the mud of Grand Criterium Sunday after the Prix de l'Arc de Triomphe at Longchamp.

Then there was his outstanding training feat with Pas de Seul, rated champion three-year-old miler in England and Ireland (with a rating of 133 from "Timeform") in 1982. In the hands of Christy Roche, Robert Sangster's Mill Reef colt had taken the Prix Eclipse (Group 3) at Saint Cloud in late September 1981, the second victory of his two-year-old career. He was then off the course for eleven months with a hairline fracture of the off-fore cannon bone, which required pinning.

He reappeared amazingly fit enough to win the Hungerford Stakes (Group 3) in mid-August 1982 at Newbury with Pat Eddery in the saddle, starting at 13-2 in a field of ten. And then, having finished fifth in the Waterford Crystal Mile Stakes (Group 2) at Goodwood on firm going, he went to Longchamp in October and on heavy going took the Prix de La Foret (Group 1) by an impressive three lengths with Christy Roche up.

David had proved that he could evaluate with uncanny accuracy the material in his yard. Before Assert had his first outing in a Maiden at Leopardstown and before he won the Group Beresford Stakes at the Curragh, David, when asked to name the best colt in his care, immediately named Assert. He was beaten by Golden Fleece in that Maiden at Leopardstown but in the Beresford trounced the previously undefeated Longleat.

While he was studying accountancy in Dublin, David found that he was "more and more often returning home to be with the horses".

"Eventually I decided training was what I wanted to do," he added.

Vincent took him under his wing as an apprentice trainer. It became a four-year course interspersed with winters in America and in Australia, where he joined Bart Cummins, an almost legendary figure Down Under. It was in Australia that he would meet Catherine, who hails from the same area near Perth as Jacqueline. Later Catherine came over to Ireland to stay with a cousin. She never went back, but married David.

Before the end of his first season training on his own, David was asked if he could foresee the possibility of handling a Classic winner in his second season and his response was: "Some of the two-year-olds have potential. I just hope they come up to the required class."

He was thinking in particular of Assert.

✳   ✳   ✳

Assert was having his first outing of the season and started at 6-1 when he ran in the Nijinsky Stakes at Leopardstown on May 8, 1982 against the Vincent O'Brien-trained Golden Fleece, who had already taken the Sean Graham Ballymoss Stakes at the Curragh on April 17. Assert was beaten two-and-a-half lengths but "Raceform" reported that "making his run on the home turn, he closed the gap with the winner very impressively from the distance and when there was no chance of victory, was gently eased close home. He will be a force in the very top class".

Golden Fleece, as a result of that victory, was installed 3-1 favourite for the Epsom Derby, his next outing. There was speculation that David was prevented from running Assert against Golden Fleece at Epsom by Robert Sangster, who owned both colts, but David flatly rejected any such suggestion. "It was never my intention to run Assert at Epsom. Assert was a big, long-striding colt. I decided that he would not be able to handle the gradients, would have difficulty coming down the Hill and might get unbalanced rounding Tattenham Corner."

Assert, having won the Prix du Jockey Club (French Derby) like a really top-class colt by three lengths, swept to an eight-lengths win in the Irish Derby. Christy Roche rode him to both victories. After being beaten by a neck by Kalaglow in the King George VI and Queen Elizabeth Stakes over twelve furlongs at Ascot, Assert came back to one-and-a-quarter miles in the Benson and Hedges at York and became the widest-margin winner of this prestigious event when drawing relentlessly clear of his rivals in the last two furlongs to beat Norwick by seven lengths, with Amyndas a neck away third.

As Christy Roche was injured, Pat Eddery took the ride at York.

With a $25 million syndication deal safely completed, Assert made his farewell Irish appearance in the Joe McGrath Memorial Stakes over ten furlongs at Leopardstown on Saturday, September 18 and got a wonderful reception from a large crowd as he toyed with the opposition to win by three lengths from King of Hush with Punctilio a further one-and-a-half lengths away third.

Assert started 5-2 favourite for the Prix de l'Arc de Triomphe as some big punters in Ireland and Britain went for a real 'touch'.

Close up on the outside until two furlongs out, Assert, in the hands of Pat

Eddery, dropped out of it quickly to finish eleventh, to the disappointment of the big Anglo-Irish following present.

Desmond Stoneham reported from Paris in the *Irish Field* that Assert's fate was sealed when at 10.30 on Saturday night the heavens opened and the already very soft ground was quickly transformed to heavy. Pat Eddery said that Assert, a light-actioned colt, could never show his true form on that soggy ground.

Would Assert have beaten Golden Fleece if the two had met in the Irish Derby? David O'Brien told me that the go-ahead had been given for the two to face each other in the Curragh Classic. However, since Golden Fleece never ran again after his Epsom Derby triumph, it must remain a matter of conjecture whether the two Robert Sangster-owned colts would have actually clashed head-on. The cynics will continue to exclaim that it was NEVER on, just as they would never have seen a repeat of the Secreto-El Gran Senor 1984 Epsom Derby clash evolving at the Curragh.

"It would have taken an exceptional horse to have beaten Assert that day at the Curragh," said David O'Brien. "We put in a pacemaker for him. It would have been a real test – a tougher test for Golden Fleece than Epsom was. The question is – would Golden Fleece's electrifying burst of finishing speed have been blunted by the time they got to the final two furlongs? They would have been going a really hot gallop the whole way.

"Assert liked it that way and would have been very much at home forcing the pace from a half-a-mile out, as Christy Roche did in the actual Curragh race, in which he had built up an unbeatable lead at the distance".

Even though Secreto gave Christy Roche the greatest day of his career as a jockey when he won the Epsom Derby by beating El Gran Senor, Christy unhesitatingly put Assert ahead of him, describing him as "a true mile-and-a-half horse".

✳   ✳   ✳

In one short season, David O'Brien had scaled peaks that many trainers could not have dreamt of reaching in a lifetime in the profession. Robert Sangster had so much faith in him that he had an interest in over half of the 50 horses in his stable.

David's dedication was such at this early stage of his career that he thought nothing of rising at 5.30 a.m. and not finishing his working day until 8p.m. This routine never changed.

Jacqueline O'Brien said to me of David: "He treated the horses in his care as individuals – feeding each one differently and planning individual training schedules suited to the personality, temperament and ability of each horse. I have never seen anyone who went to so much trouble to personally bring out the potential in each separate horse.

"I don't believe anyone else ever put on a bandage in his yard; he made up the feed himself for the horses and always did the early morning feed himself. He used to say that he could tell how the horses were by the way they behaved in their boxes after the night.

211

"Whenever we came up against a problem in either stable management or in the veterinary field," Jacqueline added, "I would go to David and expect to get a first-class answer."

✳   ✳   ✳

Those who saw "the season of Assert" as a flash in the pan, were to underestimate completely the quality of genius in David O'Brien's make-up. Nothing demonstrated this quality better than the way he prepared Secreto for the 1984 Epsom Derby and assessed that El Gran Senor could be beaten.

Like his father, David was not given to extravagant expressions of opinion. He repeatedly said however: "By the time he is finished with Secreto, El Gran Senor will know he has had a race."

Secreto was at least as well bred as El Gran Senor; indeed, in the opinion of breeding authority Tony Morris, Secreto was better equipped in this department for the Derby, being by the same great Northern Dancer, out of a half-brother to a French Derby winner and, therefore, more likely to stay. Isoble Cunningham in *The Scotsman* tipped Secreto to win on the score of breeding.

Nonetheless, the public evidence in support of Secreto's claims was limited. He had won his only race in the autumn of 1983 with ease, but it was a minor event which merited a rating of 7st 7lbs in the Irish Two-Year-old Classification, 28lbs below El Gran Senor. And while the Tetrarch Stakes, in which he ran away from Without Reserve and Deasy's Delight, over seven furlongs at the Curragh in April, showed that Secreto had a real touch of class, the Irish 2,000 Guineas, for which he started favourite, raised doubts in the minds of many experienced race-readers.

Secreto, starting 6-4 favourite, could only finish third behind Sadler's Wells and Procida, beaten a neck and one-and-a-half lengths, though it was noticeable that he was running on at the end.

The doubts raised afterwards were not shared by either David O'Brien or Christy Roche, despite the fact that they both admitted subsequently that they had considered Secreto unbeatable that day. The modest early gallop and the fact that Secreto ran too freely in Roche's opinion, combined to bring about defeat.

There was no weakening in the resolve to take on El Gran Senor. Thus it was that on a perfect summer's day the two sons of Northern Dancer, trained in neighbouring parishes in County Tipperary, were among the 17 runners that went to the start and created one of the most debated race climaxes in racing history.

"My attitude," said David, "was that I had a horse in my charge that was good enough to go for the race and, therefore, I must go for the race. I could not be influenced in that decision by El Gran Senor's unbeaten record and neither could I be influenced by sentiment, though I know some people would have found it difficult to understand why I should be taking on my father.

"I didn't feel overawed by the reputation El Gran Senor had built up. Anyway, a close study of his pedigree showed that there HAD to be a doubt

212

about his getting the distance and, furthermore, I concluded that he had shown such speed in his previous races that you had to wonder whether he could last it out up the hill.

"On breeding, I felt my horse had the better chance. So, despite the defeat Secreto had suffered in the Irish 2,000 Guineas, I was not going to be deterred.

"As to the race itself, I accept that it looked all over bar the shouting two furlongs out. It was not until I saw El Gran Senor beginning to wobble under Secreto's challenge that I knew we could beat him. The hill found him out in the end.

"I suppose I was sorry in a way to beat my father when there was so much at stake for El Gran Senor but, at the same time, it was a tremendous thrill for me to win the Epsom Derby and add it to the two Derbys I had already won. There is nothing in racing for a Flat trainer to compare with winning the Epsom Derby.

"There is too much emphasis placed on keeping Classic horses unbeaten. The way I look upon it is, you win some, you lose some. A horse, I contend, must be judged on the OVERALL record. If you try to protect a record, say after a colt has won the 2,000 Guineas and Derby, then you may never find out his true worth – what he is capable of achieving if allowed to go for the King George VI and Queen Elizabeth Stakes and the Prix de l'Arc de Triomphe, for example.

"I don't believe for one moment that it took all that much from El Gran Senor that he was beaten a short head in the Epsom Derby. To my mind, the very fact that he ran in the race after winning the 2,000 Guineas showed that he was tough enough to take plenty of racing, especially as he came out subsequently and won the Irish Derby.

"I don't think either that breeders were put off in the least by that short-head defeat. His record in the overall was outstanding – only one defeat and that by the narrowest of margins in a photo finish."

The final word on Secreto and El Gran Senor at Epsom and what might have happened if they had met again remained with Christy Roche, who said: "If the repeat of the Epsom Derby that everyone wanted had taken place at the Curragh, it would undoubtedly have been a wonderful race. I would still have favoured my one in a true test of stamina. "

Secreto's triumph at Epsom overshadowed another outstanding achievement by David O'Brien in 1984 when the filly Alydar's Best, who had been purchased at Keeneland for $625,000, won the Grand Criterium at Longchamp, beating River Drummer (Cash Asmussen) by a neck. Earlier at Leopardstown the Alydar filly out of Berkut had won the Silken Glider Stakes by three lengths on her racecourse debut.

On her reappearance in '85, she was unplaced in her first two races at Longchamp and the Curragh before winning the Pretty Polly Stakes at the Curragh on Irish Derby Day. She had to be content with runner-up position in the Irish Oaks and fourth place in the Yorkshire Oaks and her season finished with a fifth place in the Prix Vermeille at Longchamp.

Overall her second season was a disappointment, considering that it had even been suggested after she had finished unbeaten as a juvenile that she might be aimed at the Derby rather than the Oaks.

At the end of her three-year-old career she went to America where she broke down badly.

David O'Brien won the Irish 2,000 Guineas in 1985 with Triptych, wearing the colours of Alan Clore, but this brilliant mare was being trained in France by Patrick Biancone when she won the Phoenix Champion Stakes in 1987 and when she finished third to Dancing Brave in the Prix de l'Arc de Triomphe in 1986 and to Trempolino in 1987. The last of David's Classic triumphs came in 1986 when he won the Jefferson Smurfit Memorial Irish St. Leger with Authaal (Christy Roche) at 8-1 for Sheikh Mohammed.

When he made the announcement that he was quitting training, he had 29 horses registered in training, 23 of them being owned by Sheikh Mohammed. In that 1988 season – up to October – he had won 14 races with seven horses for £87,634. He had experienced a lot of problems with his two-year-olds and none of the 16 had made a racecourse appearance. That was very frustrating, because the two-year-olds provide the potential Classic challengers for the following season.

There have been admirers of David O'Brien who have argued in cold retrospect that when he saw that the material in his yard was not up to scratch he should have had a major clean-out, irrespective of the fact that so many of them were owned by Sheikh Mohammed. As a man who had proved that he could do it on the High Sierras, who had shown that he could conquer the Classic peaks, he could afford to be ruthless – could afford to let one season go completely by and start again from scratch.

As it was, he was breaking his back – and almost broke his spirit – with indifferent material. He was too good a trainer to have wasted almost an entire season before he saw that he was on a hiding to nothing.

After learning that David had decided to quit, Robert Sangster was quoted as saying: "His entire life revolved around horses. David is a very shy man and I think that perhaps he was unsuited by the hurly burly of the racing world. I also think that he was probably frustrated by the lack of success with his two-year-olds in that 1988 season."

When you have scaled the heights that David O'Brien scaled at 25 when winning two Derbys with Assert and then at 27 sealing that achievement by winning a third Derby with Secreto and when you have handled a horse of Triptych's calibre, it is extremely difficult to continue to work sixteen-hour days with horses of moderate calibre and no potential to reach the top. As Christy Roche so aptly put it, David was interested more in quality than in the number of winners he turned out.

The home-loving David came to realise that there were other things in life besides the continued quest for more Classic glory – and the constant grind that went with it.

His pursuit of excellence is now in a vineyard in France.

27

Charles Strikes Out
On His Own

Back in 1987 when Vincent O'Brien celebrated his 70th birthday, his younger son, Charles was being viewed as the Heir Apparent – the man who would succeed the Master at the helm at Ballydoyle.

That was still the assumption into the early seasons of the Nineties as Charles accompanied his father to the yearling sales and with each passing day was learning more and more about the business of training itself. However, when Vincent stepped down at the end of the 1994 Flat season, what everyone had assumed would happen, did not happen.

Charles decided to strike out on his own and established himself at Ridge Manor Stables, Rathbride in County Kildare.

The Tetrarch, dubbed by some historians the fastest horse seen on a British racecourse this century, was bred in the area by Edward Kennedy. One of his nicknames was "The Spotted Wonder" because of the peculiar white marks on his iron-grey coat. After showing fantastic speed against older horses in trials at home, he was unbeaten in seven races as a two-year-old. Sadly, he injured a foreleg in the autumn of his juvenile season and never ran again. At stud he sired the very speedy Tetratema and the brilliant filly Mumtaz Mahal.

The question naturally arises: Why did Charles O'Brien not assume his father's mantle?

When I put it to him down at the Ridge Manor Stables on a glorious day in late May, '97, he revealed that he did not want to be boss over a massive operation like Ballydoyle. "To make it viable you would need to train between 120 and 130 horses and charge fees well above the national average," he said. "There are costs in an operation of that size that have simply got to be high of their very nature because of the scale of things. If you are not able to attract owners with the financial resources to pay the fees to cover the running costs, then it's inevitable that you would find yourself in trouble from the outset."

He emphasised also that you have to be prepared to make immense sacrifices in relation to your personal life and family life, in particular in the case of taking time off. "The very demands of the job would not permit you to cut corners," he noted.

Charles, to put it frankly, was not willing to go down that road. He had a vision of what he wanted to do, the kind of life he wanted to lead. And that was to have around 50 horses in his Ridge Manor Stables, to be able to give them individual attention and not feel constantly pressurised.

He had learned in the days when he was assistant trainer to his father that "knowing your horses really well" was an essential ingredient to success as a trainer.

"You must know each horse's strengths and weaknesses. You must play to the strengths and overcome the weaknesses. Most important of all, you must be able to place them to the best possible advantage," he said.

Charles learned also from his father that you might start out at the beginning of each new Flat season with very high hopes for the material in your yard – you might even think of every horse being a champion until proved otherwise. In a word, you aimed at an Everest peak and then worked down.

But Charles learned too that you can't make a moderate animal into a champion. You were only fooling yourself and your owners – the people who pay the piper – if you did not coldly involve yourself in a weeding-out process. "Once it has become apparent that five or six are a cut above the rest and potentially very good, then these are the ones you aim at the higher targets. The others will go for run-of-the-mill races and you can only hope that by placing them in the right category, they will pay their way.

"You have got to be a realist in this business otherwise you won't get results," he added.

Another factor influencing him strongly when he decided to strike out on his own was his recollection of the fact that as soon as David began to conquer the highest peaks, there were those who asserted that it was Vincent who was training them and not him. His father in the final analysis was happy then seeing him wanting to be his own man, wanting to be in the position that if he made a success of things in County Kildare, no one could say that there was someone in the background assisting him along.

Charles had about twenty two-year-olds in his charge the day I called to see him. He was able to say that "five of them are very good" and he would be disappointed if they did not make a notable impact.

He had done very well with his three-year-olds, even better in some instances than his closest friends could have visualised at the outset of the 1997 Flat season.

* * *

Charles had carried on his young shoulders quite a deal of responsibility when his father was over-seeing the Classic Thoroughbreds operation. Recognising that his father was not one for the centre-stage spotlight and that neither was he one to relish a public relations role, Charles was quite prepared to go up front and take on an additional workload.

In the long run this was to have its own beneficial effects on his career as a trainer. He got to meet all the racing journalists on first-name terms and all the people in positions of power and influence in the racing and breeding industries. He admits to being an essentially shy person, like his brother David, but I have always felt that in a racing environment he carried himself off with admirable assurance. Certainly, he is impressive when surrounded by the circle of racing writers in the winner's enclosure after his stable has recorded another success.

I remember visiting Ballydoyle in 1991 just a week after Vincent O'Brien had celebrated his 74th birthday. He had still 60 horses in his charge – 25 of them two-year-olds – and they went out in three lots each morning, at 8.30, 10.30 and noon. "He's amazing really," said Charles of his father. "His attention to detail, his dedication and enthusiasm and the way he knows the individual traits and potential of every horse in his care hasn't diminished in the least. You would think that he was setting out to try and win his first Group or Classic race."

Vincent's summation was more simple. "It's hard to break the habits of years".

I could understand why on that lovely sun-drenched mid-April morning, for Ballydoyle, in all the sweeping grandeur of its gallops, set against the backdrop of the Knockmealdowns, the Comeraghs and timeless Slievenamon never looked better. It was not until the end of the 1994 Flat season that he finally called it a day.

Hopes were high on that morning that Sportsworld might go on to even greater success after a smooth victory on his racecourse debut as a three-year-old over seven furlongs at the Curragh. Carrying the colours of Classic Thoroughbreds, this son of Alleged out of the Nureyev mare, Gallanta built on that initial success by winning a Listed race at the same venue, then took the Gallinule Stakes by four lengths in the hands of Lester Piggott, again at the Curragh.

He was certainly bred to win a Derby. And it was no surprise that he was sent to challenge for the Budweiser Irish Derby. But, frankly, he could not be expected to beat the Epsom Derby winner, Generous, who justified even-money favouritism when winning easily by three lengths. Sportsworld had to be content with fourth place. He failed later by a neck to gain compensation for that defeat in the Desmond Stakes, losing to the Jim Bolger-trained Star Of Gdansk.

Sportsworld could be said to have justified the outlay on him but he did not realise the dream of becoming a Classic winner. Neither did Saratogan, who could have become the lifeline Classic Thoroughbreds needed (in the week when the shares jumped to 41p and the company itself was valued at £23.67 million) had he won the 1987 English 2,000 Guineas instead of finishing unplaced to Nashwan.

No one ever said, however, that the concept behind Classic Thoroughbreds was wrong. If three or four Royal Academys had been produced or even one Nijinsky, Sir Ivor or El Gran Senor, the investors, especially the "small men" would have had reason to smile.

The Classic Thoroughbreds experiment – what Dr Michael Smurfit described as "this noble and unique experiment" – impressed deeply upon Charles the value of caution. But that was something his father had always shown. The basis of the Master's approach was that "you can't turn them into Classic winners if they are not good enough." And Vincent, to his credit, had never from the very beginning raised false hopes for 'Classic'. He had been too long in the game and knew too much about its up-and-downs for that.

✳   ✳   ✳

Charles O'Brien will tell you that his father never "pushed" him towards a career in racing.

When he was eight he went off to school in England, first to Sunningdale and then Eton. He actually had the distinction of winning an Oppidan Scholarship from Sunningdale to Eton. He then went into accountancy, like David, getting his degree in due course. "I suppose the reason I went into accountancy was that my parents wanted me to make up my own mind, to see if I would prefer another life rather than racing. I am thankful to them for that. But I realised from the outset that a nine-to-five desk job was not for me, in fact would have left me stultified and very unhappy," he said. "I loved being with horses. I suppose you could say that it was in my blood."

When he was twenty, in 1987, he had a six-months sojourn at Brian Mayfield Smith's training establishment in Australia. That was followed by a spell at the Californian stables of John Gosden, who, as we have seen already, had been an assistant trainer at Ballydoyle (and is now a top trainer at Newmarket).

The sojourn Down Under and the spell in the States could be viewed as all part of the education process. But you might say that Charles took his "Master's Degree" during the years he was assistant to his father. These were the most significant and priceless days of all. And it was from these days that he acquired the authority that cannot but shine through when he dwells on the subject that is dearest to his heart.

His parents put him on the road by sending him around nine horses to train for them and Robert Sangster, who has never forgotten the debt he owes Vincent, especially from that golden era in the Seventies and early Eighties, also rowed in with support. He had two from the Al Maktoum brothers.

He counted himself lucky because, as he put it to John Karter of the *Sunday Times* in a 1993 interview, "most of my owners are family or friends, so I'm not under the same pressure".

During my own visit to his stables in the Spring of '97, I found him to be laid back in the sense that he had his priorities right and the quality of life was as important to him as achieving success as a racehorse trainer. His wife, Anne (a daughter of great racing enthusiast, Dr Andrew Heffernan and Margaret Heffernan) qualified as a doctor and is attached today in a specialist capacity at St. Vincent's Hospital and for her M.D. is pursuing research into kidney dialysis at U.C.D. The fact that they live in County Kildare allows her to be able to get home in the evenings to enjoy a normal family life and, indeed, one of the reasons that swayed Charles in opting for a County Kildare base was its proximity to Dublin. Charles and Anne delight in daughter Kate who was born in 1993. When his responsibilities and time-consuming schedule as a trainer permit he will manage to get in a game of golf (he plays to a 16 handicap).

Charles, who likes to dress in polo-neck and jeans as he works around the stables, slipped into the kitchen to make coffee while we were continuing the interview. His relaxed, easy manner would set any stranger at ease but I had known Charles from much younger days from visits to Ballydoyle.

He mentioned the fact that when he set up on his own initially, friends kept saying to him that he would feel the pressure of being a son of Vincent O'Brien and that it would colour all his efforts to climb up the ladder. He confessed that he didn't feel this pressure and saw the good side of it in that it helped open doors for him that would not be opened so readily to one who didn't have a similar leg-up.

He accepted the fact that when he aimed for a Royal Ascot winner or success in a Classic, reference would immediately be made to his father's record. He was resigned to the fact that he couldn't escape the shadow of his father but he was adamant that he wasn't going to allow himself to be pressurised by it.

Charles can relax with his music as he can relax with his golf. He laughed when he recalled how he used play tapes constantly in the car when he drove to race meetings and to the sales in Ireland with his father. "I'm afraid I used drive him mad as he was never really into music whereas I like all kinds of music."

Charles described Vincent as a "hands-on trainer" when he was starting out in Churchtown and in the early years in Ballydoyle. By that he meant that he was involved in everything, right down to the feeding of the horses and even in the secretarial work. It was a case of having to be a hands-on trainer because he did not have the financial backing then to employ the range of staff available to him later.

Later his father became a "hands-off trainer" in the sense that much of the nitty-gritty of the day-to-day responsibilities was looked after by assistant trainers and top staff and he could give his undivided attention to planning strategy and supervising, like a Commander-in-Chief, the training of the horses aimed at Classic and other tactics.

Charles noted that his father was outstanding in the way he could delegate and again, he contended, this was one of the facets that contributed greatly to his success as a trainer of Classic winners.

Charles sees himself currently as a "hands-on trainer" and is happy to be fully involved in much of the day-to-day responsibilities. He oversaw the putting in of an all-weather gallop and the development of the stables themselves.

He emphasised again that he would NEVER want a huge number of horses in his charge. Individual attention means everything to him.

He keeps about six mares and naturally would love in time to produce a champion. He acquired a great depth of knowledge of breeding from his father and this will certainly stand him in good stead in the coming years. Obviously we can look out for the name Ridge Manor Stud.

✳　　✳　　✳

His 30th birthday was just two months behind him when Charles O'Brien came within a length of winning his first Classic – the Budweiser Irish Derby – on June 28, 1997.

Dr Johnson, carrying the colours of his father (who was present with Jacqueline on the occasion) was, ironically, beaten by Desert King owned jointly by Michael Tabor and John Magnier, though carrying Tabor's colours.

Little wonder that Phonsie O'Brien should say to me in the enclosure afterwards that it was a moment of mixed emotions for him as he watched Dr Johnson being headed inside the last furlong.

By Woodman out of Russian Ballet, Dr Johnson had won three successive races before the Budweiser Irish Derby – a maiden over the full Derby distance at Leopardstown in May, then the Conrad International Dublin Silver (3-Y-O) Stakes over ten furlongs at the Curragh on Irish 2,000 Guineas Day and another twelve furlongs event at Leopardstown a fortnight or so before the Derby.

In defeat Charles O'Brien was showered with congratulations on coming so near a first Classic triumph. In August Dr Johnson gained compensation by winning the Ballycullen Stakes at Leopardstown by an impressive three lengths.

Charles had his first runner at Royal Ascot when Burden Of Proof challenged for the 1997 renewal of the Cork And Orrery Stakes – the race his father had won with College Chapel in 1993 as he had his Last Hurrah at the meeting.

Burden Of Proof, starting at 16-1, could only finish eighth behind hotpot Royal Applause, who emerged as a very impressive winner.

On the way to Royal Ascot, Burden Of Proof had proved himself a good servant to Charles O'Brien's stable, winning the Group 3 Weatherbys Ireland Greenland Stakes at the Curragh in May and earlier taking the Listed Amethyst Stakes at Leopardstown under 9-11 from English raider Wizard King.

Since he started as a trainer, Charles O'Brien has had the odd hurdler to keep things ticking over during the winter but he can visualise the day coming when his concentration will be totally on the Flat.

After Dr Johnson's run at the Curragh on Derby Day '97, it's hard to think of Charles as anything else but a Flat trainer. And one obviously going places.

28

Now The Big Break-Through

The year 1997 will be remembered as the year that Aidan O'Brien made the big break-through on to the Classic plateau as he provided first (Classic Park) and second (Strawberry Roan) in the Airlie/Coolmore Irish 1,000 Guineas, then twenty-four hours later won the Lexus Irish 2,000 Guineas with Desert King and the same colt repelled the English and French challenge when taking the Budweiser Irish Derby from the Charles O'Brien-trained Dr Johnson.

It saw the 27-year-old trainer equal the 1963 achievement of P.J. 'Darkie' Prendergast when he won the first three Irish Classics with Gazpacho (1,000 Guineas), Linacre (2,000 Guineas) and Ragusa (Irish Derby).

Whatever he achieves in the years ahead, O'Brien will always have a special place in his heart for Desert King, for this colt provided him with his first Group One success in the 1996 Aga Khan's Studs National Stakes and in a way that could be viewed as the prelude to Desert King's double strike in taking the 1997 Irish 2,000 Guineas and Derby.

Aidan O'Brien has come a long way in a short time. Back in June, 1993 when Vincent O'Brien sent out College Chapel to win the Cork and Orrery Stakes – his last Royal Ascot winner – a shy, modest but very single-minded young man was granted a licence to train at Piltown, County Kilkenny, near where his father-in-law Joe Crowley and his wife Anne Marie had trained before him.

Initially, Aidan O'Brien combined training with riding and finished the 1993-'94 season as the top amateur in Ireland with a total of 26 winners. But as the demands on his time increased, with intense training schedules, he had to retire from the saddle.

When I called to see him in Piltown in June '94, Anne Marie and himself were actually supervising three yards – Joe Crowley's original yard, then the one that was added when Anne Marie was training and then the latest one, a model of everything that one expects in a modern stable and with a capacity to accommodate 100 horses.

The day I talked to him he told me he was planning to build a lab to facilitate the taking of regular blood tests. A canteen was also being planned for the staff.

He didn't see horses as just inanimate machines. "You have got to approach it as if you are looking into their minds. You have got to make sure that they come out of their races as if they hadn't had them," he said.

He showed himself to be a great believer in feeding his horses well. He has a lot of faith in electrolytes and gives all his horses these before and after their races. "I find that it enables them to recover very quickly and run frequently."

❋   ❋   ❋

My visit to Piltown was before the call came from John Magnier that saw him enter overnight a new phase of his career. His greatest achievements up to then had been in the National Hunt sphere. Now the key challenges facing him would be on the Flat.

Vincent O'Brien had retired at the end of the 1994 Flat season and it was obvious that the showpiece gallops and other amenities would not be left idle for long.

Ballydoyle was taken over by John Magnier, the boss of Coolmore and in 1997 he would also take over the nearby establishment where David O'Brien had trained, thus enhancing still further the overall training facilities.

Naturally, Vincent and Jacqueline were delighted that Ballydoyle would remain "in the family" through John Magnier, who is, of course, a son-in-law of Vincent's through his marriage to Sue. Vincent and Jacqueline continue to live at Ballydoyle House. They are happy in the knowledge that Ballydoyle with its world-famous gallops will pass on one day from John and Sue to one of their children and, hopefully, on to a further generation. It could well happen, indeed, that a Magnier may train here one day.

It came as no surprise early in 1995 when John Magnier announced that Aidan O'Brien – no relation of the Maestro – would begin training a string of Flat horses from Ballydoyle while at the same time continuing to handle the horses that were based in the yards back in Piltown. In a word, Aidan O'Brien was to become a key figure in the operation that had been planned by John Magnier in association with Michael Tabor – an ambitious operation that stretched out to new horizons in the racing and breeding spheres and presented him with a challenge that went far beyond the mere breaking of records and the setting of new ones.

In time, Anne Marie and himself would make their new home in a house on the lands at Ballydoyle.

Quickly Aidan O'Brien was dubbed 'The new Master of Ballydoyle' by the media. And that in turn put a more intense spotlight than ever on him. Now the racing public, both in Ireland and Britain, were waiting to see whether this amazing young man could aspire on the Flat to emulate in time the feats of Vincent O'Brien, who from these same gallops had turned out horses that had achieved immortality – like Sir Ivor, Nijinsky, The Minstrel, Alleged, El Gran Senor and Golden Fleece.

John Magnier, the boss of Coolmore and Michael Tabor were providing the finance to supply the "ammunition" in the shape of choicely-bred yearlings that would give Aidan O'Brien every opportunity to reveal his genius. Tabor had sold his bookmaking chain for £26 million and was now based in Monte Carlo. Magnier and himself were combining in what can best be described as a Grand Strategy.

Basically, it was a make-our-own-stallions strategy – for John Magnier a throw-back to the Golden Era of the seventies when Vincent O'Brien, Robert Sangster and himself made their assault on the Keeneland Sales and purchased the colts who, after realising their potential at the highest level on the track, were syndicated for millions of dollars when put to stud.

Magnier knew from long experience the gamble involved. He knew, in fact, that gambling in bloodstock was certainly not a gilt-edged proposition. There was no guarantee of making easy millions.

But it represented the kind of challenge that he gloried in. And Michael Tabor, for his part, noted that in the racing and bloodstock arena it was all about putting your judgement on the line. The thrill and personal satisfaction derived from seeing your judgement vindicated was immense. If there was failure you had to learn to take it on the chin, otherwise you had no place in this business.

Magnier and Tabor didn't have to say it but it was a jungle – a jungle that had trapped the unwary and the naive again and again and yet there were always those prepared to venture into it. You had to have the resilience of an Indiana Jones to be one hundred per cent sure of coming through unscathed.

Vincent O'Brien has total respect for the knowledge that John Magnier has of breeding matters on a global scale. Indeed, he confesses that it is hard to find the words to describe his brilliance.

"John, in my opinion, will succeed in the policy he is now pursuing of making his own stallions. He has an extraordinary perception of the whole industry and what is required. The status which Coolmore has achieved on the world bloodstock stage is testament to his genius; in his hands it has become the leading international stud complex.

"I consider that Demi O'Byrne, his adviser, has no equal in selecting yearlings at the Sales world-wide. John has enormous courage to make the necessary investments and now has at Ballydoyle a world-class training set-up where no expense is being spared to have every facility known to training. John also has the greatest ability imaginable to put together a team of people and Aidan O'Brien has already proved himself an outstanding trainer."

The Magnier-Tabor partnership, with Demi O'Byrne doing the bidding, expended $8.5 million dollars at the Keeneland Select Sales in July '97 on twelve lots.

They rocked the sales ring on Monday as Demi O'Byrne, their racing manager, bidding on their behalf laid out a total of $6.9 million on ten yearlings, including two seven-figure purchases. He went to $1,050,000 for a Gulch filly and paid $1 million for a colt by Storm Cat.

There were numerous Japanese buyers present and some of the biggest High Rollers of the racing and breeding world from various parts of America itself, including Californian trainer D. Wayne Lukas. But it quickly became apparent that when the John Magnier-Michael Tabor partnership wanted a yearling they were not going to be stopped from getting it.

Roger Beasley, sales director at Keeneland, said: "When Demi O'Byrne and his group decided to buy one, they just would not give in".

On Tuesday O'Byrne paid the round million dollars for a Seattle Slew colt and went to $635,000 for a Forty Niner colt.

They had the chequebook out again at the Saratoga yearling sales at Saratoga Springs, New York in August when they went to $1.4 million, the overall top price and the highest at the Sales since 1990, to purchase a colt by Gulch (sire of Thunder Gulch) out of A.P. Indy's half-sister Weekend Storm. Bred by William Farrish and William Kilroy, the colt was consigned by Farrish's Lines' End Farm. He will be trained by D. Wayne Lukas.

Demi O'Byrne noted that it was the same cross as Thunder Gulch, who had been trained by Lukas to win the Kentucky Derby and Belmont Stakes and finish third in the Preakness Stakes, the third leg of the American Triple Crown. He also won the Travers Stakes at Saratoga and the Florida Derby at Hollywood Park as a three-year-old. He ran in the colours of Michael Tabor, though again it represented a major achievement for the Tabor-Magnier combination. Today he stands at stud at Ashford Farm, the American wing of Coolmore. He covered an exceptional book of mares in his first season at stud.

Where in the peak days and heady times of the latter half of the Seventies and early Eighties $8 million would have been way short in the hectic bidding stakes at Keeneland for a colt like Seattle Dancer, who eventually, as we have seen, was knocked down for $13.1 million, John Magnier and Michael Tabor were able to spread the risk over a nice batch of yearlings with what they expended at Keeneland and Saratoga in the summer of 1997.

It could be argued that if one or two colts' Classic winners emerged from the bunch and went on to be successfully syndicated at stud, then the outlay of close on $10 million would have been fully justified. Even if some of the colts hit the top as two-year-olds and achieved enough overall to still have potential as stallions, any substantial loss could be avoided. An outlay of $10 million might look massive to those unacquainted with the bloodstock world but the Golden Dream that drove men on was the thought of getting one that would succeed like Northern Dancer, Nijinsky or Sadler's Wells – and then the sky was the limit when reflecting on the return for the original investment or gamble if you wish to term it that.

John Magnier and Michael Tabor had from their yearling purchases given Aidan O'Brien the right kind of ammunition to "go to war" with in 1997. Expectations were high for the two-year-olds that had proved their potential in '96 or, in some instances, held out the promise on breeding and the racecourse appearances they had of going on to higher things as three-year-olds.

It must be noted that as the Magnier-Tabor partnership increased its bloodstock interests globally, Aidan O'Brien was not the only trainer engaged by the duo. As we have seen, they employed the talents of D. Wayne Lukas and, on this side of the Atlantic, the list also included Michael Stoute, Luca Cumani and Neville Callaghan, all based at Newmarket, while in France the highly-successful Andre Fabre was a key member of the training team.

Incidentally, Michael Stoute, trainer of the brilliant 1997 English 2,000 Guineas winner, Entrepreneur for the Magnier-Tabor partnership, produced Kilimanjaro to win the Vintage Inns District Top 48 Conditions Stakes at Sandown late in August '97 by eight lengths. Running in the colours of Michael Tabor, this Shirley Heights colt out of Darara by Top Ville also represents Mrs John Magnier and Lord Lloyd Webber, who now has a stud outside Fethard in South Tipperary. The Tote reacted immediately to Kilimanjaro's excellent showing by making him 16-1 for the 1998 Epsom Derby. He had been backed ante-post for the Derby on his debut in the Newbury race won by Mahoob but ran green and finished fourth. He certainly showed vast improvement in his Sandown victory, achieved in testing conditions, Michael Tabor noting that one would expect him "to go through this ground well as a son of Shirley Heights".

* * *

Aidan O'Brien had conquered everything there was to conquer in the numbers game – the breaking of records and the making of new ones. He had now entered a different league – the Premier League in which Vincent O'Brien had been such a dominant figure, basically the making of stallions League. That had to mean Classic success in the long term, if not in the short. There could be no avoidance of that goal.

I remember O'Brien saying to me before the dawn of the '97 Flat season that he did not feel under pressure, that he would do his own thing and you sensed that he had this tremendous belief in his own methods – to the extent that he would hit the jackpot in the very arena where expectations were highest.

In the eyes of informed racing men, however, he simply had to deliver with the quality of the horses he was getting and would get and with the incomparable facilities at his disposal at Ballydoyle.

The argument in the haunts where racing aficionados gather was that John Magnier and Michael Tabor would not continue to hit the yearling sales from Keeneland to Saratoga, to Newmarket and Goffs without expecting a return from the very gallops that had come to be associated in the minds of the racing public with the conquering of the highest peaks in the Flat arena.

It's a cruel age in sport. Cruel for managers in the Premiership Soccer

League in Britain, cruel for managers over county senior hurling and football teams in Ireland. A club has a magnificent stadium and a panel with players of international calibre and the directors will feel rewarded only when a high place is achieved in the League and maybe in time a title or Cup success on the domestic front and eventually in the European competitions. The manager can pay the penalty if he fails to deliver to the targets that are set.

The rewards for success are high and the media profile of those who are deemed winners is likewise pitched at the highest possible level. There is no place for losers as the Nineties give way to the new Millennium. That is the stark reality.

Aidan O'Brien went on record to state: "The facilities at Ballydoyle are second to none. You could train any horse here."

In the Spring of '97 when he followed in the footsteps of Vincent O'Brien by holding his first Open Day for the racing media, he said: "The facilities here are so good that there is no room for excuses. Indeed, there is only one person to blame when things go wrong – and that's me."

There are gallops at Ballydoyle that can be described as secondary to the main ones that many a trainer, starting off in the business, would be only too glad to utilise as his principal one. You arrive at Mecca when you arrive here and stand in awe at the finest range of gallops, semi-peat gallops and natural grass gallops.

There was no equine swimming pool at Ballydoyle in Vincent's day. Now there is one. Aidan uses it on a daily basis for many of his two-year-olds once they have reached racing fitness.

He has also come to appreciate the benefits of crushed ice. The horses' front legs are put into buckets of crushed ice after they have worked. And this extends to Classic contenders, who seemed to enjoy the experience every bit as much as a seasoned handicapper.

* * *

The weekend of the first two Irish Classics in 1997 was not alone a memorable one for Aidan O'Brien but one of profound significance. Not alone did he provide the winner of the Airlie/Coolmore 1,000 Guineas on Saturday, May 24th but the runner-up as well and then on the Sunday, May 25th, scaled another peak when Desert King landed the 2,000 Guineas.

The knockers were well and truly silenced. And it has got to be admitted that there were those only too ready to hint openly that O'Brien was heading for the chop when there was no basis in fact for such assertions.

Yes, the weekend of May 24th-25th brought a sea change overnight.

When Desert King failed in the King James's Palace Stakes at Royal Ascot to reach the frame Aidan O'Brien accepted publicly that he might not have given him enough work at home since the Irish 2,000 Guineas. It indicated that he was a big man that he could blame himself.

Desert King was back on Budweiser Irish Derby Day at the Curragh on Sunday, June 29th revealing the scintillating form that had won him the Guineas and the confidence expressed by O'Brien beforehand that he would stay the stiff twelve furlongs and still produce that admirable burst of finishing speed was fully vindicated.

So in the space of five weeks the New Master of Ballydoyle had three Classics under his belt. The question now being asked was: How many will he have garnered by the age of 47? And if he keeps going until he is 67 what will his tally be?

The road ahead could well stretch down a span of forty years...

Of course, he could NOT beat Vincent O'Brien's overall record in the National Hunt sphere and the Flat and he would not be foolhardy enough to think he could do that. He could win all the Classics not just once but a number of times but it would be drawing the long bow to bet on the possibility – even if he acquired the National Hunt material to make an all out onslaught – that he could win three successive Gold Cups and an additional one to boot, three successive Champion Hurdles and three successive Aintree Grand Nationals.

Again I must repeat that Vincent O'Brien's overall record over the jumps and on the Flat will NEVER be beaten – not in the new Millennium or beyond.

Let's not then burden Aidan O'Brien, the record-maker, with the impossible expectation that he could from the Ballydoyle gallops get near Vincent's unsurpassed and unsurpassable record. Let's rejoice in what he has done to date in keeping the Irish flag flying high with notable successes from the Curragh to Cheltenham and Royal Ascot, where he fired his initial winning salvo in June of '97.

Time is on his side and very much so.

He will stitch a lot more into the racing history books before he comes to retire.

✳   ✳   ✳

Aidan O'Brien hails from County Wexford – from the same kind of country that gave Jim Bolger to the training profession.

He actually spent three-and-a-half years working with Jim Bolger. It was then that he became acquainted with Tony McCoy who spent his apprenticeship with the Master of Coolcullen. When Aidan O'Brien was asked by one of the race writers in the winner's enclosure – after Toast The Spreece had won the 1997 Guinness Galway Hurdle in truly impressive style in the hands of British champion jump jockey, Tony McCoy – how he had opted for McCoy, he smiled and said: "It goes back to our time together at Jim Bolger's." Obviously, Aidan had been following Tony's progress up the ladder – and realised full well the unique talent he had.

Where others terminated their tenure at Coolcullen abruptly and departed with no love lost, O'Brien will tell you frankly: "Jim Bolger is a very good and a very fair man. He expects the best from you but if you respond as he wants you to respond, then he is good to you. I learnt pretty well all I know from him."

And Bolger, for his part, has nothing but the highest praise for Aidan O'Brien, naming him unhesitatingly as "one of the top three people to have worked for me since I became a trainer."

"He is a wonderful human being and one of the nicest young men I have ever come across," said Bolger. "If anyone was to epitomise the attributes of a gentleman and a scholar it is he. Aidan is intelligent and clever and picks things up quickly. Any operation with which he is associated can only prosper. His industry and dedication are tremendous. I'd have done anything to keep him working for me."

Aidan O'Brien was born in Killegney, Clonroche, near Enniscorthy. Like Jim Bolger, who was one of eight children – five boys and three girls – raised on a farm in Oylegate, he has no pretensions. There is not an ounce of affectation in his make-up. He presents a boyish and unassuming manner that surprises when you contemplate his achievements to date and the impact he has made in such a short space of time on the Irish racing scene.

That impact becomes all the more significant and praiseworthy when you reflect on the fact that unlike Dermot Weld, John Oxx, Jim Dreaper, Arthur Moore and Edward O'Grady, he did not spring from an established training family. However, his father Denis was a very keen point-to-pointer. "He rode many winners and there were always horses around the yard", Aidan told me.

O'Brien left secondary school midway through Fifth Year. "First of all I got a job weeding strawberries and later did shift-work as a forklift driver in Waterford Co-op", he recalled. The call of the horses was in his blood. Long-term he saw no other life. And already deep down the ambition to become a trainer was stirring in his veins

He got the break that was to set him on the ladder that would lead eventually to making him the most exciting talent to burst on the Irish racing scene in the Nineties when a family friend, Pat Kelly, put him in contact with Curragh trainer, P.J. Finn, a son of the legendary Tipperary hurler, Jimmy Finn, who was selected at right wing back on the Hurling Team of the Century in 1984. He was with P.J. Finn for two months before the latter opted temporarily out of the game and, fortunately for Aidan O'Brien, Pat Kelly then arranged a job for him with Jim Bolger. He was on his way.

It was on the racing circuit that Aidan and Anne Marie met and fell in love. It happened at Galway in 1989. Aidan was riding Midsummer Fun in an amateur race for the Jim Bolger stable – it came home a winner, incidentally – and down at the start his eye was caught by the dark-haired Anne Marie who also had a mount in the race. Although shy, he was so smitten by love at first sight that it was inevitable that he should take it from there and the rest is history.

Fate stepped in to cause his departure from Jim Bolger's stable in a rather unusual way. Six weeks before his wedding he broke his shoulder in a fall "and I just never went back". At that stage Anne Marie had just started training on her own and Aidan found himself completely involved in assisting her in the operation. He was the first to acknowledge that the three-and-a-half years he had spent with Jim Bolger represented "an invaluable experience" and that, having started off as a stable lad doing the most menial jobs around the yard and then being given more and more responsibility as time went on, he acquired a tremendous amount of knowledge of every facet of the training profession. "I would start work in the dark and finish in the dark. I would ride out in the morning and do just about everything", he recalled.

✳   ✳   ✳

Aidan, one might say, was carrying on where Anne Marie left off when he took over the licence from her. In the two years she was a public trainer she carved a unique niche for herself in Irish jumping history. She was Ireland's champion National Hunt trainer in the 1992-'93 season with 26 winners of 53 races earning a total of IR£206,458 in prizemoney, putting her ahead of Noel Meade, Arthur Moore and Paddy Mullins. Her father was top owner the same season.

It captured the imagination of the race writers in Britain that this girl described by one as "the 23-year-old with the stunning looks and killer instinct" should emerge overnight as the leading trainer in that area of the racing game that has generally been viewed as the natural terrain of hard bitten men heading for Cheltenham with their charges come March each year. It was in 1993 that she sent her first challengers to the Festival meeting. Much play was made in the British media of the fact that at 29 per cent, her strike rate in Ireland was better than Martin Pipe's in Britain.

The tabloids made hay of the fact that she had forsaken the catwalks for the life of a trainer. But in reality she only took modelling assignments in Kilkenny as a teenager "as a hobby" and from the outset she knew deep down that her life would be spent in racing. "I was brought up to believe that horses were part of life itself", was how she put it to me.

One of six sisters, it was from her father that Anne Marie took over the licence. Joe Crowley didn't just fade away into the background. No, he remained very much involved as did Anne Marie's mother, Sarah. The Crowley operation could best be described as a classic regime – and after Aidan married Anne Marie – bore comparison with other notable examples like the Dickinsons, the Rimmells and Reveleys.

Anne Marie's sisters could be found riding out for her and helping out in different ways when they were at home. Anne Marie herself was very successful in the saddle, riding 23 winners as an amateur, one of her happiest memories being the double she recorded at the 1991 Galway Festival meeting. Of course, when she held the licence, she partnered the stable's bumper horses.

Before assuming her father's mantle she furthered her racing education by spending some time at Jim Bolger's stable, so both Aidan and herself can be described as pupils of the "Bolger Academy".

Anne Marie readily acknowledges the debt she owes her father, recognised as one of the shrewdest characters in the game.

Now 67, he can claim the distinction of having bought and developed and eventually sold on a young horse named after the hill under which he worked his own string, namely the 1983 Cheltenham Gold Cup winner Bregawn. His most memorable triumph as a trainer was sending Ravaro to win the 1985 Irish Cesarewitch at 20-1 under 9st 12lbs.

But nowadays he is deeply respected in racing circles as one of Ireland's best judges of horseflesh and still buys a lot of horses that are trained by his son-in-law, especially the National Hunt types. Patrons of the stable have great faith in his eye and in his judgement.

Originally when they were based in Piltown, Anne Marie acted as secretary to Aidan. But now she has her hands full with the children.

Aidan has at his disposal the members of the professional and experienced secretarial staff remaining from the days when Vincent was still training out of Ballydoyle. It means that Anne Marie and himself don't have to worry about the nitty-gritty of paper-work.

Anne Marie, as we have seen, was brought up with horses and it would be impossible for her not to continue to be involved closely with Aidan in the Ballydoyle operation. While family chores monopolise quite a deal of her time, she can still make the time to watch developments on the gallops and, if Aidan is away, she can with her own experience of training take on greater responsibilities if needs be.

Team-work has always been a hallmark from the days that Anne Marie had a licence and looked to her own family to help out and it was the same when Aidan took over the licence from her. It would have been impossible for Aidan to handle all the horses under his care and supervise a number of yards in an overall singular operation unless he had the Crowleys to row in fully behind him. Today, as he moves between Ballydoyle and Piltown he appreciates the back-up support all the more. And that includes the support of Anne Marie's parents. "We all work together – we have got to, with all the horses we have," was how he put it to me.

The respect between Christy Roche and Aidan O'Brien is a deep and mutual one. O'Brien fully appreciates the depth of experience Roche brings to the task when he arrives to ride work. The two became acquainted when Roche was No. 1. jockey to the Bolger stable and O'Brien was moving up the ranks to become assistant trainer before he left. And now Roche gets immense satisfaction from every success achieved by O'Brien. He noted that this young man had a special way with horses – an understanding of them and "an uncanny ability to keep them at their peak".

"What I like about him also is that in the ring before you go out to ride one of his horses, he doesn't beat about the bush, doesn't get involved in almost lecturing you on how to ride the race. A man of few words, he says exactly what has to be said and what you want to know. He leaves the rest to your judgement and experience."

On August 15, 1994 Aidan O'Brien joined the elite band of Irish trainers who had 100 winners to their credit in a calendar year, reaching his century at Tramore through Moorefield Girl. The only other four to do so have been J.J. Parkinson, Paddy Mullins, Dermot Weld and Jim Bolger. But what made Aidan O'Brien's achievement unique was the fact that he produced the "ton" in his first FULL season as a trainer.

The following year he would smash all existing records for the total of winners on the Flat and over the jumps produced in one calendar year.

Records, it seemed, were made to be broken by Aidan O'Brien.

At the end of 1995 he stood on top of the world in the sense that he had turned out 241 winners on the Flat and over the jumps in the one calendar year – and in the process smashed all existing Irish records. Not alone that, but he eclipsed the highest winning total achieved in recent times by the current English record-holder, Martin Pipe.

O'Brien's strike rate was simply phenomenal, especially over the jumps. It had reached the point in the National Hunt sector that in the battle of the Irish Trainers' crown, he had in each of the two seasons, 1994-'95 and 1995-'96, three times as many winners as his nearest rival in the table, Arthur Moore.

On the Flat in Ireland he had become one of the "Big Four" with John Oxx, Dermot Weld and Jim Bolger. This quartet dominated the scene above all others.

O'Brien had his first significant Group success on the Flat when Dancing Sunset was awarded the Royal Whip (Group 3) at the Curragh on August 13, 1994 on the disqualification of Blue Judge. He took his first Listed two-year-old prize with Glouthaune Garden at Leopardstown on August 20, '94. And then, as we have seen, he recorded his first Group One success when Desert King won the National Stakes at the Curragh on September 21, 1996.

Dermot Weld had shown that he had the ability to turn out ten winners at a Festival meeting like Galway or Tralee (he achieved the distinction at both in '94). But Aidan O'Brien proved at Tralee '94 that he also had the ability to attain a significant total when he produced eight winners.

At Galway '97, as Dermot Weld had to be content with four winners over the six days, Aidan O'Brien emerged as top trainer with eight winners, including, as we have seen the Guinness Galway Hurdle winner in Toast The Spreece while top-weight Idiot's Venture was just touched off giving O'Brien a three-timer in the Digital Galway Hurdle, Paul Carberry riding one of the greatest races I have seen from any jockey in this event when scoring on Stroll Home for the small Cork stable of Jimmy Mangen (in the emotional Cheltenham-like scenes that followed, Aidan O'Brien pushed his way through the press of the crowds to shake Jimmy Mangen's hand in congratulations).

*   *   *

Aidan O'Brien came to know what it is to have a talking-horse in your charge when King Of Kings, carrying the colours of Susan Magnier but representing, of course, the John Magnier-Michael Tabor partnership, scored by eight lengths on his debut at the Curragh on Sunday, May 25, '97. When next the Sadler's Wells colt won the Arthur Guinness Railway Stakes at the Curragh on Budweiser Irish Derby Day he was cut to 5-1 for the 1998 English 2,000 Guineas by the big English layers, who reported that their liabilities stood at that point at £2 million, some early-birds having got in at 25-1 with Corals.

Men who had seen it all could not but reflect back at that point to Try My Best, Storm Bird, Apalachee, Danzatore and Monteverdi. The graveyard of torn anti-post dockets represented the stark reality that the foolhardy would continue to ignore.

Going for the three-timer in the Omni Racing Anglesey Stakes on July 13 – again at the Curragh – King Of Kings was sensationally beaten a short-head by the Con Collins-trained Lady Alexander. He was given a sympathetic ride by Christy Roche when he did not get the right feel. On the Monday it was reported that he had returned home a sick horse. Four horses that O'Brien had withdrawn at the Curragh Sunday meeting had been "off their feed".

The bookies quickly deposed King Of Kings as favourite for the 1998 English 2,000 Guineas. In fact, his odds slipped out to double the 5-1 on offer after his second success. Those with ante-post dockets could now only keep their fingers crossed and hope for the best.

Aidan O'Brien was not fazed by all the headlines, all the intense debate, by the reaction to what the cynics saw as another bubble bursting. Just over a fortnight after the Anglesey Stakes setback for King Of Kings he was in Galway saddling those eight winners over six days, taking the triumphant moments in his stride as he could put defeat behind him.

King Of Kings, starting at 2-9, got back on the winning trail when taking the Flame of Tara Tyros Stakes (7f) at the Curragh on Saturday, August 16 by one-and-a-lengths from English raider Sharp Play. His tendency to put his head in the air when he hit the front did not enamour him with professional race-readers but Aidan O'Brien attributed to the two-year-old's learning process. "When he goes for his race, he thinks he's done enough and starts looking around. He's just going to have to learn."

✳   ✳   ✳

We are into the age of the cult of the celebrity, into the public seemingly wanting to know all the tittle-tattle and trivia about their sporting heroes, the gossip columnists eager for any scandal.

On the eve of Royal Ascot '97, Aidan O'Brien, as he sought his first winner at this greatest of Flat meetings, got headline treatment and the words "New Wizard From Ballydoyle" were there in the headlines over a perceptive article by Colin MacKenzie in the *Daily Mail,* while the heading over Marcus Armytage's feature in the *Daily Telegraph* read: "Ballydoyle's New Master Has Much To Live Up To".

We might ask ourselves should we be concerned simply with the trainer, his art and his achievements just as in the case of a great screen actor like Humphrey Bogart or Henry Fonda or Dustin Hoffman the performance is everything – the performance that sees us getting lost in the character. In our childhood and youthful days Charlie Chaplin left an impact that could not fade. Did we care about his personal life?

The public's fascination with Aidan O'Brien lies in the fact that he is a private person like Vincent O'Brien. And this very eschewing of the centre-stage spotlight only increases the fascination.

Colin MacKenzie wrote that he "looks like an 'A' level candidate, scarcely into long trousers" and also that "the painfully shy trainer was as modest and retiring as a Trappist monk".

I got to thinking at Royal Ascot '97 that topper and tails weren't really his milieu, though he knew they were required for the occasion.

Aidan O'Brien can be totally himself in the company of racing people, and the racing writers. When he is being interviewed after a race by the media circle – whether it be at the Curragh, Leopardstown, Punchestown or Galway or even Cheltenham – he has no problem in handling the flow of questions put to him. He is in his own domain then – a racing domain.

He shows a candour that is refreshing. If one doesn't spark, he will never put up a smokescreen seeking to divert attention away from himself. If he believes the cause of failure lies in his court he is prepared to say so. For example, at Galway '97 he blamed himself for the fact that his No. 1 jockey over the jumps, Charlie Swan missed the ride on Toast The Spreece in the Guinness Galway Hurdle. "Charlie told me he would ride him if his only engagement was the Hurdle. We ran him in the McDonagh Handicap on the Tuesday evening, in which he finished 9th, so Charlie opted for Just Little in the Hurdle and she finished 8th."

Aidan O'Brien is not one I would expect to jump at the opportunity of being interviewed live on a television chat show about subjects that may not be directly related to racing – "do you take cornflakes or bran flakes for breakfast?" "And who is your favourite film star?"

If I were his personal adviser, I would certainly be the last one to advocate that he go up front for the cameras to satisfy the producer of a television chat show. I would advise also against giving an after-dinner address to some luncheon gathering. It is not his field, not his forte.

Aidan O'Brien's feats speak for him in a way that he doesn't have to be a self-publicist. Speak in the very same way that made David O'Brien, another retiring person, someone on a plane apart for what he achieved before he reached his 30th birthday.

Vincent O'Brien was always retiring and certainly not one to court the gossip columns or appear on television chat shows. In fact, I would say that he had one thing in common with Aidan O'Brien, who would assume his mantle at Ballydoyle. Neither of them could ever be classed an interviewer's dream in the mould of a Mick O'Toole or a Mick Fitzgerald. Both were happier and far more relaxed when you were with them on the gallops, no note-book in hand, just talking horses. Then they exuded knowledge – a depth of knowledge. You knew you were in the company of genius in Vincent's case and a very special talent in Aidan's.

Aidan O'Brien is very much a family man, as Vincent O'Brien has been all through his life. I have been with Aidan and Anne Marie in Ballydoyle talking horses to Aidan while one or two of the children played at his feet or sat on his knees.

They have three children now, Joseph (3), Sarah (2) and Anna (1).

He is up at 5.30 in the morning, so naturally that rules out burning the candle at the other end. It means also that in order to spend time with the children, to relax in the family circle, he cannot take in all the evening meetings that fill the calendar in the summer season.

Aidan O'Brien is a perfectionist like Vincent before him. Every horse is blood-tested before it runs and again immediately afterwards, when it goes straight into an isolation unit. Only when a horse has been tested free of infection is it allowed to return to the main yard.

O'Brien, again as with Vincent, puts great emphasis on the speed factor. "Everything is geared towards speed, speed and more speed," he told Michael Clower of the *Sporting Life* during the Open Day for the media last April. "M.V's theory was that the faster they go, the easier they will travel in a race – and the easier they travel, the further they will stay."

He has also followed Vincent's lead in keeping plenty of condition on his horses and said: "I think this is important. If you start off the season with them looking like whippets, you will end up with skeletons."

✳   ✳   ✳

On one of my most recent trips to Ballydoyle I saw the sun rise over the Old Castle and over the magnificent spread of gallops, including the famous gallop designed as a replica of the sweep to Tattenham Corner.

I stood with Aidan O'Brien as he watched some of the horses in his charge cantering up the grass. Tommy Murphy, who rode for Vincent and has forgotten more about the game than many can ever aspire to learn, is now an assistant trainer to the new Master of Ballydoyle. And the stable jockey is Christy Roche. No trainer could hope to have a jockey of greater experience or with a better ability to run the rule exactly over the potential of a two-year-old after exercise on the gallops.

Roche, now training successfully on his own at the Curragh, will continue to ride for the stable next year. It has been decided that he will take the mounts on the leading contenders on the home front while Michael Kinane will ride the O'Brien challengers in Britain and elsewhere.

You arrive at Mecca when you arrive here and stand in awe at the finest range of gallops in the world. They extend from all-weather ones to peat gallops, semi-peat gallops and natural grass gallops.

Aidan brings me out in the Land-Rover accompanied by Anne Marie and Tommy Murphy.

They talk about each horse individually as it goes by. Recognition is immediate and where it stands in its particular schedule, whether it has been backward or under a cloud and is now well on the way back. You marvel at the attention you know each horse is given.

But that attention extends to an animal back in Piltown, carrying the hopes of one owner or maybe a Syndicate, whose targets will be set well below those of the choicely-bred Flat campaigners. Each man to his own dreams and it is the trainer's job, if he can, to make the dreams become reality. Aidan O'Brien with his flow of winners has realised a lot of dreams.

Back in the house he defines for me his role as he now sees it. For the time being he wants to preserve a duality of approach – that is training both jumpers and Flat horses. Naturally, he was thrilled to turn out his first Cheltenham Festival winner in '96 when Urubande, in the hands of Charlie Swan won the Sun Alliance Novices Hurdle at 8-1 and then went on to take the Martell Aintree Hurdle at the Grand National meeting. At Cheltenham '97 there was Istabraq's wonderfully-courageous victory in the Sun Alliance Novices Hurdle in the colours of J.P. McManus after he had looked like leaving it behind him in the parade ring. There was immense satisfaction too in Life Of A Lord's brilliant win in the Whitbread Gold Cup Chase, followed by a fine performance under top weight of 12st by this ill-fated chaser in winning the Digital Galway Plate for the second successive year.

In moment's like that it's hard to contemplate Aidan O'Brien easily saying farewell to the jumping game.

But even though Vincent O'Brien set records in the National Hunt sphere that will never be broken, he eventually had to choose between giving his undivided attention to the Flat or continuing to mix it. He came down in favour of the Flat and had no reason to regret that decision.

Charlie Swan returns in triumph to the winner's enclosure after riding the Aidan O'Brien-trained Istabraq (right), in the J.P. McManus colours, to victory in the Sun Alliance Novices Hurdle at Cheltenham '97. (Pictures: Bernard Parkin)

29

Return To Churchtown

The plaque is a simple one. It can be seen now right in the centre of Churchtown – a reminder to the world that this village was Vincent O'Brien's birthplace, that it was here that it all began and, come 1998, it will be half-a-century since he sent Cottage Rake to Cheltenham to win the first of three successive Gold Cups. And from then on for a decade he would be the "King" of the Festival meeting.

I felt privileged to be there on Sunday evening, July 27, 1997, when Noel O'Brien, who today resides in the original O'Brien family homestead in Clashganniff House – about a mile and a half east of the village – where Vincent first saw the light of day on April 9, 1917, unveiled the plaque.

Also unveiled were two other plaques – one to Dr Barry Edmond O'Meara, who was born in Churchtown in 1782 and who was chosen by Napoleon to accompany him to St. Helena; he actually sailed with Napoleon on the H.M.S. Northumberland, came to be known as the former Emperor's "favourite surgeon" and later on his return to England brought out his famous *Voice From St. Helena* or *Napoleon In Exile*.

There was a plaque unveiled also to Seán Clárach MacDomhnall, also a native of Churchtown and a renowned 18th century bard-cum-gentleman farmer.

After the Chairman of the Development Association, Oliver Byrne, had addressed the people gathered in knots around the village "square", giving a brief resume of the achievements of the sons of Churchtown being honoured that evening, there was a wine and cheese reception in the Parochial Hall (the wine, incidentally, being a gift from film star Oliver Reed, who now lives at the outskirts of Churchtown and who was present for the unveiling ceremony).

The members of the Brugh Theinne Choral Society – among them Noel O'Brien's wife Margaret – gave a special recital and one of the memories that will always remain with me of the evening will be of their fine rendering of the Barcarolle from Offenbach's *The Tales Of Hoffman*.

Directing the choir was Mary Wilson from Cork, wife of Denis Wilson who delivered an absorbing talk on Napoleon's doctor, Barry Edmond O'Meara. Incidentally, the Wilsons' daughter is Fiona Shaw, the award-winning actress of stage and screen, whose credits include a role in Franco *(Romeo & Juliet)* Zeffirelli's 1996 film, *Jane Eyre,* starring also William Hurt, Joan Plowright, Geraldine Chaplin, Billie Whitelaw and Maria Schneider.

Patrick Irwin presented a slide show on Vincent O'Brien's racing days from Churchtown to Ballydoyle and beyond and he took the opportunity also to show a rare film of Loch Lomond winning the 1919 Irish Derby, proving that Vincent was fortunate to hail from an area that had bred more than one brilliant horse on the Flat and in the National Hunt sphere.

✳　　✳　　✳

In O'Brien's pub, Tom, who knows the point-to-point scene like the back of his hand and has had good ones running in the colours, is pulling pints as fast as they can be served while also putting up the inevitable "chasers".

The atmosphere is redolent with racing talk – with memories too of the era when Vincent's stable was like a small industry considering the employment it gave. How sad they were when he moved to Ballydoyle but in the final analysis they had to accept that it was inevitable. And yet it was suggested to me again that evening that if the right farm had come on the market at the critical juncture, Vincent would have stayed put for he had a deep affinity with his native area.

But would the doors have been opened that saw millionaires like Raymond Guest, Charles Engelhard, John Galbreath and John Mulcahy row in behind him to make it possible for him to hit new unimagined peaks? Would he have formed 'The Syndicate' with Robert Sangster and John Magnier with multi-millionaire Stavros Niarchos, the Greek shipping tycoon in there at one stage?

No, he might have continued as a dual-purpose trainer adding to his laurels over the jumps and on the Flat but not destined to become a global figure.

Vincent wanted each one of his trusted staff, who had soldiered with him in Churchtown, to accompany him to Ballydoyle. He was a great believer in teamwork and realised that without it you couldn't live on the High Sierras.

Vincent's assistant Maurice O'Callaghan, the faithful headman for 30 years and Danny O'Sullivan, who as we have seen, was an outstanding schooling rider, moved to Ballydoyle.

But Jimmy Gordon, viewed by Vincent as a key figure in the line-up that had known such success under his captaincy, decided to stay put. "Vincent made me a very generous offer to start anew with him in the new stables. It was very difficult to refuse but Mai, the girl that I would marry, had a grocery-cum-drapery in Churchtown and I was also thinking of setting up as a trainer myself."

"So you won't come?" Vincent said. "I'm afraid I have to say no," was Jimmy's response.

"It was the hardest things I ever had to say in my life," he added. "I knew I could never repay him for all the knowledge I acquired in those years."

Jimmy took the road to being a trainer, and knew his share of winners over a span of fifteen years, his name winning total respect especially on the point-to-point circuit. Ask him if he had any regrets from that period of his life and, acknowledging that he knew great times, he will tell you there was one – his charge Storyville with John Harty in the saddle being beaten in a blanket finish to the Galway Plate by a short head and three-quarters-of-a-length. The race went to the 33-1 outsider, Sarejay Day, carrying 9 st 7 lbs and ridden by Sammy Shields. The runner-up was the English challenger, the topweight with 12 st Larbawn, the mount of Macer Gifford. Storyville, carried 9 st 11 lbs – 2 lbs more than his allotted handicap mark as John Harty could not do the weight. It could be argued that it made all the difference in the end.

The yarns, the banter and the repartee flow in O'Brien's and Jimmy now recalls for me one of the most amazing episodes of all from Vincent's initial days as a trainer in Churchtown.

✳   ✳   ✳

In Chapter Four I related how 1949 marked the first time that Vincent O'Brien sent challengers for the Cheltenham Festival meeting by air – indeed, it was the first occasion he flew horses to a meeting in England. The three horses in question were Cottage Rake, Hatton's Grace and Castledermot.

The flight was from Shannon to Bristol in a converted bomber and it took all of three hours. On the plane were Dermot O'Brien, Jackie O'Brien, Jack Roche, Danny O'Sullivan, Danny O'Gorman and Jimmy Gordon.

Jack Roche was a farmer whose holding was not far from Clashganniff House and whenever there was even a hint of a virus hitting Vincent's yard in the countdown to Cheltenham, the challengers earmarked for the Festival meeting would be 'isolated' in the Roche's farm. Again this demonstrated that long before modern isolation units came into being Vincent was able to improvise with a natural one.

Danny O'Gorman, who lived near Buttevant, contributed to the O'Brien operation by breaking horses; indeed, he had a wonderful way with young horses and Vincent had great faith in his uncanny ability at this art and also in his healing hands. I met his son Dan on the evening of the unveiling. He is maintaining the family tradition and, as one might expect, he has a great eye too for spotting young talent and when he has broken them in he can tell which are likely to become the future success stories.

He loves the point-to-point scene and confesses that there is no greater thrill than when you see one of your own entering the winner's enclosure. Time can stand still the next day as the celebrations continue!

Jimmy Gordon was young then and the flight from Shannon to Bristol was a great adventure for him. He was responsible, as groom, for looking after Hatton's Grace and Castledermot.

Vincent's brother Dermot and Danny O'Sullivan, with help from the others, had the unenviable task of ensuring that Cottage Rake – a nervous traveller even when taken by road and sea – would not go berserk. It became a nightmare from the moment the plane gave a lurch as it was straightening out for take-off and 'The Rake' took fright and began to go down.

Dermot O'Brien and Danny O'Sullivan fought desperately to keep him on his feet and there was the sight of them almost swinging out of his tail as he trashed around and kept kicking out. "I was so innocent that I shouted at them, 'Look, my two are very quiet' and they were so occupied with Cottage Rake that they could hardly have heard what I was saying. The noise the plane made was terrible and people accustomed only to modern jet travel can have no concept what that flight was like."

Jimmy Gordon revealed that it became such a near-impossible task at one point trying to quieten Cottage Rake that the pilot indicated that the safety of passengers and crew would have to be paramount. "I think there was a gun on hand if the worse came to the worst and, as I looked at Dermot and Danny, with the sweat pouring down their faces, I realised, young and all as I was, that this was a terrible crisis and that before he ever even got to Cheltenham, Cottage Rake's prospects of landing the Gold Cup could evaporate in appalling fashion.

"Fortunately, Dermot and Danny somehow or other managed to keep matters on an even keel for the rest of the flight but, as Dermot often said to me afterwards, it was a near thing, a very near thing."

When the real moment of crisis had passed Jimmy Gordon recalls a bottle of whiskey being produced and never did men need a quick shot more than was the case then.

As the three Cheltenham challengers were being led down the ramp, after the plane had landed at Bristol, Danny O'Gorman held the empty whiskey bottle aloft, gave it a kiss and exclaimed: "But for you I would not be here."

✳   ✳   ✳

Hatton's Grace was one of the horses in the O'Brien stable that Jimmy Gordon had special responsibility for and he said unhesitatingly: "He was one of the best horses I ever put a leg across."

But then versatility was his middle name, for apart from winning those three successive Champion Hurdles he won the Irish Lincolnshire (1949) and the Irish Cesarewitch two years running (1949 and 1950).

When Jimmy Gordon got married to Mai, he was presented by Mrs Moya Keogh, in whose colours Hatton's Grace ran, with a picture of the horse winning the Champion Hurdle – in a solid silver frame.

A gesture he has never forgotten.

Jimmy said it was a far, far different Cheltenham in the late Forties than it is today. "When I returned in the past few years I could not believe the change – the vastness of the stands, with their corporate boxes, the Tote area, the new amphitheatre-like winner's enclosure, the crush of the crowds on Gold Cup Day, in particular."

"There were only cinders where Cottage Rake was led in following his first Gold Cup triumph in 1948," he added.

Jimmy Gordon smiled when he reflected on the limit of 50,000 being put on the attendance for Gold Cup Day in future.

The number of Irish jumping enthusiasts attending the Festival meeting in the initial years of the Vincent O'Brien onslaught was quite big but could not compare, of course, with the exodus each March nowadays. "Those who went over mingled with the many Irish in Britain who seemed to make it a point to try to get to Cheltenham. Remember, with so much emigration there were a lot of Irish working in England then."

Jimmy Gordon has seen a number of those who were team-mates of his in Vincent's Churchtown operation pass on – Maurice O'Callaghan, Jimmy and Danny O'Sullivan.

Today he lives with Mai in a comfortable spread at the outskirts of the village – happy to remember times past, to talk about an era when all the world was young for him and he was there for the embryonic years when Vincent was taking his first steps up the ladder that would lead in time to a level of achievement that no one could have foreseen.

He has reason to count himself one of the privileged ones – those who soldiered with Vincent before Ballydoyle even came into the scheme of things and he changed the face of Churchtown, helping to put it on the map.

Dinny Fisher, who was in school with Vincent and who played hurling with him in a field in front of Clashganniff House, had died since last I was in Churchtown. Dan Flynn had also passed on.

But I had the pleasure of renewing acquaintanceship with Jack Murphy, whose brother Bill was in the same class as Vincent. Jack and Bill were in the LDF during the Emergency with Vincent O'Brien.

Jack's son, Gerald, who is an executive with the First National Building Society in Dublin, is playing a key role in the admirable efforts at community level to revitalise the village and add to its attraction with tourists.

The Flannerys were away that evening. Edward Flannery and his wife, Mary, maintain in the Egmont Stud the proud traditions forged by this stud down the decades. The tradition goes back to 1850 when the Flannery family founded Churchtown Stud. It was reputed to be the oldest stud in Ireland. They also had the Egmont Stud at the edge of the village, dating from 1870.

The late Frank Flannery and his wife, Nell, always had very close ties with Clashganniff House. In fact, Frank's friendship with Dan O'Brien led to Dan acquiring a mare that was to bring him good fortune. Once when Frank Flannery was going to the Newmarket Sales, Dan asked him to keep an eye out for a good mare and told him to purchase it if he thought fit.

Frank duly bought the mare, Golden Emblem for 35 guineas in foal to Tetrameter. Her first foal, Golden Meter showed a lot of speed but did not stay. Dan bred her to Vesington Star, which was standing at the Flannery's Churchtown Stud and the result was first Astrometer and then Astrologer – two colts that turned out to be prolific winners, Astrometer, as we have seen, winning the Irish Cesarewitch in 1941 while Astrologer, switched to the stable of John Oxx Snr. in 1943 after the death of Dan O'Brien, won the Irish Cambridgeshire (he had been just touched off in the Irish Lincoln earlier that same year when trained by Dan O'Brien).

Edward and Mary Flannery have reason to remember 1979 for not alone did Dickens Hill, bred at the Egmont Stud, win the Irish 2,000 Guineas and finish runner-up in the Epsom Derby and Irish Derby but the Stud also had the distinction of breeding Brother Philipos, second in the Irish 2,000 Guineas.

And at Galway '97 the Noel Meade-trained Saving Bond, bred at the Egmont Stud, won the feature event on the Tuesday evening, the G.P.T. Galway (Q.R.) Handicap in impressive style in a field of 18. In the process the Digmatist gelding (out of Marine Life) was completing a four-timer.

Denis Fehan and his wife Ann missed the unveiling of the plaques as they were away on holidays. They told me, when I met them earlier in the summer, about the amazing stroke of good fortune that saw them acquire Nick Dundee very cheaply and sell him for a substantial six-figure sum.

They had joined their trainer, Eugene O'Sullivan of Lombardstown at the Tattersalls Derby Sale. "I had £10,000 to spend," recalled Denis Fehan. "There was nothing that really caught our eye and then Eugene mentioned a horse by Supreme leader out of Silent Run, a Deep Run mare that had been taken out of the ring unsold at over 5,000 guineas. He liked him.

"I looked at the horse about three times and, frankly, I couldn't make up my mind. Then Ann said 'it's time we were getting home to Churchtown – the price is right, buy him'. And I did."

After he had won a point-to-point very impressively, English trainer Tom Tate put in an enticing bid for him but Denis Fehan decided not to sell there and then. There followed Nick Dundee's very impressive victory in a bumper at Clonmel and John Magnier stepped in with a £100,000-plus offer that could not be refused.

✳   ✳   ✳

The evening in O'Brien's stretches on towards closing time amidst a wealth of racing chat, the banter and the craic. And somehow pervading all is Vincent O'Brien, though he has been unable because of family commitments to make it for the occasion (he has written a note of explanation to the Organising Committee).

I meet Willie O'Brien of Buttevant, nephew of the legendary Jackie O'Brien, who, as we have seen, played such a crucial role in putting Vincent O'Brien on the road to a training career. Willie had an outstanding record as an amateur jockey, winning no less than 200 races, and he also rode work for Vincent O'Brien when he was based in Churchtown.

I could not but notice the limp and he confessed that it was a legacy of his days in the saddle, of the falls. "I must have broken every bone in my body," he laughed. "I would say that the old collar bone was fractured thirteen times at least."

The pictures dotting the walls of his Buttevant home tell of the triumphs like the day in 1950 he rode Sharp Answer to victory at Fairyhouse for Willie O'Grady. Many others and one he takes special pride in – a framed picture of Pat Taaffee on Arkle with a personal note written on it – because Pat gave it to him at the time of his wedding. "We were very good friends," said Willie.

Willie's father, James was one of six brothers and the family was steeped in the tradition of the horse. One brother, Willie, was killed riding at a point-to-point meeting. Another brother, Tommy, was Master of Avondhu Hunt and Jackie himself was the Whip. Jackie rode to hounds with an enthusiasm that was infectious and he knew, from the knowledge bred in his bones, what you had to look for in a horse that would make a first-class point-to-point or potential star chaser.

"Jackie picked up The Harrier for my father and they still talk to this day about the record of this horse," recalled Willie O'Brien. "He ran in 22 point-to-points and won 20 of them. Yes, he had a great eye for a horse."

As we have seen already, it was Jackie O'Brien who was instrumental in alerting Frank Vickerman to the potential of Cottage Rake when the horse was owned by Dr Otto Vaughan of Fermoy.

Jackie's pet terrier seemed to go everywhere with him. He was actually a "guest" at Willie O'Brien's wedding.

"That's one of my happiest memories of the bould Jackie," said Willie O'Brien, "seeing him in full cry that day, the life and soul of the party and the terrier beside him – smoking a cigarette."

Already we have seen earlier in this book how the intrepid Willie O'Brien was runner-up to the legendary P.P. Hogan in the historic re-enactment in April, 1954 of the first steeplechase on record between two local gentlemen, Cornelius O'Callaghan and Edmund Blake in 1752 (the race was over four-and-a-half miles of country from Buttevant Church to the St. Leger Church in Doneraile and because it was from steeple to steeple, it gave the word 'steeplechase' to National Hunt racing).

The 1954 re-run was from Doneraile to Buttevant and then in June, 1996 Donal O'Keeffe organised another repeat with leading professionals and amateurs taking part and this time Jason Titley emerged triumphant in a rousing finish with Charlie Swan.

Buttevant is a town steeped in history and derives its name from the war cry of the Anglo-Norman de-Barry family who settled here in 1206 – 'Boutez en Avant!'

Today Buttevant retains many of its Norman features. Willie O'Brien and his wife, Josette run Spitalfields, a lovely 18th century country house set in its own farmland at the edge of the town and very popular with British visitors and, indeed, tourists from all parts of the globe.

✳   ✳   ✳

The railway station at Buttevant stands for me always as a monument to Vincent O'Brien's years as assistant to his father – the years before the pad at Ballydoyle from which horses were flown to challenge for races abroad was ever contemplated.

Every time I see the signalman's cabin, I think of Vincent walking horses from the Churchtown stables, managing at the same time to bring his bike with him. Then he would throw the bike into the guard's van and, having loaded the horses on to the train, he would stay with them for the journey, maybe to the Curragh.

Or the destination might be the now-defunct Miltown-Malbay track in Co. Clare, entailing a rail journey that seemed to go on forever. The final stage of it on the famous West Clare line, immortalised by Percy French, and because of its narrow gauge the horses had to be put into cattle wagons.

'Are ye right there, Michael, are ye right?
'Do you think that ye'll be home before it's light?'
''Tis all dependin' whether
The ould engine howlds together –'
'And it might now, Michael, so it might!

Raymond Guest... the millionaire racehorse owner and former U.S. Ambassador to Ireland who was associated with memorable triumphs by Vincent O'Brien.

WHEN VINCENT O'BRIEN RECEIVED DOCTORATE FROM NORTHERN UNIVERSITY

Vincent O'Brien on the day he was honoured with the Doctorate of Science by the University of Ulster. He was also honoured by the National University with the Doctorate of Law. (Picture: Jacqueline O'Brien)

EPILOGUE

The 80th Birthday Milestone

V incent O'Brien passed the milestone of his 80th birthday on April 9, 1997. Jacqueline and himself celebrated the day quietly at their holiday home in Lyford Cay, Nassau in the Bahamas.

Vincent's eldest son, David and his wife, Catherine and their four children, Andrew, Robert, Charles and Alexandra flew in from France to share the occasion and the small dinner party. "The rest of the family visited us during the Christmas holidays and Charles, his wife Anne and Kate, their daughter, spent a week here in February," noted Mrs O'Brien.

Vincent was never one to dwell on age or the passage of time. He was actually 77 when he finally decided to retire from training, having held a licence for half a century.

Now he had no wish to have the fanfares sounding because his 80th birthday loomed and that was why Jacqueline, who understands him so well, decided that it should be a low-key affair.

For Vincent the day took on the pattern and regularity of days in Lyford Cay or other centres abroad. He walked the mile he invariably walks every morning and he managed to get in his customary nine holes of golf.

Nowadays with the pressures of training off his shoulders, he is enjoying life very much. He has substantial bloodstock interests in Ireland and, as a partner in the Coolmore Stud, with its wings in the United States and in Australia, he has to attend to questions that come up from day to day.

He keeps himself fully informed and right up to date with all developments worldwide in the racing and breeding spheres. When he is abroad, he will receive each morning from Coolmore a long fax with racing news from all countries.

His son-in-law, John Magnier, the Boss of Coolmore, has always placed great store in the unparalleled knowledge and judgement that Vincent has. Together they shared moments at the Keeneland Sales with Robert Sangster that are part of the history of the bloodstock industry globally.

When the morning tasks and the correspondence have been dealt with, he makes the time to play nine holes of golf every afternoon. Always an avid reader, he continues to read a lot. He prefers biographies. Fiction doesn't appeal to him.

The all-pervading sense of family, and a very closely-knit family at that, has always struck me forcibly when I have conversed with his children about Vincent O'Brien. All five children married. The grandchildren, fifteen in all, six girls and nine boys, came to adore him. Vincent and Jacqueline in turn do not conceal their pride in their grandchildren.

Liz McClory, who now lives near Blessington, County Wicklow, has a son Sean (18) heading for University this year.

Sue and John Magnier have five children, Katie (20), Tom (17), J.P. (14), M.V. – called after Vincent – who is 13 and Samantha ('Sam'), who is eleven. The boys, who are all good golfers, are pupils of Glenstal.

Katie is studying art and antiques. Several years ago Tom was on the Irish pony three-day eventing team while J.P., M.V. and 'Sam' all ride but then a love of horses is ingrained in their blood.

Jane and Philip Myerscough have Jamie (18) headed for University; he will take a year off first and this could include working on his golf as he is tremendously keen on the game.

David (17), a very keen event rider, has an ambition to be a racehorse trainer some day. Sophie (15) is also a very keen eventer, and was a member of the Irish team that competed in the three-day under-16 European Pony Championship in Gloucestershire and acquitted herself extremely well.

Tara (9) also has a love of horses in her blood. Indeed, wanting to be with horses is part of life for the Myerscough children.

Philip Myerscough is not alone Chief Executive of Goffs but with Jane runs Ballysheehan Stud near Cashel, County Tipperary. Jane, as might be expected of a daughter of Vincent O'Brien, is very good with the yearlings. Philip, despite all his other commitments, threw himself wholeheartedly into the efforts to uplift the Curragh racecourse and increase attendances. If today the Headquarters venue for Irish Flat racing presents a new image to the racing public, a deal of the credit must go to what Philip Myerscough achieved during his time as Chairman of the Curragh Committee.

Vincent O'Brien takes a deep personal interest in Charles's progress as a trainer. He is in constant touch with him about the horses in his charge. His parents have supported Charles by sending him horses to train for them. It was a proud Budweiser Irish Derby day for Vincent and Jacqueline in '97 when they saw Dr Johnson, carrying Vincent's colours, come within a length of lifting the principal Irish colts' Classic but then it had to be a moment of mixed feelings and emotions as Sue Magnier was involved with the winner, Desert King.

When I asked Vincent for his reaction to Dr Johnson coming so close to victory – having led one and a half furlongs out – he said that he was thrilled to see the colt improve so much, even though he didn't actually emerge the winner.

Vincent and Jacqueline are proud that David has made such a success of his new role as a wine-maker in the South of France and that the wines produced at the famous Chateau Vignelaure are developing new markets with each passing year. Almost a decade has passed since David gave up training. But he left footprints on racing's sands of time that will never fade.

Liz... Sue... Jane... David... Charles. And the family line continuing through the grandchildren and in time through their children.

Christmas figures strongly in the childhood memories of all the O'Brien children. Jane recalled the thrill it gave her writing to Santa and then examining the presents on Christmas morning. "They came for each of us in a pillow case."

Sue too remembers Christmas times past with a special clarity as she recalls her own special memories of growing up in Ballydoyle. "I remember Mum playing the organ in the little Church in Rosegreen. We joined in the hymns, *Silent Night* and *Adeste Fidelis,* and then being brought to the Crib. Dermot and his wife, Jean and Phonsie and his wife, Ann, joined us for the Christmas dinner and I can recall the laughter around the table as the turkey was brought in. Later the Christmas pudding and then the slices of Christmas cake and all the minerals that we kids could consume.

"We would put on our own little theatrical production during the Christmas period; I played the piano, David was on the trumpet, Liz played the viola and Jane the violin. We took it very seriously. We made the stable lads pay going in! It was all good fun and there was even a ballet performance as part of the production."

She recalls from childhood days Dad coming up to read bedtime stories to her, *Winnie the Pooh,* and other timeless favourites such as *The Wind in the Willows.* "What I liked even more than these was when he talked to us about his own childhood days, when he talked too about the War years, the rationing of tea and cigarettes, the clothes coupons and his days in the LDF. He brought back the veil on a lost world to us – something it is not easy to imagine today. It all seemed so wonderful because he had made it so real and in many ways so simple and different.

"I remember how the characters he knew in Churchtown and Buttevant became for me, in the telling, people I felt I knew all my life, he painted such a picture of them. And I remember laughing at funny happenings and funny sayings and being sad, too, when he related tragedies that befell friends of his in the community. He had such an exact feeling for that area of County Cork."

She recalled too being taught how to play cards by her father. "But, strangely enough, he never played children's card games. If he played with us, he played poker – and he played it seriously. He had learned how to play cards, he told us, from his own father.

"As a family man, I don't think there was anyone like him. And, now as a grandfather, he has been simply wonderful to our children, Katie, Tom, John Paul, Michael Vincent and Samantha."

Did she really call one of the boys Michael Vincent?

"Yes, and he so quickly became 'M.V.'," she laughed.

There could be no finer tribute by John and Sue to Vincent than that one of the Magnier boys already being known as 'M.V.'

Birthday parties, too, have a special place in the storehouse of memories of the O'Brien children. One party, for example, that will always be recalled by Jane is the evening her father celebrated his 70th birthday in April, 1987 and the celebratory dinner took place in Ballydoyle House (where the 80th birthday because of the circumstances of the moment was celebrated in Lyford Cay). "It was a wonderful party, a purely family occasion. I think Dad really enjoyed it," added Jane.

Vincent and Jacqueline believed in protecting the children when they were too young to appreciate, or cope with, certain happenings. Liz recalled the time that Vincent lost his licence over the "Chamour Affair".

"Nanny had been told not to breathe a word about it to any of us children. I can remember an awful lot of secret whispering and wondering what it was all about. Then we were having tea in the Nursery with Nanny – that is us children – and suddenly over the radio came the news that Dad had lost his licence and I think it was mentioned that we would be moving out of Ballydoyle.

"I remember Nanny literally flying to the radio and trying desperately to switch it off before we could hear any more. I can still see the exact spot in the Nursery where the radio was that evening. You never forget things like that."

Yet as they got older they were included in every family conversation over meals. "Nothing was held back from us," said Liz, "and I think this cemented the closeness of the family as a unit."

Jane recalled the pressures created on her father whenever he had a horse that emerged good enough to win a Classic and that pressure became all the more intense the better the horse was, especially if it was in the Sir Ivor, Nijinsky or Golden Fleece class.

"I always noticed that he grew tense when one of the outstanding two-year-olds of the previous season came out and won as a three-year-old and then the spotlight came on it as a possible 2,000 Guineas and Derby winner. Strangely enough, he took defeat in his stride. He was more relaxed after a bad day than he was when victory meant that he had a horse in the yard that created all the security problems surrounding a well-fancied candidate, maybe even a warm favourite for one of the Classics. He became pre-occupied with the planning ahead, with concentrating on every detail, ensuring that nothing would go wrong if he could possibly help it."

✳   ✳   ✳

It's coming up to half a century since Vincent O'Brien, from his Churchtown base in County Cork, made his initial assault on Cheltenham. For ten years he was King of the March Festival meeting. Before his 38th birthday and over a span of twelve years, he sent out the winners of 22 races at Cheltenham. Again we can only speculate on how many more big races over the jumps, including further Grand National triumphs to add to the Gold Cups, Champion Hurdles and Gloucestershire Hurdle victories – he would have achieved had he not switched in 1959 to concentrate completely on the Flat.

Naturally Cheltenham retains a special place in his affections. He made a nostalgic return visit in March '95 after being away for a number of decades from the scene of his great triumphs. He was guest of honour at lunch on Gold Cup Day and was acclaimed by well-wishers when he entered the parade ring after the big race.

While still on holiday in Lyford Cay in the Bahamas, he was able to get the result of all the races at Cheltenham '97 and listened each day on the phone to the commentaries on the most important events.

In his absence, his daughter Jane Myerscough presented the trophy for the Vincent O'Brien County Handicap Hurdle on Gold Cup Day.

On the day of his 80th birthday, very special memories of times past crowded into his mind – memories, in particular, of the great moments at Cheltenham, including four Gold Cups and three successive Champion Hurdles. Then too Quare Times's win at a rain-soaked Aintree in 1955 that completed three Grand Nationals in a row; Nijinsky – the colt that Vincent picked out because he had "the look of eagles" – winning the Triple Crown; also the other Epsom Derby victories and Alleged, in the hands of Lester Piggott, winning the Prix de l'Arc de Triomphe two years running (1977 and '78). Outside of racing he was moved at being given the Doctorate of Law by the National University and the Doctorate of Science by the University of Ulster – "two very special occasions," to quote Jacqueline.

Vincent was also very touched to have been made an Honorary Life member of the Turf Club in 1997.

Twenty-five years on from the day that Nijinsky won the King George VI and Queen Elizabeth Stakes in 1970, Vincent was the recipient of the Forte Crest Legend in Sport award. The beautiful insribed crystal trophy was presented to him at a luncheon in the Forte Crest Hotel, Dublin Airport by then Minister for Justice, Mrs Nora Owen T.D.

The first recipient of the award was Jonjo O'Neill and in July, '97 Sir Peter O'Sullevan became the latest recipient – a fitting tribute to the man who was retiring at the end of the 1997 Flat season as "The Voice of BBC Racing" and who over a span of half-a-century as a commentator for radio and television had given brilliant commentaries on many of Vincent O'Brien's most notable victories over the jumps and on the Flat.

Vincent O'Brien considered himself very lucky to be spending his 80th birthday with Jacqueline after being married 46 years. "Jacqueline has been my right arm and looks after me so well," he said in spontaneous tribute to her. "Of all the things that have happened down the years, our marriage was the single most important one for me. And I thank God every day for the wonderful family we have – the grandchildren as well as the children. My greatest pleasure now is to see how the young ones are developing."

Jacqueline paid her own birthday tribute to Vincent: "I cannot praise him highly enough. He had a small stroke recently which he faced with great courage and he did everything possible to undo the effects. Although it affected his right arm, he was soon back playing golf every day.

"He has great faith in God and this is a great help to him. I think he is enjoying his retirement. He was never one for the social round and still is not. He is happiest with plenty of exercise and a very quiet life."

Jacqueline, for her part, is not working on any book at the moment but, with her amazing energy, she is doing two courses with the Open University on the Renaissance. "I find these courses very interesting and more than enough to cope with," she said.

Incidentally, when they are at their holiday home in Lyford Cay, Vincent and Jacqueline lead a very quiet life and, contrary to what people might think when they hear mention of the Bahamas, they do not get involved in the "social round". They like, for example, to dine with Alec and Ghislaine Head, who have a house there. Alec has been a friend of Vincent's for over forty years. His daughter Criquette and son Freddie may also join them at dinner.

Vincent and Jacqueline may also have a quiet dinner with Dr Tony O'Reilly and his wife Chryss. Vincent, of course, trained for Dr O'Reilly.

Long-standing friends who invariably renew acquaintanceship with the O'Briens when they come to Lyford Cay on holidays are Nick and Kitty Brady. Nick Brady was Secretary of the U.S. Treasury under President George Bush. He is son of James Cox Brady for whom Vincent trained Long Look to win the 1965 English Oaks at 100-7 with Australian Jack Purtell in the saddle

.

*   *   *

When Vincent O'Brien retired at the end of the 1994 Flat season, he was showered with tributes from colleagues in the racing world.

Robert Sangster said simply: "I could talk all night about Vincent and what he achieved, but I am only going to give you two words: The Greatest."

Henry Cecil described him as an "unbelievable trainer," adding one sentence that summed it up very cryptically: "He started it all."

Jim Bolger said: "For the whole of my life Vincent has been on the top rung and he retires there, too. He was the world's greatest – there was no second to him. He was the Christopher Columbus of Irish racing."

Dermot Weld said Vincent O'Brien was a legend in his own lifetime who would go down as being one of the greats. Irish racing owed him a tremendous debt for the lasting status that he gave to Pattern races in the Irish calendar through the outstanding horses from his stable that won them.

Weld too was only too conscious of the trail-blazing approach by Vincent O'Brien as he bid for targets not alone in England and France but in the States and twenty-two years after Vincent O'Brien sent Sir Ivor to win the Washington DC International Stakes, Weld made history by becoming the first European trainer to win a leg of the American Triple Crown when Go

And Go took the 1990 Belmont Stakes, beating both the winners of the Kentucky Derby and Preakness Stakes.

And then in 1993 came Weld's epoch-making and historic achievement when Dr Michael Smurfit's Vintage Crop won the Melbourne Cup with Michael Kinane in the saddle – the first time a horse from the Northern Hemisphere had made such a stunning break-through Down Under.

John Oxx, who had his own moment of international glory when Ridgewood Pearl, ridden by John Murtagh, scored a famous victory in the 1995 Breeders Cup Mile at Belmont Park, said in tribute to Vincent O'Brien: "He has been the greatest ambassador for his profession and for the Irish bloodstock world. His fellow trainers in Ireland owe him a great deal."

John Reid noted: "He was a legend before I came into the game and it was a pleasure to be able to work for a legend. When I was a kid, I never thought I would ride for him and it was a great honour, even though it was in the twilight of his career."

Cash Asmussen said: "What he did, not only for Irish racing but racing around the world, will probably never be equalled. I think there are a lot of people who could thank him for that.

"The champions that were trained at Ballydoyle speak for themselves. They represented Vincent's achievements and if I tried to describe those achievements they would only be cheapened by my words. His horses did the talking far better than I could."

Tommy Stack, who, as the rider of a Grand National winner in Red Rum, knows better than anyone the true significance of Vincent O'Brien winning three successive Grand Nationals with three different horses, commented: "Vincent is the man for whom I have had the most admiration in racing. He understands the whole business from A-to-Z."

Edward O'Grady described it as "the end of an era, the end of a glorious era".

※   ※   ※

The impact that Vincent O'Brien made in his long career as a trainer on those involved in racing and breeding world-wide was borne home to me quite forcibly on a Sunday morning in March 1990 as I sat talking to Charles Taylor, President of Windfields Stud Farm and Chairman and Chief Steward of the Jockey Club of Canada, in his home in Toronto (he died in the summer of 1997 after losing a nine-years battle with cancer).

Charles, son of the legendary E.P. Taylor (whose name will always be linked with the peerless sire, Northern Dancer, and with colts like Nijinsky and The Minstrel that helped put Vincent O'Brien on a pedestal apart as a Flat trainer) and a former foreign correspondent of *The Globe and Mail* in his own right, said in tribute to the Master of Ballydoyle: "I like to quote my late father, who always said, 'there is no greater trainer in the world than Vincent O'Brien'. And then he would add with a knowing twinkle in his eye, 'The only reason I do not say he is the greatest is that I do have many other trainer friends!'

"I share the total respect my father had for Vincent. What always struck me during my visits to Ballydoyle was the meticulousness and thoroughness of the entire training operation and the total attention to detail. I have never seen anything like it anywhere else in my lifetime."

Charles Taylor recalled being at Epsom the day El Gran Senor and Secreto, both bred at Windfields Farm, fought out their memorable finish to the 1984 Derby. "I remember David saying to his parents, 'I'm sorry', but of course they were both thrilled for their son."

Sir Peter O'Sullevan has known Vincent O'Brien for close on half-a-century. "As a visitor to Ballydoyle from the early Fifties one of the features which, to me, reflected the prosperity generated by M.V.'s talent was the speed with which the personnel's bicycle shed gave way to a carport," he said.

He went on: "It should always be remembered that Vincent and his long-time contemporary, Paddy ("Darkie") Prendergast, did more than any other personalities to put Ireland on the international racing map."

Brough Scott has always had a way of capturing a moment in singular fashion and with an individuality of style that can be lasting in its impact. As Vincent stepped down he said in tribute: "There have been, and will be, many great trainers through the ages but there will be only one Vincent O'Brien. For me he has been unique, in both the range and manner of his achievement. He was the pioneer.

"No one else had so completely conquered the high ground of the jumping game and then moved to similar eminence on the Flat. And he was the first to develop the high-tech, high-finance blending that has become the modern training norm.

"But for all his energy and ambition, the real key to Vincent's success lay in something you will never find in books or ledgers, something he was born with, something as Irish as Tipperary: a genius with a horse.

"When it's all over, that will be the part of the O'Brien's legacy which many will seek but none can find. It's that which sets a standard against which all greatness will be judged."

Brough noted that when the flow of Derby and other Classic winners had stopped in the twilight days in the late Eighties and early Nineties, the magic had already been demonstrated. "We always want to return to where the story started. To marvel at the sheer improbability of those first achievements. To think of those early, hungry years in Southern Ireland when the targets were so few that missing them was out of the question. When the whole future depended on putting the money down. So the memory wants to go back to the beginning. Back to where the magic all began."

Appendix 1
Big Race Successes At Home

ON THE FLAT

IRISH 2000 GUINEAS
1959 El Toro (T. P. Burns)
1978 Jaazeiro (L. Piggott)
1981 King's Lake (P. Eddery)
1984 Sadler's Wells (G. McGrath)
1988 Prince of Birds
     (D. Gillespie)

IRISH 1000 GUINEAS
1966 Valoris (J. Power)
1977 Lady Capulet (T. Murphy)
1979 Godetia (L. Piggott)

IRISH DERBY
1953 Chamier (W. Rickaby)
1957 Ballymoss (T. P. Burns)
1970 Nijinsky (L. Ward)
1977 The Minstrel (L. Piggott)
1984 El Gran Senor (P. Eddery)
1985 Law Society (P. Eddery)

IRISH OAKS
1964 Ancasta (J. Purtell)
1965 Aurabella (L. Ward)
1969 Gaia (L. Ward)
1979 Godetia (L. Piggott)

IRISH ST LEGER
1959 Barclay (G. Bougoure)

1966 White Gloves (L. Ward)
1969 Reindeer (L. Ward)
1975 Caucasus (L. Piggott)
1976 Meneval (L. Piggott)
1977 Transworld (T. Murphy)
1980 Gonzales (R. Carroll)
1985 Leading Counsel
     (P. Eddery)
1988 Dark Lomond (D. Gillespie)

TETRARCH STAKES
1968 Harry (L. Ward)
1969 Sahib (L. Ward)
1971 Minsky (L. Piggott)
1972 Homeguard (J. Roe)
1973 Dapper (L. Piggott)
1974 Cellini (L. Piggott)
1982 Achieved (P. Eddery)
1983 Salmon Leap (P. Eddery)
1985 Northern Plain (P. Eddery)
1988 Prince of Birds (J. Reid)
1989 Saratogan (J. Reid)
1990 Royal Academy (J. Reid)
1993 College Chapel (W.J.
     Supple)

ATHASI STAKES
1962 Lovely Gale (T. P. Glennon)
1968 Rimark (L. Ward)

1972 Arkadina (J. Roe)
1974 Lisadell (L. Piggott)
1979 Godetia (L. Piggott)
1990 Wedding Bouquet (J. Reid)

TRIGO STAKES
1957 Ballymoss (J. Power)
1960 Die Hard (G. Bougoure)
1962 Larkspur (T. P. Glennon)
1965 Donato (J. Purtell)
1966 Beau Chapeau (L. Ward)

DERRINSTOWN STUD
DERBY TRIAL STAKES
(Formerly Nijinsky Stakes)
1972 Boucher (J. Roe)
1974 Hail The Pirates (L. Piggott)
1976 Meneval (L. Piggott)
1982 Golden Fleece (P. Eddery)
1983 Salmon Leap (P. Eddery)
1984 Sadler's Wells (G. McGrath)
1987 Seattle Dancer
     (C. Asmussen)
1988 Kris Kringle (J. Reid)

GALLINULE STAKES
1953 Chamier (W. Rickaby)
1965 Baljour (J. Purtell)
1969 Onandaga (L. Ward)
1970 Saracen Sword (N. Brennan)
1971 Grenfall (J. Roe)
1973 Hail The Pirates (L. Piggott)
1974 Sir Penfro (T. Murphy)
1975 King Pellinore (T. Murphy)
1976 Meneval (L. Piggott)
1977 Alleged (L. Piggott)
1978 Inkerman (L. Piggott)
1980 Gonzales (L. Piggott)
1984 Montelimar (P. Eddery)
1987 Seattle Dancer
     (C. Asmussen)
1991 Sportsworld (L. Piggott)

PRETTY POLLY STAKES
1959 Little Mo (G. Bougoure)
1964 Ancasta (J. Purtell)

1967 Iskereen (L. Ward)
1969 Rimark (L. Ward)
1979 Godetia (L. Piggott)
1980 Calandra (L. Piggott)
1988 Dark Lomond (J. Reid)

DESMOND STAKES
1964 Restless Knight (J. Purtell)
1966 White Gloves (L. Ward)
1967 White Gloves (L. Ward)
1969 Reindeer (L. Ward)
1972 Boucher (J. Roe)
1973 Hail The Pirates (L. Piggott)
1974 Sir Penfro (T. P. Burns)
1976 Niebo (L. Piggott)
1977 Be My Guest (T. Murphy)
1981 Belted Earl (P. Eddery)
1985 Sunstart (P. Eddery)
1986 Wise Counsellor (P. Eddery)
1987 Entitled (C. Asmussen)
1992 Via Borghese (W. Carson)

BLANDFORD STAKES
1959 Little Mo (G. Bougoure)
1961 Silver Moon (G. Bougoure)
1965 Donato U Purtell)
1968 Wenona (L. Ward)
1970 Riboprince (L. Ward)
1971 Wenceslas (J. Roe)
1972 Manitoulon (J. Roe)
1974 Richard Grenville (L.
     Piggott)
1975 King Pellinore (L. Piggott)
1980 Gonzales (T. Murphy)
1981 Magesterial (P. Eddery)
1982 Lords (P. Eddery)
1983 South Atlantic (P. Eddery)
1988 Kris Kringle (J. Reid)
1992 Andros Bay (L. Piggott)

BALLYMOSS STAKES
1967 White Gloves (L. Ward)
1969 Selko (L. Ward)
1973 Cavo Doro (L. Piggott)
1982 Golden Fleece (P. Eddery)

JOE McGRATH MEMORIAL STAKES

1978 Inkerman (L. Piggott)
1979 Fordham (T. Carberry)
1980 Gregorian (G. McGrath)
1981 King's Lake (P. Eddery)

PHOENIX CHAMPION STAKES

1984 Sadler's Wells (P. Eddery)

PHOENIX STAKES

1976 Cloonlara (T. Murphy)
1981 Achieved (P. Eddery)

RAILWAY STAKES

1962 Turbo Jet (T. P. Glennon)
1965 Glad Rags (J. Purtell)
1968 Sahib (L. Ward)
1969 Nijinsky (L. Ward)
1970 Minsky (L. Ward)
1971 Open Season (J. Roe)
1975 Niebo (L. Piggott)
1976 Brahms (L. Piggott)
1978 Solar (T. Murphy)
1980 Lawmaker (T. Murphy)
1982 Ancestral (P. Eddery)
1983 El Gran Senor (P. Eddery)
1984 Moscow Ballet (P. Eddery)
1991 El Prado (L. Piggott)

ANGLESEY STAKES

1959 Arctic Sea (G. Bougoure)
1962 Philemon (T. P. Glennon)
1965 Bravery (J. Purtell)
1969 Nijinsky (L. Ward)
1970 Headlamp (L. Ward)
1971 Roberto (J. Roe)
1973 Saritamer (L. Piggott)
1975 Niebo (L. Piggott)
1977 Solinus (T. Murphy)
1980 Storm Bird (T. Murphy)
1982 Caerleon (P. Eddery)
1984 Law Society (P. Eddery)
1985 Woodman (P. Eddery)
1987 Lake Como (C. Asmussen)

MOYGLARE STUD STAKES

1981 Woodstream (P. Eddery)
1990 Capricciosa (J. Reid)

NATIONAL STAKES

1967 Sir Ivor (L. Ward)
1971 Roberto (J. Roe)
1972 Chamozzle (J. Roe)
1973 Cellini (L. Piggott)
1975 Sir Wimborne (L. Piggott)
1979 Monteverdi (R. Carroll)
1980 Storm Bird (T. Murphy)
1982 Glenstal (V. Rossiter)
1983 El Gran Senor (P. Eddery)
1984 Law Society (P. Eddery)
1985 Tate Gallery (C. Asmussen)
1987 Caerwent (C. Assmussen)
1988 Classic Fame (J. Reid)
1991 El Prado (L. Piggott)
1992 Fatherland (L. Piggott)

BERESFORD STAKES

1947 Barfelt (G. Wells)
1962 Pontifex (T. P. Glennon)
1967 Hibernian (L. Ward)
1969 Nijinsky (L. Ward)
1970 Minsky (L. Ward)
1971 Boucher (J. Roe)
1972 Chamozzle (J. Roe)
1973 Saritamer (L. Piggott)
1979 Huguenot (T. Murphy)
1980 Euclid (G. McGrath)
1982 Danzatore (P. Eddery)
1983 Sadler's Wells (P. Eddery)
1984 Gold Crest (P. Eddery)
1988 Classic Fame (J. Reid)
1991 El Prado (L. Piggott)

BIRDCATCHER NURSERY STAKES

1962 Turbo Jet (T. P. Glennon)
1966 Theo (L. Ward)
1977 Pull The Latch
      (T. Carberry)
1981 Afghan (T. Murphy)

1982 Treasure Trove
(P. Eddery)
1983 Western Symphony
(C. Roche)
1988 Kyra (D. Gillespie)

IRISH LINCOLNSHIRE
1949 Hatton's Grace (M. Wing)
1950 Knock Hard (T. P. Burns)

IRISH CAMBRIDGESHIRE
1944 Dry Bob (M. Wing)
1957 Courts Appeal (J. Power)
1961 Travel Light (G. Bougoure)
1968 Hibernian (L. Ward)
1979 Habituate (D. Hogan)

IRISH CESAREWITCH
1944 Good Days (M. Wing)
1947 Cottage Rake (G. Wells)
1948 Hot Spring (M. Wing)
1949 Hatton's Grace
(M. Molony)
1950 Hatton's Grace
(M. Molony)

NAAS NOVEMBER HANDICAP
1946 Cottage Rake (J. Tyrrell)
1949 Wye Fly (H. Holmes)

LEOPARDSTOWN
NOVEMBER HANDICAP
1959 Coologan (A. Briscoe)

✳ ✳ ✳

UNDER NATIONAL HUNT RULES

THYESTES CHASE
1956 Sam Brownthorn (T. Taaffe)

LEOPARDSTOWN CHASE
1953 Lucky Dome (P. J. Doyle)

IRISH GRAND NATIONAL
1952 Alberoni (L. Stephens)

GALWAY PLATE
1952 Alberoni (L. Stephens)

GALWAY HURDLE
1951 Wye Fly (M. Molony)

Appendix 2
Big Race Successes Abroad

ENGLAND
ON THE FLAT

THE 2000 GUINEAS
1968 Sir Ivor (L. Piggott)
1970 Nijinsky (L. Piggott)
1983 Lomond (P. Eddery)
1984 El Gran Senor (P. Eddery)

THE 1000 GUINEAS
1966 Glad Rags (P. Cook)

THE DERBY
1962 Larkspur (N. Sellwood)
1968 Sir Ivor (L. Piggott)
1970 Nijinsky (L. Piggott)
1972 Roberto (L. Piggott)
1977 The Minstrel (L. Piggott)
1982 Golden Fleece (P. Eddery)

THE OAKS
1965 Long Look (J. Purtell)
1966 Valoris (L. Piggott)

THE ST LEGER
1957 Ballymoss (T. P. Burns)
1970 Nijinsky (L. Piggott)
1972 Boucher (L. Piggott)

CORONATION CUP
1958 Ballymoss (A. Breasley)
1973 Roberto (L. Piggott)

HARDWICKE STAKES
1977 Merleval (L. Piggott)

ECLIPSE STAKES
1966 Pieces Of Eight (L. Piggott)
1977 Artaius (L. Piggott)
1983 Solford (P. Eddery)
1984 Sadler's Wells (P. Eddery)

KING GEORGE VI AND QUEEN ELIZABETH STAKES
1958 Ballymoss ((A. Breasley)
1970 Nijinsky (L. Piggott)
1977 The Minstrel (L. Piggott)

SUSSEX STAKES
1973 Thatch (L. Piggott)
1977 Artaius (L. Piggott)
1978 Jaazeiro (L. Piggott)
1981 King's Lake (P. Eddery)

WATERFORD CRYSTAL MILE
1975   Gay Fandango (P. Eddery)
1977   By My Guest (L. Piggott)

BENSON & HEDGES GOLD CUP
1972   Roberto (B. Baeza)
1983   Caerleon (P. Eddery)

CHAMPION STAKES
1966   Pieces Of Eight (L. Piggott)
1968   Sir Ivor (L. Piggott)

ST JAMES'S PALACE STAKES
1973   Thatch (L. Piggott)
1978   Jaazeiro (L. Piggott)

RIBBLESDALE STAKES
1975   Gallina (L. Piggott)

CORONATION STAKES
1974   Lisadell (L. Piggott)

GREAT VOLTIGEUR STAKES
1977   Alleged (L. Piggott)

KING'S STAND STAKES
1962   Cassarate (N. Sellwood)
1973   Abergwaun (L. Piggott)
1977   Godswalk (L. Piggott)
1978   Solinus (L. Piggott)
1987   Bluebird (C. Asmussen)

JULY CUP
1973   Thatch (L. Piggott)
1974   Saritamer (L. Piggott)
1978   Solinus (L. Piggott)
1979   Thatching (L. Piggott)
1990   Royal Academy (J. Reid)

WILLIAM HILL SPRINT CHAMPIONSHIP
1978   Solinus (L. Piggott)

VERNONS SPRINT CUP
1972   Abergwaun (L. Piggott)

GEOFFREY FREER STAKES
1977   Valinsky (L. Piggott)

QUEEN'S VASE
1958   Even Money (A. Breasley)
1975   Blood Royal (L. Piggott)

ASCOT GOLD CUP
1958   Gladness (L. Piggott)

GOODWOOD CUP
1958   Gladness (L. Piggott)

QUEEN ANNE STAKES
1975   Imperial March (G. Dettori)

JERSEY STAKES
1956   Adare (W. R. Johnstone)
1975   Gay Fandango (L. Piggott)

CORK and ORRERY STAKES
1970   Welsh Saint (L. Piggott)
1974   Saritamer (L. Piggott)
1975   Swingtime (W. Carson)
1979   Thatching (L. Piggott)
1993   College Chapel (L. Piggott)

DIADEM STAKES
1971   Abergwaun (L. Piggott)
1972   Home Guard (L. Piggott)
1974   Saritamer (L. Piggott)
1975   Swingtime (L. Piggott)

COVENTRY STAKES
1977   Solinus (L. Piggott)

QUEEN MARY STAKES
1964   Brassia (J. Purtell)

NORFOLK STAKES
1984   Magic Mirror
         (L. Piggott)

CHERRY HINTON STAKES
1977   Turkish Treasure
         (L. Piggott)

CHAMPAGNE STAKES
1981   Achieved (P. Eddery)

**FLYING CHILDERS
STAKES**
1981   Peterhof (E. Hide)

MIDDLE PARK STAKES
1978   Junius (L. Piggott)

CHEVELEY PARK STAKES
1967   Lalibela (L. Piggott)
1981   Woodstream (P. Eddery)
1990   Capricciosa (J. Reid)

DEWHURST STAKES
1969   Nijinsky (L. Piggott)
1973   Cellini (L. Piggott)

1976   The Minstrel (L. Piggott)
1977   Try My Best (L. Piggott)
1979   Monteverdi (L. Piggott)
1980   Storm Bird (P. Eddery)
1983   El Gran Senor (P. Eddery)

ROYAL LODGE STAKES
1975   Sir Wimborne (L. Piggott)

OBSERVER GOLD CUP
1973   Apalachee (L. Piggott)

WOKINGHAM HANDICAP
1975   Boone's Cabin (L. Piggott)

EBOR HANDICAP
1958   Gladness (L. Piggott)
1961   Die Hard (L. Piggott)

✳   ✳   ✳

FRANCE
ON THE FLAT

PRIX DU JOCKEY CLUB
1983   Caerleon (P. Eddery)

**PRIX DE L'ARC DE
TRIOMPHE**
1958   Ballymoss (A. Breasley)
1977   Alleged (L. Piggott)

1978   Alleged (L. Piggott)

GRAND CRITERIUM
1967   Sir Ivor (L. Piggott)

PRIX MAURICE DE GHEEST
1993   College Chapel (L. Piggott)

✳   ✳   ✳

USA
ON THE FLAT

**WASHINGTON DC
INTERNATIONAL STAKES**
1968   Sir Ivor (L. Piggott)

BREEDERS' CUP MILE
1990   Royal Academy (L. Piggott)

ENGLAND
UNDER NATIONAL HUNT RULES

THE GRAND NATIONAL
1953   Early Mist (B. Marshall)
1954   Royal Tan (B. Marshall)
1955   Quare Times (P. Taaffe)

KING GEORGE VI CHASE
1948   Cottage Rake (A. Brabazon)

CHELTENHAM GOLD CUP
1948   Cottage Rake (A. Brabazon)
1949   Cottage Rake (A. Brabazon)
1950   Cottage Rake (A. Brabazon)
1953   Knock Hard (T. Molony)

CHAMPION HURDLE
1949   Hatton's Grace (A.
       Brabazon)
1950   Hatton's Grace (A.
       Brabazon)
1951   Hatton's Grace (T. Molony)

GLOUCESTERSHIRE HURDLE
1952   Cockatoo (Mr A. S.
       O'Brien)
1954   Stroller (P. Taaffe)
1955   (Div I) – Vindore
       (Mr A. S. O'Brien)
       (Div II) – Illyric
       (T. P. Burns)

1956   (Div I) – Boy's Hurrah
       (Mr A. S. O'Brien)
       (Div II) – Pelargos
       (Mr A. S. O'Brien)
1957   (Div II) – Saffron Tartan
       (T. P. Burns)
1958   (Div I) – Admiral Stuart
       (T. P. Burns)
       (Div II) – Prudent King
       (T. P. Burns)
1959   (Div I) – York Fair
       (T. P. Burns)

SPA HURDLE
1954   Lucky Dome (T. P. Burns)

BIRDLIP HURDLE
1955   Ahaburn (T. P. Burns)

NATIONAL HUNT CHASE
1949   Castledermot (Lord
       Mildmay)
1954   Quare Times (Mr J. R. Cox)

NATIONAL HUNT HANDICAP CHASE
1952   Royal Tan (Mr A. S.
       O'Brien)

Appendix 3
Year-by-Year Irish Record

	RACES	MONEY	POSITION
1943	1	£74	—
1944	10	£1206	—
1945	14	£1710	19th
1946	16	£2360	18th
1947	21	£4725	5th
1948	21	£3779	15th
1949	35	£7659	5th
1950	52	£9435	2nd
1951	42	£7279	4th
1952	26	£7113	3rd
1953	24	£12196	2nd
1954	17	£2996	20th
1955	15	£2669	17th
1956	29	£5295	9th
1957	40	£15571	2nd
1958	21	£4097	14th
1959	52	£23793	1st
1960	11	£4248	11th
1961	28	£8104	6th
1962	47	£27743	2nd
1963	27	£14417	3rd
1964	30	£24857	3rd
1965	36	£48643	2nd
1966	24	£35423	3rd
1967	27	£29088	3rd
1968	28	£26607	2nd
1969	44	£80533	1st
1970	30	£90928	1st
1971	49	£58474	2nd

	RACES	MONEY	POSITION
1972	48	£65059	1st
1973	41	£62413	2nd
1974	30	£43552	5th
1975	38	£71497	2nd
1976	31	£73969	3rd
1977	33	£192820	1st
1978	47	£144976	1st
1979	43	£233224	1st
1980	45	£193930	1st
1981	40	£218000	1st
1982	49	£232486	1st
1983	28	£203411	2nd
1984	42	£769478	1st
1985	21	£415888	2nd
1986	21	£134219	9th
1987	43	£474552	1st
1988	33	£623017	1st
1989	27	£150112	7th
1990	37	£266857	4th
1991	36	£324205	6th
1992	19	£228294	5th
1993	6	£44574	—
1994	4	31905	—
TOTAL	**1529**	**£5,759,460**	

LANDMARK YEARS:
His winnings topped the half million pound mark in 1970; the million pound in 1977; the two million pound in 1982; the three million pound in 1984; the four million pound in 1987 and the five million pound in 1990. In money terms, he was the champion trainer on 13 occasions, finished 2nd 11 times and 3rd 6 times. He twice won more races than any other trainer.

Vincent O'Brien won 25 races at Royal Ascot and 23 races at the Cheltenham National Hunt meeting, including Cottage Rake's 1949 Gold Cup triumph which came a month later as Gold Cup Day had been lost during the Festival meeting itself because of frost.

Appendix 4
Memorable Seasons In Britain

UNDER NATIONAL HUNT RULES

	RACES	MONEY	POSITION
1948-49	6	£10869	5th
1952-53	5	£15515	1st
1953-54	8	£14274	1st
1954-55	8	£12426	2nd

ON THE FLAT

	RACES	MONEY	POSITION
1958	9	£67543	3rd
1962	2	£36891	9th
1966	8	£123848	1st
1968	5	£99631	2nd
1970	5	£162286	2nd
1972	11	£154719	2nd
1973	8	£112098	4th
1975	15	£73549	9th
1977	18	£439124	1st
1978	8	£155405	10th
1983	5	£306682	8th

Irish-born millionaire John Mulcahy, the man who during a day's fishing with Vincent O'Brien advised him that he must "take a piece of the action" in the great horses he trained and it changed matters dramatically for The Master of Ballydoyle.

BEFORE IT'S GONE...

Only a limited number of copies are now left of the second edition of Raymond Smith's acclaimed 300-page book, *Better One Day As A Lion* which captures all the excitement engendered at Cheltenham '96 as a result of Imperial Call's epic victory in the Gold Cup.

There is a chapter also on the amazing comeback of Danoli, "The People's Champion" from a near-fatal injury while a special spotlight is put on the Edward O'Grady-trained Golden Cygnet and the lasting imprint he created before that fateful moment at Ayr in April, 1978. Read too about the exploits of the High Rollers of our time, including J.P. (The Sundance Kid) McManus, Barney Curley and Noel Furlong.

Retailing at £9.95 it is available from Easons and other leading bookshops in Dublin, Cork, Limerick, Galway, Belfast. In Britain it can be purchased through W.H. Smith's bookshops, also Turf Newspapers, J.A. Allen (The Horseman's Bookshop), London, Foyles, London and Sports Pages, London and Manchester, Tindall's, Newmarket, or direct for £10 (including postage) from:

SPORTING BOOKS PUBLISHERS,
4, Sycamore Road, Mount Merrion, County Dublin, Ireland.

265

John Magnier (fourth from left) and J.P. McManus (second from left) share with their great friend, Dermot Desmond (arm aloft in victory salute) the moments of joy in the winner's enclosure at Cheltenham '97 after his Commanche Court, trained by Ted Walsh (left), had won the Elite Racing Club Triumph Hurdle.

Brian Palmer (left) and Tony Weir of the Golden Step Racing Syndicate lead in Toast The Spreece (Richard Dunwoody) after he had won the Guinness Galway Hurdle at Galway '97, yet another big-race triumph for Aidan O'Brien's Ballydoyle stable.

WHEN COTTAGE RAKE WAS KING OF THE GOLD CUP SCENE

Fifty years have passed since Cottage Rake gave Vincent O'Brien his first big-race triumph in England by winning the 1948 Cheltenham Gold Cup. Here a young Vincent pats the three-times Gold Cup winner in his stables at Churchtown, County Cork. Also pictured Sidney Ryan (The Rake's lad), Maurice O'Callaghan (Headman) and Vincent's brother Dermot.

Vincent O'Brien was at Royal Ascot '97 with Jacqueline in the role of spectator, having turned out 25 winners at the meeting as a trainer. He saw his son Charles's Burden of Proof (pictured below winning the Amethyst Stakes at Leopardstown) contest the Cork & Orrery Stakes. (Pictures: Bernard Parkin and Peter Mooney)

Vincent O'Brien showing all the control and unsurpassed knowledge of a master of his profession, talking to John Reid after a race at the Curragh and (right) Charles. Thatching, standing at Coolmore and top-class sire of 39 Stakes winners, is pictured below winning in the hands of Lester Piggott. He was champion European sprinter in his prime.

Bibliography

Francis, Dick. *Lester: The Official Biography* (Michael Joseph, 1986 hardcover and Pan Books, 1987 paperback).

Francis, Dick. *The Sport of Queens* (Michael Joseph, 1976).

Herbert, Ivor and O'Brien, Jacqueline. *Vincent O'Brien's Great Horses* (Pelham Books, 1984).

Holland, Anne. *Grand National: The Official Celebration of 150 Years* (Macdonald Queen Anne Press, 1988).

Lee, Alan. *Cheltenham Racecourse* (Pelham Books, 1985).

MacGowan, Kenneth. *The Rock of Cashel* (Kamac Publications, 1985).

Mortimer, Roger with Nelligan, Tim. *The Epsom Derby* (Michael Joseph, 1984).

O'Donnell, Augustine. *Saint Patrick's Rock* (The Cashel Press, 1979).

O'Sullevan, Peter. *Calling The Hores: A Racing Autobiography* (Stanley Paul, 1989).

Piggott, Lester. *Lester: The Autobiography of Lester Piggott* (Partridge Press, 1995).

Robinson, Patrick Nick. *Horsetrader: Robert Sangster And The Fall of The Sport Of Kings* (Harper Collins, 1993).

Slattery, Finbarr. *Horse Racing* (Killarney Race Committee, 1984).

Slattery, Finbarr. *Following The Horses* (The Kerryman, 1996).

Tanner, Michael. *The Champion Hurdle* (Pelham Books, 1989).

Watson, S. J. *Between the Flags* (Allen Figgis, 1969).

Welcome, John. *The Cheltenham Gold Cup* (Constable, 1957).

Wilson, Julian. *100 Great Horses* (Macdonald Queen Anne Press, 1987).

Wilson, Julian. *Lester Piggott: The Pictorial Biography* (Macdonald Queen Anne Press, 1985).

Wright, Howard. *The Encyclopaedia of Flat Racing* (Robert Hale, 1986).

Also *Ruff's Guide to the Turf; Timeform Publications* (including Timeform Black Book and Racehorses); *The Irish Racing Annual; Raceform Note-Book; The Racing Post, The Sporting Life, The Irish Field, The European Racehorse.*

Select Index